Dear Eddie,

A Matter of Moral Justice

Thanks
for coming to
the talk!
to meet you!
Nice

In Solidarity,

Jenny Carson

THE WORKING CLASS IN
AMERICAN HISTORY

Editorial Advisors
James R. Barrett, Julie Greene, William P. Jones,
Alice Kessler-Harris, and Nelson Lichtenstein

*A list of books in the series appears
at the end of this book.*

A MATTER OF
MORAL
JUSTICE

Black Women Laundry Workers
and the Fight for Justice

JENNY CARSON

**UNIVERSITY OF
ILLINOIS PRESS**
Urbana, Chicago, and Springfield

Publication supported by a grant from the
Howard D. and Marjorie I. Brooks Fund
for Progressive Thought.

Library of Congress Cataloging-in-Publication Data
Names: Carson, Jenny, 1972– author.
Title: A matter of moral justice: Black women laundry
    workers and the fight for justice / Jenny Carson.
Description: Urbana: University of Illinois Press, [2021]
    | Series: The working class in American history |
    Includes bibliographical references and index.
Identifiers: LCCN 2021005238 (print) | LCCN 2021005239
    (ebook) | ISBN 9780252043901 (cloth) | ISBN
    9780252085895 (paperback) | ISBN 9780252052804
    (ebook)
Subjects: LCSH: African American laundresses—United
    States—Social conditions—20th century. | Laundry
    workers—Labor unions—United States—History—
    20th century.
Classification: LCC HD8039.L32 U593 2021 (print) | LCC
    HD8039.L32 (ebook) | DDC 331.4/78166713097309043
    —dc23
LC record available at https://lccn.loc.gov/2021005238
LC ebook record available at https://lccn.loc.gov/
    2021005239

Contents

Acknowledgments

A book is indeed a labor of love, one that cannot be completed alone. My mother often says that this book is my fourth child. It began as my first child, but three little boys came along and decided that she would have to wait, and so she became my fourth child. She and I have been on a journey that began decades ago during graduate school when my first mentor, Margaret Kellow, suggested that I write about the Women's Trade Union League (WTUL). I eagerly dove into the WTUL records, where I soon encountered the laundry workers, a group about whom relatively little had been written but who have so much to tell us about the "arc of the moral universe." In the first half of the twentieth century the African American women who grace the pages of this book led a militant battle to secure racial and economic justice, a battle that in many ways mirrors the one taking place today in 2021. The historical precedents of Black Lives Matter extend back to Jamestown, where white colonial settlers built an economy and society based on the forcible removal and genocide of Indigenous peoples and the labor of enslaved African peoples. Resistance began when slavery and displacement began and has continued ever since. The women in this book, including Charlotte Adelmond and Dollie Robinson, were inspired by the celebrated leaders of this resistance: Marcus Garvey, A. Philip Randolph, and Adam Clayton Powell Jr., among others. But they too were leaders of movements, part of the continuum of resistance that stretches from Harriet Tubman to Alicia Garza and to all of those unrecognized women in between. As Black female unionists and activists they fought for economic justice at work, civil rights in their union, an end to police brutality and segregation (both de jure and de facto), the right to exercise political power when and how they deemed fit, and, finally, the right to live their lives with dignity and respect. The laundry workers then are the very obvious progenitors of Black Lives Matter.

These acknowledgments are dedicated first and foremost to the women who fought these struggles: Charlotte Adelmond, Dollie Robinson, and their coworkers. They inspired me to write this history, and they inspire me every day. I am grateful to Robinson's daughter, Jan Robinson, and to Jan's husband, Melvin McCray, for generously sharing with me their excellent documentary on Dollie Robinson and patiently answering my questions.

Movements often have allies, and this was certainly the case for the laundry workers. In the 1930s and 1940s white Jewish radical workers Jessie Taft Smith and Beatrice Shapiro Lumpkin, deeply committed to worker power and racial justice, joined the laundry campaign. I have been fortunate enough to interview both women over a number of years. Their insights not only filled in important blanks in this story but also deepened my own knowledge of and commitment to social justice. I thank them deeply for opening their homes and minds to me. I would also like to thank Jessie's son, Russell Smith, and partner, Jane LaTour, also a historian, for providing records, images, and support. Similarly, I would like to thank Beatrice Lumpkin's beloved grandson Soren Kyale for providing images and for being a good friend.

The epilogue of this book briefly discusses a contemporary campaign to organize laundry workers employed at Cintas, the nation's largest industrial launderer and uniform rental provider. My deep gratitude goes to the Cintas workers who kindly and courageously allowed me to interview them, despite their well-founded fears of employer retaliation. A very special thank you to my husband, Hugo Leal Neri, who joined me on this particular research trip to get a break from his labor law job but who spent the entire trip translating from Spanish to English and English to Spanish for me. Never once did he complain. I would also like to thank union organizers and officials Katie Unger, Doria Barrera, Jorge Deschamps, Carmen Western, and the late and much missed James Thindwa for talking to me about laundry workers and organizing.

I have been blessed to have wonderful mentors and academic supporters and friends, starting with Margaret Kellow, who introduced me to women's history. Her impact on my career cannot be underestimated. Jack Blocker and Ian Steele, also at Western University, London, Ontario, taught me how to do history: how to ask the right questions and assess evidence. At the University of Toronto my PhD supervisor, John Ingham, taught me how to tell the important story and provided unflagging support and intellectual rigor. Thank you also to his wonderful wife, Lynne Feldman, also a historian, who provided insights, support, and friendship then and now. Elspeth Brown came on board my dissertation committee immediately upon arriving at U of T as an assistant professor. Now that I have been an assistant professor I know how hard those first years are, and I am even more grateful and amazed that she found the time to bring so much insight to my work and to support me as I learned to navigate academic politics. Franca Iacovetta read much of my work and always believed in the project. I would also like to thank Rick Halpern for serving on my committee and especially for suggesting that I apply for a Fulbright at Columbia University, where I worked with indomitable Alice Kessler-Harris.

Despite being chair of Columbia's history department and already a supervisor to a large number of graduate students, Alice graciously agreed to take me on as an exchange student. She critiqued all of my work, made available her vast networks, and invited me into her wonderful dissertation group, where new connections were forged. I left New York after a year, but Alice never left the project or me! She brought me onto panels at conferences, served as commentator on many of those panels, and helped me refine and sharpen my work. Most importantly, when I felt overwhelmed with being a full-time professor and full-time mother to three little boys she reminded me that the system was not built for working mothers and that it was the system, not me, that was at fault. (Her research tells us this, but it was a gift to hear it directly from her.) She was right, and one of these days we need to change the system.

Alice introduced me to the wonderful and brilliant Annelise Orleck, who generously shared her time and enthusiasm for this project. Annelise agreed to serve on my dissertation committee despite the fact that my dissertation was almost six hundred pages long(!). She graciously noted that she too "wrote long." Annelise not only read that tome but also, like Alice, stuck with me and the project, shaping its direction and helping to bring it to fruition today. Through Alice I also met fellow laundry scholar and now research director at the Communications Workers of America, Nell Geiser. Nell wrote a brilliant undergraduate thesis on laundry workers, and we became fast friends and collaborators, publishing an article together in *Labor: Studies in Working-Class History*. I am also grateful to fellow laundry historian Arwen Palmer Mohun for speedily answering my emails and sharing her expertise. At the beginning of this project Eric Arnesen generously shared his research and insights on the laundry workers.

I owe deep intellectual debts to the following scholars, who read my work and cheered me along: Franca Iacovetta, Ester Reiter, Rob Teigrob, Jennifer Guglielmo, Premilla Nadasen, Stephanie Ross, Steve Tufts, and the Toronto Labour Studies group, in particular, Craig Heron, Ian Radforth, Susana Miranda, Cindy Locke-Drake, Katrina Srigley and Jason Russell. I was fortunate to have most of my records housed at the Kheel Center at Cornell University, where the incomparable Patrizia Sione helped me make sense of the mountains of records on the laundry workers. Steve Calco did a last-minute intervention during COVID to secure some final images. Thank you! I would also like to thank the staffs at the Schomburg Center for Research in Black Culture in Manhattan and the Tamiment Library at NYU for their research support.

I was incredibly fortunate to be hired by the Department of History at Ryerson University in Toronto, where I turned an unwieldy dissertation into this book. The Faculty of Arts and the Centre for Labour Management Relations at Ryerson provided funding for research, conferences, image collection, and indexing. This funding enabled me to hire excellent research assistants and editors, including Kristina Fuentes, Mark Abraham, Supriya Latchman, Rabiah Choksi, and Daniel Guadagnolo. Their skills and expertise were critical to this book's completion. I am particularly fortunate in my job to have had female leadership that recognizes that scholars wear multiple hats: thank you to my equity-oriented dean and fellow labor scholar and friend, Pam Sugiman, and to my supportive chair and friend Catherine Ellis. Thank you Nicole Neverson and Andie Noack for being on the tenure journey with me and sharing our tenure party! And thanks for making the tenure party so great and being friends as well as colleagues: Rob Teigrob, Tammy Landau, Pam Sugiman, Mary Beth and Klaas Kray, Catherine Ellis, Kathryn Rowan, Anne-Marie Singh, Jean Li, Miriam Anderson, Art Blake, Ross Fair and Jenn Bridges, Joey Power, Ingrid Hehmeyer, Fatima DaSilva, Rahul Sapra, Doreen Fumia, Mustafa Koç, and Sedef Arat-Koç. A very, very special thanks to my colleague Myer Siemiatycki, who combines a number of roles: colleague, research collaborator, cheerleader, friend, mentor, and model for how to combine academia and social activism for the enrichment of both.

The editors at the University of Illinois Press have been a dream to work with, beginning with Laurie Matheson, who embraced the project and was so excited about the workers and their activism. When she moved to the position of director I was fortunate to have in a new editor someone just as excited and enthusiastic about the project, James Engelhardt. James was everything one could ask for in an editor: enthusiastic, knowledgeable, patient, yet persistent. Alison Syring has handily taken over in this final phase, and I am grateful for her support and wisdom. Many thanks as well to the reviewers of the manuscript for their insightful comments and suggestions and especially to Mary M. Hill for her careful and thoughtful copyediting.

Behind every set of working parents are caregivers, including family, teachers, and workers. I could not have held down my job without the full-time labor of incredible caregivers Veron Lucas, Bonnie Knox and Muna Muhammed Nuru, who at different times looked after my children so that I could be a scholar and a mother. And thank you to my therapist, who knows who she is, for keeping me steady as I navigated the often conflicting and always hard to balance demands of work and home.

I am blessed to work at Ryerson, where we have an incredibly active and diverse student body. I have learned and continue to learn so much from my students, and I consider it a privilege to teach them and watch their careers soar, including but certainly not limited to Chris Wright, Anna Bridges, Christina

Ailes Smit, Rabiah Choksi, Hareda Fakhrudin, Katie Flinn, Chanele Rioux-McCormick, Becky Wiltshire, Hakim Murray, Dan Darrah, Shebli Zarghami, Shameez Rabdi, Eliany Guardez Suarez, Julian Reid, Kyle Resendes, Angela Wallace, and so many others.

I am equally fortunate to have wonderful friends who sustained me in so many ways. Natalia Crowe is like a sister and is a wonderful godmother to my children. We are so lucky. Christa Short, my oldest friend, deserves special thanks for always graciously hosting me in her home in New York City and for taking an interest in my work despite our different fields. Ilyana Karthas and I met at Columbia, finished our PhDs, started our families together, and have shared this journey. I met so many wonderful friends in my graduate school days who sustained me then as now: Mary Kate Arnold, Dorothy Lo, Sarah Finkelstein, Tan Bao, Bronwyn Singleton, Heather Schramm, Alice Taylor, Katrina Srigley, and Jelica Zdero.

Thank you to the many friends who have sustained me since motherhood, my tribe who bring over meals when there's no food left and gin when it's just too much: Alanna Lammens-Davis, Heather Conway and Greg Gray, Kelly and James Hayes, Blair Irwin, Susana Miranda, Anne Baranowski and Marilyn Mc-Callum, Rob Teigrob and Suzanne Zerger, Catherine and Matthew Ellis, Chris Wright and Justin Zelasko, Katherine and Gene Zubovich, Miriam Anderson, Jean Li, Anne Smith and Chris Fernandes, Christina Schloen, Rita Jakorta, Susie Heintzman, Sean Patterson, Leah Tussman, Kathleen Fortune, Kristina and Al Fuentes, the Twin Mom Crew (always and especially Alanna Lammens-Davis, Jenny Richmond-Bravo, Tracy Michalak, Audrey Gavin, and Sera Vavala Jilek), the Riverdale Crew (Kris Olson, Josie Hughes, Sheila Ritson-Bennet, and Jess Ardanaz), and the Degrassi Crew.

And last but not least, thank you to my amazing family. My mom, Kate Kirkpatrick, and my stepfather, David Kirkpatrick, have been rooting for this project from its inception. They always believed that it would see the light of day, even and especially when I started to wonder. And special thanks to David, a fellow writer, for his editorial expertise! Margaret Kirkpatrick has been a wonderful source of history and always lots of fun. Katie Kirkpatrick Sorrell is a lovely niece/cousin whose passion for history makes me so happy. And thank you to my Mexican family, Paz Neri Giacinti and Igor Leal Neri, for cheering me on from afar and sharing with me the great gift of my husband.

Hugo Leal Neri has sustained me in countless ways both big and small. Sixteen years ago we began a conversation about social justice that is still going on. His enthusiasm for this project and shared commitment to social justice are a source of joy. From editing my work to doing more than his fair share of the household laundry, he has supported me in more ways than I could ever hope to describe here. But most importantly, thank you for our precious boys, Teodoro, Matias, and Nicolas. They are the lights of my life.

A Matter of Moral Justice

Introduction

It was June 16, 1937, the twilight of the Great Depression, when more than one thousand laundry workers gathered in the auditorium at New York City's Rand School of Social Science for what would later be remembered as the workers' "day of independence." Most of the participants, significant numbers of whom were Black, came from the Brownsville section of Brooklyn, where they had recently led a fourteen-week strike against abusive working conditions and sweatshop wages.[1] One of the leaders of that strike was Trinidadian transplant and longtime laundry activist Charlotte Adelmond. A militant Garveyite who was known for using "head butts" to slam abusive bosses to the ground, the thirty-two-year-old Adelmond had been trying to organize her coworkers since 1933, using her own home as a campaign base.[2] One of the few recognized female leaders of the movement and of the union it produced, Adelmond represented the inside workers: the mostly women and people of color who worked inside the plants washing, folding, drying, and ironing clothes and linen. She was joined by African American laundry worker and socialist Noah C. Walter of the Harlem-based Negro Labor Committee and Louis Simon, secretary treasurer of Teamsters' Local 810, the union that represented the drivers.[3] Representing different constituencies and ideological commitments, the three worker—activists were united by their recent activism on the picket lines and by their determination to halt the downward spiral in wages and working conditions that accompanied the Depression. Most significantly, by 1937 they enjoyed the support of rank-and-file workers radicalized by fourteen-hour workdays, racist and sexist treatment, and poverty wages.

The employers were not the only target of the workers' ire that summer. Adelmond, Simon, and their coworkers denounced the American Federation of Labor (AFL) for its tepid trade unionism and reliance on a craft union model that divided the workers along occupational and, by extension, race and gender lines. The auditorium pulsated with the energy of workers who had learned the value of interracial and militant organizing by marching together on picket lines and by engaging in direct and sometimes violent confrontations with their employers and the state. Eager to formalize these new solidarities, white and Black, female and male, and inside workers and drivers voted unanimously to abandon the AFL and affiliate directly with the newly—organized Committee for Industrial Organization (CIO). Within a year their nascent union—the Laundry Workers Joint Board (LWJB) of Greater New York—represented most of New York City's thirty thousand laundry workers and had affiliated with the powerful Amalgamated Clothing Workers of America (ACWA), one of the founding members of the CIO.[4] Understanding how these workers—the majority of whom were women and people of color—came to join the CIO and ACWA, how the industrial union movement both nurtured and constrained their activism, and, finally, how their battle to win economic dignity and racial and gender equality enriched, challenged, and at times threatened the industrial union project forms the heart of this story.

The road to unionization for New York's laundry workers was a long and arduous one that spanned many decades and elicited the intervention of some of New York's most prominent laborites, including New York Women's Trade Union League (WTUL) president Rose Schneiderman; ACWA president Sidney Hillman and his wife and fellow labor leader, Bessie Abramowitz Hillman; Negro Labor Committee president Frank Crosswaith; and a cadre of committed African American and communist organizers. The campaign took place during a period of cataclysmic change for American workers, one that saw the birth and growth of industrial feminism; the Great Migration of more than six million Black southerners to the urban industrial centers of the North and West; the rise of the "New Negro," inspired by mass migration, Marcus Garvey's Black nationalist movement, and the explosion of Black trade unionism; the emergence of the CIO and New Deal order; the heyday of Communist Party organizing; two world wars; and the burgeoning civil rights and women's movements. Spanning this period of transformative change, an examination of the laundry industry and its workers' multidecade organizing campaign contributes to our understanding of how race and gender shaped working conditions, the formulation of union tactics, and the struggle for union control and union power in modern America. Following the union as it transitioned from its radical, grassroots, community-based origins into a bureaucratic organization led by white men illuminates some of the benefits and limitations of the industrial union movement for women and people of color employed outside the traditional bulwarks of industrial unionism.

Charlotte Adelmond and her good friend and fellow laundry worker, African American Dollie Lowther Robinson, are at the center of this story. In 1930 at the age of thirteen Robinson migrated with her mother from North Carolina to New York City, six years after Adelmond had made the trek from Port-of-Spain, Trinidad, to Harlem. Despite the two women's very different backgrounds and migration paths, Robinson and Adelmond began their working lives in New York City in power laundries, a function of their shared skin color and gender—by 1930 the power laundry employed more Black women than any other industry in the United States—and their settlement in New York City, one of the leading centers of the industry.[5] Adelmond and Robinson were connected in other important ways. Both women became leaders in the union they helped organize; both women practiced a civil rights–based trade unionism, pursuing race and gender equality, as well as economic dignity; and both women faced predictable but disappointing challenges as they navigated union politics in the 1940s.[6] Alongside their radical allies in the Communist Party, Robinson and Adelmond challenged the liberal reformism of the industrial union movement, putting the CIO's commitment to antiracist principles and union democracy to the test, even when that meant risking their jobs. Their social justice–oriented unionism and intersectional organizing, a response to their lived experiences of race, class, and gender as "interlocking systems of oppression" and as identities around which they could mobilize for change, challenged the working-class politics of the mid-twentieth-century labor movement.[7]

As workers who labored at the intersection of the industrial and service sectors performing historically undervalued and oftentimes invisible work, power laundry workers have received relatively little scholarly attention. Yet they have much to tell us about how labor markets, union organizing, and labor politics are organized around race and gender.[8] Power or industrial laundry workers have made brief and fleeting appearances in surveys of African American and women's labor history, where they are offered as evidence of the persistence of occupational sex and race typing and of the dubious nature of Black women's occupational advancement in the urban industrial North, where most power laundries were located. Black women fell into power laundry work, scholars and contemporaries argue, because of the dangers and difficulties of the work; because Black women had long washed clothes for white families, and because the laundry was one of the few industries in which African American women were in demand.[9] A Matter of Moral Justice challenges this narrative of passivity and victimization by demonstrating that Black women actively sought jobs in power laundries, seizing the opportunities provided by urbanization, industrialization, and mass migration to propel themselves out of the cotton fields and kitchens of white America and onto the industrial ladder, albeit at the lowest rungs. In many cities the power laundry served as the vehicle through which African American women first escaped domestic service and entered the industrial workplace, a transition described by historian Joe Trotter as "proletarianization." In New York City the laundry was also the vehicle through which Black women including Dollie Robinson and Charlotte Adelmond first entered the union movement.[10]

This book focuses on the experiences of laundry workers in New York City, but because of the dearth of scholarship the early chapters explore the industry from a national perspective. Employed in a fiercely competitive, labor-intensive, and decentralized industry that serviced rather than manufactured a finished product, laundry workers encountered erratic and often long hours of work, hot, sweaty, difficult, and dangerous working conditions, and abusive employers. Workers in the marking department, where the garments began their journey through the plant, sorted through bags of laundry so filthy that workers were not surprised to find worms and cockroaches buried in the piles. Workers in the washing department described walls and ceilings that sweated and heat and humidity so intense that workers fainted. Conditions were especially difficult in the ironing department, where most of the workers were Black women. After long days on their feet, the workers limped out of the plants in their sweat-stained clothes complaining of burning lungs and aching muscles and strategizing about how to put food on the table, a particularly daunting task for the women and people of color assigned the lowest-paying and least desirable positions in the ironing department.[11] An exploration of the shop floor conditions and social division of labor that emerged during the laundry's formative years, the topics of chapters 1 and 2, illuminates how the workers understood and negotiated the gendered and racialized assumptions about skill that undergirded the laundry's occupational structure and wage scales.[12]

Beginning with chapter 3, the story shifts to New York City, a leading center of the industry and one of the few places where the workers formed a union. At first glance, unionization appeared to be the result of the CIO's interracial and industrial organizing, but this book demonstrates that this victory was in fact nearly thirty years in the making, born of a variety of worker mobilizations and alliances that stretched back to 1912, when the laundry workers launched their first general strike. In 1912 women laundry workers collaborated with their male coworkers in the AFL-affiliated Laundry Workers International Union but also drew support from the Progressive Era women's labor organization, the Women's Trade Union League. Founded in 1903 by working women and their middle- and upper-class female supporters, or "allies," as they were called, the WTUL sought to empower working women through unionization and education and by securing protective labor legislation.[13] An exploration of the 1912 laundry strike illuminates some of the impediments to women's early unionism and allows us to assess the efficacy of the WTUL's gender-based and cross-class organizing.

In the 1920s, as the laundry workforce transitioned from predominately white to interracial, a product of the Great Migration and employer and worker preferences, new occupational configurations emerged, sparking a new union drive that attracted additional allies to the campaign, including the socialist-led Trade Union Committee for Organizing Negro Workers. With the support of WTUL president Rose Schneiderman, in 1924 African American women laundry workers founded a short-lived AFL-affiliated local.[14] An examination of their campaign brings into focus Black women's activism during the 1920s, the nadir of the labor movement, and allows us to consider how white women labor leaders and African American women workers interacted, sometimes effectively and sometimes not. Chapters 3 and 4 demonstrate that the gender- and race-conscious organizing of worker leaders and their feminist and Black allies in the early 1900s produced important coalitions and contributed to an emerging union consciousness, but it did not produce a mass mobilization among the workers or result in lasting union gains. Those failures in turn prompted the intervention of white Jewish communists in the early 1930s, the topic of chapter 5.

In the early 1930s a small but dedicated group of communist laundry workers and organizers supported a grassroots uprising of laundry workers in Harlem and the Bronx. One of these organizers, seventeen-year-old Jessie Taft Smith, who was a member of the Young Communist League and a recent graduate of Harlem's Wadleigh High School, spearheaded the formation of a new organization: the Laundry Workers Industrial Union, an affiliate of the Communist Party's Trade Union Unity League (TUUL).[15] Following the Communist Party's Third Period directive to organize independent industrial unions, the Left-led laundry union united the mostly women and people of color inside the plants with the more highly paid white male drivers. Using militant tactics that included putting stink bombs under the doors of strikebreakers and relying on the support of the Left-led women's and unemployed councils, Smith and her coworkers led a series of strikes that shut down some of the largest plants in Harlem and the Bronx.[16] The Left-led mobilization demonstrates that in semi-skilled and unskilled industries with largely moribund AFL unions, communist organizing during the sectarian Third Period provided important support for workers who had already begun mobilizing at the shop-floor level practicing a more inclusive and radical trade unionism.

In 1934 the wave of strikes that had begun in upper Manhattan and the Bronx spread to Brooklyn, where the workers, including a teenage Dollie Robinson, took to the streets demanding higher wages and better treatment. Organizers and allies from the WTUL joined the workers on the picket lines and at the

Regional Labor Board, where the workers demanded that the state enforce their newly won labor rights, including the right to strike. With the WTUL's support, the workers demanded and won representation on New York State's recently formed laundry wage minimum board, where they secured a minimum wage of thirty-one cents an hour. The laundry wage code, part of the New Deal initiative to improve conditions in low-wage, female-dominated industries, fueled the wave of strike activity that was transforming the industry.[17] Chapters 5 and 6 demonstrate that Depression-era conditions, New Deal labor legislation, and communist organizing supported a rank-and-file uprising that nurtured the activist solidarities that would lead the laundry workers into the CIO and ACWA in 1937.

Historians have situated the ACWA, which began organizing laundry workers in 1937, as the driving force behind the unionization of New York City's laundry workers, casting Robinson and her coworkers as the beneficiaries of a powerful international union that took in a poor and demoralized workforce as part of its broader commitment to industrial unionism and racial justice. The ACWA, according to this narrative, provided the money and expertise to organize a low-wage, low-skilled workforce that included significant numbers of African Americans.[18] This interpretation, which hews closely to that of resource mobilization theorists who posit that social movements are most successful when adequate resources—in particular, money and labor—are deployed to facilitate collective action, erases the decades of worker organizing that preceded the ACWA's intervention.[19] This book argues that the CIO laundry campaign succeeded because a core group of worker leaders had already forged a culture of solidarity and resistance at the grassroots level. The simultaneous presence of organizational resources *and* internal activist solidarities, the latter of which are identified by collective identity theorists as critical to a movement's success, facilitated the unionization of New York's laundry workers.[20] In 1937 radical laundry workers, including Jessie Smith and her good friend Beatrice Shapiro Lumpkin, Black nationalists such as Charlotte Adelmond, African American socialists such as Noah Walter of the Negro Labor Committee, and longtime AFL laundry unionists, joined forces to organize their coworkers, part of the mass movement that would soon transform organized labor into a powerful political and economic force.

I had originally intended to conclude this book on a triumphant note with the success of the union campaign in 1937 and with the subsequent achievement of industry-wide agreements that secured higher wages, shorter hours, paid vacation and sick days, arbitration machinery to mediate workplace grievances, and a closed shop, important victories by any measure.[21] However, by glancing ahead in the union records I sensed that this triumph was short-lived and that an equally important story about what happened to the laundry workers after unionization was waiting to be told. Extending the book into the postwar period meant that the laundry workers could become a case study for assessing the relationship between the industrial union movement and women and people of color employed in the traditionally low-wage industrial service sector.

Early scholarship on the CIO praised industrial union leaders for organizing industries with large numbers of Black workers, for hiring African American organizers, and for their commitment to rooting out racial discrimination. Under collective agreements Black union members won unprecedented wage gains, pensions, and a degree of job security previously unimaginable.[22] As scholars have documented, however, industrial unionists' commitment to racial justice varied widely across and within unions and was embraced most vigorously by Black workers themselves and by Left-led unions such as the United Packinghouse Workers and the National Maritime Union. Many CIO unionists refused to prioritize the dismantling of racist job structures and wage scales, to support Black workers' aspirations for leadership, or to engage in civil rights advocacy. As labor historian Marshall Stevenson notes, like most other American organizations and institutions, the CIO went through "historically exclusive and inclusive phases of African-American participation."[23]

The scholarship on the CIO and gender exposes a similarly mixed record. Labor sociologist Ruth Milkman argues that the CIO lacked a "special commitment to challenging sexual inequality" and that industrial union leaders remained wedded to a male breadwinner model that cast women in secondary roles. Men dominated leadership positions, even in unions with majority-female memberships, and supported women's demands for equality only insofar as they advanced men's own interests. But despite these shortcomings, industrial unionism went far beyond craft unionism by creating spaces where women could mobilize in pursuit of equity. Opportunities for women were especially abundant during World War II, when a robust women's culture flourished in unions such as the United Auto Workers and the United Electrical Workers. Barriers to women's unionism persisted, but as historian Dorothy Sue Cobble argues, such barriers often served to reinforce women's escalating demands.[24]

A Matter of Moral Justice contributes to this scholarship by examining the relationship between Black laundry activists, described by Dollie Robinson as the "democratic initiative," and their white male union leaders at the local (LWJB) and national (ACWA) levels in the 1940s. Under the leadership of Charlotte Adelmond, the democratic initiative pursued a civil rights agenda that included equal pay for equal work, the promotion of African American men into driving positions, the inclusion of a nondiscrimination clause in the collective agreements, and expanded social supports within the union.[25] During and after the war the democratic initiative challenged the racist practices of private institutions such as the Red Cross, passed resolutions in support of the anticolonial struggles being waged by people of color abroad, collaborated with civil rights groups to end racial discrimination and violence, and demanded access to leadership positions in the union so that they could pursue this agenda. Black workers' civil rights unionism, as labor scholars Robert Korstad and Martha Biondi have demonstrated, gained its power from its expansive social vision and broad coalition building, including, at least initially, the alliance between labor, the Left, and African Americans and its commitment to interracial organizing.[26] As chapters 8 and 9 reveal, African American laundry workers and their radical allies—before the ACWA ejected the communists from the laundry union in 1941—contributed to the dynamic civil rights unionism animating the postwar urban North, what historian Jacquelyn Dowd Hall describes as the "decisive first phase" of the modern civil rights movement.[27]

The final two chapters of this book explore how white male industrial union leaders and white workers responded to the democratic initiative's civil rights unionism, exposing a disappointing but familiar pattern of union racism, union sexism, and union bureaucracy. In the 1940s the ACWA leadership—composed primarily of white male professional unionists—imposed an organizational structure and vision on the union that privileged labor peace and stable contractual relations over meaningful gains at the bargaining table or racial justice for Black workers. Race- and gender-based job assignments and wage scales remained intact in the postwar era, and women and people of color continued to earn less than subsistence-level wages. The conflicts that ensued between Black workers demanding racial and economic justice and their white male union leaders culminated in 1950 with the ousting of Adelmond, Robinson, and other Black activists from the union. This outcome exposes some of the very real differences and interests among white and Black workers and their union leaders and suggests that the industrial union movement fell short of its commitments to women and people of color.[28]

Despite the disappointing outcome, this story is not without hope. These tenacious and outspoken Black working-class women overcame seemingly insurmountable odds and used the openings provided to mobilize in pursuit of equal treatment and dignity at work. Their stories challenge assumptions about worker passivity and about the inability of the most exploited to organize. Resurrecting these moments of resistance complicates the history of the industrial union movement and provides insights on organizing in the twenty-first century, when women and people of color in the postindustrial service and care sectors have been leading some of the militant battles for economic and social justice.

Uncovering this story has been a challenge, not because the Laundry Workers Joint Board did not leave behind copious union records but rather because those records focused on the accomplishments of the mostly white men who ran the union. Women and Black workers appear in the union records either as loyal trade unionists and helpmates who unquestioningly supported union policy—a formulation that mirrors the traditional interpretation of Black women as "ground troops" or "bridge leaders" rather than as leaders of their own movements—or as agitators and troublemakers whose understanding of the industrial union project and their place within it was deeply flawed.[29] Recovering the role of women and African Americans as leaders with significant rank-and-file support required looking at a different set of sources, including the records of the Women's Trade Union League and the Communist Party. Oral histories conducted by me and others have been particularly valuable in restoring the place of women and African Americans in this story, as has the communist and Black press, in particular the *New York Amsterdam News*, which followed the laundry union closely. A fifty-page legal memo compiled by Black feminist and civil rights lawyer Pauli Murray, who represented Charlotte Adelmond, provides a searing account of the racial abuses Black workers suffered under the union's local and national leadership.[30] Taken together, these sources allow us to consider some of the tensions that emerged within the industrial union movement between Black workers and their white union leaders and between workers committed to rank-and-file control and grassroots democracy and those intent on consolidating their personal power. At the same time, they reveal the extraordinary activism of a group of workers who, in the face of incredible odds, tried to build a democratic union committed to racial justice, economic dignity, and gender equality.

CHAPTER ONE

"We Win a Place in Industry"

Black Women and the Birth of the Power Laundry Industry

In 1924, at the age of sixteen, Sylvia Woods moved with her husband from New Orleans to Chicago, part of the Great Migration that saw six million African Americans abandon the Jim Crow South between 1915 and 1970 for the urban industrial centers of the North and West.[1] Only days after her arrival Woods approached one of the local laundries that dotted the city landscape and waited outside the plant for the foreman to appear. Although the foreman informed her that there were no jobs for an inexperienced worker and sent her on her way, Woods, who was not one to be deterred (as a teenager she had refused to sing "The Star-Spangled Banner" in school because she did not feel free in a land where she was forced to attend a segregated school and forbidden from playing in the fancy "white" park), showed up the following day and the one after that, biding her time until the foreman finally relented and hired her.[2] If she had peered inside the grimy windows, Woods would have seen the sorters and markers, hunched over piles of dirty laundry, sorting the garments by color and fabric and the washers, white and Black men, standing in deep puddles of water loading garments into the large rotating cylindrical washing machines. Down the hall she would have seen the starchers with their cracked hands dipping dress shirts into vats of boiling starch and the ironers wearing bandanas and gloves to protect their hands and faces from the scorching heat and steam. As a Black woman Woods would have paid particular attention to the ironers, knowing that this was the position she would most likely be assigned. In the relatively peaceful room at the back of the plant, Woods would have seen the mostly white women folding and packaging the freshly laundered pieces for return to the customer.[3]

In the 1920s power laundry work represented a relatively new employment opportunity for African American women. Had Woods arrived in Chicago ten years earlier she most likely would have worked as a domestic servant in a white household. Compelled by wartime labor shortages to hire nontraditional sources of labor, power laundry owners, like many other industrial employers, first opened their doors to Black women during World War I. But unlike most other industrialists, power laundry owners continued to employ African American women after the war. As a result, by the beginning of the Great Depression, the power laundry had become the leading industrial employer of Black women in the United States, surpassing both the garment and tobacco trades. In New York, Chicago, and other leading centers of the industry (and of the Great Migration), power laundries would serve as vehicles of proletarianization, enabling African American women like Woods to escape the much despised field of domestic service and take their place, albeit on the lowest rungs of the industrial ladder.[4] Understanding how Black women came to work in power laundries in such large numbers and how they understood that work highlights the complex ways in which race, gender, and migration shape urban labor markets and illuminates how Black wage-earning women balanced their income-earning needs with their desire for autonomy and dignity within a labor market narrowly circumscribed by race and gender discrimination.

The Technological and Social Roots of the Laundry Industry

In 1924 Woods owed her employment to a complicated web of technological developments and social changes. By the end of the 1800s large mechanical washing machines; flat-work ironers, which pressed sheets and towels between padded rollers and steam-heated chests or cylinders; centrifugal drying machines, which spun clothes at high speed; and steam presses could wash, dry, and iron clothing and flat work in a portion of the time it took the home laundry worker or housewife. Originally, workers operated the machines by using hand cranks, foot treadles, or hand levers; by the 1920s many of the machines were operated by pushing a button. Mechanization and the construction of urban water systems in the mid- and late nineteenth century, which were made available first to factories and businesses such as power laundries, hastened the removal of the work from the home to the factory.[5]

While legend had it that an enterprising miner constructed the first power-operated washing machine in the United States in 1851 in Oakland, California, designed to cater to the men flocking West in search of gold (often without female kin), historians Arwen Palmer Mohun and Carole Turbin locate the origins of the industry not on the "masculinized frontier" but rather in eighteenth-century textile production. Mohun demonstrates that as early as 1800 at least one English textile manufacturer had developed a system of steam-powered machinery capable of washing and drying laundry in an institutional setting. British and American firms offering commercial laundry machinery came on the market in the middle of the nineteenth century, and within a few decades steam laundries (so-called for their reliance on steam power) had become publicly recognized as a "distinct commercial enterprise." In the mid-1800s these enterprises consisted of small-scale operations that employed relatively few workers.[6]

In the United States, the laundry industry's origins date back to the 1850s in Troy, New York, the center of the nation's shirt, collar, and cuff industry. (For much of the nineteenth and early twentieth centuries men wore shirts with detachable cuffs and collars to reduce the amount of laundering and to enhance the possibilities for variations in style.) According to Turbin, in the 1850s a collar manufacturer in Troy constructed what is believed to be the nation's first commercial laundry. Troy's collar laundresses, as they were called, washed, starched, and ironed the newly manufactured dress shirts, work that required considerable skill. (Laundries as centralized workspaces where at least some of the work was done by machine would be variously and rather imprecisely referred to as steam laundries, power laundries, commercial laundries, industrial laundries, and in Troy in the mid- and late nineteenth century, collar laundries.) In 1860 Troy was home to fourteen collar laundries employing six hundred workers. By 1886 many of Troy's large shirt and collar factories had constructed their own laundry departments, where they employed as many as two hundred workers (per employer).[7]

Troy's laundry workers, nearly all of whom were Irish immigrant women, inhabit a special place in the history of the laundry industry and in the women's labor movement, evidence of the possibilities of women's unionism in nineteenth-century America. In 1864 collar laundresses Esther Keegan and Kate Mullaney formed the Collar Laundry Union, which, Turbin argues, marked the beginning of the women's labor movement. In the same decade women compositors in New York City organized the Women's Typographical Union No. 1, women shoe workers in Lynn, Massachusetts, organized the first local of the Daughters of St. Crispin, and women cap makers and parasol and umbrella sewers in New York City organized locals. Part of this regional network of women's labor activism, Troy's laundresses engaged in significant labor militancy for the next two decades, launching strikes to win higher wages and protest the implementation of machinery and attendant wage cuts.[8] Turbin attributes the women's early militancy to the homogeneity of the workforce (most of the collar laundresses were Irish immigrant women); to the city's unionized and skilled male Irish molders, who supported the women's activism; to Irish cultural, religious, and political traditions that imbued the women with a strong sense of class consciousness; and to being part of a tight-knit immigrant community in which relatively skilled workers of both sexes supported one another.[9]

Troy's laundries served as important precursors to the more technologically sophisticated laundries of the twentieth century where workers labored in specialized departments performing a single task under the direct supervision of a foreman or supervisor. As laundry machinery became more complex and expensive in the 1910s and 1920s, laundries grew in size and scale. By the 1930s most power laundry workers labored in large, corporate-owned, and highly mechanized establishments alongside dozens or even hundreds of other employees. Yet small laundries where a handful of workers used less sophisticated machinery, often bought on the second-hand market, or did some of the work by hand, persisted well into the twentieth century. As a result, laundry workers labored in a variety of settings, from the tiny laundry shop where workers performed a multitude of tasks to the sprawling plant with dozens of departments and a highly detailed division of labor.[10]

Power laundries did not immediately displace the traditional labor of the home laundry worker or laundress, as she was often called. In 1900 335,000 women made their living washing clothes for wages in private homes, of whom 200,000 were African American.[11] Home laundry work as an occupation remained most prevalent in the South, where nearly all of the workers were African American women. In fact, the widespread availability of African American laundresses who preferred home laundry work over domestic service, the major occupational field for Black women in 1900, impeded the development of the power laundry industry in the South.[12] In the urban centers of the North, immigrant and Black women who were shut out of other occupations took in laundry well into the 1930s and beyond, preferring laundry work over live-in domestic service and sometimes over industrial jobs, given that washing at home provided opportunities to combine wage earning with domestic responsibilities. In her 1911 study of Black Harlem, *Half a Man: The Status of the Negro in New York*, socialist and NAACP cofounder Mary White Ovington observed that for African American women, "laundry work is an important home industry, and one may watch mothers at their tubs or ironing boards from Monday morning until Saturday night." Ovington described laundry work as New York City's "great colored home industry."[13] Power laundries, then, were competing not only with one another but also with home laundry workers. The complexity of the trade—small and large shops competing with home laundresses and even housewives who during hard economic times could opt to do the work themselves—contributed to the low wages that would become a defining feature of power laundry work.[14]

The contraction of domestic spaces that accompanied urbanization created the concentrated markets necessary for the growth of the laundry industry. While the rural housewife or home laundry worker had ample space to wash and iron multiple loads of laundry, cramped urban living spaces, air pollution, and unreliable or nonexistent residential water supplies convinced many a city dweller to send their laundry to a commercial establishment where piped-in water and sealed windows provided optimal conditions for cleanliness.[15] In 1899 the *New York Times* reported on the growing number of laundry establishments sprouting up across the city that were patronized by apartment dwellers eager to avoid having to haggle with their neighbors over roof space to hang their freshly washed garments or risk having their clothes "surreptitiously appropriated."[16] Residents who had once relied on home laundry workers would increasingly turn to power laundries rather than risk having their clothes misappropriated or contaminated in the squalid tenement dwelling of the neighborhood laundress.[17]

While power laundries would become fixtures of the urban industrial North, they remained relatively uncommon in the South. In 1930, when New York City boasted four hundred power laundries and twenty-five thousand power laundry workers, the entire state of Alabama was home to only fifty-six laundries and fewer than three thousand power laundry workers. The persistence of rural and small-town life and the widespread availability of African American laundresses, who because of lack of employment opportunities took in bundles of family wash for as little as a dollar or less (cleaning a large family bundle could take days to complete), undermined the financial viability of the power laundry in the South.[18] For most of the early and mid-1900s New York City led in the number of power laundries and employees, followed closely by Chicago and Los Angeles.[19]

Urbanization spurred the laundry industry in other important ways. Streetcars, factories, and other urban fixtures left residents covered in soot and grime. At the same time, rising standards of cleanliness, a matter of both aesthetics and public health, and the expansion of individual wardrobes made of cotton, an easily washed fabric—the result of the post–Civil War ready-to-wear clothing industry—increased the amount of clothing that Americans regularly washed and ironed. Eager to divest themselves of this onerous household chore (housewives frequently listed laundry work as their most burdensome domestic task), housewives were among the power laundry's first customers.[20] Because men's dress shirts were particularly difficult and messy to wash at home—cuffs and collars had to be starched and ironed—they were often the first item to be sent out. Laundry owners catered to housewives and men living alone by offering the bachelor bundle service, in which shirts or detachable collars and cuffs were washed, dried, and ironed, and customers paid for them by the piece. For single men, the bachelor bundle took the place of a wife or a servant.[21]

Commercial and service establishments comprised a second and initially even larger market for industrial laundry services. In the early twentieth century, laundries received the bulk of their business from hotels, restaurants, and steam ship companies, businesses that produced large amounts of linen or flat work (sheets, towels, and other flat pieces) that required frequent washing and ironing.[22] To capture a larger share of the family market in the 1910s, power laundrymen introduced the wet wash or damp wash service, in which families could send their garments and flat work in net bags to be put through the washing machines and returned damp and unironed. Wet wash, which cost significantly less than fully finished work, in which everything was washed, dried, and ironed, appealed to working-class families and those on a budget. Customers paid for the work on a per pound basis that varied depending on the finishing option requested, the most expensive being having everything returned washed and ironed.[23]

The introduction of more affordable finishing options led to an explosion in the family service laundry trade, which by 1930 had surpassed the linen trade. Estimates suggest that by the 1930s approximately one-third of all American families used power laundries on a regular or part-time basis. In 1940 the laundry trade journal the *Laundry Age* estimated that close to three-quarters of city residents sent part or all of their laundry to an industrial establishment. As a result, by 1930 the majority of power laundry business came in the form of family wash rather than linen from commercial establishments.[24]

Doing the Dirty Work:
The Construction of a Workforce

The expansion of the laundry industry depended on the availability of workers willing and able to perform the hot, difficult, and sweaty jobs that power laundries created. As the family trade increased in the early 1900s, so too did the demand for workers. From 110,000 workers in 1910, the first year that census takers included power laundries in the US census, the industry exploded to 233,000 workers by 1930.[25] With labor costs constituting 50 percent of all business costs, industrial laundry employers actively recruited low-wage workers, who were structurally disadvantaged by their gender, ethnicity, race, and other social variables. Here laundry employers had both tradition and history on their side.

As a home-based occupation that involved performing ostensibly unskilled work related to the maintenance of the family, laundry work had long been gendered women's work. In 1900 335,000, or 87 percent, of the nation's laundry workers were women, most of whom washed clothes by hand in private homes.[26] In the early 1900s wage-earning women followed the work as it moved into the factory, where employers, most of whom were white men, employed women for all but the most skilled jobs. In 1909 the laundry was one of the few industries covered by the manufacturing census in which female employees exceeded men, a reflection of the work's domestic and female-gendered roots. In 1930 two-thirds of power laundry workers were women.[27]

Prior to 1920 most power laundry workers were white, a function of the industry's concentration in the urban North, where before the Great War relatively few African Americans lived and worked, and of the racist hiring practices, which kept Black workers on the margins of the urban industrial economy everywhere. In 1910 57 percent of the nation's 110,000 power laundry workers were native-born white, 19 percent were foreign-born white, 13 percent were Black, and 11 percent were Chinese. Prior to World War I, most power laundry workers in the Northeast and Midwest were of northern European descent. In New York City, immigrants from northern Europe worked alongside Italians and Russian Jews.[28] Tensions, documented by reformers such as Women's Trade Union League (WTUL) upper-class ally Carola Woerishoffer and muckraker Dorothy Richardson, predictably erupted. Woerishoffer, who worked in sixteen laundries over four months in 1909, described the laundry as a "small unit fiercely competitive multi-nationalities industry" marked by "deep-rooted" antagonisms between the Irish and Italian workers, who "clubb[ed] together from the different departments in separate bands." Italians ranked lowest on the occupational ladder and earned the lowest wages simply because they were Italian.[29]

Labor shortages brought on by World War I, the reduction in emigration from Europe, and the migration of 1.5 million African Americans from the rural South to the North contributed to the laundry's transformation from a predominantly white to an interracial workforce. In 1919 the Chicago Commission on Race Relations reported that wartime labor shortages had forced power laundry owners to "tap this reserve labor supply."[30] By the end of the war Black workers played a larger role in the industry than immigrant workers. In 1920 one-quarter of the nation's eighty-one thousand women laundry workers were African American, compared to 15 percent who were foreign born (the remainder were native-born white). Between 1910 and 1920 the increase in the percentage of Black workers in laundries exceeded that of all other occupations except barbers and hairdressers.[31]

The employment of Black women in power laundries coincided with the broader movement of women and African Americans into industry, but the laundry was exceptional in that Black women did not lose the foothold they had gained in the industry during the war. A Women's Bureau Department of Labor study conducted in 1920 concluded that African American women "did not have a permanent footing in industry."[32] Increased mechanization in the 1920s eroded Black women's already tenuous industrial foothold, eliminating many of the low-skilled jobs they had held. As unemployment rose in the late 1920s and especially in the early 1930s, African American women would be squeezed out of the industrial workplace altogether.[33]

The power laundry represented an exception to this broader pattern of industrial exclusion. Between 1920 and 1930 the number of Black women in power laundries jumped from twenty-one thousand to close to fifty thousand. By the beginning of the Depression, 30 percent of the nation's 160,000 women laundry workers were African American, 11 percent were foreign-born white, and the remainder were native-born white.[34] In the South, where the industry remained marginal, four out of every five power laundry workers were African American, and in the cities that dominated the Great Migration, including Chicago and New York, Black women comprised up to one-half or more of the workforce.[35] In 1930, when only one hundred thousand Black women worked in industry in all of the United States, close to fifty thousand worked in power laundries, more than two times as many as in the tobacco trade and three times as many as in the clothing industry.[36]

While Black workers provided much of the labor that fueled the growth of the laundry industry, African Americans were rarely able to raise the capital needed to open their own laundries. In 1928 the *New York Amsterdam News* reported that there were only four African American–owned power laundries and fourteen Black-owned hand laundries (small shops, introduced in chapter 3) in Harlem, where they served a mostly Black clientele excluded from the pickup routes of white-owned laundries. Black Americans were unable to compete with the better-capitalized laundries owned and operated by white businessmen who were able to offer the same services at lower prices.[37]

"This Was Completely Jim Crow": Black Women and Power Laundry Work

In his 1921 tome on World War I and Black workers, George Haynes, head of the Division of Negro Economics in the Department of Labor, attributed Black women's employment in power laundries to the "difficulties and dangers of the work" and to the "traditional linking of Negro women to such tasks."[38] The "linking" of Black women to laundry work began during the period of racial slavery, when slave women were required to wash the household linen and clothing, and it persisted into the postemancipation era, when white southerners hired Black women to perform the difficult and backbreaking labor involved in preindustrial washing. As a home-based occupation, laundry work involved procuring, transferring, and heating hundreds of gallons of water, lifting and scrubbing heavy wet clothing over washboards, and wielding piping-hot irons, work deemed too heavy and too menial for native-born white women. In 1900 laundry work employed the smallest percentage of white women of native parentage and the third largest group of Black women in the United States.[39] Because of the work's early association with female slave labor, white workers' aversion to laundry work was particularly acute in the South. Polly Stone Buck of Atlanta, Georgia, explained that in the Jim Crow South, "no white family ever did its own washing." When Buck's father's death left the family in financial straits they still found the money to hire an African American laundress. Buck explained that "even at the time when we were poorest, the soiled clothes were regularly 'counted out.'"[40] In 1950 laundry historian and publicist Fred DeArmond observed that of two women of the same social status, one from the North and one from the South, "the southern white woman will find some way to hire her washing done, while the northern woman is much more likely to do it herself." DeArmond attributed the difference to the "servant tradition carried over from slavery days in the South." As DeArmond understood it, the employment of Black laundresses enabled white southerners not only to avoid an onerous household chore but also to lay claim to one of the privileges of whiteness. The African American laundress or washerwoman, as she was commonly called, served as a critical link to a racial past in which all Black people were subordinate to and purportedly eager to serve all white people.[41]

The historical association of washing with women of color contributed to the work's undesirability and to African American women's ability to obtain such work as it moved from the home to the factory. In 1908 Elizabeth Butler of the New Jersey Consumers' League observed that the power laundry attracted women who were "least able to choose their kind of employment." The specter of the wash tub and all that it implies, she explained, are "irksome to many ambitious girls."[42] New York City laundry worker and radical organizer Jessie Smith observed that "the average white person wouldn't go work in a laundry. . . . This was completely Jim Crow." Smith explained that the laundry was "not considered prestigious" because of the "idea of the product." Although she worked in a laundry during the Great Depression, Smith wondered "who would go into that, that's a dirty business. You're picking up dirty clothes." As someone who was exposed to African American history through the Communist Party, Smith understood that tradition and racism, as well as poor working conditions, contributed to Black women's employment in power laundries. In the South, Smith explained, "that was what they all [Black women] did, laundry. Or they nursed or were maids and they did people's laundry in order to get a dollar. . . . [A]ll through that period, probably for 100 years, they did the dirty work. So the laundries, they came up here."[43] An astute student of history, Smith understood that Black southern women had long been assigned society's "dirty work," a reality that shaped their employment opportunities in the North, where migrants seeking economic empowerment confronted the weight of history.

Black women's employment in power laundries was a function of employer preferences, as well as history. In an intensely competitive industry, laundrymen eagerly recruited traditionally low-wage workers. This was especially true in the 1920s, when laundrymen faced new financial challenges as progressive states such as New York and California implemented minimum wage laws. Laundry owners were also victims of their own success. By the 1920s supply had exceeded demand as aspiring entrepreneurs flocked to the industry, opening small, underfinanced shops that competed with the larger and more highly mechanized plants.[44] Laundry owners who had first hired Black women during the war quickly gleaned the financial advantages of employing them long term. To capitalize on the large-scale migration of Black workers to New York during and after the war, in the 1920s, some laundry owners moved their plants to Harlem and Brooklyn's Brownsville—home to large and growing Black populations—and, according to Black socialist Frank Crosswaith, "specialized in giving employment only to Negroes."[45] In 1924 investigators from the New York Department of Labor noted the concentration of laundries in the "very oldest and poorest loft buildings available, where rentals are lowest, and local, especially foreign and colored help is to be had at low wages."[46]

In addition to hiring workers disadvantaged by racial and ethnic discrimination, power laundry employers hired older women and wage-earning wives and mothers, workers also on the margins of the urban industrial economy. Nationally, in 1920 19 percent of women laundry workers were forty-five or older; only a little over one-third were under the age of twenty-five, compared to almost one-half of all women employed in manufacturing and mechanical pursuits. African American women laundry workers were likely to be younger than their white female counterparts, evidence that racial discrimination limited the employment opportunities of Black women of all ages.[47] After her journalistic foray as a laundry worker, muckraker Dorothy Richardson reported that "the regular workers are old women. . . . Young women will work in such places only as a last resort." One of the workers told her that the laundry was simply "no place for a young girl to work."[48] In the early 1930s a sixty-five-year-old laundry worker named Mrs. Wolfe told investigators from the consumer activist organization the League of Women Shoppers that she would not allow her young girlfriends to work in the laundries but instead helped them secure more respectable employment at the telephone company: "I'd say, 'I want you to be ladies, not like me. You got an education. I'm an old woman and can't start out new, but you're young.'"[49] As historian Alice Kessler-Harris argues, wage-earning women like Wolfe "developed hierarchies of desirable occupations" shaped by "class, ethnic and racial distinctions in the work force," as well as their own preferences for work deemed respectable.[50] For Wolfe, keeping her young friends out of the laundry was critical to maintaining their respectability and status as "ladies."

Power laundries hired relatively large numbers of wage-earning mothers and wives, as well as older and racialized workers. In 1910 a little over one-quarter of women laundry workers were married; by 1930 the percentage had jumped to 43, and an additional 20 percent reported their status as widowed or divorced.[51] Despite the laundry's difficult working conditions, wives and mothers found some aspects of the work amenable to their domestic roles. Because laundries were scattered across the city, serving the local population, wage-earning mothers could easily obtain work close to home. In the 1930s, activist and educator

Anna Arnold Hedgeman of the Negro Branch of the Young Women's Christian Association (YWCA) in Jersey City, New Jersey, noted that many of the laundry workers who frequented the YWCA were mothers who went home at lunch to feed their babies, despite being worried about the quality of their "hot, tired milk."[52] The laundry's work schedule and convenience attracted wives and mothers. As the clothes had to be washed at the start of the day, a job that was done by men, the women's workday (with the exception of sorters) often began midmorning, giving them time to perform household tasks before the start of their paid workday. And because laundries were nearly always hiring—a function of the poor working conditions and low wages—white mothers and wives and to a lesser extent Black women could easily obtain work in response to a family emergency. In 1914 a twenty-seven-year-old woman who had worked in laundries since the age of thirteen explained that when she married she returned to the laundry only for short periods to help out in emergencies. When she turned thirty-four financial circumstances forced her back into the laundry, where she worked full time until she died of tuberculosis five years later, likely related to her unhealthy working conditions. In 1911 a thirty-nine-year-old African American mother of one explained that she took in laundry "excepting occasional days, when she goes into the laundry for a few days at a time."[53] Until power laundries and home washing machines rendered the occupation of home laundering obsolete in the 1950s, working women could move between power and home laundry work to accommodate the needs of their families and maximize their wage-earning potential.[54]

Proletarianization and the Meaning of Power Laundry Work to Black Women

Scholars have interpreted African American women's employment in power laundries as evidence of their continued exploitation in the labor market, situating the laundry along a continuum of low-paying, low-status service or service-related work, what feminist scholar Evelyn Nakano Glenn describes as "back-room jobs," jobs traditionally assigned to racial-ethnic women. In her pioneering work on Black women's labor, historian Jacqueline Jones argues that African American women's employment in power laundries "reveals the doubtfulness of their advancement as factory workers."[55] Jones's analysis underscores the undesirability of power laundry work relative to many other industrial occupations, as well as to white-collar work, but minimizes the ways in which African American women embraced power laundry work as a rare and coveted opportunity to leave domestic service.

At the beginning of the Depression three in five Black women worked in the domestic and personal service sector, primarily as servants in private homes.[56]

Subject to the direct supervision of their employers and isolated from other workers, domestics were acutely vulnerable to sexual and physical abuse, degrading treatment, and overwork. An employer's requirement that a woman wear a uniform, enter by the back door, act deferentially, and make herself invisible were intended to reinforce the domestic's subordination and undermine her sense of humanity.[57] Harlem activist Florence Rice, who worked in household service in the Bronx before securing a job in a power laundry during the Depression, reported that she had to fend off the nearly daily advances of her white male employer, an experience she did not have in the laundry. Rice, who noted the difficulties of power laundry work, nonetheless insisted that it "was better than domestic work, certainly."[58]

Panamanian-born garment activist Maida Springer remembers that her mother, Adina Stewart, quit her job as a domestic servant because of the low wages and humiliating treatment and obtained work at a Park Avenue laundry, where she earned higher wages ironing pleated nightgowns and fine embroidered linens. New York's laundry employers, who understood that Black women such as Rice and Stewart preferred laundry work over domestic service, exploited this preference when their workers demanded better conditions. Anna Hedgeman of the Colored YWCA reported that the laundry bosses would respond to the women's complaints about low wages and poor working conditions with the "reminder that laundry jobs were better than domestic work."[59]

White women who enjoyed more and better employment opportunities quickly abandoned domestic service when jobs became available in the manufacturing and white-collar sectors. As a result, between 1920 and 1930 the percentage of Black women in domestic and personal service rose by 50 percent. By 1920 African American women no longer constituted a regional servant class. As they came to dominate domestic service, African American women successfully challenged the occupational requirement to live in, a victory that advanced their struggle to win greater autonomy in the workplace and to protect their bodies.[60] They would also actively pursue jobs outside of domestic service, including in the laundry. The Chicago Urban League reported that while it had "great difficulty" meeting the demand for domestic servants and home laundresses during World War I, it had no difficulty filling job openings in power laundries. The Chicago Commission on Race Relations similarly reported that Black women embraced jobs in power laundries during the war, "eager to desert work as domestic servants and 'family washer-women,' with the social stigma and restricted human contact involved." The women explained to investigators from the commission that the power laundry's relatively autonomous working conditions and the "association with fellow-workers" combined to "enliven the work day."[61] Of 211 women interviewed by the Women's Bureau of the Department of Labor for a

1930 study of power laundry work in twenty-three cities across the country, 90 percent reported that they preferred laundry work over domestic service, citing higher pay, shorter hours, no Sunday work, and more freedom.[62]

Domestic workers from Washington, DC, interviewed in the 1980s by historian Elizabeth Clark-Lewis, similarly recalled that their coworkers abandoned domestic service as soon as jobs became available in power laundries in the 1920s. Exposing intraracial divisions within the Black community, some of the domestic workers complained that laundry owners only hired northern-born Black workers. Southern-born household worker Ora Fisher complained: "I remember when they first started taking coloreds at the laundries or to work cleaning government buildings. Every one of them that got on came from here [Washington]. They had been to school more, that was the reason. They sure couldn't work no better than us the world knows." Mathilene Anderson similarly explained that household employers only hired Black women "born and trained-up in the South," knowing that northern-born domestics would abandon household service as soon as jobs in laundries and other more desirable workplaces became available.[63] The workers' observations reveal the desirability of laundry work over domestic service, as well as industrialists' preference for hiring African American workers trained and educated in the North, those who were most likely to be familiar with industrial work routines and discipline.

In 1929 an article in the National Urban League's *Opportunity* celebrated the employment of Black women in power laundries with the title "We Win a Place in Industry."[64] That the Urban League, an organization committed to improving the economic and social status of Black migrants, would frame power laundry work as a victory suggests that Black workers and their advocates embraced industrial laundry as a new and welcome employment opportunity. For Rice, Woods, and the tens of thousands of other African American wage-earning women who had traditionally worked as domestic servants, the power laundry provided an opportunity to earn marginally higher wages, exercise greater workplace autonomy, and find solace in the social networks they would develop on the shop floor and in some places in the union hall. Beginning in the 1920s, the power laundry served as a vehicle of proletarianization, facilitating African American women's transition from sharecropping and low-paid personal service work into the urban industrial sector. In contrast to white workers, for whom historian Joe Trotter argues proletarianization often involved a loss of autonomy over land and skilled crafts, for African American women it represented an upward occupational shift, an opportunity to leave jobs most reminiscent of slavery and enter the industrial workplace.[65] It was within this context that Black women pursued power laundry work and that the Black community celebrated such work as a victory.

CHAPTER TWO

A Miniature Hell

Working in a Power Laundry

In 1938 Vivian Morris of the Works Progress Administration (WPA) visited a laundry on West 41 Street between Tenth and Eleventh Avenues. Despite the laundry's midtown location, most of the workers came from Harlem. The WPA writer, who had borrowed a union card from an unemployed worker to get inside the plant, recalled her shock upon entering the ironing department. Morris described the "gushes of damp heat [that] pushed at you from some invisible force in the mechanism of the machine." The "smooth, shiny-faced women," Morris wrote, "work in silence, occasionally dropping a word here and there, slowly wiping away dripping perspiration" as they wearily pushed twelve-pound irons while listening to the "hiss of steam" and the "clanging of metal as the pistons bang into the sockets."[1] As Morris quickly deduced, ironing jobs were among the most difficult in the plant, and the positions most likely to be assigned to Black women. In contrast, employers hired white men to perform the ostensibly skilled jobs of machine washing and driving and paid them two to three times more than the ironers. White women worked as ironers, but, unlike Black women, they also obtained jobs as markers and sorters, highly coveted positions that paid more than ironing. By following the laundry as it moves through the plant, this chapter explores how cultural assumptions about the relationship between skill, ability, and a worker's racial and gender identity shape the social division of labor that emerges during an industry's formative years. An in-depth analysis of the laundry's working conditions and occupational structure also sheds light on some of the factors that impeded the workers' unionism in the first three decades of the twentieth century.

FIGURE 1. A driver and driver's assistant at the Avenue Industrial Laundry, New York City, undated. Credit: Photographer Sam Reiss. Folder 1, box 51, 5743 P, ACWA Photographs, Kheel Center, Cornell University, Ithaca, NY.

Blue Monday: Men with Trucks

The laundry's workweek began early Monday morning with the drivers, who picked up laundry from individual families and institutional customers and delivered it to the plant. Drivers or outside workers comprised 10 percent of the workforce and were all white men.[2] In small laundries one or two drivers handled all of the routes, while large laundries had fleets of drivers and trucks that were serviced by their own mechanics. Most drivers had established routes with regular customers that they serviced on a weekly basis. Even after motor vehicles replaced horse-drawn wagons in the 1920s, the men started as early as seven in the morning to accommodate their customers' work schedules and worked well into the night returning bundles of clean laundry. Bleary from lack of sleep, the men lugged bags of laundry that weighed as much as sixty pounds up and down narrow apartment stairwells while haggling with customers over prices. Because drivers took money, settled complaints about missing pieces or improperly washed items, and engaged in sales work, laundry worker and organizer Beatrice Shapiro Lumpkin insists that drivers "had some character-istics of small businessmen."[3] Women's Trade Union League (WTUL) president and longtime laundry organizer Rose Schneiderman similarly reported that "the drivers were always able to hold their own with the employers, for they were really salesmen and employers depended on them to bring in business."[4]

As the only workers who interacted directly with the customers, drivers did indeed enjoy significant bargaining power over the employer. A disgruntled delivery man could take his customers elsewhere or, because of the relatively low start-up costs, open his own plant. Although laundry machinery could be expensive—in 1910 a machine for a single process could cost as much as $200—and large laundries spent considerable money purchasing new machines to keep pace with changes in fashion, owners of small laundries made do with only a few machines, often bought on the second-hand market, and had their employees do some of the work by hand.[5] Drivers in possession of their own trucks also had the option of "bobtailing," collecting laundry from customers and then patronizing whichever plant offered the lowest rate, keeping the dif-ference for himself. Eager to appease these workers, employers gave the drivers preferential treatment, including higher wages and a commission for securing new customers, as well as access to facilities such as coat closets.[6] In most cities, drivers earned two to three times more than the inside workers. In Depression era Chicago, drivers earned average weekly wages of thirty-four dollars, com-pared to eleven dollars for the inside female workers.[7]

Laundry employers, who were almost always white men, hired white men as drivers. Women and people of color were considered neither desirable as ambassadors of the industry nor capable of learning the complicated routes that depended on mastering the geography of the city. Since drivers interacted with customers, many of whom were white housewives, in intimate domestic spaces such as apartment hallways and door stoops, Black men's exclusion from driving jobs was also a function of Jim Crow. In 1950 trade historian, publicist, and laundry owner Fred DeArmond warned his fellow laundry owners not to employ drivers whose "dialect and racial characteristics are notably at variance" with those of their customers. DeArmond added, "Ability can overcome all handicaps, just as true love can make an interracial marriage a success, but why assume an extra hazard?"[8] DeArmond's reference to interracial marriage belied his fear that the employment of Black men as drivers could lead to consensual or, consistent with the racist trope of the Black beast rapist, a fiction used to enforce white supremacy through lynchings, nonconsensual relations between Black men and white women. The employment of drivers handicapped by race posed an unnecessary hazard. A smart businessman, DeArmond argued, would voluntarily police the sexual boundaries between white women and Black men in conformity with the racial etiquette of Jim Crow.[9]

It is also possible that Black men would have been refused entry into the buildings where many of the customers lived. In 1944 industrial relations scholar Herbert R. Northrup attributed the exclusion of Black men from driving positions in the laundries to white women who "object to their presence at the door." Radical laundry organizer Jessie Smith similarly believed that Black men would have been refused entry into many of New York's residential buildings.[10] A combination, then, of employer and customer prejudices and gendered and racialized assumptions about skill and presentability led to the exclusion of women and people of color from driving positions.

This Place "Wasn't Fit for Animals": Life inside the Plants

Inside workers, who accounted for close to 90 percent of the power laundry workforce, labored inside the plants out of sight of the public in what Evelyn Nakano Glenn describes as "back-room" jobs. Eight out of ten inside workers were women, and all of the Black workers in the industry worked inside the plants.[11] Inside workers labored in a variety of settings, from the tiny storefront shop to the sprawling power laundry that encompassed an entire city block. As the cost of machinery increased in the 1920s many small laundries went bankrupt or merged with larger laundries. As a result, by 1930 most laundry workers labored in corporate-owned plants that employed fifty or more workers. Small, poorly run, and undercapitalized laundries did not disappear, however, but remained on the margins of the industry driving down profits and wages.[12]

Despite the differences in scale and size, laundries shared certain commonalities, including hot, wet, and difficult working conditions. In the early 1900s few laundries were housed in spaces equipped to handle the heat and humidity generated by the machines and wet clothing. More commonly, laundries were found in garages, poorly ventilated factories, and even cellar basements, where rent was cheap.[13] Beatrice Lumpkin remembers working in a Bronx laundry in the 1930s that was formerly an auto repair shop, with no provisions for ventilation or drainage. She described the working conditions as "kinda fierce."[14] African American laundry worker and union leader Dollie Robinson recalled that many of her coworkers developed rheumatism, a condition she attributed to "handling all these wet clothes, one of the hazards of the job." Hot, humid working conditions and heavy lifting resulted in high rates of respiratory diseases, sciatica and neck pain, high blood pressure, colds, varicose veins, and rheumatism. Harsh cleaning chemicals burned the workers' hands and lungs, and accidents on improperly guarded machines and slippery floors were alarmingly common.[15]

The laundry's location at the nexus of the industrial and service sectors led to unpredictable work schedules and often long workweeks. A successful promotion, a large convention, or the arrival of a steamship on a tight schedule led to overwork, while a downturn in the economy could reduce business by as much as half. The housewife's traditional practice of doing laundry on Monday contributed to a lopsided workweek: twelve-, thirteen-, or even fourteen-hour days at the beginning of the week were followed by short days or no work at all.[16] Even after factoring in the lopsided schedule, hours in the laundry were typically long. In 1923 half of New York City's women laundry workers worked more than fifty hours a week, compared to only 18 percent of women employed in four manufacturing industries (tobacco, shirt and collar, paper box, and confectionary).[17] The 1930 Women's Bureau survey of 290 laundries in twenty-three cities determined that 40 percent of women laundry workers worked at least fifty-four hours a week. Hours were longest in the South, where most of the workers were Black. In good economic times, laundry workers could expect to enjoy relatively stable employment, for laundry was a year-round business.[18]

Since most laundry work was unskilled or semiskilled and could be learned in a few days, employers had little incentive to provide "perks" such as lunchrooms or welfare programs to reduce labor turnover. In 1939, African American laundry worker Evelyn Macon insisted that the toilet in her laundry "wasn't fit for animals, much less people." When she complained the boss told her there were not many places paying ten dollars a week, thus ending her protests.[19] Smith, who worked in a number of laundries in the Bronx in the 1930s, remembered that "there was no such thing as a lunch room." The workers ate "right on the counter where you happened to be working, or on a bench or a table." In one plant her coworkers warmed food such as spaghetti on the pipes. Smith lamented that in most laundries there was "no air conditioning, no air of any kind. And there were no rest periods, no breaks, and if you had to go to the bathroom you'd have to get permission."[20]

Abusive treatment and sexual harassment exacerbated the laundry's already poor working conditions. Lumpkin remembered that the foreman was "king" and that a woman could be fired for refusing to go out with him.[21] In the 1930s

African American laundry worker Nettie Wilson of New York City explained that if one of the bosses "likes a girl, she got to go to bed with him or lose her job." She also noted that "us colored girls gets treated worst of all." Workers at the National Laundry in the Bronx warned about a foreman who "doesn't like dark-skinned girls and lets them know it."[22] In a 1936 editorial in the *New York Amsterdam News* African American laundry worker Emma Cosby reported that if a woman wanted to keep her job, she had to be "friendly with the foreman, or even the employer." Racist and sexist stereotypes that cast Black women as Jezebels or whores—constructions deployed to justify white men's access to and abuse of Black women's bodies—underpinned and magnified the economic and sexual vulnerability of Black women in the laundries.[23]

From the Marking Department to the Finishing Room

Inside work began with the markers or checkers, who were usually white women. Markers received the bundles of clothing that had been delivered by the drivers or dropped off at the plant by customers eager to save on delivery costs. The checker recorded all the items on a laundry list and weighed the pieces so that the office workers could calculate the cost (most customers paid for their laundry on a per-pound basis). Using visible or invisible ink, a pin, or a temporary label or tag to mark the articles with the owner's name, the marker sent the items to a sorter, who sorted the laundry by color, fabric, and finishing service.[24] Marking required knowledge of fabrics, legible handwriting, bookkeeping skills, and, in plants where customers dropped off their laundry, presentability. Because markers sometimes interacted with the public and because the job included aspects of white-collar work, employers hired white women as markers. The 1930 Women's Bureau survey of 290 laundries found that only 5 percent of the African American women surveyed worked as markers or sorters, compared to 20 percent of the white women.[25] Because they recorded information, markers had some characteristics of clerical workers and earned the highest wages of the inside female workers. In 1930 white female markers and sorters earned $17.35 a week, compared to $14.55 for white female flat-work ironers. To reduce labor costs, in the 1920s many laundries acquired marking machines, which automatically imprinted a symbol on the article.[26]

Checkers and markers had the most intimate contact with the dirty laundry. Lumpkin described the work as relatively light but "nasty-dirty." She still remembers the customer who sent in sheets covered in feces. In 1930, a Cleveland laundry worker complained that some of the clothes contained worms and that the stench made it nearly impossible to breath.[27] With medical experts confirming workers' fears that contagious diseases were communicable through clothing, some workers refused to handle laundry from red-light districts. The employers' failure to provide protective gear such as gloves and aprons—a privilege that was sometimes accorded to white women but not African Americans—intensified the workers' fears of contagion. The Cleveland laundry worker complained that the bosses provided white women with sturdy "Hoover aprons," while the Black women were given only "bungalow aprons which are made just like nightgowns."[28]

Markers sent the pieces by cart, drop chute, or conveyer belt to the washing department or, as it was called, the "kitchen." White men worked as head washers, and, consistent with Jim Crow practices, Black men worked as assistant washers under the supervision of the head washer. In multistoried laundries, employers placed the washing department in the basement or on the first floor so as to avoid rotted floors collapsing onto the workers below. Such practices meant that the heat and steam generated from the machines rose to the floors above. Washers did the bulk of their work at the beginning of the week. Lumpkin remembered that many of the kitchen workers stayed overnight on Monday and Tuesday "catching what sleep they could stretched out on bags of wash."[29]

The washing department was a hot, wet, and noisy place to work. In the 1920s the metal washers that replaced the earlier wooden machines filled the laundry with the sound of clanging metal. Before loading the clothes into the machines, the washers prepared the washing solution, a mixture of bluing, water, bleach, chloride, ammonia, caustic soda, and other cleaning agents (premixed solutions would become available in the 1920s). The chemical solution produced noxious odors and took a toll on the workers' hands. The wife of one washer complained that her husband's arms "look like a butcher shop—all burned and seared from the chemicals."[30] After loading the dirty garments into the hatches at the top of the machine, the washer poured in the soap solution and then used a valve to add water and adjust the temperature level. Before the development of automatic washing machines, washers had to drain the machine by pressing a pedal. Despite the men's best efforts the machines constantly overflowed. In 1936, one washer complained that "your feet stay wet all the time. They're so wet they feel numb." The rubber boots the workers wore increased the likelihood of accidents on the wet, slippery floors.[31]

Pullers or wringers, often Black men, removed the freshly washed garments and flat pieces. Because the clothes were wet, washers described pulling as the most difficult job. An African American puller explained, "I have to put my head in the hole to pull them out and all the water runs down over my head. . . . I stay wet all day."[32] By the 1930s self-dumping washing machines that unloaded the clothes into basket containers and transferred them via monorail or conveyer belt to the extractor had largely eliminated the job of pulling.[33] Power laundry owners, at least those with the means, embraced the development of new technologies that promised to reduce labor costs.

FIGURE 2. Washer in a New York City laundry, 1937. Credit: Jane Filley and Therese Mitchell, *Consider the Laundry Workers*, New York, League of Women Shoppers, 1937.

Social and cultural assumptions about skill and physicality led to the regendering of washing in the power laundry as a man's job. While all laundry work involved some physical labor, washing jobs were particularly onerous. On any given day a washer was likely to lift upward of five tons of wet laundry, work that investigators from the New York State Department of Labor insisted only "sturdy" men could do.[34] Lumpkin explained that the effort involved in washing "far exceeded any other job in the laundries" and that "only big, strong men worked in the kitchen."[35] Robinson was one of the few workers to challenge this view. She pointed out that "lifting was a problem with men *and* women, you know, really and truly. . . . [T]here were some men that just couldn't lift as much as some of the women even."[36] The more common view, though, was that women were too weak to work as washers.

Gendered assumptions about men's greater capacity to perform scientific and technologically skilled work also contributed to women's exclusion from the washroom. Laundry owners, workers, and labor investigators alike described machine washing as both a technical and a scientific process. In 1924, labor investigators reported that machine washing was a "very exact procedure, requiring both technical information and conscientiousness on the part of the laundryman."[37] In the course of a day, a washer was required to mix a variety of chemicals and washing agents: too many bleaching agents would harm the garment, while too few would produce an improperly cleaned product. In some cities, washers had to soften hard water by adding chemicals or soda. The workers had to calculate the correct ratio of water to garments to ensure that the machines did not overflow, work that was compared to that of a chemist. In 1936, unionized male washers in San Francisco justified their high wages on the grounds that the work "requires skill and good judgment" to avoid overflowing the machines.[38] DeArmond insisted that "the heart of the laundry is its washroom, and the basis of good laundering is good washing."[39] Now deemed skilled and even scientific work, industrial washing had become men's work. Redefined as a man's job, the work rose in status and was assigned the highest wages of the inside positions. In most power laundries, the head washers earned two to three times more than the other inside workers and more than the assistant washers and pullers, who were often Black men. In 1940 in New York City head washers earned thirty dollars per week, while women workers received sixteen dollars per week. Assistant washers earned twenty dollars per week.[40]

Washers sent the flat pieces and garments to the extractors, usually men, who operated the centrifugal drying machines, which spun the pieces at high speed to eliminate the excess water. Because of the speed at which the machines revolved some of the industry's most serious accidents took place at the extractors. Broken bones resulted when workers accidentally stuck their arms into the spinning machines. Because extracting was related to both washing (men's work) and ironing (women's work), it was one of the few jobs performed by both women and men, although most were men.[41]

Shakers, who were usually women, removed and untwisted the avalanche of damp, tangled garments that came out of the extractors. To handle large pieces such as bed sheets, the women worked in teams. Smith described shaking as both monotonous and hard because "you're standing on your feet all day and it's killing. Your back is killing 'cause you have to bend down and pull it out." One employer admitted that his shakers never lasted more than three days.[42] Shaking was one of the least skilled and lowest-paying jobs in the plant, so employers assigned new workers and older women with no industrial experience to shaking. One worker reported that it was pitiful to see older women who "should have been retired standing in that hell-like heat" shaking clothes.[43] Workers whose race, ethnicity, or nationality gave them more status refused shaking jobs. Interviewed in the 1920s, immigrant women in Philadelphia reported that "Americans" refused to shake.[44] To "break up the boredom," the shakers in Smith's laundry chatted with each other and tried to have "a little fun." She remembers that the bosses would place workers from different nationalities next

FIGURE 3. Starchers in a New York City laundry, 1937. Credit: Jane Filley and Therese Mitchell, *Consider the Laundry Workers*, New York, League of Women Shoppers, 1937.

to one another to try to prevent them from talking but that the women still found ways to communicate: "In the meantime . . . they don't want you to talk . . . so you would. You'd have an Italian and a what-do-you-call-it and you'd talk, kid around. . . . You'd learn the various words in the language that are not spoken. . . . But they'd always be observing you."[45] Despite the boss's best efforts, group work such as shaking provided opportunities for the workers to socialize, even across linguistic divides, and, in the hands of skilled organizers like Smith, for the creation of group solidarity.

Garments that required starching, such as shirtwaists and collars (until the 1920s some men wore business shirts with detachable collars), went to the starchers, who were usually white women. Before the 1920s, workers had to make starch from scratch, mixing wheat or corn with water and then cooking the solution in a special starch cooker or pan placed on top of a stove. The workers submerged the articles in washtubs full of the boiling starch or fed the garments into starching machines, where rollers rubbed in the starch and a drum squeezed out the excess starch. Fumes from the starch burned the workers' skin and left them nauseated.[46] Although cold starch carried fewer health risks, employers rarely used it, because it cost more. Evelyn Macon recalled that the women in the starching department put camphor ice on their hands before submerging them in the boiling starch. They also sang spirituals such as "Go Down Moses" and "Down by the Riverside" to make the work more bearable.[47] Because starching required skill—workers had to know how much water to add to the starch solution, what temperature to heat the starch to, and how much starch to apply—employers usually hired white women and paid them more than flat-work ironers (the lowest-paying job) but less than markers and sorters. In 1930 white starchers in the Northeast earned $15.85 a week, compared to $13.50 for white flat-work ironers and $16.30 for white markers.[48]

Pieces that required drying went to the drying closets, where workers hung the items on hooks attached to revolving racks. Some of the closets included conveyer belts that slid in and out of the closet, while others required the workers to manually hang and retrieve the articles, a dangerous job, given that the temperature inside the closets reached as high as 300 degrees Fahrenheit. At the end of their time in the closets the articles dropped automatically into a basket and were dampened before being sent to the ironers. By the 1920s many laundries had acquired rotary tumbling dryers, into which workers loaded the garments for drying, rendering obsolete the drying closets. Men usually operated large tumblers, while women operated smaller machines.[49]

Starchers and driers sent the articles to the ironing department, which, as one of the largest and busiest parts of the plant, provided employment to dozens and sometimes hundreds of workers. Most of the ironers were women, and nearly all of the African American women in the industry worked in the ironing department, most commonly in the much-despised position of flat-work ironer, or "mangler," as they were sometimes called. In 1912 Elizabeth Butler of the New Jersey Consumers' League observed that "the mangle girls rank lowest among laundry workers." She reported that when there was a difference in nationality, the bosses assigned immigrant women, including in New York Italian women, rather than "white American" women to flat-work ironing. Butler's observation suggests that Italians, alongside other "new" immigrants from southern and eastern Europe, inhabited a liminal or "in-between" racial status, above African Americans and Asian Americans on the socially constructed racial hierarchy of turn-of-the-twentieth-century America but below native-born white and older immigrant groups from northern Europe.[50] In the 1920s Black women would take their place alongside immigrant women on the mangles. The 1930 laundry study found that 50 percent of Black women worked as flat-work ironers compared to 40 percent of white women. In the Northeast nearly all of the Black women in the industry worked on the flat-work machines, the second-lowest-paying position (after hand washing and hand ironing). Smith remembers that it was mostly strong Black women working on the flat-work irons. In 1930, Black flat-work ironers earned $8.65 per week, compared to

FIGURE 4. Feeders (flat-work ironers) in a New York City laundry, 1937. Credit: Jane Filley and Therese Mitchell, *Consider the Laundry Workers*, New York, League of Women Shoppers, 1937.

$11.90 for marking and sorting. White women flat-work ironers earned $14.55, compared to $17.35 for marking and sorting.[51]

Unlike washers, who were busiest early in the week, ironers received the bulk of their work midweek, after the garments had been washed. Flat-work ironers fed sheets, pillowcases, tablecloths, and other flat items into the feeding roller or revolving belt, where the garment was dried and ironed between heated cylinders or padded rollers and steam-heated chests. To handle large pieces such as bed linen, two or three feeders worked together feeding the pieces into the mangle. With the machine's rollers moving at a rate of eighty feet a minute pressing upward of a thousand pounds of material, the feeders had to be careful to keep their fingers away from the revolving belt. As many of the machines lacked finger guards, a small slip could lead to a lost finger or worse.[52] Anna Hedgeman, who worked for two weeks on the mangles, explained that "the hot steam, the damp floor and the constant movement of my arms created an indescribable weariness." Before working in a laundry, Hedgeman had criticized the women who frequented the Colored YWCA where she worked in the 1930s for not following through on social activities they had planned during the week.

After working on the flat-work machines (flat work ironers were one kind of ironing machine in the ironing department) for two weeks—at the suggestion of the women—Hedgeman conceded that she was too exhausted to do anything at night other than sit and commiserate with the other workers. With a better understanding of the workers' situation, Hedgeman railed against the unions for ignoring the plight of the laundry workers and the Black church for preaching a message of love but failing to deliver a social message "except at moments of special crisis in the Negro community."[53]

On the other side of the flat-work ironing machine receivers or folders received, inspected, and folded the finished products. Robinson described receiving as the hardest part of the job "because it was hot. You see, you were getting the steam from the mangle. . . . [Y]ou were working in 106 and 126 degree heat all the time."[54] Hedgeman remembered getting blisters from catching the hot towels rolling out of the ironer. Some of her coworkers wore gloves to protect their hands and handkerchiefs to protect their eyebrows. In the 1940s many laundries acquired flat-work ironing machines with attachments that fed the material into the ironer and received and folded the pieces on the other side.[55]

Articles that were not flat (e.g., shirts, pajamas, dresses, and suits) went to the press operators, who earned more than flat-work ironers but less than markers and sorters. Most pressers were women, and after flat-work ironing and hand ironing, pressing employed the third largest group of Black women.[56] Owners of small laundries relied on a few general multipurpose presses, while large, well-capitalized laundries had dozens of specialized presses. One article might go through as many as five operations, passing through the hands of five workers. Smith described pressing as assembly-line work: one worker ironed the cuffs and sleeves, another ironed the collar, and yet another ironed the body of the shirt. Pressers placed the garment on the machine's steam-heated bed or padded table and used a hand lever or foot pedal to lower the metal pressing head onto the garment. Before automation some presses required as much as one hundred pounds of pressure to operate.[57] In 1911, a twenty-eight-year-old Polish woman complained that the levers produced "swelling of the muscles and pains in ankles and bowels." She was so sore at the end of the day that she could "hardly bear her clothes across her." Reproducing popular stereotypes about immigrant hardiness, in 1908 one manager insisted that "no American can stand this. We have to use Hungarians or other foreigners. It seems to be unhealthful."[58] Constructed as beasts of burden or "mules" naturally equipped to perform hot and heavy physical labor, immigrant and later Black women would be assigned ironing jobs, work deemed too "unhealthful" for white Anglo women.[59]

Dress shirts that had been machine pressed went to the shirt ironers, who used heavy hand-held irons to press any parts of the shirt that had been improperly finished. Shirt ironers had to perform a multitude of operations quickly with a heavy, piping-hot iron, work that required physical strength, endurance, and manual dexterity. Lumpkin explained that although the workers used their arms and hands, their feet never stopped moving in a kind of "unchoreographed dance."[60] Because shirt ironing was skilled work, shirt ironers, who were often paid by the piece (only 10 percent of laundry workers were piece workers), earned significantly more than the flat-work ironers and machine pressers. Because turning out a properly ironed men's dress shirt was essential to a laundry's success, shirt ironing was the only ironing position for which employers hired both men and women.[61]

Most power laundries employed women to wash and iron by hand anything that could not be put through the machines or that had been inadequately washed or ironed. Hand washers washed fine linens, silks, and other "fancy" pieces in a tub, sometimes with the use of a washboard and wringer, while hand ironers used crimping or fluting irons to iron garments with ruffles, lace, or frills. Because they were often paid by the piece, hand ironers despaired at receiving fussy, time-consuming articles. In 1936, one worker explained that "when we get them beautiful little baby dresses it's like taking bread out of our mouths. So we just pray for heavier things that ain't half so pleasant to do."[62] Because hand ironing so closely resembled work performed in the home, employers hired older women with no industrial experience and African American women, some of whom were experienced laundresses, as hand ironers. Hand ironing employed the second largest group of African American women, after flat-work ironing. In 1930 Black women hand ironers earned median weekly wages of $7.95, compared to $8.65 for Black flat-work ironers. White women hand ironers earned median weekly wages of $16.60, more than double that of their Black counterparts. As a job that was in part dependent on weather and fashion—customers rarely wore frilly clothes in the winter—hand ironing often provided only part-time work, a fact that contributed to the higher levels of part-time work among Black as compared to white women laundry workers.[63]

In the sorting department, described by observers as a "comparatively quiet and comfortable" part of the plant, the mostly white female sorters and checkers ensured that all of the garments had been properly washed and finished and that no items were missing.[64] In some plants the sorters, who usually earned as much as the markers, the highest-paid inside female workers, refused to socialize with their coworkers. In 1908, Elizabeth Butler described the checkers and sorters as the "aristocrats of the trade."[65] Once all of the pieces were accounted for, wrappers or packers put the wet wash in oiled bags and the remainder in paper or cardboard boxes. At this point the clothes were ready to be sent to the delivery department, where they would begin their journey back to the customer.[66]

Inside workers also included foremen or supervisors whose duties included hiring and firing workers, organizing and supervising the labor process, and maintaining production records. Depending on a laundry's size, hiring was done through a shape-up or by recruiting workers through job advertisements placed in local newspapers such as the *New York Amsterdam News*.[67] Workers also used their own networks to obtain jobs in the industry. In 1930 a Polish immigrant worker from Philadelphia explained that "my Polish friend know the laundry and take me there the day after I come." While friends helped newcomers secure laundry work, lack of English sometimes kept them there. Another Polish woman, also from Philadelphia, explained that although the work "almost killed her," she stayed in the laundry for four years because the boss spoke Polish. Over time she learned that there were "nicer" places to work, especially for a white woman, and quit.[68]

Large laundries had a foreman or department head for each department, while in smaller laundries a superintendent or the owner oversaw the entire plant.[69] Of the approximately six thousand laundry foremen or overseers in the United States in 1930, thirty-five hundred were women, and most were native-born white; only 2 percent of laundry foremen were Black.[70] New Orleans transplant Sylvia Woods had been working in a Chicago laundry for a few years when the white male foreman quit. Although most of her coworkers were African American women, the boss hired a white woman to replace the foreman. Outraged, Woods and her coworkers stopped working and refused to leave the plant. When the police arrived the women threw things at them and "wrecked" the place. When union organizers arrived at the laundry where Woods got her next job (after being fired) she was the first to join the campaign.[71]

Alongside foremen, nonproductive inside workers included engineers or mechanical workers who installed and repaired equipment. Most of these workers were white men who earned more than productive workers, including head washers, but less than drivers.[72] Office employees, nearly always white women, kept records, tabulated prices, and dealt with customer complaints about improperly cleaned clothing and missing pieces. Removed from the washing and ironing machines, office workers enjoyed better working conditions and higher status, and they earned higher wages.[73]

Race and Gender in the Laundry

What did the race- and gender-based occupational assignments mean for the laundry workers in the first half of the twentieth century? First, it meant that Black women performed the most difficult jobs in the ironing department, where they earned the lowest wages. In most cities, Black women earned approximately one-third of the wages of their white male coworkers. They also earned less than Black men and white women, although the gender-based wage gaps exceeded the race-based wage gaps.[74] Most departments were interracial.

Black and white men worked side by side in the washroom, and Black and white women worked together in the ironing department. The sorting and checking departments and office were the most racially segregated parts of the plant, staffed primarily by white women.

While nearly all the laundry's departments were interracial, very few included both women and men. Interracial but gender-segregated departments emerged as the norm in the industry. Some employers reinforced this occupational pattern by limiting opportunities for social interactions off the shop floor. In 1928, Charles Vita, the white superintendent of the Carolyn Laundry in Harlem, informed the *New York Amsterdam News* that "mixing of the sexes on or near the premises is strictly forbidden. The men and women each have a separate stairway."[75] Although he did not elaborate, it is likely that Vita wanted to prevent the Black men from socializing with the white women, a practice that would have violated Jim Crow etiquette and inflamed white racial prejudices. When Smith began organizing in Harlem and the Bronx in the early 1930s, she approached the African American women but not the men, explaining that she "would have been out of a job" had she been caught talking to her African American male coworkers.[76] In some laundries employers tried to limit interactions between white and Black workers by providing separate entrances and racially segregated eating spaces. Robinson remembered that at the Colonial Laundry in Brooklyn in the 1930s white and Black workers were not allowed to eat in the same room.[77]

The race- and gender-based occupational divisions and wage scales implemented during the early 1900s survived the Great Depression and World War II (and to a large extent remain intact today) when the imperatives of the economic crisis and wartime labor shortages should have led the employers to replace their higher-paid white male drivers and head washers with lower-paid Black and female labor. That the occupational structure remained in place reveals the resiliency of the sex- and race-typing that occur during an industry's formative years. Labor sociologist Ruth Milkman's study of the auto and electrical manufacturing industries reveals that once a job is labeled female or male, the demand to fill that job becomes sex-specific and, over time, extremely resistant to change. Once they have taken root, Milkman explains, "traditions of sex-typing" shape employment decisions and day-to-day managerial practices.[78] In 1950 Fred DeArmond wondered if the industry was moving into a period of consolidation but concluded it was not, because insufficient numbers of men had come forward during the war to operate the large tumbling machines required by larger plants. DeArmond never considered that women might operate the machines. Gendered assumptions about skill and physicality and their attendant occupational patterns had taken on the weight of tradition, and employers showed little interest in tampering with them even to reduce costs.[79] Even during the Depression, when many laundries tottered on the brink of bankruptcy, laundrymen did not hire Black workers as drivers or head washers, and Black women remained concentrated in the ironing department.

As in other industrial workplaces, white male laundry workers embraced an occupational structure transposed from above. Lumpkin and Smith remember that the drivers refused to organize or socialize with the inside workers. Smith believes that the drivers saw themselves as superior to the inside workers. The drivers, she explained, believed they "had more class or whatever they felt." Describing the drivers' behavior as "completely Jim Crow," Smith insisted that they "didn't want to be part of the Black people in the laundry." Lumpkin similarly recalled that the drivers lived in a world apart.[80] In New York and many other cities, drivers organized with the International Brotherhood of Teamsters rather than with the inside female and Black workers under the AFL-affiliated Laundry Workers International Union. The men's sexist and racist behavior—masked as craft unionism—enabled them to protect their privileged occupational and economic status while distancing themselves from workers they considered socially inferior. For white men working in a female-gendered and racialized field, policing the boundaries of their work was especially important.[81] The race- and gender-based occupational structure implemented from above and defended from below would both complicate the workers' organizing, at times hopelessly impeding the development of workplace solidarities, while simultaneously providing opportunities for women and people of color to mobilize in independent and oftentimes empowering spaces where they forged race- and gender-based coalitions with allies in the labor movement.

CHAPTER THREE

The 1912 Uprising of New York City's Laundry Workers

On January 1, 1912, 650 laundry workers from twenty-five of Manhattan's power laundries walked off the job. Within a week six thousand workers were on strike, prompting the *New York Times* to report that the city was "nearer a dearth of clean shirts and collars than ever before."[1] Among those workers was Irish immigrant laundry worker Margaret Hinchey. As a forewoman in a laundry Hinchey earned more than her coworkers, but when the strike began she immediately walked off the job, proclaiming that "no one could be so mean as to go to work in a laundry now!"[2] Hinchey reported to strike headquarters at Goetz Hall on Eighth Avenue near 127th Street, described by the *Times* as "about the liveliest place in the city." Journalists reported a festive atmosphere as workers "kept coming in groups, many of them young women, all through the day." Taking respite from the bitter cold of the picket lines, the strikers "laughed and chatted together and occasionally had a dance," reclaiming control over bodies normally ravaged by long, hot days in the laundries.[3]

Organizers from the Laundry Workers International Union (LWIU), which was affiliated with the American Federation of Labor (AFL), rushed to the scene, eager to assert control over the strike, but it was the middle—and working-class leaders of the Women's Trade Union League (WTUL) that the women turned to for support. It had been nearly three years since WTUL leaders had helped bring industrial unionism to New York City's garment workers, and WTUL activists were keen to apply the knowledge and skills they had amassed during that pivotal campaign to another group of workers also in need of organization. Hinchey worked late into the night alongside wealthy and well-connected WTUL president Mary Dreier and WTUL organizer and socialist Leonora O'Reilly planning parades, organizing picket lines, and liaising with churches and other community institutions.[4] For nearly a month New York's laundry workers filled the streets and pages of the *New York Times*, determined to win better working conditions and higher wages. The alliances they forged during this strike underlined the vitality of the Progressive Era women's labor movement and its potential to empower the most exploited workers, but they also exposed the women's marginality on the edges of a labor movement led by and for men.

The Hand Laundry Trade

In the early 1900s laundry worker organizing in New York and elsewhere was complicated not only by occupational and social divisions among the workers but also by competition between hand and power laundries. By 1910 nearly every American city boasted at least a few dozen and in some cases hundreds or even thousands of hand laundries, small storefront shops where the owner and sometimes a worker washed and ironed garments from the surrounding neighborhood. In the 1910s New York was home to an estimated twenty-eight hundred hand laundries. (Because of hand laundries' ephemeral nature, statistics on hand laundries were notoriously unreliable and were not included in the census.)[5] Because of the relatively low start-up costs—a 1900 account estimated the value of the average hand laundry at $500—the trade attracted aspiring entrepreneurs with few resources. Typical was Beatrice Lumpkin's father, Morris Shapiro, an immigrant from Russia who opened a small hand laundry in the East Bronx in 1913. Lumpkin remembers that her family lived adjacent to the shop in spite of laws that required a separation of the two. Her mother hung a curtain to separate the workspace from the living space. The Shapiros used the front room for receiving customers and the back rooms for sorting, washing, hanging, ironing, and packaging the garments. Lumpkin remembers that most of her parents' customers were Jewish factory workers who lived in the surrounding neighborhood. Beatrice was born in 1918, and once she was old enough she helped her mother iron delicate pieces while her father was out on deliveries. Despite her parents' dreams of occupational mobility, Lumpkin insists that they did "harder physical work and made less money than if they had stayed in the factory."[6]

Dreams of economic independence and occupational mobility also inspired Chinese men to enter the laundry field, but it was their exclusion from almost all other occupations that led to their concentration in the laundry trade. Failing to find their fortune on California's "Gold Mountain," in the mid- and late 1800s Chinese immigrant men entered the laundry trade, where, because of the shortage of women in the mining towns of the West, they faced little resistance.

As they moved eastward and southward in the late 1800s Chinese men opened small hand laundries in New York, Boston, Chicago, and other urban centers where they settled.[7] By 1930 close to thirteen thousand Chinese men owned or worked in laundries nationwide, mostly in small hand laundries. One Chinese laundryman described the hand laundry business as the "lifeline of the Chinese community," with "wives and children back home depend[ing] on it."[8]

In small cities and towns, hand laundries provided a full range of services, while in large cities, including New York, they served as receiving stations for wholesale laundries, power laundries that catered exclusively to hand laundries. Lumpkin's family sent everything they collected except delicate pieces to a wholesale laundry for washing and drying. The articles came back to the family shop clean and ready to be ironed by Lumpkin's mother. Like Morris Shapiro, many hand laundry owners relied on family for help; those without family support hired an employee to sort, iron, and package garments. With very few exceptions, hand laundrymen employed no more than one or two workers, and in some cases the owner did all of the work himself.[9]

Hand laundries that provided a full range of services competed directly with power laundries by offering lower prices; those that sent the washing out incited competition between wholesale laundries by patronizing whichever plant offered the lowest price. White power laundry owners solicited work from hand laundries while simultaneously lobbying municipal authorities to eliminate them altogether and, when that failed, by targeting Chinese hand laundries with racist advertisements that portrayed their shops as dirty and disease-ridden.[10] Despite such campaigns, hand laundries persisted well into the twentieth century, adding to the chaotic and competitive nature of the industry and its narrow profit margins. Power and hand laundry owners also competed with their own customers who might decide to do the wash at home or take their clothes to a home laundry worker. In 1910 half a million women washed clothes by hand for wages in private homes.[11]

By the time the strike erupted in 1912, New York was home to well over two thousand hand laundries and one hundred power laundries. More than twenty thousand workers, half of whom were women, worked in the trade.[12] Half of the workers were foreign-born, a little over one-third were native-born white, 16 percent were Chinese (hand laundry owners and workers), and a little under 10 percent were Black.[13] As the different branches of the industry began to take shape, laundrymen formed local trade associations to coordinate prices, develop industry-wide standards of service, and maintain the open shop. It was the proposal of one such association—the New York Laundrymen's Association—to form a trust to control the city's wholesale power laundries that incited the strike.[14]

The Laundry Workers International Union

By all accounts the 1912 strike was a grassroots uprising sparked by worker fears that the proposed trust would lead to a series of amalgamations that would result in job losses. When reports of the uprising reached the front pages of the *New York Times*, the LWIU, which had jurisdiction over the workers, speedily dispatched its organizer, Vernon B. Smith, to New York City. Founded in 1900 by workers from sixteen locals in the Northeast and Midwest and headquartered in Troy, New York, where Irish women collar laundresses had been organizing since the mid-1860s, the LWIU was a conservative craft union led by white men.[15] With limited resources and narrow vision, the LWIU in 1912 claimed few members outside of a local in San Francisco, where the live-in working conditions, a strong local labor movement, progressive labor legislation, and a homogeneous workforce of mostly native-born white and North European immigrant workforce created the conditions for organizational success. LWIU officials do not appear to have initiated the strike, and in fact organizers from Troy had to rush to New York after the workers walked off the job.[16]

At the time of the strike, New York was home to three small laundry locals: uptown Manhattan Local 126, comprised of wholesale power and hand laundry workers; Brooklyn Local 37, composed of power laundry workers; and Local 34, which represented the male shirt ironers who worked in the city's hand laundries ironing men's dress shirts.[17] Little is known about Locals 126 and 37, both of which would disappear after the strike. In contrast, we know that Local 34 had been founded in 1901 by Harry Levine, a Russian immigrant and longtime laundry worker.[18] Shirt ironers, who in the non-Chinese owned hand laundries were almost always white men, used heavy gas-heated or electric hand-held irons or small mangle machines to iron men's dress shirts. The work was detailed and skilled-collars and cuffs had to be starched and ironed to perfection to produce a glossy appearance—and physically onerous. The workers developed calluses and swollen feet from standing all day, but as skilled workers, they could earn wages as high as ten cents a shirt. (Most ironers were paid by the piece.)[19] Gendered assumptions about who was capable of skilled heavy work led white hand laundry owners to hire white men for shirt ironing, many of whom were Jewish immigrant men who had served apprenticeships in Europe. Chinese hand laundry owners hired their own kin or friends to work in their hand laundries, often as an avenue to facilitate their immigration to the United States. In the 1910s an estimated one thousand to two thousand mostly Jewish men worked as shirt ironers in New York hand laundries, in addition to the Chinese workers employed in the Chinese-owned hand laundries, the latter of whom did not participate in the strike.[20] With headquarters at 62 Pitt Street on the Lower East Side, by 1912 Local 34 claimed a few hundred members.[21]

While the proposed laundry trust precipitated the strike, it was the abysmal working conditions that convinced the workers to walk off the job. The strikers, described by observers as Italian, German, American, Irish, and Jewish, reported working in water an inch deep, losing fingers in the revolving rollers, and sustaining burns on unguarded machinery. Hannah Gilette, who testified before the State Bureau of Mediation and Arbitration, reported that during the Christmas period she worked ninety hours a week, well in excess of the state's sixty-hour maximum for women and minors, and she earned only four to five dollars a week. Male power laundry workers, in contrast, earned between twelve and twenty-four dollars, a consequence of their monopoly over the highest-paying machine washing, truck driving, and shirt ironing positions.[22]

A joint strike committee of the three locals, composed entirely of men and chaired by local AFL organizer Jacob Tazelaar, drew up a list of demands that included a maximum fifty-four-hour workweek; safeguards on the machines; a closed shop and twenty-five dollars a week for collar and shirt washers (male); and a scale running down to six dollars a week for the "mangle girls," or flat-work ironers.[23] The demands reflected the leadership's determination to maintain the occupational wage differentials that saw men earning as much as four times more than their female coworkers.

From the original group of 650 workers the strike quickly spread, and within a week an astonishing 6,000 laundry workers, around one-third of the city's laundry workforce, were on strike. Within two weeks twenty of Manhattan's twenty-five wholesale laundries and three of Brooklyn's four wholesale laundries had been forced to shut down, in addition to eight hundred Manhattan hand laundries. Most of the strikers were inside power laundry workers and shirt ironers from the hand laundries. In what would become a familiar pattern, most of the drivers, who enjoyed higher wages and better treatment, refused to join the strike. The *Times* reported that a group of angry strikers "roughly handled" some drivers and threw their laundry into the streets. The close attention the *Times* paid to the strike and the panic that ensued as abandoned clothes lay rotting in washing machines underlined the public's growing dependence on the laundry industry and the workers' potential to leverage this dependency.[24]

Although there is no direct evidence of a connection between the laundry strike and the 1909 uprising of twenty thousand garment workers, it is unlikely that the laundry workers were unaware of the strike. For eleven weeks young immigrant women, aided by the New York Women's Trade Union League, had filled the streets of the Lower East Side demanding safer working conditions, higher wages, and union representation. The strike swelled the ranks of the nascent International Ladies' Garment Workers' Union (ILGWU) Local 25 and laid the foundation for industrial unionism in the garment industry.[25] In 1912 New York's women laundry workers could look to the example set by their sisters in the garment trades, who similarly toiled in a competitive industry where men monopolized the highest-paying jobs and controlled the union.

Women Laundry Workers and Their Feminist Labor Allies: The Women's Trade Union League

Founded in 1904 by working women and their middle- and upper-class female "allies," the New York WTUL, as a local branch of the national organization, had by 1912 almost a decade's experience supporting women's labor activism. Working-class leaders and allies helped working women found or join existing unions, often in the face of male opposition, including from AFL leaders who only barely tolerated the WTUL and never considered its mission to organize working women a priority. When women workers struck, WTUL allies joined them on the picket lines, sometimes in their fur coats, and used their social stature to generate publicity for the workers. In the absence of organization—often hard to achieve in the low-wage industries in which women labored—WTUL leaders lobbied the government to pass protective labor legislation as an immediate remedy to industrial abuses such as overwork. As part of the process of empowerment the WTUL provided working women with educational training, as well as access to social and cultural activities not typically enjoyed by the working class. Finally but not less importantly, WTUL activists mentored budding young women unionists, some of whom would go on to assume leadership positions in the labor movement and in the government, where in the 1930s they would help build the modern welfare state. The WTUL's vision, described by historian Annelise Orleck as "industrial feminism," combined union consciousness with a feminist sensibility and relied on organizing strategies often eschewed by the AFL.[26]

WTUL leaders had been watching New York's laundry workers closely, alarmed by the emergence of yet another female-dominated sweatshop industry. In January 1912, when the workers struck, New York WTUL president and ally Mary Dreier rushed to the scene, where she found the workers holding meetings in a dingy pool hall. After a decade of organizing in the labor movement (a large family inheritance enabled Dreier to serve as president of the New York WTUL from 1906 until 1914), Dreier understood women's reluctance to meet in traditionally male spaces such as bars, and so the president promptly secured a more hospitable location for the workers.[27] At the first meeting convened by the WTUL, one of the women gave a rousing speech "full of wit and humor." To the surprise of everyone there, she announced that it was the first time she had ever given a speech.[28] By creating spaces where women felt empowered to give speeches and articulate their grievances, the WTUL helped foster what historian Lara Vapnek describes as the new climate of self-expression taking root among working women in the early 1900s.[29]

Eager to raise public awareness about the conditions in the laundries and build solidarity among the workers, WTUL leaders helped the workers organize a series of auto parades in the neighborhoods where workers were on strike. A group of women strikers decorated the cars of Mary Dreier and ally Josephine Morgenthau, wife of American businessman and diplomat Henry Morgenthau, with "pink bunting" and signs that announced "'Laundry Strike,' 'Don't Be a Scab' and '200 Laundries Organized.'"[30] The gaily decorated pink cars stood in stark contrast to the traditionally masculine symbols of labor, highlighting women's participation and leadership in the strike. As WTUL organizers had hoped and expected, the pink cars and the cross-class alliances that produced them generated significant media attention.

As well as logistical support, the WTUL provided critical financial support for the laundry workers. For the duration of the strike the organization provided strike relief of five dollars a week for workers with families and three dollars a week for those without families. No doubt aware of the relatively high numbers of wage-earning mothers in the laundries, WTUL leaders rejected the traditional practice of allocating strike relief on the basis of sex and instead dispensed relief on the basis of family status.[31] As industrial feminists with a broad vision of working women's rights—most memorably articulated by garment activist and WTUL organizer Rose Schneiderman in 1911 when she insisted that "the woman worker needs bread, but she needs roses too"—WTUL leaders used the strike as an opportunity to introduce the laundry workers to some of the social and cultural activities the city had to offer. WTUL organizers hosted parties where the workers kept the organizers busy providing copies of labor songs such as "Toilers Arise!" Dreier and other allies organized an outing to the Hippodrome Theatre in midtown Manhattan. One of the strikers remarked that the trip was "worth the whole strike and it's as good as seeing the Lakes of Killarney."[32] WTUL leaders arranged for the workers to be treated to a benefit show put on by vaudeville actors who played a group of laundry workers who stampeded off the stage when the union called a strike. The backdrop was the inside of a laundry constructed from striker accounts. Live theater and song and dance enhanced the appeal of union organizing and provided the "roses" that Schneiderman insisted working women deserved.[33]

In recognition of the importance of community support to women's labor activism, WTUL leaders worked closely with the women to solicit financial and moral support from external allies, including local clergy. In January the workers wrote a fiery letter to local ministers accusing them of neglecting their religious duties by not supporting the strike. The women insisted that the strike posed a "moral question that should be taken up by preachers in their pulpits." On Janu-

ary 14 WTUL secretary Helen Marot and two laundry workers, one a widow
with two young children and the other an elderly woman, told congregants at the
Episcopal Church of the Ascension about working in heat so intense that some
of the workers were "prostrated in the Summer." The women's moving testimony
convinced a number of congregations to contribute money to the strike.[34]

As industrial feminists who combined a union consciousness with a feminist
sensibility, WTUL leaders arranged for British suffragette and socialist Sylvia Pankhurst to address the workers. Pankhurst told a group of two hundred
women laundry workers to remain resolute in their fight for "political equality"
and "industrial rights" and recounted that a recent strike in England had been
won because the workers had stuck together. Margaret Hinchey listened raptly as
Pankhurst spoke, and with the support of former shirtmaker Leonora O'Reilly,
who by 1912 was one of the city's most influential labor and suffrage activists,
Hinchey secured a job as a paid organizer with New York's Woman Suffrage
Party (WSP), an affiliate of the National American Women's Suffrage Associa-
tion (NAWSA).[35] Hinchey was among six working-class suffragists, including
Schneiderman, to speak to an overflow crowd at a mass suffrage rally at Cooper
Union in April 1912. The rally was organized by the Wage Earners' Suffrage
League (WESL), and the speakers challenged the arguments put forward by
antisuffrage state legislators who insisted that "ladies" belonged in the home.
Drawing on her experiences in the laundry, Hinchey argued that the home was
not a vocation for working-class women but rather a place where they went to
rest their "weary bones" before returning to work.[36] Working women needed the
vote, Hinchey argued, so that they could elect politicians who would support
their efforts to earn fair wages and combine wage earning with domestic responsibilities, the latter of which sometimes included earning a family wage. By
increasing women's exposure to the suffrage movement, WTUL leaders nurtured
the laundry workers' political and feminist consciousness while simultaneously
broadening the suffrage movement's predominantly middle-class base.[37]

As the strike continued into its second week the workers remained resolute,
sticking to their pickets and visiting the union headquarters, where they chatted and occasionally had a dance. As public pressure mounted, New York State
labor commissioner John Williams directed the State Board of Mediation and
Arbitration to conduct hearings with a view to brokering a settlement. A long
line of witnesses testified about the unsanitary and dangerous working conditions in the laundries. Hinchey reported that her boss forced the women to
work seventy-two hours a week. The erstwhile forewoman also complained
that the men had access to the women's dressing room, a veiled reference to the
women's sexual vulnerability and their determination to protect their bodies
and reputations. Hinchey of course knew that popular stereotypes cast working

women, especially those in factories, as morally dubious, assumptions that only intensified when they took to the streets to demand union representation.[38]

The Board of Mediation ultimately sided with the workers and recommended that the employers establish a minimum wage of six dollars for a maximum fifty-four-hour workweek, install safety guards on the machines, and recognize the union. But as the board had no mechanism to enforce the recommendations the employers simply ignored them.[39] And although the board determined that the employers had violated state maximum-hour and child labor laws, as well as factory inspectors' orders, the labor commissioner decided not to prosecute on the grounds that many of the employers were of "long standing" in the community. Paul Kennaday, the secretary of New York's Association for Labor Legislation, wrote a scathing editorial in the *Times* condemning the commissioner for his cowardly failure to enforce the laws and hold the employers accountable.[40] As Kennaday predicted, the state's inaction emboldened the employers, who continued to bring in strikebreakers and harass the strikers. Dreier reported that the police arrested picketers "wherever possible" and even helped carry bundles of wash into the plants. Hinchey, who was arrested during the strike, spoke of the injustice of being fingerprinted and jailed as if she had committed a "terrible crime."[41]

With little recourse a month after they had walked off the job, the workers called off the strike. The three laundry locals lay in shambles. Charles Bailey, secretary treasurer of the LWIU, blamed the women for being overly timid and uninterested in the labor movement—an assessment contradicted by the women's demonstrated activism on the picket lines and willingness to testify before the state.[42] Hinchey and Dreier more accurately attributed the outcome to the drivers who continued to deliver laundry to the strikebreakers, thus enabling the employers to remain open and to employer antiunionism.[43] In 1914 the AFL ensured that the de facto divisions that had emerged between the drivers and inside workers in 1912 would become permanent when they allowed the men to organize independently of the inside workers under the Brotherhood of Teamsters, Chauffeurs and Helpers.[44]

The end of the strike precipitated a wave of mergers as disgruntled laundry owners pooled their resources to purchase new equipment in anticipation of future union drives. In 1912 six of the city's large flat-work laundries (flat-work laundries washed and ironed linen, often from businesses such as hotels and restaurants) merged to form the Great Eastern Laundry Company with a combined capital pool of $1.3 million. Having been in "ill-shape to fight the demands of their employes" in 1912, the owners explained that the merger would allow them to eliminate the ruinous competition that drove down profits and prepare for future union drives.[45]

In 1918 the WTUL initiated a new laundry campaign, but after a few weeks on the job they abandoned the drive, explaining that the "large number of married women and many old people," as well as the varied "nationalities[,] complicate this situation."[46] In 1920 one-third of New York's women laundry workers were married, and of those, one in three was over the age of forty-five.[47] With domestic responsibilities and dependents at home, the women had little time for union organizing and few resources to sustain themselves and their families during strikes. The relatively large numbers of married women in the laundries help explain why, unlike New York's shirtwaist makers, women laundry workers were unable to form a lasting union in the 1910s. And although there is no evidence of ethnic tensions during the 1912 strike or during the short-lived campaign of 1918, the WTUL's reference to "varied nationalities" suggests that the laundry's diverse workforce contributed to the workers' organizational difficulties.

Assessing the Strike and the Potential of Cross-Class Feminist Labor Alliances

Although it produced no lasting union gains, the 1912 strike forged new ground for the laundry workers by educating the public about the unsanitary and abysmal working conditions in the laundry industry. Housewives and churchgoers listened to harrowing stories about workers losing fingers in the machines and widowed mothers slaving over scorching irons for ninety hours a week. The strike introduced the laundry workers to the labor movement and created opportunities for activist workers like Hinchey to develop their organizational and leadership skills. Hinchey explained that before the strike "I never knew I could talk in public before. Then I started making speeches along the picket lines."[48] The strike initiated what would become a lasting relationship between New York's women laundry workers and the WTUL. When the employers blacklisted Hinchey after the strike the WTUL hired her as a full-time organizer. Four years later Hinchey was arrested outside of Brooklyn's Cascade Laundry, the city's largest laundry, for defying a police order and setting up picket lines in front of the plant. From 1912 to 1918 she served on the WTUL's executive board.[49]

Finally, through their participation in the strike women laundry workers gained additional exposure to the suffrage movement, where they contributed a class-based analysis to the fight for suffrage. In 1914 Hinchey participated in a delegation of workers to the White House, where she urged President Wilson to support a federal suffrage amendment, the goal of Alice Paul's Congressional Union for Woman Suffrage, the delegation's sponsor.[50] While in Washington Hinchey addressed the Wage Earners' Suffrage League with a speech entitled "Why the Laundry Workers Need the Ballot." Linking women's economic exploitation to their political disenfranchisement, Hinchey argued that without the vote working women would continue to be abused by their employers and dismissed by politicians.[51] As economic and political power were intertwined, Hinchey understood, suffrage would allow working women to defend their interests as women, as wage earners, and as breadwinners.

Hinchey's activism as both labor leader and suffragist reflects the complex ways in which working women's class and gender interests intersected. Hinchey explained that "I broke into suffrage when I broke away from slavery," a reference to her decision to strike against the abusive and even slave-like conditions in the laundries. Her economic stand led her into the suffrage movement, where, as a working-class suffragist, she highlighted the connection between political and economic rights, framing female suffrage as a vehicle to women's economic empowerment.[52] Her working-class feminism also brought her into conflict with the predominately middle-class leadership of the movement. While attending a NAWSA conference in December 1913, Hinchey wrote to Leonora O'Reilly:

> I feel as if I have butted in wher I was not wanted. Miss Hay gave me a badge was very nice to me but you know they had a school teacher to represent the Industrial workers if you ever herd her it was like trying to fill a barrell with water that had no bottom not a word of labor spoken at this convention so far. you would have to be a real politician now to be a suffrage. . . . I am not goying to wait for sunday meeting I am goying home satturday.[53]

Hinchey felt relegated to the margins of a movement that, despite recruiting working-class women, continued to be controlled by professional women. Even after the formation of the labor-friendly Woman Suffrage Party, historian Meredith Tax argues that NAWSA remained "uncongenial to working women," especially to immigrant and Black women.[54] Hinchey complained about having to educate middle-class suffragists about why working women needed the vote. "I have noticed," Hinchey reported, "many well-dressed women in my audiences, both in Washington and other cities who have apparently been shocked by what I have said, but, nevertheless, every word is true."[55] For working women like Hinchey, the vote was both the means to achieve political equality and a vehicle to eradicate the sweatshop conditions and poverty wages that their middle-class sisters could barely imagine.

Hinchey would also have a falling out with the leaders of the WTUL. In 1917, after her work in the suffrage movement dried up, Hinchey tried once again to secure a full-time job organizing for the WTUL. Rose Schneiderman, who assumed the presidency of the New York WTUL in 1917 (a position she would hold until 1949), declined to hire her, likely because of Hinchey's opposition to protective labor legislation, a longtime goal of WTUL leaders who saw legislation as an interim solution until working women organized unions. In Hinchey's view, maternalist legislation based on arguments about female fragility and reproductive capacities undermined women's competitiveness in the labor market and limited their wage-earning opportunities, a particularly problematic outcome for women who supported families on their wages.[56] Rebuffed by the WTUL, Hinchey ended up back in a cellar laundry, working "long hours in darkness." She wrote to her good friend and mentor, Leonora O'Reilly (who also had a history of butting heads with socialites in the movement), that "I lost my bread and also lost the light or sunshine when I lost my work." With profound disappointment, Hinchey insisted that the WTUL was "not a League for the Working women only a Political Org so we will have to find an org that will stand by the working women that we can trust wont sell us out while our nose is to the grinding stone."[57] The laundry worker felt betrayed by an organization that professed to support working women's right to represent their own interests but that provided little space for dissenting views, especially those of its working-class members. Hinchey's involvement in the WTUL and the suffrage movement, then, illustrates some of the tensions that animated the cross-class feminist alliances of the Progressive Era women's labor and suffrage movements.

Ultimately, despite the activism of worker leaders like Hinchey and the support of their feminist labor allies, in the 1910s the laundry workers lacked the resources to build a stable union. Without the drivers' support the inside workers were unable to bring the employers to the bargaining table. Evidence moreover suggests that Hinchey's activism was exceptional, the result perhaps of her ethnic background, which, as Carole Turbin demonstrates in her study of collar laundresses in Troy, New York, imbued Irish immigrant workers with a heightened sense of class consciousness and a propensity to organize.[58] In 1912 a widely rooted oppositional consciousness had not yet taken root among the laundry workers. Employer antiunionism, poverty wages, police brutality, and internal divisions undermined unionization. In 1918, six years after the first general strike, half of New York's women laundry workers earned less than eight dollars a week, and one-quarter earned less than six dollars. At the time, the cost of living for a single woman was $11.70 a week. Only 20 percent of women laundry workers earned enough to survive on their own, let alone provide for a family.[59] Determined to win higher wages and aided once again by the WTUL, the workers would launch a new campaign in the 1920s, by which time large numbers of Black women had entered the industry. The inclusion of Black workers would both complicate and enrich the union campaign.

CHAPTER FOUR

The Rise and Fall
of Local 284

Black Women Laundry Workers'
Activism in the Era of the
Great Migration

With forty dollars in her pocket, in 1924 nineteen-year old Charlotte Adelmond boarded the SS *Vandyk* in Port-of-Spain, Trinidad, headed to New York City. The young woman was among the forty thousand immigrants of African descent to leave the Caribbean for Harlem between 1900 and 1930. Arriving at her sister's apartment at the corner of Nicholas and 136th Streets during the height of the Harlem Renaissance, Adelmond would have been mesmerized by the large crowds that congregated daily to listen to Garveyites preach a message of Black unity and economic nationalism; to Black trade unionists and socialists extoll the benefits of working-class unity; and to Caribbean radicals preach a philosophy of "race first" and Black self-determination. Like many of her fellow migrants, Adelmond joined the Black nationalist and Pan-Africanist Garvey movement, inspired by its message of race pride and Black solidarity. She would also join the thousands of other Black women entering the laundry industry, taking a job in a power laundry in Harlem and later, after she moved out on her own, in Brownsville, Brooklyn, where she met her good friend and fellow union activist Dollie Robinson.[1]

Black workers' entry into the laundries raised new questions about how to forge solidarities among workers already divided along gender and occupational lines. It also injected new energy into the campaign, spurring the formation of a new laundry local, this time in the hand laundries and this time led by Black women. Black workers' presence in the industry also attracted new allies to the campaign, including the short-lived Trade Union Committee for Organizing Negro Workers, led by Black socialists and trade unionists A. Philip Randolph and Frank Crosswaith, as well as longtime allies from the WTUL. Supported by allies with different interests and agendas and inspired by different ideologies and philosophies, women laundry workers would gain important organizational experience in the 1920s that they would harness to organize their coworkers in the 1930s.

The Great Migration and the Laundry Industry

The Great Migration, the mass movement that would see more than six million African Americans leave the Jim Crow South between 1916 and 1970 for the urban industrial centers of the North and West, led to an explosion in New York City's Black population from fewer than one hundred thousand in 1910 to more than three hundred thousand in 1930. Most of the migrants settled in Harlem, attracted by the social and cultural opportunities the Black capital provided and excluded by racist real estate practices from most other areas of the city. Southern-born Black migrants mingled with the fifty-five thousand Black people from abroad who lived in New York in 1930, most of whom hailed from the British colonies of the Caribbean.[2] Puerto Ricans fleeing unemployment at home comprised a large proportion of New York's African diaspora, especially after the 1917 Jones Act granted Puerto Ricans US citizenship. By the beginning of the Depression, fifty thousand Puerto Ricans lived in New York City, where they comprised the largest Spanish-speaking group.[3]

Adelmond was unique in that relatively few Caribbean migrants came from Trinidad. While Adelmond's homeland had experienced centuries of European exploitation, its economy was much more diversified and less dependent on the sugar market than the older British colonies. With its small population, fertile land, and oil reserves, Trinidad attracted workers from the rest of the Caribbean and relied on indentured servants from the Indian subcontinent. With job opportunities at home and relatively high wages, those who did emigrate tended to be more middle class than migrants from the rest of the diaspora.[4] Given that Adelmond's mother, Mrs. Clamence Adelmond, paid for her passage (a ticket could cost as much as sixty-five dollars, the equivalent of almost $1,000 today) and that Charlotte listed her occupation as seamstress, a skilled occupation, it is unlikely that Adelmond came from the poor working class.[5]

The decision to emigrate was a difficult one. Emigrants left behind family and friends and faced the daunting task of navigating the United States immigration system. US government notices printed in Caribbean newspapers such as the *Jamaica Gazette* made clear that the immigration process was rigorous, especially for single women, who were required to provide proof that a family member was meeting them in New York. In 1917 twenty-year-old Amy Ashwood, the future wife of Marcus Garvey, fretted, "I cannot get passage alone." But despite the warnings and the very real possibility that she would be turned away at Ellis Island, in 1924 Adelmond boarded the SS *Vandyk* to join her sister, Mrs. Iria Borde, in Harlem. Although we do not know for certain, it is likely that Adelmond decided to emigrate in 1924 in anticipation of the passage of the restrictive 1924 Immigration Act, which favored emigration from northwestern Europe.[6]

Adelmond listed her occupation at Ellis Island as a seamstress, so why, unlike her soon-to-be—friend Panamanian-born Maida Springer, did she not obtain work in the garment industry? One answer is that in 1924 power laundries were actively recruiting Black workers. As competition intensified in the 1920s some laundry owners moved their plants to Harlem and Brownsville to facilitate the recruitment of (low-wage) workers of color. In contrast, Black women had to fight their way into the garment trades. A Caribbean pioneer of the needle trades remembers reading signs in the garment shops in the early 1900s that announced that "colored people weren't wanted." She also reported that she and other Black migrant women tore down the signs and marched into the plants: "You bet, we got the jobs." Black women's determination to work in the garment industry and the support they received from radical Jewish union allies eventually forced New York's garment manufacturers to open their doors to Black women.[7]

Outside of the laundries and garment shops, few other industries were hiring Black women in the 1920s. This was especially true in New York City, which was not home to the large industries that would provide some occupational mobility for Black workers in other northern cities. In 1930 manufacturing provided employment to only one-third of New York City's entire workforce, less than in any other northern city.[8] If Adelmond had needed to supplement her sister's family's income quickly or wanted to become financially independent, in 1924 the laundry provided a relatively quick path to employment outside of the much—despised field of domestic service.

Drawn by lower rent and more spacious living conditions, as well as the completion of the Eighth Avenue subway, in the mid-1920s Adelmond joined the small migration of Black people from Harlem to Brooklyn. By 1930 sixty-eight thousand Black people lived in Brooklyn, primarily in Stuyvesant Heights and Brownsville, where Adelmond found an apartment on Thatford Avenue. The Trinidadian laundry worker and Garveyite had perhaps been drawn to Brownsville because of its history of radical politics and strong union presence.[9] Since the early 1900s Brownsville's radical Jewish unionists and housewives, including the indomitable Clara Lemlich Shavelson, the leader of the New York shirtwaist strike of 1909, also known as the Uprising of the 20,000, had been organizing strikes, consumer boycotts, demonstrations, and sit-ins to combat high food prices, greedy landlords, and abusive employers.[10] Black workers both contributed to and were influenced by this radical organizing. When Dollie

Robinson moved from North Carolina to Brownsville in 1930, she described the working-class neighborhood as "labor-conscious" and ready to organize.[11]

As New York City's population exploded in the 1920s, so too did the demand for laundry services. By the decade's end New York was home to four hundred power laundries employing close to thirty thousand workers.[12] Rapid growth in the industry led to fierce competition, exacerbating the already narrow profit margins and low wages. In 1928 Rose Schneiderman described the laundry industry as "overbuilt, wasteful, unscientific and without any pretense of standards."[13] As in most other cities in the 1920s, New York's power laundries were also still competing with home laundresses. The *New York Times* reported that wet wash laundries (plants that provided washing but not ironing services) received a boost in 1921 when home laundresses raised the price of family wash from $3.50 to $4.10 a load.[14] At the time, ten thousand women worked as home laundresses in New York City, close to half of whom were African American (most of the remaining were immigrant women).[15]

It was likely the laundresses' economic and familial responsibilities that prompted them to raise the price of wash in 1921. White middle-class housewives balked and turned to wet wash laundries instead, eventually forcing the city's laundresses to drop their prices. Yet the *Times* predicted that the days of the home laundress were ending and that within a few years, yet another household industry would be "neatly lifted out of the home, almost without our knowing it."[16] The *Times* was of course correct to predict the home laundress's demise but wrong to assume that laundry work would permanently leave the home.

The explosion of the laundry industry and migration of Black workers to New York led to a sharp increase in the numbers of Black women working in laundries. From fewer than seven hundred in 1910, six thousand Black women worked in New York's power laundries by 1930, and an additional two thousand to three thousand worked in the hand laundries. In 1930 close to one-half of New York City's female power laundry workers were Black, one-third were native-born white, and 20 percent were foreign-born white. By the beginning of the Great Depression the power laundry had become the leading industrial employer of Black women in both New York City and in the United States. Black men also obtained jobs in power laundries, although on a lesser scale than Black women. Of the thirteen thousand men working in New York City's laundries in 1930, only 12.5 percent were Black. The largest proportion—close to 40 percent—were foreign-born white, 14.5 percent were Chinese hand laundry workers, and the remainder were native-born white.[17]

Alongside African Americans a small number of foreign-born Black workers, primarily from the Caribbean, worked in New York's laundries. In 1925 Schneiderman described the predominating "races" in the laundries as "Colored and Italian with a few Spanish," a reference to the small but growing Puerto Rican presence in the trade (and evidence of how Americans used race, nationality, color, and language in imprecise and often overlapping ways).[18] Employers exploited tensions between workers from different backgrounds to depress wages and impede the development of shop floor solidarities. A 1932 article in the communist *Liberator* noted that it was not uncommon for an employer to "fire out a department of Negro workers and hire white workers. Then he will fire out the white workers and hire Spanish-speaking workers and hire Negroes again, at a cheaper scale."[19] In 1936 an African American laundry worker told investigators from the consumer activist organization the League of Women Shoppers that "the boss kept encouraging a fight between the foreign and American Negroes. He'd make nasty cracks about one to the other behind their backs." She also noted that African Americans refused to perform certain jobs, insisting that they be given to West Indians.[20] In the 1920s New York's laundrymen capitalized on the large-scale migration of Black people from the South and abroad, who were forced to compete for scarce housing and jobs, to create a workforce that was divided along multiple lines, including race, nationality, language, and gender.

Constructing a Workforce: Race and Gender in the Hand Laundries

With the exception of a brief strike in 1919, the 1910s saw little formal trade union activity in the laundries. The end of the war, the continued mistreatment of the workers, and the entry of Black workers into the industry precipitated a new union campaign, this time originating in the hand laundries.

By 1920 New York was home to at least five thousand hand laundries, most of which were small storefront shops where the owner and an employee took in laundry from the surrounding neighborhood. Chinese men owned at least half of the shops, while Italian and Jewish immigrant men eager to avoid the garment trades and win social and economic mobility as small businessmen operated most of the remaining shops.[21] Beatrice Lumpkin, who worked in her father's Bronx hand laundry in the 1920s, remembers that the Chinese and Jewish hand laundry owners "lived in a world apart." It was "very apartheid," Lumpkin recalls, as Chinese and Jewish owners accused one another of driving down standards by cutting rates.[22]

In New York City hand laundries served primarily as receiving stations for the wholesale power laundries, which provided washing but not ironing services. The hand laundry owner or worker received clothing and linen at the front of the shop, or in some cases provided pick-up and delivery services. Jessie Smith, who worked briefly in a hand laundry in the early 1930s, remembers that the bulk of the business came in the form of men's dress shirts and linens such as sheets, towels, and pillowcases. Once collected, the items were sent to a wholesale power laundry for washing. The pieces came back to the shop clean, ready to be ironed, and packaged for return. Many hand laundry owners employed a shirt ironer to starch and iron men's dress shirts and other garments. Because the work was skilled, hand laundry owners hired white men for shirt ironing, some of whom were Jewish immigrant men with prior experience in the laundry trade.[23]

In 1901 the shirt ironers had founded the first known laundry local in New York City, Local 34, affiliated with the Laundry Workers International Union. The local participated in the 1912 strike, and the men remained quasi-organized in the 1910s. Eager to reduce their reliance on their union-conscious shirt ironers and cut costs, hand laundry owners created the position of family ironer in the 1920s and hired Black women for the job. Family ironers were responsible for ironing everything but dress shirts, which remained the domain of the shirt ironers. In contrast to shirt ironers, who were paid ten cents a piece, family ironers received an hourly wage that saw them earn significantly less than the shirt ironers.[24] The employers' decision to retain white men as shirt ironers suggests that racist and sexist assumptions about Black women's ability to perform skilled work trumped financial considerations. It is equally likely that hand laundry owners feared losing business should the customers learn that Black women were ironing dress shirts, a symbol of white middle-class professionalism and respectability.[25]

In November 1921 the shirt ironers founded Laundry Workers International Union Local 280 to replace the defunct Local 34. In January 1923 AFL general organizer Hugh Frayne estimated that Local 280 had three hundred members. WTUL leaders who had been watching these developments closely reported that the men had "been able to maintain conditions and to set up certain standards as to hours and wages."[26]

Although there is no explanation for why the shirt ironers chose 1921 to resurrect their local, it is likely that the entry of an estimated one thousand to two thousand Black women into the hand laundries prompted their decision. Communist laundry workers, who comprised a small but vocal faction within Local 280, accused their fellow shirt ironers of trying to convince the employers to fire the women. Only when that failed did the men consider organizing the women, but, unwilling to take on the work themselves, the shirt ironers called on the WTUL for help.[27]

Rose Schneiderman and the Founding of African American Laundry Local 284

By 1921 the WTUL had undergone significant changes, most evident by the fact that the organization was now headed by Rose Schneiderman, a working-class activist with roots in the Jewish socialist Left rather than a middle-class ally. Born in 1882 in the Polish village of Saven, Schneiderman immigrated to New

York City with her family at the age of eight, settling on Manhattan's Lower East Side, where many of the city's one million Jewish residents lived and worked in the needle trades. Like many of her fellow migrants, Schneiderman was exposed to Marxism at an early age and embraced socialism as a vehicle to eradicate the inequities of industrial capitalism. Tragedy struck when in 1892 her father, a tailor, died of meningitis, leaving his pregnant wife, Deborah Schneiderman, with three children to support. Deborah took in boarders and laundry, but she was unable to earn a family wage, and so in 1895 at the age of thirteen Rose Schneiderman was forced to leave school and enter the workforce. At her mother's urging Schneiderman took a position as a sales clerk in a department store, a job deemed more respectable than factory work. But after three years of low pay Schneiderman left for a higher-paying job in a cap-making factory. Angered by the abysmal working conditions and the sexist treatment of women, who were excluded from the highest-paying positions, in 1903, at the age of twenty-one, Schneiderman organized her shop for the socialist United Cloth Hat and Cap Makers' Union.[28] It was within the socialist milieu of the Lower East Side's garment trades that Schneiderman would develop an ethic of social justice and a political worldview connected to the Jewish tradition of helping others.[29]

Schneiderman's involvement in the Cap Makers' Union brought her into the orbit of the WTUL. The fiery socialist organizer initially harbored doubts about a labor organization that included middle- and upper-class socialites who had never set foot on a shop floor, but she was impressed enough by the WTUL's contributions to the 1905 cap makers' strike to join the organization. Only a few months later she was elected to the executive board and in 1906 won the position of vice president. In 1908 Schneiderman permanently left the ranks of the industrial workforce when she accepted a position with the WTUL as a full-time organizer in the ladies' garment industry. After a brief hiatus to organize with the International Ladies' Garment Workers' Union (ILGWU) and the New York Woman Suffrage Party, in 1917 Schneiderman was elected president of the New York WTUL, a position she would hold until 1949. While she retained a connection to the socialist Left, the former shop floor radical was increasingly drawn into the world of middle-class social reform.[30]

In 1921 Schneiderman eagerly responded to the shirt ironers' call for help, a reflection of the WTUL's continued commitment to the laundry workers and of Schneiderman's particular commitment to workers of color. In 1909, after the uprising of garment workers, Schneiderman had urged the ILGWU to support Black women's efforts to obtain work in the garment industry and lobbied the WTUL to reach out to African American women.[31] Schneiderman was an early supporter of the Black railroad union, the Brotherhood of Sleeping Car Porters (BSCP), founded in 1925 by Black socialist and trade unionist A. Philip Randolph. When she resigned from public life in 1949 Randolph recalled that

Schneiderman had supported the union "in the early days when friends were few and hard to find."[32] It was her support of New York's laundry workers, though, that most clearly demonstrated her commitment to racial justice.

Schneiderman embraced the hand laundry campaign as an opportunity to try to convince Black women, who were well aware of organized labor's history of racist and sexist exclusion, of the potential benefits of trade unionism. In the spring of 1923 she and other WTUL organizers started canvassing the hand laundries and launched a fund-raising campaign to secure the support of "people who were interested in the colored workers." In letters to potential contributors, Schneiderman emphasized "what it would mean to have a strong and powerful organization of colored women—how that would react on the psychology and status of other colored women."[33] When, to Schneiderman's great satisfaction, the family ironers responded positively to the WTUL's overtures, the WTUL president approached the shirt ironers about admitting the women into their local. But, much to her dismay, the men refused. With no other option, in November 1923 the WTUL helped the family ironers charter a separate local: Laundry Workers International Union Local 284, composed of family ironers, markers, and sorters. Most of the potential members of the new local were Black women (a small number of markers and sorters in the hand laundries were men).[34]

Local 284 was in essence a gendered Jim Crow local that fit squarely within the parameters of a labor movement that marginalized or outright excluded workers of color. Alongside the Hotel and Restaurant Employees' International Union and the Tobacco Workers' Union, the LWIU established Jim Crow locals in cities where white workers refused to admit Black workers.[35] In 1933 a laundry worker from Birmingham, Alabama, insisted that the LWIU's practice of "maintaining and supporting the jim-crow policy" had forced Black workers into the lowest-paying and least desirable positions in the laundries.[36] As the founding of Local 284 illustrates, biracial unionism was not confined to the South.

Longtime laundry worker and African American Delia Haren served as the local's first and only president. Under Haren's leadership Local 284 began holding weekly meetings. The women drew up a list of demands that included a maximum eight-hour workday and forty-hour workweek, double pay for work on holidays, time and a half for overtime, and a "standardized minimum wage for the various kinds of ironers." The final demand underlined the women's determination to eliminate the occupational and, by extension, gender- and race-based wage differentials between the shirt and family ironers. Describing their workplaces as cramped, dirty, and stuffy, they also demanded improved sanitary conditions.[37]

The women's demand for better sanitary conditions might have been an allusion to an even more serious problem in the hand laundries, one identified by

Jessie Smith. Interviewed in 2006, Smith still distinctly recalled the insidious sexual abuse that Black women experienced in the hand laundries: "There were a lot of problems with the owners, you know, abusing them [the Black women] sexually, and I heard stories like that." Some of the employers, Smith argued, "forced the women to sleep with them to keep their jobs. And they had a good opportunity because the women worked right in the back there." Smith understood that Black women ironers were sexually vulnerable because, like domestic workers, they labored under the direct supervision of their employers in intimate settings. Smith, who was also sexually harassed, insisted that "every woman was a lay. That's what it was. I'm sorry, that's what it was."[38] While Smith recognized the sexual vulnerability of all women, she understood that Black women were especially vulnerable because they confronted both racism and sexism.[39]

In December 1923, a month after Local 284 was chartered, a group of power laundry workers chartered LWIU Local 290. A month later workers in the wet wash laundries founded Local 201. Schneiderman attributed the upsurge to the "wholly unstandardized conditions" and to the "long years of educational work" undertaken by laundry allies, including the WTUL. In 1923 the drivers chartered Teamsters' Local 810 and by the end of the year had five hundred members. In November 1923 the new locals formed the Laundry Allied Trades Council to coordinate organizing efforts and in December 1923 held their first mass meeting. Two organizers from the LWIU headquarters in Troy, New York, came to New York City to support the campaign.[40]

In an enthusiastic start to 1924, Schneiderman attended Local 284's weekly meetings, helped the women write a news bulletin, hosted parties at the WTUL's Lexington Avenue clubhouse, and secured funds to pay Haren twenty-five dollars a week to work as a full-time organizer, at least double what she earned in the laundry. Haren and Schneiderman employed a rank-and-file intensive approach that relied on person-to-person contact and small group meetings to build solidarity among the workers. In January 1924 the WTUL reported that Haren "was doing splendid work" and had managed to reach over four hundred women in 312 hand laundries. By June 1924 seventy-two women had filled out applications for union membership. Schneiderman was optimistic but nervous, describing this period as "the most difficult time in the life of a new union," when the membership was not strong enough to make demands of the employers but simultaneously was growing impatient at "marking time and wanting results for the dues they pay." She also noted that it was at this juncture that the WTUL was most needed to "stimulate" the members and hold them together.[41]

As someone who understood firsthand how ethnic and racial identities could be harnessed to empower workers and augment their class-conscious organizing, Schneiderman, alongside Haren, employed race-conscious organizing strategies that included forging coalitions with Black community and labor organizations.[42] In April 1924 Schneiderman and Haren convinced the New York Urban League (NYUL), a local chapter of the National Urban League, formed in 1910 by white and Black social reformers eager to support Black southern migrants as they made the transition to urban industrial life in the North, to donate a meeting room for Local 284. Schneiderman correctly predicted that the women would be more likely to attend meetings at the NYUL's Harlem headquarters than at the WTUL's downtown Lexington Avenue clubhouse. Schneiderman and Haren also convinced the social organization to donate a room for a short-lived employment office for the laundry workers.[43] It was during this period of cooperation that NYUL chairman and architect Arthur Holden admitted to Schneiderman that his organization was "way behind on what should be done" to support African American women workers. Holden further informed Schneiderman that "Colored Women will probably be more easily organized than men," a statement that was contradicted by Black women's experiences in the union movement.[44] In 1919 the New York Consumers' League conducted a study of 2,185 African American women in 217 industrial establishments in New York City: only .003 percent were organized. Investigators noted that even in shops where white women were organized, Black women "seldom held union membership."[45] Holden's comments suggest both a lack of attention to gender as a category of oppression and his organization's minimal focus on unionization as a vehicle of racial empowerment. It would take the devastation of the Depression and the resurgence of the union movement to convince the NYUL to actively support Black trade unionism.[46]

In April 1924 Local 284 suffered a blow when after six months on the job Haren resigned from her position as organizer. WTUL records do not specify why Haren left, but a number of explanations exist. Organizing workers who were geographically dispersed across the city in small shops was nothing less than a herculean assignment; building solidarity among them even more challenging. WTUL leaders described "a great deal of indifference" among many of the women, a sentiment they attributed to long hours of work and poverty wages, which made paying union dues almost impossible. Schneiderman further hypothesized that the abysmal working conditions had produced a "psychological inability to realize that anything so bad can be bettered, even with the union."[47] Haren was likely as frustrated or even more so by the shirt ironers' lack of solidarity. Although Local 280 contributed $100 to the campaign, the men did little else to support the new local.[48]

By the beginning of 1925, approximately one year after the founding of Local 284, Schneiderman and Haren, who by this time was serving on the New York WTUL's executive board, reported that Local 284 was "down and out." WTUL leaders blamed the shirt ironers for refusing to admit the women into their local. In her analysis of Local 284's demise, Schneiderman accused the men of engaging in sexist behavior, but she did not explicitly discuss the role of race in the campaign or describe the men's behavior as racist.[49] While the WTUL president was more attuned to issues of race than many of her fellow industrial feminists, because she was entrenched in the women's labor movement, she would interpret Black women's organizational difficulties through a gendered lens, even as she deployed organizing strategies attentive to the centrality of race in their lives.

In contrast, communist laundry workers interpreted the shirt ironers' behavior as racist. In a 1933 retrospective article on Local 280 in the communist *Harlem Liberator* entitled "The Role of Local 280 in the Laundry Industry," the communists proclaimed that the shirt ironers "always thought that Negroes were too stupid to understand what a union is and what a union can do for workers." The article described Local 280 as an organization that "never has, never can and never will serve the interests of the Negro laundry workers."[50] The different interpretations, one that read the men's actions as sexist and the other that read them as racist, reflected the WTUL and communists' different priorities and agendas, explored more fully in the following chapters, as well as the myriad of factors that impeded the women's unionism.

While the shirt ironers drew most of Schneiderman's ire, she secondarily blamed the communists in Local 280 for Local 284's demise. The WTUL president reported to her colleagues that "quarrelling between the 'lefts' and the 'rights'" in shirt ironers' Local 280 had disrupted the campaign. At a time when factional battles between a communist left-wing and mostly socialist leadership was tearing apart the ILGWU, Schneiderman feared that similar battles could erupt in the already precarious laundry locals.[51] In the 1930s Schneiderman's relationship with radical laundry workers would deteriorate as their influence grew.

The "New Negro" in Harlem:
The Trade Union Committee for
Organizing Negro Workers

On the heels of Local 284's demise, WTUL organizers shifted their attention to the power laundries, where Locals 290 and 201 and Teamsters' Local 810 were eager to launch a new drive supported by the recently formed Laundry Allied Trades Council.[52] Fortuitously for the power laundry workers, the new campaign coincided with the formation of the Trade Union Committee for Organizing Negro Workers (TUC), an interracial central labor body formed in 1925 by delegates from thirty Black and white local and international unions, including representatives from shirt ironers' Local 280. Funded initially by the American Fund for Public Service and headquartered at 2380 Seventh Avenue in Harlem, the TUC compared its work to that of the WTUL and during its brief tenure supported campaigns launched by diverse groups, including Black motion picture operators, elevator operators, and laundry workers. Most of the TUC's work was carried out by socialists A. Philip Randolph and Caribbean immigrant and ILGWU organizer Frank Crosswaith, the latter of whom was dubbed the "Negro Debs."[53] Randolph and Crosswaith urged unions and social-ists to prioritize the battle against racial discrimination, a focus that diverged from the Socialist Party position developed under party leader Eugene V. Debs, which held that Black workers should be organized into unions and the party as workers, without special attention to race.[54] ILGWU leader Maida Springer recounted that while others had tried to convince her of the virtues of socialism, it was Crosswaith and Randolph who introduced her to a socialist philosophy that she was willing to support.[55]

The Trade Union Committee reflected the new assertiveness taking root among African Americans in the interwar years. In 1925 Howard University professor Alain Locke coined the term "New Negro" to describe a young gen-eration of Black northern urbanites mobilizing against racial injustice in their communities and workplaces and at the voting booth. The "New Negro" found expression in the works of Harlem Renaissance artists like Langston Hughes; in the formation of radical leftist organizations such as the African Blood Broth-erhood; and in the unions and labor organizations founded by Black workers and socialists, including the Brotherhood of Sleeping Car Porters. It also found expression in the raucous street parades launched by Jamaican immigrant and Pan-Africanist Marcus Garvey.[56]

In 1918 Garvey founded the New York chapter of the Black nationalist Uni-versal Negro Improvement Association (UNIA). The charismatic leader quickly amassed a large base of mostly working-class followers among Harlem's West Indian immigrant and African American populations. The New York chapter alone had thirty thousand members. The UNIA was particularly popular among Black workers who were angered by the persistence of economic discrimina-tion and the mistreatment of Black World War I veterans and less connected to middle-class civil rights organizations such as the NAACP. Garvey's message of racial empowerment through economic self-sufficiency and Black unity and his embrace of Africa's rich past served as a "beacon of hope" for Black Americans who after World War I faced intensifying anti-Black racism as the economy contracted and as a response to Black mobility.[57] Promoting racial uplift through Black enterprise, Garvey opened the Negro Factories Corporation, which in-cluded Black-run grocery stores, restaurants, a clothing factory, a printing press, and a power laundry. With their meager wages, Black workers bought thousands of shares in Garvey's Black Star shipping line, which promised to build Black power by promoting trade across the African diaspora.[58]

Inspired by Garvey's message of Black pride, self-determination, and decolonization, Adelmond was among the thousands of Harlemites to join the movement. Like many of Garvey's followers, Adelmond was impressed by Garvey's bombastic, militant, and unapologetic promotion of Black rights and his denunciation of the abuses perpetrated against Black people globally. In Harlem and elsewhere, members of the UNIA's Universal African Legion and Black Cross Nurses marched through the city streets in full military regalia, demanding "Africa for Africans" and "Liberty or Death." With its strong female leaders, including Marcus Garvey's wife, Amy Jacques Garvey, the UNIA provided Black women with strong models of female activism and leadership.[59] Robinson insists that Adelmond's uncompromising critique of American racism and militant defense of worker rights drew inspiration from her participation in the Garvey movement. Robinson explained that because Adelmond was a Garveyite, a movement comprised primarily of Black workers committed to economic and racial empowerment, she "was very much interested in the black workers, and all workers."[60] Interviewed in the 1970s, Springer described Adelmond as a fierce nationalist who was "uncompromising of any form of racial discrimination." Springer scoffed at "these kids today [who] think they're nationalists? Shucks. They don't know. She was outspoken, outrageous."[61] In the 1920s Garvey introduced workers like Adelmond to a language of empowerment and autonomy that they would employ in their own battles for racial and economic justice.

A "Backbone or a Wishbone": The Power Laundry Workers

In 1925 the newly formed Trade Union Committee joined the laundry campaign, injecting a perspective that reflected the assertiveness of the "New Negro" movement. A TUC campaign poster asked the laundry workers, "Have you a backbone or a wishbone? Do you want a voice in regulating your hours, your wages and your working conditions? THEN ORGANIZE, YES ORGANIZE." In the summer of 1925 the TUC, the WTUL, and representatives from Locals 280 and 290 and two new Engineers' Locals, 20 and 56 (like the drivers, white male engineers who fixed and maintained laundry equipment would organize independently of the mostly women and people of color on the shop floor), formed a joint organizing committee with the plan of initiating a new union drive. Schneiderman served as chairman and Crosswaith as secretary. Crosswaith estimated that of the thirty thousand laundry workers in New York City, twenty thousand were African American, most of whom were young women.[62] WTUL organizers took on the typically female gendered work of arranging for speakers, drafting circulars, distributing literature, and finding spaces to hold meetings.[63]

Crosswaith, Schneiderman, and Haren approached prominent African

American leaders and ministers to build community support for the campaign. Campaign organizers distributed thousands of circulars outside of laundries and in front of Black churches, held meetings at the Colored YWCA, and showed motion picture slides on trade unionism in Harlem movie theaters. Schneiderman organized a party for the workers at the Henry Street Settlement.[64] In February 1926 the joint committee arranged for Gertrude Elise McDougal Ayer, an industrial secretary in the local branch of the National Urban League, to address the workers. A teacher by training, Ayer was devoting most of her time by the 1920s to the trade union movement.[65] Much to the campaign leaders' disappointment, however, few workers attended the meetings or social events. The *New York Times* reported that a mass meeting at the YWCA at 137th Street in Harlem "called to stir up the enthusiasm of the 20,000 negro laundry workers" brought out only twenty workers. Those who did respond to the call were men.[66]

Women laundry workers had many reasons to be wary about joining the campaign. Those who were the heads of their families risked jeopardizing their families' economic survival. Concentrated in the unskilled positions in the industry, they understood that they were far more expendable than the strategically located drivers and washers, whose support the women could not depend on.[67] It is also possible that the campaign did not succeed because the organizers did not explicitly address the racist hiring and employment practices in the laundries. In 1926 the *New York Amsterdam News* reported that the AFL and the WTUL were trying to organize the city's twenty thousand African American laundry workers. (The article did not mention the TUC, likely because its participation was fleeting.) Instead of celebrating the campaign, however, the article asked why the organizers were not demanding that Black laundry workers be promoted into skilled positions in the industry with "commensurate pay and equalized conditions of labor." Pointing out that there was "no especial reason why the colored workers should have the 'corner' on the profession of washing and ironing any more than the white should have it on electricians and pipefitters," the authors noted that "a bit of suspicion irresistibly attaches itself to a movement to organize the sisters and brothers, while, at the same time, they are frequently barred from other branches of the union." The critique captured the widely held belief among Black workers—born of lived experience—that unions existed to protect white workers' monopoly over the highest-paid trades and positions.[68]

After only a few months on the job the TUC withdrew from the campaign so that Crosswaith could work full-time on the campaign launched in 1925 by the Black porters who served the white passengers on the Pullman railway cars. The national scope of the Pullman porter campaign, which would result in the formation of the Brotherhood of Sleeping Car Porters, likely explains why the

TUC chose to support the porters over a local campaign to organize a group of poorly paid African American women.[69] The laundry workers' needs were certainly as great as those of the porters, and their wages were much lower. In 1925 a porter could earn as much as seventy dollars a month, far less than the thirty-three dollars a week needed to support a family of four in Manhattan, but far more than the ten dollars a week or less that Black women laundry workers earned.[70] Black male trade unionists, like their white working-class brothers, would prioritize the organization of men and the attainment of a family wage that would render the employment of women unnecessary. For Black men whose wage-earning wives and mothers were so often the victims of workplace sexual violence, winning a family wage would enable them to protect their female kin—an obligation and a right of manhood—while also benefiting from their reproductive labor in the home.[71]

While the WTUL remained on the campaign, little activity took place until February 1928, when a group of power laundry workers in the Bronx struck after the employer fired a driver who was an active unionist. Three hundred workers from four Bronx laundries controlled by the Manhattan and Bronx Laundry Association (one of the city's many employers' associations) walked off the job in solidarity.[72] Half of the striking women were African American, while many of the remaining were Jewish and Italian. Schneiderman and WTUL organizer Sadie Reisch worked around the clock, conducting daily strike meetings, picketing with the workers, and raising funds. The WTUL hired an African American organizer, Floria Pinckney, to work with the women.[73]

As in 1912 the employers refused to meet with the workers and hired strikebreakers, who attacked the picketers in full view of the police.[74] Despite the violence, the women continued on the picket lines, but the strike was lost when the men negotiated a private settlement with the employers. Schneiderman was incensed both at the men and at the LWIU, which had refused to send an organizer from Troy to New York during the strike.[75] As was the case in the hand laundries, the men's lack of solidarity would undermine the incipient unionism emerging among women power laundry workers.

The Successes and Limitations of the 1920s Laundry Campaign

In many regards, the women's inability to establish a stable union or launch a successful strike is less surprising than the fact that during the 1920s, a decade in which labor was in retreat across America, African American and white women laundry workers were organizing at all. In the 1920s, on the heels of the Bolshevik Revolution, capital exploited fears of the Left and launched an open shop drive. Corporate attacks on labor, supported by the state, and high unemployment rates reversed many of the gains organized labor had made in the 1910s. Against this reactionary backdrop women laundry workers were attending shop committee meetings, signing union cards, going out on strike, and, in the case of the African American women family ironers, founding their own local.[76] While many of the women were reluctant to join the campaign, some did, risking their jobs and families' well-being. In contrast to the 1910s, when white immigrant women such as Maggie Hinchey had led the campaign, in the 1920s Black women such as Delia Haren assumed leadership roles. African American women laundry workers' lack of employment alternatives and the economic needs of their families help explain why some would choose to devote their limited time and resources to union organizing. But white ethnic women did not disappear from the union campaigns. In the 1930s white Jewish communist women, including Jessie Smith and Beatrice Lumpkin, would also emerge as shop floor leaders, organizing alongside and with their African American female coworkers.

On a less celebratory note, the campaign supports Alice Kessler-Harris's contention that in the 1920s male trade unionists missed a golden opportunity to bolster labor's economic power. As the case of the laundry workers illustrates, women workers were both class conscious and ready to organize. Women's continued marginalization and exclusion from the labor movement represented a missed opportunity that hurt both male and female workers.[77]

The 1920s laundry campaign uncovers an important, although largely overlooked, moment of interracial cooperation between New York City's African American women laundry workers and the WTUL's predominantly white working- and middle-class leadership. While WTUL leaders failed to challenge the racist job assignments or analyze the campaign in an intersectional way, to focus only on these shortcomings is to overlook an important moment of interracial cooperation. In the 1920s, by which point many scholars dismiss the WTUL as little more than an effective lobbying organization, the WTUL was at the forefront of the campaign to organize New York City's laundry workers.[78] With Schneiderman at the helm the WTUL employed race-conscious organizing strategies that included hiring African American organizers, collaborating with Black trade unionists and social reformers, and conducting events and meetings in the communities and spaces where Black women developed their class consciousness and understanding of the labor movement.[79]

The WTUL's commitment to African American laundry workers owed much to the intervention of Schneiderman, who, like the Yiddish socialist garment workers described by historian Daniel Katz, was exceptional in her efforts to support other racial-ethnic minority groups. Born in the same year that the Russian emperor Alexander III issued the May Decrees, which reinforced civil restrictions on Jews and contributed to a new wave of pogroms and expulsions,

Schneiderman understood racial discrimination, lynchings, and other state-sanctioned racial violence as analogous to the persecution Jews experienced in czarist Russia and later under Hitler. In a speech to the National Conference of Christians and Jews in 1944, Schneiderman denounced the wartime race riots and pointed out that "economic and political discrimination on account of race or creed is in line with the nazi program." As an international power, the United States could not allow itself to "become the stronghold of bigots."[80] Schneiderman understood from an early age that racism and anti-Semitism sprang from the same ugly roots and had to be fought vigorously and consistently.

Schneiderman's concern for African American women workers also sprang from her personal experiences with gender discrimination. As a young girl she watched as many of her Yiddish sisters were denied an education because of their gender and kept out of the skilled trades by the men who controlled them. But she also benefited from having strong female role models in the Jewish women who led garment unions, in the housewives who led militant protests against exorbitant rent and food prices, and in the countless other women, her own widowed mother included, whose wage-earning activities sustained their families. The fiery organizer butted heads with male trade unionists in the Jewish labor movement and in the AFL when they underestimated women's capacity to organize and excluded them from leadership positions in the unions they did organize. Her experiences as a Jewish immigrant woman and socialist organizer sensitized her to the intersecting forms of oppression that women of color experienced—even if she lacked the language to articulate it—and made her a valuable ally of the laundry workers.[81] In spite of this support and their own activism, however, women laundry workers in the 1920s remained excluded from the small and fractured laundry locals led by men. Except for the shirt ironers, all of New York City's laundry workers were unorganized in 1928.[82] It would take the devastation of the Depression to inspire a new surge of union organizing that would this time result in unionization.

CHAPTER FIVE

"It Was Up to All of Us to Fight"

Communist Laundry Organizing during the Great Depression

In 1931, after her father lost his job as a garment worker, Jessie Taft Smith got a job working as a sorter and packer at the National Laundry in the Bronx. Smith, who lived across the street from the plant, had long peered inside the grimy windows to watch the mostly Black workers wash and iron clothes. Once inside the plant, Smith, a member of the Young Communist League (YCL), began organizing her coworkers. With the support of the communist shirt ironers from hand laundry Local 280, Smith began leafletting the large plants in Harlem and the Bronx, where she talked to the workers about the benefits of unionizing.[1] Inspired by the workers' enthusiastic reception, in 1931 Smith and her comrades founded the Laundry Workers Industrial Union, which would affiliate with the communist Trade Union Unity League (TUUL). Recognizing the importance of industrial unity and consistent with Communist Party directives, the Left-led union united the inside workers with the drivers. With support from radical allies, including the Left-led Women's Councils and Unemployed Councils, in the early 1930s the laundry workers took to the streets to halt the downward spiral in wages and working conditions that accompanied the Depression. In 1933 the left-led union launched a series of strikes that shut down some of the largest plants in Harlem and the Bronx.[2] Instead of crushing the incipient unionism in the laundries, the Depression set the stage for the largest revolt yet. The militant industrial and interracial organizing of the workers and their communist allies in the early and mid-1930s helped forge the activist solidarities that would lead the laundry workers into the CIO in 1937.

The Great Depression and
the Laundry Workers

Even before the official onset of the Depression the laundry industry had begun to feel some of the effects of the structural weaknesses of the 1920s economy. Between 1927 and 1933 gross national laundry sales plummeted from $500 million a year to less than $300 million. In New York City the industry operated at a loss between 1931 and 1934.[3] Because few of the Lumpkins' neighbors could afford to send their laundry out, Beatrice Lumpkin's parents were forced to close their Bronx hand laundry in 1932 and go on relief. As unemployment soared, housewives who had once patronized power laundries did the wash at home themselves or hired a laundress or domestic worker.[4] With the rise of New York's "street corner markets" or "slave markets," so named for their tragic resemblance to slavery, where Black women congregated, waiting to be hired for a day's work, the housewife could employ a domestic servant for as little as a dollar a day.[5]

The early 1930s brought a second related blow to the laundry industry as garment manufacturers introduced women's clothing made from lightweight fabrics, a development that reduced the cost of the family bundle (customers usually paid by the pound). Desperate to stave off bankruptcy, some laundry owners branched out into dry cleaning services; others focused exclusively on household linen, offering both rental and laundry services. Some laundrymen went the traditional route of buying new machinery in the hopes of reducing labor costs; others replaced their white workers with lower-paid Black workers.[6] In one Harlem laundry the employer replaced his white workers with Black women, explaining that he "could get more work out of them." As an added incentive he served a chicken dinner on Saturdays in a small restaurant in the garret of the factory.[7] Older women who had been all but guaranteed work in power laundries were replaced by younger, more "desirable" workers who, in the face of mass unemployment, were now willing to work in laundries.[8]

Stories about employers replacing longtime African American workers with white workers occasionally surfaced. In October 1931 the employer of the Saratoga Laundry in Brooklyn fired longtime African American worker Clara Smith, a widowed mother of one, and three of her Black coworkers. On her way out of the plant Smith met the four white replacement workers. When given the opportunity, some laundrymen replaced their African American workers with white workers who, during the Depression, were willing to take jobs in laundries.[9]

Those fortunate enough to remain employed experienced speedups and wage cuts typical of the early days of the Depression. An African American sorter saw her quota increase from fifty-five to ninety bundles a day. In at least one plant, the owner required his workers to bring in their own laundry and pay for its cleaning; other employers forced workers to perform "wash-overs" of particularly dirty clothing while off the clock.[10] New York Department of Labor investigators reported that the Depression had created two extremes in the laundries: excessively long or excessively short workweeks.[11] Wages meanwhile plummeted from around twelve dollars to fourteen dollars a week in the late 1920s to as little as six or seven dollars a week in the early 1930s. When Dollie Robinson began working at Brooklyn's Colonial Laundry in 1931 she earned six dollars a week and was expected to work seventy-two hours. Robinson, who insisted that "existence was almost . . . impossible," reported that when the workers complained the bosses got "very abusive and raised their hands."[12]

Laundry drivers, the highest-paid laundry workers, also experienced wage cuts. Before 1930 most drivers earned a fixed salary, as well as a commission for securing new customers. With the onset of the Depression many employers forced their drivers to buy their trucks and routes on credit and work on straight commission. The men were allowed to keep the difference between what the customer paid and what the laundry charged. In the 1930s milk, bakery, laundry, and other drivers' wages plummeted as their employers transformed them into "independent" contractors forced to carry part of the risk of the business.[13] It was not until World War II that the industry fully recovered. In New York State, laundry sales rose from a little over $100 million in 1939 to $136 million in 1944, a 30 percent increase.[14]

Laundry workers survived the vagaries of the Depression by relying on family and friends for help, by supplementing their paltry wages with relief from local charities, and by engaging in collective activities in the workplace. A laundry worker who lived in a cold-water flat reported that she survived by taking "cast-off" clothing and furniture from her friends. In one laundry six women organized a one-dollar club. Each week the women pooled one dollar of their earnings. At the end of six weeks the women drew numbers from a hat to determine the order in which they dispensed the money. The worker who drew number 1 received the first week's collection of six dollars, the person who drew number 2 received the second week's collection of $6.00, and so on until everyone had enjoyed a week of six dollars, at which point the drawing was repeated.[15] In the West End Laundry in the Bronx, African American Evelyn Macon and her coworkers sang spirituals such as "Go Down, Moses," "Down by the Riverside," and "The Heavy Iron Blues," songs that tapped into an African American oppositional consciousness born during slavery and nurtured by American racism. Macon recalled "the feeling they used to put in their singing. As tired as we were, those spirituals lifted up our spirits. . . . While singing we would forget our miserable lot."[16] Through informal organizations such as the dollar club and by singing on the job, laundry workers nurtured a group consciousness based on their shared experiences of oppression and determination to survive the Depression.

The Reds in the Laundries

Depression-era conditions ushered in a new wave of organizing in the laundries, this time supported by communist laundry workers and organizers. Founded in 1919 by radicals from the left wing of the Socialist Party, the Communist Party USA included by the late 1920s a small cadre of skilled Black organizers and intellectuals attracted to the party's opposition to imperialism and racism. With the Bolshevization of the party under way in the mid- and late 1920s, party leaders in New York created the consolidated multinational Harlem Section, in which white and Black communists joined interracial neighborhood-based street units or shop units at work. By 1928 white and Black radicals were working together in Harlem to support Black tenants facing eviction and to campaign for party members running for political office, including William Z. Foster, the future chairman of the party.[17]

In 1928 the Communist Party adopted the "Black Belt thesis," calling for an independent Black nation in the southern Black Belt, desegregation in the North, and racial justice everywhere. The party's support for Black autonomy and self-determination resonated with African Americans and compelled white communists to prioritize the struggle against racial injustice.[18] The Black Belt thesis was also, as African American studies scholar Erik McDuffie notes, the first Communist International (Comintern) resolution to specifically reference Black women, describing them as a "powerful potential force in the struggle for Negro emancipation." Black women were in fact already among the party's most effective organizers, especially at the grassroots level, where they mobilized around day-to-day issues such as job discrimination, housing evictions, and rising food prices.[19]

Home to the nation's largest Black community and to a small but deeply committed Black radical leadership, Harlem was chosen as the "concentration point" for the party's campaign to recruit Black workers. Most of the white communists who organized in Harlem were young Jewish radicals who attended Columbia University or City College or who came from the immigrant neighborhoods surrounding Harlem.[20] While white communists' commitment to civil rights varied significantly—in 1929 one white party member attacked a Black man for sitting with two white women in the cafeteria of a party-affiliated fraternal organization—at least some, including those who had been exposed to militant and revolutionary activities in their neighborhoods and workplaces, took seriously the directive to organize Black workers, especially as the Depression wreaked havoc among Black Harlemites.[21] In 1930 the party organized the Upper Harlem Council of the Unemployed to help Black workers fight evictions, resist police brutality, and challenge discriminatory relief and employment practices.[22] The collaborations forged between Harlem's Jewish and Black radicals during

FIGURE 5. Jessie Taft Smith in Harlem, New York, ca. 1934.
Credit: Courtesy of Jane LaTour and Russell Smith.

the Depression, historian Mark Naison argues, both invigorated the party and
represented its continued marginality in American society.[23]

While communists prioritized the organization of Black workers and the battle
against racial injustice, party leaders paid less attention to gender as a system of
oppression. Attributing women's subordination to their status as unpaid housewives and poorly paid wage laborers, party doctrine held that women would be
liberated through their participation in the revolutionary struggle. The party
advocated for equal pay for equal work, for the organization of women into
unions, and for progressive goals such as maternity benefits and access to birth
control, but in reality "women's" issues remained a low priority.[24] In 1937 Com-

munist Party leader Earl Browder admitted that many of his male comrades were more than willing to postpone the question of women's oppression to "a more favorable moment, which never comes."[25] For Black women, the most serious and sustained critiques of their "triple oppression" as workers, as women, and as people of color came from the party's handful of Black female leaders, including Trinidadian-born Claudia Jones. Jones's intersectional analysis of the "super-exploitation" of Black women "as workers, as Negroes, and as women" expanded Marxist thought and provoked important conversations about how race, class, and gender oppression simultaneously disadvantaged women of color.[26]

The inauguration of the Communist Party's Third Period, as well as the party's commitment to antiracist organizing, contributed to the leftists' intervention in the laundries. Motivated by the deepening economic crisis and the rise of fascism, in 1928 the Comintern ordered communists everywhere to sever ties with social democrats, liberal reformers, and trade unionists unwilling to support the impending revolution. Under this ultraleftist line, the Comintern instructed American communists to abandon "reformist" and "corrupt" AFL unions and organize independent, Left-led unions dedicated to revolutionary struggle and industrial trade unionism.[27] In response, in August 1929 American communists formed the Trade Union Unity League (TUUL), an umbrella organization for the "red" unions they would establish in meatpacking, tobacco, textiles, and other industries. The most powerful TUUL Council was in New York City, headquarters of the Communist Party USA. By 1933 the TUUL claimed one hundred thousand workers nationwide in unions such as the Fur Workers Union, the Food Workers Industrial Union, and the Needle Trade Workers Industrial Union.[28] Less well known is the fact that the party also worked with New York's laundry workers to establish a TUUL-affiliated union spearheaded in part by young Jewish radical women committed to interracial organizing and racial justice.

Red Feminists in the Laundries:
Jessie Taft Smith and Beatrice Shapiro Lumpkin

By the time Jessie Taft Smith helped launch the laundry campaign in 1931, her father, communist garment worker Morris Taft, former manager of Tuckers, Pleaters, and Hemstitchers ILGWU Local 41, had been ousted from the garment union, a casualty of the factional battles taking place in the 1920s. During the Depression Morris Taft struggled to support his family of six by teaching English to immigrants and working as a fundraiser for the International Labor Defense (ILD), the legal arm of the Communist Party. In his spare time he taught classes on Marxism and wrote poetry. Smith described her father as "always active," promoting socialism. Smith's mother, Rebecca Bernard, immigrated to

New York City from Russia after the failed 1905 anticzarist revolution. Bernard worked before marriage as a custom dressmaker sewing women's clothing. Like millions of other immigrant housewives, she took in boarders and did piecework at home to support her four daughters during the Depression.[29]

Smith, who joined the communist youth organization, the Young Pioneers, in 1925 at the age of eleven, was still in high school when the Depression began, but she spent more time on picket lines and at the Communist Party's headquarters at 26 Union Square than she did in the classroom. From a young age she joined her father when he stood on stepladders on Bronx's busiest street corners to extol the benefits of socialism. Smith, who graduated from the Young Pioneers to the YCL when she became a teenager, attributes her activism to being "brought up with labor" and insists that she "was proud to be a daughter of a worker. I wasn't ashamed. And I thought that the worker was the best kind of human being to be." Smith argued in 2006 that classism was a form of prejudice as dangerous as racism. She attributed the low political tone in the country to "social brainwashing" that elevated business people over workers. "The idea of being a worker is not something that gets any honour," Smith lamented. Whenever the garment workers went out on strike, members of the YCL at Smith's Bronx high school, PS 61, would rush out to the picket lines, where they were later picked up by truant officers. Smith was suspended from school in 1929 for distributing communist literature, and at the Board of Education hearing to consider her suspension, Smith's teachers used her laudatory composition about party leader William Z. Foster as evidence to uphold the suspension.[30]

As a rising star in the party and as YCL trade union director for New York City, Smith attended the Communist Party's national convention in New York City in 1929. Taking the stage after party founder and national secretary Jay Lovestone, who would soon be expelled from the party by Stalin, Smith told the audience about the problems confronting youth, including teachers, principals, and truant officers. In May 1929, after a confrontation with the police outside party headquarters, Smith was charged with juvenile delinquency.[31] A few months later she joined an interracial youth delegation headed to the 1929 International Conference of Young Pioneers in Moscow. Singing "The Internationale" and shouting "Down with the United States!," she and her comrades boarded the ship's third-class gangway waving red bandanas in place of the red banners the police had confiscated.[32] In the Soviet Union, Smith attended talks and visited Soviet schools and workplaces with youth delegates from around the world. She explains that it was through the Young Pioneers and the YCL that "I learned to stand on my own two feet and make decisions." Throughout her life of activism (Smith left the party in the 1950s but remained politically active for progressive causes until her death in 2015 at the age of one hundred), Smith was able to withstand the Red-baiting and other forms of persecution because she "led a life with a purpose." Making the world a better place for workers was, Smith explained, her religion.[33]

While Smith developed valuable political and organizational skills on the picket lines and in the union hall, she also benefited from the party's cultural and intellectual activities. Smith explains that through the movement "you became a thinking person." It was through the party that Smith was introduced to a version of American history that included slavery, the Civil War, and Reconstruction. Even before Smith learned this history, as someone who lived and worked in Harlem and the Bronx and saw firsthand the pernicious impact of racial discrimination, Smith was convinced that the "biggest problem" facing the working class was racism. "I mean," Smith explained, "the whole idea of the Civil War—they were the most exploited part of the working class. And when the blacks came up from the South, they would use them as scabs whenever there was a strike. So if you were going to be successful, it was important." As someone who understood racism as a system designed to maintain white supremacy and capitalism, Smith insisted that fighting racism "made common sense from the point of view of justice. . . . I mean, there were some Black organizations too. But it was up to all of us to fight."[34]

Although deeply immersed in the party, Smith always made sure to mingle with the "common people" and explained, "I just didn't stay with what you call 'movement people' only. No, I was always part of the people. 'Cause you can, I think, become very narrow." Smith criticized her comrades for being patronizing toward those not in the movement and asked, "How can you organize people when you think they're stupid? So the fact is that I was always a good neighbor and a good citizen." Smith also confessed that she enjoyed socializing with non-movement people because of the freedom it provided: "I loved to dance and liked to go out and act stupid and nuts. And I figured that I wouldn't feel comfortable [with movement people]." Smith made an exception for the rent parties held on Saturday nights in a comrade's apartment. "We'd make spaghetti, and you'd pay for your drinks and the food, and we'd raise money." An outgoing, gregarious and charismatic person with a wide social circle, she also joined her sister, who lived in Harlem and exclusively dated African American men, at Harlem's interracial Savoy Ballroom. Smith remembers that in the 1930s wealthy white people would come up to Harlem to "get entertained at nightclubs . . . [like] the Cotton Club and Savoy."[35] In the 1930s Smith saw up close the poverty and the despair of Depression-era Harlem, but she also saw the vibrancy and dynamism that drew people, including voyeuristic whites from across the city and beyond.

As one of the most active young women in the party, Smith tried to raise awareness about issues affecting women, a feminist consciousness nurtured by her mother, whom Smith described as modern and secular. Smith recalled that her mother, who attended night school to learn English, was the first woman in their Bronx neighborhood to bob her hair. As a YCL leader Smith wrote plays and skits that celebrated the accomplishments of famous American women such as Molly Pritchard, Harriet Tubman, Susan B. Anthony, and Jane Addams. At the 1930 YCL convention the sixteen-year-old Smith arranged for a gynecologist to speak to the girls about sex but was dismayed when the doctor criticized sexually active single women. Smith was equally disturbed by the assumption, held by some of her male comrades, that radical women would be sexually promiscuous. She remembers going to parties where everyone was having sex, "where it ended up that all the couples were doing it." She criticized her male comrades for bragging about their sexual conquests and treating women like "used goods."[36] Peggy Dennis, a communist activist from Los Angeles and longtime partner of Eugene Dennis, general secretary of the Communist Party from 1945 to 1957, similarly described a culture of sexism and argued that trading sex was often the only way a woman could move up "in our movement as elsewhere." Dennis complained that radical women were pressured to relinquish their positions in the party once they married, an expectation that did not apply to men.[37] Smith, Dennis, and other female activists gained valuable organizational experience in the party, and some assumed leadership positions, yet they also confronted very typical elements of sexism. It was perhaps this awareness that led Smith to mentor other female party members, including fellow laundry worker Beatrice Shapiro Lumpkin.

Born in 1918, fours years after Smith, Lumpkin was the daughter of Russian revolutionaries Ruhd-eh Chernin and Avrom Hirschenhorn, both members of the Jewish socialist Bund in Soviet Byelorussia. Hirschenhorn was arrested during the 1905 Russian Revolution. His comrades, including his future wife, broke him out of jail and provided him with a passport in the name of Morris Shapiro and steerage to the United States. A year later Dora Chernin joined him in York City. (A clerk at Ellis Island read her name, listed as Roda, as Dora, thus beginning her American life as Dora.)[38]

Lumpkin's parents settled in the East Bronx, where they quickly became immersed in the neighborhood's vibrant Jewish Left community. Dora Chernin Shapiro joined one of the Jewish sections of the communist mutual benefit and fraternal order, the International Workers' Order (IWO), while Morris Shapiro became an intellectual figure in the community. Lumpkin explains that it was her mother who did the "Jane Higgins work for progressive organizations." (Jimmy Higgins was the name used to refer to the average rank-and-file worker who did the grunt work.)[39] Lumpkin attributes her passion for social justice to her parents' influence and to growing up in a "class-conscious, socialist, communist-oriented" community of predominantly unionized Jewish garment workers.[40] Although her parents did not join the Communist Party because they were too busy raising children and trying to make a living, Lumpkin explains that they "always maintained a contact with the left forces in the Jewish working class" and

FIGURE 6. Beatrice Shapiro Lumpkin with Hunter College contingent at May Day march in New York City, May 1, 1936. Courtesy of Beatrice Shapiro Lumpkin.

were avid readers of the Communist Party's daily Yiddish-language newspaper, *Freiheit*. Lumpkin explained that she was "born knowing which side I was on."[41]

Like Smith, Lumpkin quickly developed a feminist consciousness, something she also attributed to her mother's influence. During the 1905 Revolution a young Chernin had delivered ammunition hidden in her long skirts to soldiers on the front lines, all the while dodging bullets from the Cossack troops. Once settled in New York, Chernin Shapiro took her daughter out canvassing and ringing doorbells to recruit members for the IWO. Lumpkin remembers that her mother found time for such activities even though she was "always working," first in the needle trades—Chernin Shapiro narrowly escaped death in the 1911 fire at the Triangle Shirtwaist Factory, where she worked, because she was heavily pregnant and at home at the time of the fire—and later in the family's hand laundry. Lumpkin, who recalled that Shapiro was the first woman in their Bronx neighborhood to cut her hair short (like Smith's mother) and shorten her dresses, insisted that it was her mother who taught her to think for herself.[42]

Lumpkin's feminism grew as a result of her exposure to Orthodox Judaism. In 1924 Lumpkin's grandfather moved to New York City from Byelorussia. At the age of eight, Lumpkin was tasked with taking him to his daily prayers. As her parents were nonbelievers—Lumpkin remembered that some of her parents' friends were "militant atheists" who held anti-Seders and ate ham sandwiches—the chore gave her an opportunity to learn more about the religious aspects of Judaism. Lumpkin remembered being shocked to discover the men praying on the main floor of the synagogue while the women were relegated to the balconies, where they prayed behind curtains. She described the "second-class status of women in the synagogue" as "strange and repulsive." Her initial response was confirmed when she later learned about the sacrifices that pious Jewish women were expected to make, including shaving their heads after marriage and taking monthly baths for cleansing after menstruation. Lumpkin explained, "I don't know exactly what shaped it but I grew up militantly feministic. Now if it had been the modern, reformed Jewish synagogue I might have had a different reaction."[43]

In 1927 Lumpkin's parents moved to the Bronx's Hunts Point neighborhood, where they opened a new hand laundry. Lumpkin learned how to use a mangle machine and joined her father picking up and delivering bundles of laundry. A year later, at the age of eleven, she joined the Young Pioneers and took her first train ride to Passaic, New Jersey, to support striking textile workers there. In 1927 she was suspended from her all-girls junior high school (PS 60) in the Bronx after skipping class to attend an International Workers' Day march. She was thrilled when she was able to transfer to James Monroe High School, where she reveled at the opportunity to take science classes and organize a YCL group. When not in school Lumpkin and her comrades were out on picket lines, marching for relief and food for the unemployed, circulating the *Daily Worker*, or attending one of the many YCL parties, dances, or dinners. As a young teenager she attended the IWO's Camp Kinderland and at age eighteen graduated to Camp Unity, where she worked as a waitress.[44]

To deepen her knowledge of the class struggle Lumpkin studied Marx and Lenin at the Workers' School in downtown Manhattan. It was there that she first read Frederick Douglass's autobiography. In nice weather she and her comrades met in the park and took turns reading and debating Marx. When they were unsure of how to approach an issue or needed money, they went to the Communist Party headquarters for advice. Lumpkin recalled the thrill of attending the "grownups' meetings" and of being given the opportunity to debate with the adults.[45]

Lumpkin insisted that the most valuable lesson she learned in the party was that the "biggest barrier to uniting workers was, and still is, racism." Lumpkin described growing up in a community where "memories of the Russian czar's pogroms against Jews were still strong" and being deeply disturbed by the racist treatment of African Americans. Lumpkin understood Jim Crow segregation and the formation of Black "ghettos" as analogous to the persecution Jews experienced in Europe and elsewhere. Like Rose Schneiderman, Lumpkin understood that racism underpinned both the murderous attacks on Jewish ghettoes conducted by the czarist troops and the heinous acts of racial violence perpetrated by white supremacists in full view of the state.[46]

Lumpkin's intersectional understanding of oppression grew under the tutelage of party luminaries such as Claudia Jones. Lumpkin described the Trinidadian-born theoretician, feminist, and party leader as brilliant, gorgeous, and an accomplished orator.[47] Jones, who had worked briefly in a laundry after immigrating to New York in 1924, the same year as Adelmond, joined the party in 1936, inspired by its leadership in the campaign to free the Scottsboro Nine, the nine Black youth falsely accused of raping two white women in Alabama. Jones quickly moved up the party ranks and in 1941 became educational director of the YCL. In 1945 the party elected her a full member of the National Committee of the Communist Party USA.[48]

Jones's articulation of Black women's triple oppression or "super-exploitation" anticipated the work of Black feminist scholars in the 1960s and 1970s and shaped Lumpkin's own ideas about oppression. In line with Marxist ideology, Jones located Black women's oppression in the capitalist system, but she drew attention to their super-exploitation as workers concentrated in low-paying, degrading service work, where they faced the threat of rape, and as mothers compelled to accept such work to support their families and communities. Jones criticized white female communists who failed to acknowledge differences among women and who argued that Black women were too inexperienced or too busy raising children to become party leaders. Jones understood that Black women's lived experience at the intersection of race, class, and gender oppression situated them to lead battles for economic justice, women's liberation, and civil rights.[49] While Jones's critique alienated some white communists, Lumpkin, who was already grappling with how to develop a theoretical understanding of race, class, and gender and apply it to her everyday organizing, reveled at the opportunity to learn under Jones's tutelage.[50]

When Lumpkin graduated from high school in 1934, she enrolled at Hunter College, the "poor girls' Radcliffe." Disappointed that the all-women's school did not offer a physics program, she settled on a combined degree in history, political science, and economics and began organizing. In 1934 she led a successful milk boycott against the administration after they raised the price of a half pint of milk from five to six cents. When the dean suspended her for leading a group of Hunter students to the National Student Strike for Peace Lumpkin used her spare time to become a YCL advisor for a Bronx high school, where she took on the role of mentor. She was arrested for the first time in 1935 while picketing in front of Ohrbach's Department Store on 14th Street. A few months later the police picked her up for "peddling" the *Daily Worker* on city property in front of the New York Public Library. In 1935 the dean of Hunter College suspended Lumpkin for a second time for organizing the Conference against War and Fascism to generate support for Ethiopia and Republican Spain.[51]

It was in Harlem at a march denouncing Italy's invasion of Ethiopia that Lumpkin was first exposed to Garveyism. She remembers being shocked and upset to hear Marcus Garvey urge Black people to return to Africa, a strategy she compared to Zionism, another movement she disliked. She explained, "Why should they go someplace else, you know? Stay here and fight for your rights!"[52] Later in her life, after learning more about Garvey, she came to understand why his nationalist message of race pride, Black unity, and self-reliance resonated so strongly with Black people. Garveyism, Lumpkin explained in 2009, "instilled a type of confidence and rejection of this whole psychology of the politics of inferiority." She admitted, moreover, that her initial perspective may have been colored by the fact that Garvey's race-first philosophy did not align with the Communist Party's commitment to class solidarity and that the two movements were competing for the same followers.[53]

In 1933, within months of joining the YCL, Lumpkin learned of the strikes erupting in Harlem and Bronx laundries. It was through these strikes that she met Smith, whom Lumpkin described as her first mentor. She remembered the calls coming into the YCL office asking for recruits to join the picket lines sprouting up at laundries in Upper Manhattan and the Bronx. Lumpkin believed that the party supported the laundry workers because of its commitment to antiracist organizing and to the most marginalized workers. The young activist would join many of the picket lines in front of the National and other uptown laundries in the early and mid-1930s, but it was not until 1937, when she took a leave of absence from college, that she would devote herself full time to the laundry campaign.[54] Alongside Adelmond, Robinson, and Smith, Lumpkin would play a leading role in the organization of New York City's laundry workers.

"We'd All Go In": The Formation of the Left-Led Laundry Workers Industrial Union

With her father out of work, in 1931 Smith got a job at the Bronx's National Laundry on Wilkins Avenue, across the street from her family's apartment. The National, which employed a mostly Black workforce, was part of the Consolidated, a laundry corporation that employed three thousand workers across seventeen plants.[55] Consolidated workers complained of bosses who pitted white workers against Black workers and who used "stool pigeons" to spy on the workers. A worker at the National reported that a white woman had been fired for speaking to her African American coworker. Smith, who described the laundry as "real modern," was able to get hired immediately by standing outside the plant in the hiring line.[56]

As a white woman, Smith was offered a job as a packer earning fourteen dollars a week, significantly more than her Black female coworkers in the ironing department earned. As a packer who wrapped the laundered goods, Smith appreciated being able to work with the "clean clothing" in a relatively nice room set off from the heat and humidity of the rest of the plant. She also remembered being shocked at the speed at which the flat-work ironer revolved and of the intensity of the heat and steam generated by the machines.[57]

Fresh out of high school—she was seventeen at the time—Smith explained that she "had a lot to learn about the work, myself, and the people there." Alongside the other communist laundry workers, most of whom were shirt ironers, drivers, and delivery men, Smith formed a "nucleus" to discuss conditions in the industry and to plan a union campaign. The radicals decided to focus on the small- to medium-sized plants that employed between 40 and 180 workers (by this time a handful of plants employed as many as 1,000 workers) and described their strategy as shop based rather than industry based. Campaign records note that the drive revolved around "get[ting] first one and then more contacts."[58] To facilitate this rank-and-file intensive approach, Smith approached her Black female coworkers at lunch (as inexperienced as she was, Smith understood that she would have been fired had she been caught talking to her Black male coworkers), and she and her comrades visited the workers at night in their homes. The leftists reported significant worker interest, which Smith attributed to the fact that there were "already big movements all over the United States." Labor activism was "in the air."[59]

With the workers responding enthusiastically to the radicals' overtures and consistent with the policies of the Third Period, in September 1931 Smith and her comrades founded a new union: the Laundry Workers Industrial Union. With headquarters at 138th Street and Third Avenue, the union included both inside workers and drivers, some of whom were former members of Teamsters Local 810.[60] Deteriorating working conditions and internal union problems convinced some of the drivers to abandon Teamsters Local 810 and organize industrially with the inside workers during the Depression.

In 1931 a group of laundry drivers accused Samuel Rosenzweig, one of the leaders of Local 810, of colluding with the employers' associations and with well-known racketeer and gangster Larry Fay. Fay ran a collusive trade association of milk dealers.[61] According to the communists, the drivers, determined to clear the "union from the taint of gangsterism," asked the radicals to help them organize the Members Take Over committee. Fay allegedly retaliated by ordering the beating of the disaffected laundry drivers. A few years later the

Bronx Home News reported that six men associated with Fay had been arrested for assaulting a group of laundry drivers who had refused to join the Teamsters, suggesting the leftists' accusations were true. Smith insisted that the Teamsters had always been corrupt.[62]

Laundry driver and communist Samuel Berland served as president of the newly organized Laundry Workers Industrial Union, and fellow comrade and driver Leon Blum served as secretary. Smith accepted a job as a full-time organizer earning five dollars a week, a third of what she earned at the National. Smith described Blum as an intelligent and thoughtful man, a "true man who believed in equality" and who quickly won the workers' trust. Smith similarly described Berland as smart and dedicated but reported that he sexually harassed her. Although Berland was married, Smith remembered that he was "always grabbing me, and . . . wanna go to bed? And buggin' me and buggin' me all the time."[63] When she was interviewed in 2006, Smith also remembered that some of her comrades sexually harassed the Black women laundry workers with whom they were organizing. Smith attempted to intervene but recalled that

> I didn't have many voices to back me up, but I knew that it was wrong what they were doing. Wrong, well, I say wrong. They were treating the women like anybody else who, you know, what do you call it? White supremacists, whatever you call it. But I never made that thesis. I always was given accolades and recognition in the movement all the time as a leader and a trade unionist and a woman. I met all the categories, and nobody ever, I mean never, nobody ever challenged me as a woman that politically, ever. Like, even I went to the Soviet Union as a Pioneer.[64]

Smith's recollection suggests that she understood that Black women's devaluation within a white supremacist and patriarchal society underpinned the sexual violence they experienced in the union and beyond. While she also complained about being subjected to sexist behavior and expectations, she acknowledged the accolades she received as a radical organizer and the opportunities she enjoyed, advantages related to her white-skin privilege. Smith's racial privilege also afforded her the space to use what she described as her "big dirty mouth." "One of the best protections" against sexism, Smith insisted, was "being able to curse out loud, every dirty word."[65]

With the communists at the helm, the new union employed a rank-and-file intensive approach that included talking to the workers about the importance of organizing on an interracial and industrial basis.[66] Consistent with the party's antiracist commitments, the union demanded that African Americans be hired as drivers and washers and that "equal pay for equal work" be given to all workers, irrespective of race and sex. In the fall of 1931 Smith addressed a mass meeting of laundry workers in Harlem where she urged the workers to support the

Scottsboro Nine.[67] In December 1931, only a few months after its founding, the Left-led union was listed as one of the expected participants at the Communist Party's National Hunger March to Washington, DC.[68] In March 1932 the union held a ball at the Ambassador Hall. Social activities such as balls and dances provided opportunities for the radicals to demonstrate their commitment to interracialism and social equality.[69] By February 1932 the Laundry Workers Industrial Union reported membership of four hundred members.[70]

With the Left-led laundry campaign gaining steam, in 1932 African American party leader Maude White wrote a series of articles on the laundry workers for the party's *Harlem Liberator*. Originally from Chicago, White married white party activist Arthur Katz in the late 1940s. Alongside Claudia Jones, White Katz belonged to a relatively small but influential group of Black female party activists who historian LaShawn Harris argues combined leftist reform with the traditions of Black women's community-based organizing.[71] White, who described the laundry as a "Negro industry" in which African Americans worked longer hours and for less pay than their white coworkers, reported that the campaign would succeed only if it addressed the racist inequities in hiring and employment practices. Smith, who remembered seeing White around the laundries, described her as a valuable ally of the laundry workers.[72]

In the spring of 1932 the radicals started calling "running strikes" at the Bronx's Active, Pretty, and Superfine Laundries, where at least half of the workers were Black. Despite having little money, the workers—white and Black—stayed out on the picket lines for days.[73] In a letter to party headquarters, Berland celebrated the growing solidarities among the workers, pointing out that after an employer fired an African American laundry unionist, all the workers—white, Black, and Spanish—walked off the job in solidarity. Fifteen of the workers were arrested on felony assault charges, and eight served two weeks in jail while awaiting trial. Smith remembered that "leaders were getting arrested every other day." "They'd bring us into the court, the whole picket line," Smith recalled, and "we'd all go in. Even if they didn't put 'em in." Berland wrote to party headquarters that for the first time ever white laundry workers had gone to jail in defense of their Black coworkers. The significance of these developments intensified Berland's frustration when he was unable to secure an appointment with New York State party chairman Israel Amter.[74] Amter was perhaps preoccupied with his job as prosecutor in a 1932 party trial designed to root out white chauvinism, a task that left little time for the arguably more important work of responding to local calls to support Black workers' organizing.[75] Despite officialdom's lack of support, by the summer of 1932 the radicals reported that the laundry union had an active membership of one thousand drivers and inside workers, the latter of whom were predominantly African American.[76]

The Uprising of 1933:
The Laundry Workers
Industrial Union on Strike

In June 1933, mere days after President Franklin D. Roosevelt signed into law the National Industrial Recovery Act (NIRA), which included a provision guaranteeing workers the right to form a union (7a), Bronx laundry workers and their communist allies launched the largest walkout since 1912.[77] Between twelve hundred and fourteen hundred laundry workers, two-thirds of whom were Black, walked off the job. Twenty-one-year-old African American laundry worker Alberta Anderson took charge of one of the strike headquarters, from which she organized picket lines and canvassing committees and straightened out grievances among workers. Anderson's mother had worked as a laundress to provide her daughter with an education so that she would not have to make a "living the hard way." While Anderson did not end up washing clothes by hand for white families, she did end up in a power laundry, a testament to both the limited employment opportunities available to women of color and the racialization of laundry work. Anderson quickly emerged as a shop floor leader. At the end of the strike the workers elected her secretary of the Laundry Workers Industrial Union. She also joined the ILD to work on the campaign to free the Scottsboro Nine and served as a delegate to the Baltimore Anti-Lynch Conference.[78] As historian Martha Biondi argues, the interracial organizing and civil rights advocacy of the Left and Black workers like Anderson contributed to New York's emergence as an early locus of the civil rights movement.[79]

With communists at the helm, workers from fourteen laundries demanded union recognition, employer contributions toward the establishment of a relief fund for unemployed workers, an end to discriminatory wage scales and hiring practices, an eight-hour workday, a forty-four-hour workweek, and a 20 percent wage increase. The strikers formed a strike committee that included representation from each of the laundry's twenty-five departments. Most of the representatives were Black women.[80] Smith explains that decisions were made collectively and democratically: "You talk and you meet and you argue and you settle and you discuss," and then you "finally decide what you're going to do." The shirt ironers, likely the communist faction from Local 280, lent the union money so that it could provide strike benefits of three dollars a week to the women and five dollars to the men. The gendered relief differentials reflected the party's greater valuation of men's wage earning and stood in contrast to the WTUL, which in 1912 had dispensed relief based on family status rather than sex.[81]

With the support of the radicals the workers employed a militant industrial union strategy that included violent confrontations with strikebreakers, employers, and the police. Smith and her comrades formed "squads" that put "stink bombs" under the doors of strikebreakers, most of whom were Black and Italian workers. Smith believes that the employers used agencies such as the New York State Employment Service in Harlem to bring in strikebreakers.[82] The young activist took work as a strikebreaker so that she could sabotage the plants. At one laundry Smith mixed up all the tags that identified which pieces of laundry belonged to which customer, leaving the employer with the unenviable task of having to reunite piles of anonymous laundry with their owners. Smith, who recalls being "escorted" out of more than one laundry, became so well-known for such tactics that she had to start using aliases to get jobs in the industry.[83] The *Bronx Home News*, which followed the strike closely, reported the arrests of hundreds of workers on charges of disorderly conduct and felony assault. On June 26 the police arrested twenty-one women and men who were part of a group of one hundred strikers parading "boisterously" in front of the Mott Haven Laundry while calling on the workers inside to join the strike.[84]

Smith and her comrades organized auto parades in the neighborhoods where laundry workers were on strike and approached Columbia University students to coordinate a boycott of the Adelphia Laundry, which the university patronized.[85] The Left-led Women's Councils and Unemployed Councils, formed during the Depression to support unemployed workers, ran soup kitchens and provided other services to the workers. Smith insisted that "you couldn't operate just outta the union headquarters, with no [community support], no matter how many members" you had.[86] Smith recalled that "we always had the community behind us. And we always had the women—women's groups would set up a kitchen when we went on strike and get food, and the strikers would have—go there and eat." The communists' community-oriented unionism created space for and depended on the neighborhood networks forged by radical feminist organizers like Clara Lemlich Shavelson, a leader of the housewives' movement.[87] At a strike at the Bronx's Pretty Laundry the *Daily Worker* reported that housewives chased a group of strikebreakers from their homes. In 1932 the union established a Laundry Workers Women's Council to support the strikers.[88]

The Interborough Laundry Board of Trade, which alleged that only 225 workers were on strike, refused to meet with the strikers, claiming it would bargain only with representatives from the AFL.[89] Midway through the strike the police arrested Leon Blum, the union's secretary, for a parole violation. Smith and her comrades believe the employers had colluded with the police to remove Blum. Blum was found guilty of making threats against strikebreakers and inciting violence; he was sentenced to three years in jail (he would serve one year in state prison).[90] With the employers remaining intransigent, on July 6, 1933, a month after the strike began, the workers met at the Ambassador Hall on Third

Avenue and voted to end the strike. It was a disappointing although not surprising conclusion, given the high levels of employer resistance, police brutality, and lack of funds.

Understanding the 1933 Laundry Uprising

While the 1933 strike did not end in a union agreement or union recognition, it broke new ground as the first time that the drivers and inside workers had joined forces to challenge the employers. Black and white workers paraded shoulder to shoulder in front of some of the largest laundries in the Bronx, inspiring the wrath of their employers and the police. Black laundry workers joined a Left-led union, and at least a few, including Anderson, joined the Communist Party. The mass mobilization demonstrates that in semiskilled and unskilled industries with largely moribund AFL unions, Communist Party organizing during the sectarian Third Period helped forge the interracial activist solidarities that would bring the workers into the CIO in 1937.[91]

There is little evidence to suggest, however, that more than a handful of laundry workers joined the Communist Party. Party reports and newspaper articles from 1933 and 1934 lament that the upsurge in the laundries did not produce a similar increase in Black party membership. Party leaders excoriated members for not paying enough attention to the "special problems" of Black workers, for engaging in white chauvinism, and for neglecting the important work of recruitment.[92]

For Robinson, who did not join the party, the issue was one of tactics. Robinson argued that the communists "would fight to a point, and it was very good, we liked that—but their techniques of elimination turned us off." Robinson criticized the harsh and sometimes "dishonest" methods communists employed when severing ties with former allies, as well as their intolerance of political opponents. She explained that the "way you eliminate them [opponents] means something to me, you see. If you eliminate them without disgracing them or something, or trumping up something, at that point when you trumped up, it was dishonest as far as I could see."[93] Her good friend Pauli Murray, the civil rights activist and lawyer, shared Robinson's assessment. Murray complained that during the Depression communists used sneaky tactics to gain control of a number of unions. When they were unable to outvote their opposition, Murray argued, they accused their rivals of being "social fascists."[94] ILGWU leader Maida Springer argued that while the communists were saying all the right things in terms of racial equality, they were more "concerned with an international political agenda" and with destroying liberal organizations than they were with supporting Harlem's Black workers. Despite their repeated and fervent attempts to recruit her, Springer refused to join the party.[95]

In 1933 lack of recruitment among African Americans was a function not only of tactical and ideological differences but also of local leaders' decisions to prioritize the immediate needs of workers over the larger imperative of party building. Smith, who described herself as a "rank-and-file person who worked in the community" rather than a "political leader" (a devaluation of her actual role and typical of women organizers), did not remember ever engaging in recruitment. She insisted that "it wasn't that a lot of people would run to headquarters to get advice on what to do."[96] Smith's comments underline the autonomy with which some members of the Harlem Section of the party operated, especially during the early 1930s, when the party was unusually decentralized and when some of its working-class members were open to coalitions with allies from diverse ideological backgrounds. At the beginning of the Depression, radicals like Smith had some space to prioritize local struggles over party recruitment, space that would contract after the summer of 1933, when the party's Central Committee installed new leaders with the goal of transforming the Harlem Section into a more disciplined body focused on recruitment.[97]

While communist organizers like Smith helped launch the Bronx uprising, African American laundry activism was also inspired by the broader culture of radicalism taking root in Harlem during the Depression. Black Americans responded collectively to the ravages of the Depression with Don't Buy Where You Can't Work campaigns and by founding organizations such as the Harlem Housewives League and the Negro Labor Committee. Black churches, the NAACP, the Urban League, and other established organizations adopted more confrontational tactics, including picketing and mass demonstrations. The National Urban League, which by 1935 had forty-two Workers' Councils in seventeen states, instructed African Americans to "get into somebody's union and stay there."[98] Many of Harlem's most prominent churches hosted progressive speakers, including African American James W. Ford, head of the Harlem section of the Communist Party.[99] Interviewed in 1936, one African American laundry worker explained that "things are changing. Now in churches and clubs they teach Negroes to be union conscious. They're more ready to organize today than they were six months ago."[100]

In 1935, after conducting a survey of three hundred unions in New York City, Columbia University researcher Charles Franklin reported a "slight shift" among African Americans "from race consciousness to class consciousness," a shift he attributed to the primacy of economic issues and to the slow but steady decline of racial barriers in the union movement as white workers realized that the "horrors of industrial slavery" would not be eradicated "so long as black labor is not elevated."[101] The economic crisis, the industrial and interracial unionism of the communists, and Black working-class militancy contributed to the growing activist solidarities among the laundry workers.

The Laundry Workers' Popular Front

In order to capitalize on their recent mobilization and in response to the Popular Front, in 1934 the communists invited representatives from hand laundry Local 280 and Teamsters Local 810, as well as from a recently formed local in Brooklyn, Local 135, to a Unity Conference to discuss a merger.[102] The proposal anticipated the official inauguration of the Popular Front in the summer of 1935, when the Comintern directed its members to form broad alliances with socialists, trade unionists, and liberals in the battle to defeat fascism. Robinson remembered the Popular Front as a period in which "all of the 'isms' were together—the Left, the Far Left, and the Near Left."[103]

AFL laundry leaders refused to meet with the Left-led union, but a group of shirt ironers from Local 280, likely the communist contingent, joined the Laundry Workers Industrial Union.[104] The unity group, half of whom were African American, retained the designation Local 280 and elected a new slate of leaders.[105] William Collins, an AFL special representative and organizer in New York City, installed the new officers of the reorganized local. Smith served as financial secretary, and Berland served as manager. Smith also took on the job of "dispatch," sending out unemployed workers for jobs. It was in this role that she met her first lesbian, a short dark-skinned African American woman who had recently broken up with her girlfriend. Smith and the woman went out for walks, and Smith remembered that the laundry worker kissed her and tried to convince her to stay overnight, promising her a good time. Smith, who described the woman as nice, recalled that she "just wasn't ready to do that." An African American served as vice president of Local 280's executive board, and Black workers served as chair shop persons.[106] Smith reported that the grievance board, which included two Black and three white members, had "satisfactorily settled misunderstandings among workers and at times between the employer and Negro workers when the boss abused them with unkind words or added to their work." To maintain the local's oppositional character, Smith and her comrades held fraction meetings outside of the formal shop and union meetings usually on a Sunday night in one of the drivers' homes, where they served herring and boiled potatoes.[107]

The AFL-affiliated Laundry Workers International Union (LWIU) immediately went on the offensive, claiming that the communists had hijacked Local 280. Joseph Mackey, the LWIU vice president and eastern representative, sent out an emergency appeal for funds, writing to AFL president William Green that "either intentionally or through stupidity," the president of Local 280 had "wished on us enough communists to swamp out all our conservative A.F. of L. minded members."[108] Mackey also took aim at the workers, describing them as "over placent [*sic*], indifferent and overworked slaves" who lacked "education advantages," an overtly racist and inaccurate portrayal of New York's laundry workers.[109] When Charles Franklin conducted interviews in 1935 for his *Negro Labor Unionist of New York*, he interviewed Smith about the laundry union, not Mackey. Franklin's choice suggests that the leftists rather than the AFL were the recognized leaders of the laundry workers. Smith described the Irish-born Mackey as "just an old geezer" who did no organizing. According to Smith, he was an AFL bureaucrat with a title and pay.[110]

Strife between the communist leaders and the AFL laundry leaders culminated in November 1935, when Mackey revoked the Left-led Local 280's charter, ostensibly for failure to pay per-capita dues. In a letter to Green, Mackey confessed that he had revoked the charter because "there were too many communists in that organization that have managed to gain all key positions."[111] New York AFL representative Collins urged Green to ignore Mackey, whom he described as "not a very strong character," and explained that the charter was being held as a political "football" in the battle between socialist and communist laundry workers.[112] A staunch anticommunist, Green instructed New York official and AFL vice president Matthew Woll to help Mackey expel the radicals from the laundry union. Despite the turmoil, the communists continued to organize and in January 1936 reported that they had recruited 250 new members and won wage increases in over fifty shops.[113]

In January 1936 the *New York Amsterdam News* reported that socialist Frank Crosswaith, chairman of the recently organized Negro Labor Committee (NLC), had hosted a conference of laundry unionists with the goal of uniting the different factions. The location of the conference at the Harlem Labor Center signaled Black workers' growing power in the union and was the result of the specific intervention of African American socialist Noah Walter, a longtime laundry worker and organizer for the NLC. Walter would play a leading role in the formation of the CIO laundry union. In 1936 Crosswaith appointed William Conway, executive board member of Musicians' Local 802, and Jack Butler of the Taxi Chauffeurs' Union to chair an investigating committee tasked with uniting the various factions in the laundry. In the meantime, AFL unionists used the Harlem Labor Center as its headquarters.[114]

Power laundry Local 290, which engaged in little activity in the early 1930s, remained under the control of the AFL. In 1935 the local boasted 250 members, 60 percent of whom were Black. An African American served as vice president and treasurer, and of the forty executive board members, fourteen were African American.[115] In 1935 Walter, who served on Local 290's executive board, told Charles Franklin—somewhat optimistically—that "the industry is in perfect harmony; there is no dissension." He also insisted that he had never witnessed "discrimination, segregation or anti-Negro feeling" in the AFL union. Walter's rosy picture defied his own experiences. Despite having a college degree, Walter was unable to obtain a job as a driver, in part because the union failed to challenge Black workers' exclusion from driving positions.[116] While interracial solidarities were certainly emerging, especially under the leadership of radical organizers, racism and sexism continued to limit the opportunities available to women and people of color. For the next few years, communists, socialists, AFL trade unionists, industrial feminists, and Black laundry workers would vie for control over the insurgent movements emerging from the shop floor. At the same time, Brooklyn would emerge as a hotbed of activism, adding a second front to the laundry workers' battle to win union representation.

CHAPTER SIX

"Aristocrats of the Movement"

The Uprising of Brooklyn's Laundry Workers

In January 1934, during one of the worst years of the Depression for job scarcity, over four hundred laundry workers from the Sunshine and Colonial Laundries in Brooklyn walked off the job. Included among the strikers was the teenage Dollie Robinson, who had only just begun working at the Colonial. Interviewed many decades later, Robinson remembered that the workers were very militant and insisted that "you were an aristocratic of the movement if you could get arrested." Fresh out of high school and one of the youngest workers on the picket line, Robinson reminisced that the older women would always find an excuse to send her away just before an arrest was about to be made.[1] Although Robinson was not arrested, her participation in this groundbreaking strike catapulted her to the forefront of the laundry campaign and launched her long and successful career in the labor and civil rights movements.

The Sunshine and Colonial employers' refusal to pay the workers thirty-one cents an hour, the new minimum wage established by New York State's recently formed Minimum Fair Wage Advisory Committee, precipitated the strike. The New Deal legislation was the culmination of decades of advocacy by industrial feminists and unionists to set a floor beneath wages in low-wage, female-dominated industries, but it was also the specific culmination of Rose Schneiderman's commitment to the laundry workers. As a member of the committee, Schneiderman convinced her colleagues to choose the laundry industry for its first minimum wage investigation.[2] Schneiderman was convinced that once the workers saw they had the support of the state, they would be willing to take the risks associated with organizing, an analysis confirmed by the events of 1934. Eager to support the women, Women's Trade Union League

(WTUL) organizers rushed to Brooklyn, where they helped set up soup kitchens and solicited the support of wealthy Brooklyn allies, some of whom joined the workers on the picket lines ensconced in their mink coats. WTUL ally Eleanor Roosevelt lent the workers her Secret Service agents, while Grace Childs, the wife of business scion Richard S. Childs of Childs Restaurants (and heir to the Bon Ami scouring powder fortune), organized a boycott of hotels that patronized the Sunshine and Colonial Laundries. The mobilization demonstrated the symbiotic relationship between union organizing and legislation and the efficacy of elite support in amplifying the workers' voices. It also revealed a growing ideological rift between increasingly radicalized workers determined to engage in militant action to enforce their newly won right to organize and their allies in the WTUL who continued to promote orderly, respectable behavior to win public sympathy and state support for women's unionism.[3]

A New Deal for the Laundry Workers

Laundry workers nationwide benefited from President Roosevelt's National Recovery Administration (NRA) codes of fair practice. Operating under the assumptions of Keynesian economics, the industry-wide NRA codes mandating minimum wages, maximum hours, and labor's right to bargain collectively were intended to eliminate unfair trade practices, reduce unemployment, and bolster purchasing power. Laundry workers, who were among the twenty-two million workers covered by NRA codes, were particularly fortunate to have an ally in the New Deal administration. By 1930 Rose Schneiderman had become a close friend of the Roosevelts. Eleanor Roosevelt joined the WTUL in 1922, after which she became one of its most effective allies and fundraisers. Eleanor introduced Schneiderman to her husband in the mid-1920s, and, as Annelise Orleck argues, even Eleanor was surprised by how quickly FDR took to Schneiderman. Labor reformer Frances Perkins, whom FDR would appoint US secretary of labor in 1933, credits Schneiderman and her partner, socialist WTUL leader Maud Swartz, with educating FDR about the proper relationship between government and labor. In 1933 President Roosevelt appointed Schneiderman to the NRA's Labor Advisory Board, where she served as the sole female member.[4]

In the spring of 1933, at the Laundryowners National Association (LNA) headquarters in Joliet, Illinois, employer representatives and workers began the process of developing industry-wide codes for the laundry industry. Although initially suspicious of the NRA, many laundry owners saw the codes as an opportunity to eliminate the chiselers who had long operated at or below the cost of production. As in most other industries, the employers dominated the code negotiations, but in contrast to other sectors, they insisted on drafting regional rather than national codes of practice. After months of difficult negotiations, the NRA laundry board requested wage codes that varied across six regions and by population size, ranging from fourteen cents per hour in the South, where four out of five of the workers were Black, to thirty cents per hour in the Northeast and Far West. The board justified the lower southern rate on the grounds that prices were lower in the South, for which they blamed African American laundresses for taking in bundles of family wash for as little as a dollar or less.[5] Led by Clark Foreman, advisor on the economic status of the Negro in the Department of the Interior, and his assistant Charles Weaver, labor, women's, and civil rights groups mounted a spirited challenge to what they described as the code's race-based wage differentials.[6] An outraged Elizabeth Lawson of the Left-led National Negro Congress insisted that the wage differentials were based solely on the fact that "the women who rub your clothes in the South are practically all Negroes." The Communist-led Laundry Workers Industrial Union described the southern laundry code—the lowest code proposed by any employer group—as a "direct attack against the living standards of the Negro workers" and a terrible "precedent in the oppression of the Negro people."[7] Women's Bureau director Mary Anderson pointed out that the laundry codes were lower than those established in other low-wage occupations, including hotels, restaurants, and five-and-ten-cent stores.[8] Tellingly, despite the hearing's focus on Black women, not a single African American woman testified in Washington. The middle-class reformers and labor leaders who spoke on their behalf perpetuated the myth that Black working-class women were incapable of representing their own interests.[9]

Despite widespread opposition, the laundry board approved the proposed codes with the wage differentials intact in February 1934. In June of the same year President Roosevelt made the codes mandatory. Although in no region of the country was a fully functional compliance system in place by May 1935, when the Supreme Court declared the National Industrial Recovery Act (NIRA) unconstitutional, the codes nonetheless raised wages in the laundry industry.[10] A 1935 Women's Bureau investigation of 348 laundries across the country found that the NRA codes had "exerted a marked influence upon rates." In many cities the code rate had become the prevailing rate. Even in the South, most of the employers paid the new fourteen-cent hourly minimum, despite their previous insistence that it would lead to bankruptcy. Codes limiting hours of work to forty per week were less widely observed, however, especially in the South and especially in the flat-work department, where most of the workers were Black women. Women's Bureau investigators also determined that retail prices were not in fact lower in the South. As the code's critics had argued, the southern wage was based not on what consumers were willing or able to pay but rather on what southern laundrymen were willing to pay their mostly African American workforce.[11]

As a result of both the NRA and the longtime efforts of industrial feminists, including Frances Perkins, to establish minimum wage boards at the state level, in April 1933 New York State passed a minimum wage law for women and minors and created the Minimum Fair Wage Advisory Committee. New York State governor Herbert Lehman appointed Schneiderman and Mary Dreier to the committee. At Schneiderman's prodding the committee chose the laundry for its first minimum wage investigation. ILGWU leader Pauline Newman would soon replace Schneiderman on the Minimum Wage Laundry Board when President Roosevelt called her to Washington to serve on the NRA Labor Advisory Board.[12] Schneiderman (and then Newman), AFL laundry unionist Joseph Mackey, and Mrs. Mae Epple, an employee of the Killip Laundry and president of the YWCA Industrial League of Albany, represented the workers. Jessie Smith, who had not been invited to the hearings, showed up nonetheless, demanding to speak, a request the board denied. An article in the *Daily Worker* that appeared shortly after the hearings blasted Schneiderman for being a "close friend of the A.F. of L. machine" and for "subscribing to all its betrayal politics."[13]

After a series of hearings the board recommended a minimum wage of 31 cents an hour, or $12.40, for a forty-hour workweek in New York City—1 cent higher than the NRA laundry code—and 27.5 cents, or $11.00, a week for women and minors in the rest of the state. On October 2, 1933, the wage rates, which applied to both power and hand laundries, became effective under a directory order. On August 6, 1934, the order became mandatory. Eager to eliminate the ruinous competition that had long plagued the industry and cognizant of worker discontent, most of the city's employers complied with the order, even during the nine-month directory period.[14] Within a month of the order's passage, median weekly wages for New York City's laundry workers rose from $10.77 to $12.54, a 17 percent increase. The percentage of women earning less than eight dollars a week dropped from 22 to 12, and hours of work declined. And, much to the relief of the WTUL, the minimum wage did not lead to the displacement of women with men, the result of the rigid sex typing in the industry and of the men's unwillingness to work for minimum wage. The men, a state labor investigator reported, simply refused to work for less than sixteen dollars a week.[15] Employers who did not comply with the order earned the wrath of their fellow laundrymen, who reported them to the state Department of Labor, which in turn issued subpoenas that usually triggered compliance. Those who refused to comply with the order had their names placed on a boycott list published in local newspapers.[16] Noncompliance was more common in the hand laundries and in particular in the Chinese-owned hand laundries, although it is unclear whether this was actually the case or whether (white) state labor inspectors—at the urging of white laundry owners—targeted Chinese laundries more often.[17]

Brooklyn Laundry Workers and
Their Feminist Labor Allies

In December 1933, two months after the New York State minimum wage order for laundries went into effect and six months after the passage of NIRA section 7(a), which protected workers' right to unionize, 150 workers at Brooklyn's Independent Laundry walked off the job. Two organizers from the WTUL rushed to Brooklyn to help the workers organize picket lines. Schneiderman used her influence at the Regional Labor Board to wrest a settlement from the employer that included payment of the thirty-one-cent minimum wage, a forty-five-hour workweek, and union recognition.[18] With the new settlement in hand, the workers chartered AFL Laundry Workers International Union Local 135, with an interracial membership of three hundred, and elected African American laundry worker Mervin J. Sutherland as president. In an article entitled "Laundry Union Wins War for Pay Boost," the New York Amsterdam News celebrated Sutherland's election as the first time an African American had ever headed a laundry union in Brooklyn. African Americans Thomas O. Quashie and Herbert Hoyle served respectively as financial secretary and recording secretary of the local. Radical leaders from the Laundry Workers Industrial Union extended their greetings to the new local and offered to provide organizing tips.[19]

In 1933, around the time of the Independent strike, Charlotte Adelmond approached a group of drivers from Teamsters Local 810 to ask for assistance in organizing her coworkers. The men dismissed the Trinidadian activist and told her to organize the shop herself. Beginning with seven workers, Adelmond began holding union meetings at night in her Thatford Avenue home in Brownsville. The Amalgamated Clothing Workers of America (ACWA) would later pay homage to Adelmond, noting that the nucleus of workers who began gathering in her home in 1933 "set the ball rolling, later to stage the famous Brownsville strike."[20]

In January 1934, a month after the Independent strike, two hundred mostly white workers at the Sunshine Laundry in Williamsburg, Brooklyn, walked off the job when the employer refused to pay the minimum wage. The Sunshine was a large linen supply laundry that laundered sheets, pillowcases, and other items for upscale hotels.[21] The WTUL sent recently hired organizer Eleanor Mishnun to the plant. Mishnun, the daughter of Russian revolutionaries, grew up on Manhattan's Upper West Side, where her family owned a stationery store.[22] Although too busy to do political work, Mishnun's parents retained their socialist outlook and introduced their daughter to radical politics at an early age. Mishnun remembers hearing socialist leader Eugene V. Debs, who ran for president in 1920 from jail after his conviction under the Espionage Act for opposing the Wilson administration's war efforts, speak at Madison Square Garden and attending talks with her parents at the socialist Rand School of

Social Science.[23] Mishnun was active in the Socialist Party when she attended Wadleigh High School in upper Manhattan in the mid-1910s. As a student at Cornell University in 1918 she tried to organize a chapter of the Young People's Socialist League. After a brief hiatus in Europe, she enrolled at New York University in 1927, and upon graduation her sister's friend, socialist WTUL education director Elsie Glick, recommended her for a job with the WTUL. Mary Dreier hired her on the spot.[24]

Mishnun and Glick represented a new generation of WTUL organizers, many of whom were socialists and some of whom would clash with "old-timers" such as Rose Schneiderman. By the 1930s Schneiderman had become firmly ensconced in the social democratic world of the Roosevelts. Her close relationship with the president, commitment to the New Deal order, and fresh memories of the devastating factional battles that had racked the ILGWU in the 1920s made her reluctant to associate the WTUL with any of the radical movements of the 1930s.[25] In contrast, socialists like Mishnun were more ambivalent about the New Deal, which she argued "took a lot of starch out of the Socialist movement," and were eager to embrace a more radical politics. Roosevelt's policies, Mishnun insisted, "really bolstered the capitalist system."[26]

Ideological and generational differences between old-timers and younger organizers were exacerbated by the latter's identification with class over gender, a position that Annelise Orleck argues alienated industrial feminists like Schneiderman who had oriented their personal and professional lives around the all-female networks they developed.[27] Schneiderman's reluctance to embrace the CIO in 1937 and her continued deference to the AFL, despite its abject failure to support women's unionism, alienated younger members who had hoped to "modernize" the organization by forging alliances with socialists, communists, and CIO activists. Glick was incensed when in the 1930s the WTUL continued to offer "fluff" courses like pottery and dancing, better suited, she insisted, to the YWCA. When the leadership dismissed her concerns Glick resigned from the WTUL. As young leaders left, the WTUL would come to be associated with older women, a reality that hastened its demise in 1949.[28]

Schneiderman's rejection of radical politics contributed to the tense relationship between the WTUL and the Communist Party. In the mid-1930s Schneiderman would use her influence as a longtime laundry organizer to minimize the communists' role in the newly organized CIO laundry union.[29] In turn, Jessie Smith denounced the WTUL as a conservative organization that pressured working women to cooperate with the AFL. Smith described the WTUL and Schneiderman as "very middle of the road kind of people" who always "stuck" with the AFL. When she was interviewed in 2007 she insisted that they were not "women libbers in any sense." WTUL leaders, Smith argued, "weren't doing anything. They were just part of the publicity."[30] A 1932 Trade Union Unity

League report accused the WTUL of focusing only on skilled workers and intellectuals such as teachers and of suppressing women's efforts to organize "fighting unions."[31] While such comments did not provide an accurate or complete portrayal of the WTUL's activities, they did capture the wide ideological gulf that separated the communists from many of the WTUL's founders and upper-class allies.

"Bloody" Brooklyn: The Sunshine and Colonial Laundry Strikes

In 1934 Mishnun's first job with the WTUL was in the laundries. The organizer remembered being shocked to learn that in January 1934, at the height of the Depression, hundreds of poor laundry workers from Brooklyn's Sunshine Laundry had walked off the job. Mishnun described the workers as desperately poor and "scantily clad" and recalled that the only time she ever suffered frostbite was during the 1934 laundry strike. When she discovered that most of the women lived in cold-water flats without heat she immediately set out to secure a warm meeting room for the workers, a task that proved challenging. Interviewed in 1985, before the collapse of the Soviet Union, Mishnun argued that "being a striker in those days was like being a bomb throwing Communist today." Mishnun was appalled to learn that the women worked sixty to seventy hours a week for as little as three or four dollars, a violation of the minimum wage law. Mishnun, who reported the violations to the Regional Labor Board, recalled that not a single worker ever asked her for money. In 1985, more than fifty years after the strike, she still wondered how they "managed to survive and eat."[32]

The strike quickly spread to the Colonial Laundry in Bedford-Stuyvesant after the owner of the Sunshine Laundry sent his laundry there. (Both employers belonged to the Brooklyn Employers' Association.)[33] Fifteen years old, Robinson was one of the youngest workers at the Colonial, which employed a mostly Black workforce. She had started working in the industry during the summers while attending Brooklyn Girls High School during the school year. (It was the superior educational opportunities in New York that had led her mother to leave North Carolina in 1930.)[34] After graduation Robinson took a full-time job in a laundry while also taking night classes at Brooklyn College, where she organized a Negro Problems Club.[35]

Mishnun and one of the Sunshine workers rushed to the Colonial, where a young and "intelligent" African American worker named Slim informed them that "of course we're going on strike" but explained that they first needed to get the support of the head washer, the only worker who knew which sheets belonged to which hotels. Mishnun convinced the head washer to join by giving him twenty-five dollars a week. With the head washer on board the two hundred mostly African American laundry workers at the Colonial voted unanimously to strike.[36]

Mishnun described the ensuing strike as violent and "bloody" and insists that she would have been "bumped off" had she not been employed by the WTUL. In Brooklyn laundry workers confronted not only the familiar cast of antiunion employers but also known racketeers, including Jacob Mellon and Anthony Carfano. In the 1920s Mellon had helped some of Brooklyn's laundry owners establish the Brooklyn Neighborhood Laundry Owners' Association, which sought to control entry into the trade and fix prices.[37] After receiving a flood of complaints about the association, city officials initiated hearings in 1930 into racketeering in the laundries. Terrified Brooklyn laundry owners testified that Mellon and his associates burned down the plants of competitors who refused to join the association and pay dues. In May 1933 the state indicted Mellon and three of his associates on conspiracy charges in connection with laundry racketeering. Citing Mellon's history of violence and jury tampering, the judge took the unusual step of sequestering the jury in a hotel under police protection.[38]

The subsequent trial, which received considerable media attention, revealed Mellon's connection to Anthony Carfano, also known as Little Augie Pisano, a well-known gangster with ties to Al Capone and the Chicago Outfit. Carfano, who ran a large crew in Brooklyn, rose to power in the late 1920s as a captain in the Genovese crime family. Among other enterprises, Carfano was involved in Brooklyn's laundries and in Teamsters Local 810. Smith remembered that after Prohibition Carfano got into the "rackets, into the union."[39] Robinson recalled being told by an Italian woman known as Mama that a Brooklyn laundry she was trying to organize in the late 1930s was controlled by "Little Augie . . . one of the, you know, bad guys in Brooklyn." Robinson continued collecting union cards but was never able to organize the workers because it was a "controlled plant." She recalled being amazed that her good friend Charlotte Adelmond was able to hold her own among the gangsters in Brownsville, a strength she attributed to the Trinidadian's participation in the Garvey movement and commitment to Black nationalism.[40] Laundry workers who struck in Brooklyn in January 1934 could hardly have been unaware of the connection between the laundry industry and organized crime. That they would risk their jobs and potentially more is a testament to their determination.

In 1934 violence quickly erupted on the picket lines when the thugs hired by the Sunshine and Colonial employers to escort the strikebreakers into the plants attacked the workers. Mishnun remembers arriving early one January morning to find one of the picketers, an African American woman, bleeding from a stab wound inflicted by a strikebreaker. When Mishnun took the injured woman to the nearest doctor, an African American, the physician refused to treat the worker, explaining that he did not want to get involved. Despite the violence outside the plants, initiated by the employers, Mishnun counseled the workers not to retaliate and lectured them on how to avoid getting arrested by using appropriate language. While taking a labor law class at Columbia University, Mishnun had learned that workers could be arrested for calling strikebreakers "scabs." At the request of the WTUL, she arrived promptly at the picket lines at 5:00 every morning to make sure the workers yelled "don't be a scab" instead of "scab."[41]

The WTUL's promotion of law-abiding, restrained behavior stood in stark contrast to that of the communists, who encouraged the workers to engage in confrontational tactics and celebrated arrests as evidence of the workers' radicalization. Robinson's and Mishnun's recollections reveal that by 1934 at least some of Brooklyn's laundry workers also wanted to engage in combative tactics. Robinson described those who were arrested as the aristocrats of the movement and lamented that her older and protective coworkers would send her away just before the arrival of the police, thus preventing her from earning this distinction.[42] Mishnun had to frisk Slim's wife, who came to the picket lines every morning armed with sticks and other weapons hidden in her coat, just "in case it came to a fight." Mishnun complained that Slim's wife "just couldn't accept the fact that you can't fight back in this kind of situation."[43] The workers' preference for militant action and self-defense brought them into conflict with WTUL leaders, who were committed to maintaining order on the picket lines.

Tensions over what constituted acceptable behavior were sometimes the result of class differences between the workers and their feminist labor allies. A 1933 WTUL report on the NRA noted that some of the WTUL's friends were "disturbed over the many strikes which have developed recently." WTUL ally and laundry supporter Cornelia Bryce Pinchot, wife of Pennsylvania governor Gifford Pinchot, advised ACWA female picketers to "be patient under provocation."[44] Upper-class allies who were comfortable joining peaceful picket lines or lobbying the state feared the social chaos that accompanied the more radical and often grassroots uprisings of the early and mid-1930s. Dependent on the financial support of these allies, WTUL leaders discouraged militant behavior that could jeopardize elite support.

It is also possible that WTUL leaders were attempting to police Black women's behavior either out of paternalism, or as a means to counteract racist assumptions about Black women's propensity for disorder and immorality, or a combination of the two.[45] Like the Black middle-class female reformers described by historian Evelyn Brooks Higginbotham who counseled their working-class sisters to adopt a demure, modest, and feminine public persona to counter racist and classist stereotypes about Black working-class women, WTUL leaders perhaps believed that such behavior would demonstrate the women's worthiness and entitlement to public and allied support and respect, a privilege that was automatically bestowed on white middle- and upper-class women.[46] Conversely, emboldened by their newly won right to organize and inspired by the growing radicalization of their communities, some of Brooklyn's African American women laundry workers embraced confrontational tactics in their battle to win union representation and enforce the minimum wage.

Tensions between WTUL leaders and some of the workers also reflected differences over strategy as Black workers turned to one another for support and solidarity. Grace Klueg, WTUL member and president of the Brooklyn Machinist Union's Women's Auxiliary, described the high levels of camaraderie among the workers, who swapped rubber boots and heavy coats when their turn came up to picket. Slim's wife not only joined her husband on the picket lines armed with sticks but also offered the couple's tiny, dark, cold apartment as a resting place for the strikers. After visiting Slim's apartment, Klueg insisted that "never have I thought that my neighbors *could possibly be so poor,* and yet so happy, so kindly, so friendly to each other, as those starved, neglected laundry workers were."[47] When Klueg, Glick, and Childs formed a laundry auxiliary to raise money and secure food and clothing donations for the workers, Klueg distinctly recalled that the workers insisted that those with children be supplied first.[48]

As a member of the NRA's Labor Advisory Board, Rose Schneiderman sailed to Puerto Rico during the strike to investigate industrial conditions on the island. Well versed in using the media to generate public sympathy for workers, she invited a group of laundry workers to see her off. The *New York Times* reported that Schneiderman "was chatting with a group of friends when more than 100 striking laundry employees from Brooklyn arrived to bid her good-bye."[49] The *World Telegram* recounted that the arrival of hundreds of "poorly clad striking laundry workers from Brooklyn . . . predominately women and many of them Negroes," changed the "character of the occasion from one of polite bon voyages and seemly handshakes into one of militant and aggressive trade union warfare." Schneiderman left "her richly gowned friends flat" and told the workers to "go back to your picket lines and fight on. And remember you are fighting for the President of the United States."[50] The public event highlighted Schneiderman's ability to unite the worlds of upper-class social reform and the working poor and to harness the former in service to the latter.

Calling in the Mink Brigades: The Laundry Workers and Their Elite Allies

While the workers relied on their own solidarity and militancy, Mishnun turned to the WTUL's upper-class allies for support. Mary Dreier visited the police commissioner and convinced him to allow the strikers to increase their picket lines from two to four and to remove the police that had been protecting the company trucks that brought in strikebreakers.[51] Eleanor Roosevelt, the WTUL's most prominent ally, loaned her Secret Service agents to Mishnun to provide protection for the workers. It is possible, even probable, given the First Lady's support for civil rights, that she intervened in the laundry strike because many of the picketers were African American women. When the Sunshine employers hurled "vile language" at the workers and called Mishnun and Roosevelt a "couple of dirty Reds," Roosevelt's Secret Service agents had the men hauled off to jail. The head of the police subsequently gave Mishnun permission to give what must have been a very satisfying lecture to the police about the workers' legal right to picket.[52]

As the strike dragged into the second week the WTUL called in the "mink brigades," first used during the garment strikes in the 1910s. In 1934 Dreier, Childs, and Pinchot joined the workers on the picket lines in a show of cross-class solidarity. Pinchot was a longtime supporter of the WTUL, and in 1935 she joined the consumer activist organization known as the League of Women Shoppers. An erstwhile suffragist who had marched in parades, Pinchot was famous for her "fiery red hair," red dresses, and "bright red automobile."[53] On January 24 the *New York Times* reported that Mrs. Pinchot arrived at the Colonial Laundry at 8:05 a.m. in a limousine with the Pennsylvania license plate "P.1." Carrying a strike placard, the First Lady of Pennsylvania informed the strikers that she was with them in their fight against "outrageous and un-American wage standards." After twenty minutes she went to the Sunshine Laundry and repeated the speech and then headed to union headquarters, where she instructed the workers to continue organizing for better conditions.[54] Before heading back to Pennsylvania she recorded a Movietone News newsreel that showed her picketing at the Quick Service Laundry in Manhattan, where workers were also on strike. Schneiderman lauded elite allies like Pinchot and other members of the mink brigades for bringing an "aura of respectability" to the workers' demonstrations, an analysis that hinted at her own struggle to balance a public image of respectable womanhood with an unconventional personal and professional life that included both public activism and a long-term personal relationship with Maud Swartz.[55]

The most influential upper-class intervention came during the second month of the strike, when the WTUL had run out of money and Mishnun was about to suggest calling off the strike. Dreier urged Mishnun to visit Grace Childs, the WTUL's treasurer. The wife of businessman Richard S. Childs, Mrs. Childs had worked briefly as a social worker before becoming a full-time philanthropist. Mishnun reluctantly agreed to call on Childs, unsure of how she could help, and was shocked when she encountered no fewer than three servants during her short visit at the Childses' spacious Brooklyn brownstone. Mishnun was even more amazed when Childs withdrew $500 from her housekeeping account for the strike. Childs confessed that she was unable to approach her husband directly for the money because he was an antiunion Republican.[56]

When Mishnun quickly used up the $500, Childs offered to participate more directly in the strike. Sporting a fur coat, Childs snuck out of her brownstone early one morning to join the workers on the picket line. The patrician wore a sign made by the Young People's Socialist League with the caption "I can't live on $5 a week—can you?" Mishnun reported that Childs's husband "nearly went crazy the next day" when every couple of minutes someone in his office presented him with another edition of another newspaper with his wife's picture plastered on the front page. Mishnun, who described Richard Childs as "no great worldshaker," acknowledged that Grace Childs's activism came at a personal cost, since she was, "after all," in love with her husband and continued to live with him.[57]

When the employers remained intransigent Childs called the Hotel St. George, one of the Colonial Laundry's customers, and demanded that it stop patronizing sweatshop laundries. When the manager refused to intervene Childs marched down to the hotel armed with a one-page circular about wages and working conditions and personally informed the guests about the abysmal conditions under which their sheets and pillowcases were being washed. Dreier and Glick, alongside WTUL members Mary Rouse and Bertha Paret, picketed the Taft Hotel, another customer of the Colonial and Sunshine Laundries. Reporters flocked to Brooklyn, eager to capture pictures of elite women picketing tiny hotels on behalf of poor African American women workers. Determined to increase the pressure, Childs and other prominent WTUL members, along with members of other Brooklyn organizations, formed a "nuisance campaign" during which "practically every prominent person and organization in Brooklyn and New York, not omitting the Junior League," called the St. George and Taft Hotels at ten-minute intervals to ask why they continued to patronize laundries where workers were on strike against starvation wages.[58]

In the end, the WTUL's political connections provided the leverage that brought the employers to the bargaining table. When Mishnun discovered that the owners of the Colonial and Sunshine Laundries owed the city a combined $37,000 in back taxes she and Schneiderman visited Mayor Fiorello La Guardia, who, Schneiderman recalled, "in typical La Guardia fashion" called the owner and "read the riot act to him."[59] The laundry workers had an important ally in the mayor, a staunch supporter of the New Deal who amassed a strong record in defense of labor and civil rights.[60] At the ACWA's biennial convention in 1938, Mayor La Guardia proudly recalled that in 1934 he had given "those birds just 24 hours to settle with the workers and settle with the city." He boasted that the laundry owners were "so busy with the strike that they did not know it was a new administration. So I shut off the water and they found out." Many years later, Robinson recalled that "great help for that strike was given by LaGuardia."[61]

Eager to reopen their plants, the employers signed an agreement with the Regional Labor Board to comply with the minimum wage law and settle all future disputes through the board. The *New York Times* reported that the agreement marked the first time that a strike had been brought to close through the city's use of its tax machinery.[62] The employers agreed to fire the strikebreakers and rehire their former employees, and many of the women saw immediate wage increases of as much as 50 percent. The strike also led to a dramatic increase in the membership of Brooklyn Local 135. Starting with a group of nine members, by the end of the strike eight hundred workers belonged to the local.[63]

Hoping to maintain the momentum from the strike, WTUL leaders began preparations to conduct classes for the laundry workers in trade unionism, public speaking, economics, and English. As the workers could not afford the ten-cent carfare to the WTUL's Lexington Avenue clubhouse, WTUL organizers held the classes in Brooklyn under the auspices of the Affiliated Summer Schools.[64] The initiative underlined the WTUL's long-standing commitment to education as a tool to empower working women. A WTUL report described the twenty women who enrolled in the courses as "very enthusiastic."[65]

The workers' and their allies' jubilance quickly wore off, however, when two weeks after the settlement the most active trade unionists had yet to be rehired. And to recoup the costs of paying the minimum wage, the employers slashed the men's wages and harassed and threatened those who dared complain to the labor inspectors. Regional Labor Board inspectors in any event were not necessarily sympathetic. One inspector informed the women that they would have to work harder for the thirty-one cents an hour they would now be receiving.[66] Even progressive states like New York with long histories of factory legislation had spotty records when it came to labor enforcement, gaps the employers eagerly exploited to circumvent the laws and intimidate their workers. By September 1934, six months after the strike's conclusion, Brooklyn Local 135's membership had plummeted from eight hundred to one hundred members.[67]

Assessing the Strike: Aristocrats and Allies

The 1934 Brooklyn strike reveals both the determination of increasingly radicalized laundry workers and the benefits and limitations of the cross-class feminist labor coalitions that animated the women's labor movement. Harnessing the social and political power of its upper-class allies, the WTUL generated significant media attention in 1934 for the laundry workers while also securing the support of influential allies such as Eleanor Roosevelt, Grace Childs, and Mayor La Guardia. WTUL organizers helped the workers navigate the Regional Labor Board and provided protection from some of the violence of the picket lines. Lavish displays of elite support cloaked the workers' activism in the mantle of middle-class respectability. By the end of the strike Mishnun's early skepticism about the role of elite women in the class struggle had largely vanished. Interviewed in 1985, Mishnun explained, "These women, some of them . . . in a way really made history. I'm not saying it wouldn't have been made by somebody else at some other time. But there's no question . . . they did play an important role."[68] The WTUL's female alliances and gender-based strategies generated significant leverage for the laundry workers.

Worker-elite alliances were not unproblematic, however. Middle- and upper-class allies and organizers could be patronizing toward workers and often sought to impose their own ideas on campaigns. The extravagant displays of support that included mink coats and limousines highlighted the class- and race-bound power imbalances between impoverished Black laundry workers and their white upper-class allies. And as Alice Kessler-Harris notes, the WTUL's reliance on the state and upper-class allies confirmed male unionists' perception of working women as outsiders who needed the special protection of the state and the benevolence of elite women rather than as partners in the class struggle.[69] And while WTUL organizers no doubt believed they were helping the workers by moderating their behavior and keeping them out of jail, it was often such militancy that created organizing momentum and leadership capacity, a reality that Robinson recognized when she lamented that her coworkers would not allow her to get arrested and take her place among the strike aristocracy.[70]

In Harlem and the Bronx, the communists had made race central to the laundry campaign, demanding the promotion of Black workers into the washing and driving positions and linking the workers' battle against poverty wages to broader struggles against racial injustice. Although at least half of the strikers in Brooklyn were Black, the WTUL did not explicitly address issues of racial discrimination. In January 1936 at a membership meeting to discuss the lack of new recruitment, WTUL member Bertha Butler asked whether the WTUL admitted Black women.[71] The question was answered in the affirmative, but the fact that it had to be asked suggests that there were no African American women in active membership roles in 1936 (this would soon change as Black women laundry workers joined the WTUL and joined the board).

Despite the grassroots organizing of the workers and the support provided by communists in Harlem and the Bronx and by industrial feminists in Brooklyn, in 1935 fewer than fifteen hundred of New York's thirty thousand laundry workers were unionized. Employer antiunionism, the workers' destitution, and the state's unreliability as an ally of the working class impeded organization. Labor scholars and social movement theorists argue that union campaigns are most likely to succeed when they benefit from both resources and activist solidarities.[72] In 1934 and 1935 laundry workers were mobilizing in unprecedented ways, but solidarity was not widespread, and worker leaders lacked the resources necessary to sustain strikes and launch an industry-wide campaign. It would be under the more visionary Second New Deal (1935–36) that the workers would finally win union recognition. Still, the organizing that took place in the early 1930s helped forge the interracial activist solidarities that would bring the workers into the CIO later in the decade.

CHAPTER SEVEN

"It Was Like the Salvation"

New York City's Laundry
Workers Join the CIO

In the fall of 1936 a defiant Jessie Taft Smith chained herself to a mezzanine pillar in the Taft Hotel (chosen for their shared name), where she delivered an "uninterrupted protest" against the hotel's use of the Sutton Superior Laundry, where workers were on strike against abusive conditions and substandard wages.[1] Less than a year later, Smith, Charlotte Adelmond, Noah Walter, and hundreds of other laundry workers crowded into the socialist Rand School of Social Science, where they voted unanimously to abandon the AFL and join the newly organized Committee for Industrial Organization (CIO). Adelmond contributed some of her own money toward the cost of the local industrial union charter. After a few months of organizing under the banner of the CIO, the workers agreed to affiliate with the powerful men's clothing union, the Amalgamated Clothing Workers of America (ACWA). The ACWA provided the resources for the workers to conduct a citywide campaign that harnessed the workers' growing solidarities and the expertise of worker leaders such as Smith and Adelmond.[2] It was under the garment union that the laundry workers finally won union recognition, higher wages, and better working conditions. An examination of this dramatic union victory demonstrates that the simultaneous presence of adequate union resources, internal activist solidarities, and state support enabled the workers to overcome the long-standing divisions along race, gender, and occupational lines and build a movement powerful enough to bring the city's antiunion employers to the bargaining table.[3]

A New Era: The Promise of the Wagner Act

In 1935 no one would have predicted that by decade's end most of New York's laundry workers would be organized. In May 1935 the Supreme Court invalidated the National Industrial Recovery Act (NIRA) and in June 1936 upheld the New York Court of Appeal's decision to repeal the state minimum wage law for women and minors.[4] Overnight, New York's laundrymen slashed wages and increased hours of work. Within six months of the Court's ruling, the percentage of women laundry workers in New York State earning less than thirty-one cents an hour—the old minimum wage—jumped from 1 to 16. By the end of 1936 three-quarters of New York's women laundry workers earned less than fifteen dollars a week, and the League of Women Shoppers reported weekly wages of as low as six dollars.[5] Letters poured into the New York Department of Labor from angry laundry workers and their families, some of whom reported that the employers had the gall to demand that the workers return the "extra" money they had received under the minimum wage law. Georgette Johnson of Harlem urged the judge who had struck down the law to consider the impoverished women who would now be ironing his dress shirts for seven dollars a week. African American laundry worker Dorothy Maynard wrote an editorial in the *New York Amsterdam News* urging her fellow workers not to wait for new legislation but rather to "be prepared to help ourselves."[6]

The workers' plight caught the attention of the League of Women Shoppers (LWS), the consumer activist organization founded in May 1935 by fifty prominent women, many from the elite ranks of society. Comprised of middle-class housewives, socialites, professionals, socialists, and communists alike, the LWS used direct-action tactics to promote ethical consumerism and support workers' union organizing. In the tradition of the National Consumers' League (NCL), LWS members sought to educate housewives about their responsibilities and power as consumers, but, moved by Depression-era worker suffering and inspired by the New Deal (many LWS members were liberal Democrats, and some were married to or themselves members of the Roosevelt administration), they also offered direct support to workers, joining them on picket lines and conducting labor investigations that garnered public attention and action. Historian Kathy Higgins argues that the LWS differed from the National Consumers' League in their use of direct-action tactics and attention to race as a category of oppression. The LWS, Higgins argued, eschewed "overbearing maternalist ideology in favor of empowering themselves and the workers they supported."[7]

Considerable overlap in the memberships of the LWS and the WTUL existed, including notable "star" members such as Cornelia Bryce Pinchot. The LWS also included radicals, some of whom identified with the Socialist or Communist Party. The organization's leftist activism and membership made it a target of the anticommunist Dies Committee, a precursor to the House Un-American Activities Committee, and the organization would dissolve in 1949 in large part because of red baiting.[8]

Smith fondly remembered radical LWS activist Jane Filley, who in the mid-1930s attended the laundry workers' meetings and helped organize boycotts of laundries where workers were on strike. Born in Chicago to a middle-class family, Filley's family disowned her when she married a Communist Party leader.[9] In 1936 and 1937, working on behalf of the LWS, Filley and Therese Mitchell conducted an investigation of New York's power and hand laundries that culminated in the powerful exposé, *Consider the Laundry Workers*. The 1937 report included interviews with workers and concentrated on the mistreatment of African American and Puerto Rican workers, highlighting the employer practice of pitting white workers against Black workers. The authors' concern for workers of color was consistent with the LWS's commitment to racial justice. After reading the report, Eleanor Roosevelt lauded the LWS in her May Day newspaper column, noting its "service to industry, the public and to labor."[10]

In 1935 the LWS was not alone in its concern for workers reeling from the repeal of the NIRA. In response to the Supreme Court ruling in 1935, President Roosevelt ushered through the passage of the National Labor Relations Act (NLRA) or Wagner Act, the most sweeping labor reform yet. The Wagner Act guaranteed workers the right to form unions and bargain collectively, to strike, to boycott, and to picket, and it prohibited employers from engaging in unfair labor practices such as blacklisting and intimidating union activists, all long-standing practices in the laundry industry. The act gave workers the right to hold representation elections and compelled the employers to bargaining collectively with the victorious group, a provision designed to end company unionism. The act established the National Labor Relations Board (NLRB) to oversee union elections and collective bargaining and to arbitrate unfair labor practices against employers, workers, or unions. Unlike the NIRA's National Recovery Administration, the NLRB had broad investigative and enforcement powers, and once the Supreme Court validated the Wagner Act in April 1937, NLRB staff vigorously pursued unfair labor practice cases against employers. In industries such as steel, fired union activists returned triumphantly to work with back pay in their pockets, visible proof that the NLRB had teeth.[11]

The Formation of the Negro Labor Committee

The promising political climate and growing mobilizations of Black workers in New York City, including the laundry workers, inspired the formation of a new organization committed to Black workers and interracial unionism: the Negro Labor Committee (NLC). One of the NLC's founders was Black laundry worker Noah Walter, a longtime socialist with deep roots in the laundry industry. Born and raised in Brooklyn, Walter obtained a teaching degree from Bluefield State Teachers College in West Virginia in the mid-1920s. Upon returning to New York City, he attended the Rand School of Social Science and, alongside Frank Crosswaith, spearheaded the Socialist Party's efforts to organize and recruit African American workers. As a Black man with limited employment opportunities, Walter made his living in a laundry. Dollie Lowther Robinson, who described Walter as an "excellent person, an excellent leader," lamented that despite having a college degree he worked in the laundries.[12]

Alongside socialist garment worker Frank Crosswaith, who had organized for the short-lived Trade Union Committee for Organizing Negro Workers in the mid-1920s, Walter helped found the Harlem-based Negro Labor Committee in 1933. The organization advocated for Black workers in much the same way that the United Hebrew Trades did for Jewish workers and the WTUL did for women workers.[13] Founded with financial support from the ILGWU, the ACWA, the National Urban League, and the NAACP, the socialist-led organization supported and led union drives among barbers, painters, bakers, pharmacists, library workers, funeral chauffeurs, and, in 1935, the staff at the antiunion *New York Amsterdam News.* NLC leaders offered seminars, conferences, and classes on trade unionism at their Harlem Labor Center headquarters. Headed by Crosswaith, the NLC had close ties with the ILGWU and relied heavily on the garment union for financial support.[14]

From the outset, the Communist Party attacked the NLC, arguing that the new organization would create segregated unions and undermine the interracial unity emerging in industries like the laundry. NLC leaders countered that communists ought to support an organization dedicated to interracial unionism and Black leadership.[15] Crosswaith had long been critical of the communists for what he saw as their opportunistic work among African Americans and vicious treatment of political opponents, criticisms shared by Robinson and Maida Springer. Alongside fellow socialist A. Philip Randolph of the Brotherhood of Sleeping Car Porters, Crosswaith denounced the communists for their support of the authoritarian Soviet regime and for using undemocratic means to gain control of leftist organizations. Beatrice Lumpkin described the divisions between socialists and communists as one of "humanities' great tragedies."[16]

With the Wagner Act in hand and in response to the shop floor mobilizations of the workers, in 1935 Joseph Mackey of the AFL-affiliated Laundry Workers International Union called on the NLC to help launch a new laundry drive. The NLC agreed to release Walter, the NLC's secretary and staff organizer, to work full-time on the campaign.[17] Walter and Schneiderman headed the campaign, and the WTUL provided $100 in seed money. Working out of the Harlem Labor Center, the two unionists established an organizing committee comprised of representatives from the WTUL, the AFL laundry union, the United Hebrew Trades, the Central Trades Council, and the ILGWU.[18] At a mass meeting in Harlem led by Smith's friend Sabina Martinez, a Black laundry worker, the committee decided to focus on Brownsville, Harlem, and the Bronx, where workers were already organizing. Worker leaders, including communists Samuel Berland and Jessie Smith, began visiting the workers in their homes and calling meetings to generate support for the drive.[19] WTUL organizers Eleanor Mishnun and Helen Blanchard raised money, organized shop committees, and prepared courses on current events, labor issues, and public speaking. By December 1936 the WTUL reported that the AFL laundry union had members in seventeen shops.[20]

Although Robinson was younger than most of her coworkers—in 1936 she was eighteen—she responded enthusiastically to the call to organize. She explained that "I became interested in organizing because I met people who were talking about organizing, and they asked me to help." She described herself as "active, and I was big, and I was interested, and I talked," but she also recalled the challenges she faced. Interviewed in 1976, she explained that in the 1930s some of the people in her neighborhood thought she was a "real freak, because I was out organizing. I led picket lines; I had literature." But the budding trade unionist persevered, and throughout her long career as a labor activist she would make considerable efforts to forge connections between the labor movement and local communities.[21]

Facing Down "Fear, Force and Poverty!": Joining the CIO

On March 15, 1937, AFL hand laundry Local 280, which had recently merged with power laundry Local 290, called a general strike of Brownsville's laundry workers. Within a few days two thousand workers, more than two-thirds of whom were Black, were on strike. With headquarters at the Brownsville Labor Lyceum, the workers demanded union recognition, a 25 percent wage increase over the old minimum wage of thirty-one cents an hour, and a forty-hour workweek for women and forty-five for men.[22]

Brownsville's working-class community quickly rallied to the workers' support. Anna Piatoff of the Socialist Consumers' Union worked with the wives of Brooklyn workers to bring food to the picket lines and help the strikers fight eviction notices.[23] The Brooklyn Union Label Club served upward of seven hundred free meals a day, while the Brownsville Labor Lyceum gave the workers the use of three halls and a kitchen at no cost. WTUL organizer Helen Blanchard explained that "everywhere we went everyone seemed anxious and ready to help bring this strike to a successful close." The WTUL provided $550 of its own funds, and Schneiderman convinced the ILGWU to donate the same amount. The broad community support and the workers' determination convinced the employers at nineteen of the twenty-nine laundries to settle with the workers. The women won wages of at least thirty-one cents an hour (the old minimum wage), and the men won increases of between one and three dollars a week, significantly more than the women. Most importantly, the employers' associations agreed that once the union had organized 90 percent of Brownsville's cash-and-carry laundries, they would reopen negotiations.[24]

Concurrent with the Brownsville strike, in March 1937 the Supreme Court reversed its previous ruling in a case that involved the minimum wage law of the state of Washington and upheld the constitutionality of state minimum wage laws. The New York State legislature immediately enacted a new minimum wage law for women and minors and once again chose the laundry for its first minimum wage board.[25] The board appointed WTUL Vice President Pauline Newman and Charlotte Adelmond to represent the laundry workers.[26] The WTUL described Adelmond as "a young negro woman" whom Blanchard had "discovered" during a recent strike. While the WTUL may have "discovered" Adelmond in 1937, by then she had been working in the industry for more than ten years and organizing her coworkers in Brownsville for at least four years. The New York Amsterdam News celebrated Adelmond's appointment, noting that as the only Black member of the board she would represent more than eighty thousand laundry workers statewide.[27] Recognizing her tremendous talents as an organizer and shop floor leader, the WTUL provided funds for Adelmond to attend the Bryn Mawr Labor School. The Trinidadian activist officially joined the New York WTUL in January 1938, when Pauline Newman and Berthe Daniel endorsed her application. A little over a year later, Adelmond was nominated to the WTUL's executive board, where she delivered regular updates on the laundry workers.[28]

At the 1938 meeting, where Adelmond joined the WTUL, a proposal from the National Urban League asking that the WTUL hire a Black woman organizer to visit "groups of Negro women in churches, fraternal organizations, clubs etc. to spread a knowledge of trade unionism and labor objectives" was read into the minutes. WTUL leaders sympathized with the request but ultimately rejected it, likely because of financial constraints. By 1938 donations from wealthy allies, including Eleanor Roosevelt, were keeping the WTUL afloat. But it is strange that the leadership so quickly dismissed the request, especially given that they were organizing laundry workers, domestic workers, and beauty parlor operators in Harlem, all groups comprised primarily of African American women.[29]

Radicalized by their recent victory in Brownsville, on June 16, 1937, laundry workers from Local 280 and drivers from Teamsters Local 810 met at the Rand School of Social Science. With special police protection to allow for a free election, the drivers met in one room and the inside workers in another. Twenty years later the ACWA would report that "they sat in separate rooms, but their purpose was the same. That night they voted overwhelmingly to throw out the racketeers and to join together into one industry-wide union representing *all* laundry workers." Laundry workers, the ACWA insisted, had come together to face down "fear, force and poverty!" Walter and Louis Simon, a driver from the

Superfine Laundry and secretary treasurer of Local 810, took to the stage that night, urging affiliation with the recently formed CIO.[30]

Spearheaded by John L. Lewis of the United Mine Workers, the CIO was born in November 1935 when the AFL refused to abandon its craft union model and organize industrially, including and especially among mass production workers, who were mobilizing in unprecedented ways. Some of the new organization's leaders, including ACWA president Sidney Hillman and ILGWU president David Dubinsky, were nominal socialists. Rivalry between the AFL and CIO, industrial workers' embrace of the new organization, and the creation of the CIO-led Steelworkers Organizing Committee in 1936 resulted in the official departure of the CIO from the AFL in November 1938.[31]

The CIO's model of social unionism, historian Dennis Deslippe argues, rested on the premise of inclusion and fair treatment of workers of all skill levels and backgrounds, as well as an expansive vision of the labor movement as a vehicle of social change, both radical departures from the AFL's business unionism. The new organization supported progressive social reform, advocated on behalf of prolabor candidates, and, in states like New York, supported the short-lived American Labor Party. Finally, although not always consistently, the CIO promoted interracial organizing and the equal treatment of Black workers. Inspired by the ideals of industrial unionism and long disenchanted with the AFL, African Americans would embrace and in some cases lead the new unions formed under the CIO's umbrella. Between 1930 and 1940 Black union membership in the United States increased tenfold, in part because of the CIO.[32]

The CIO, at least in its infancy, appeared to hold out relatively less promise for women workers. Historian Robert Zieger notes that while the CIO was cautious on issues of race, it was "virtually silent regarding gender." The CIO's founding convention included only four women delegates. Not a single resolution on women's issues was adopted. With a few exceptions, CIO leaders relegated women unionists to secondary roles in the movement, where women's issues remained a low priority. The CIO, Zieger explains, had not intended to start a revolution in labor's "relationship to distinctly disadvantaged and vulnerable groups."[33] That such groups would find space within the movement to pursue their race and gendered interests is a testament to their determination to hold the CIO accountable to its commitments.

It was the CIO's commitments to inclusion that drew the laundry workers to the new organization. In June 1937, when the inside workers and drivers met at the Rand School of Social Science, they unanimously voted to leave the AFL.[34] George Schuyler of the *Pittsburgh Courier* described the vote as a foregone conclusion, given that the AFL laundry union had done "practically nothing" except collect union dues. The AFL, Schuyler argued, had pursued a policy to "never organize Negroes if possible," thereby fanning the flames of race prejudice. Sabina Martinez similarly framed the vote as a rejection of the "Jim-Crow policies of the high executives of the A.F. of L., which ignored the Negro people."[35] The CIO provided the laundry workers with a local industrial union charter, issued by CIO regional director Allan Haywood, one of more than six hundred granted that year. The newly formed United Laundry Workers Local 204 included both inside workers and drivers.[36]

With a membership of a little over one thousand, Local 204 initiated an organizing drive among the city's ten thousand linen supply laundry workers. Noah Walter ran the campaign out of the NLC's Harlem headquarters. Robinson explained that Walter was chosen because of his "advanced knowledge and because of his training in the Socialist Party."[37] Workers from two large unionized plants loaned the local money to conduct the drive under the banner of the "Forgotten Men of Labor." The campaign title offered important early clues about how women would be excluded from the union's founding narratives.[38]

Emboldened by the Wagner Act, the recent union victory in Brownsville, and the emergence of the industrial union movement, thousands of laundry workers joined Local 204. Walter, Simon, and other leaders set out to secure a contract for the workers and submitted draft resolutions to the employers' associations. Louis Paul Nestel, an industrial relations scholar who produced a study of the union in 1950, reported that although the employers were terrified that the "emotional climate" of 1937 would result in a crippling strike, they nonetheless refused to negotiate with what they saw as a new and "irresponsible" union and raised money for a defense fund. At the same time, though, the employers, through their representative Herman Brickman, indicated to the leaders of Local 204 that they would be willing to negotiate with the workers if they agreed to affiliate with a "responsible, highly successful, and bona fide union" such as the ACWA.[39]

Narratives of Affiliation:
How the Laundry Workers
Came to Join the ACWA

In the ACWA's telling of the ensuing negotiations that led the laundry workers into the ACWA, Myer Bernstein, manager of the Washable Jackets, Knee Pants and Novelty Workers Local 169, had been watching the laundries closely and communicating with Brickman. Local 169 represented the white duck workers who manufactured aprons, uniforms, and other linen for commercial establishments and who sometimes engaged in laundering. Conversations between Bernstein and Brickman "started the ball rolling," and in 1937 the ACWA agreed to extend a charter for United Laundry Workers Local 300 with jurisdiction over the city's inside power and hand laundry workers, as well as drivers. ACWA accounts report that once the laundry workers learned they had the support of the garment union they "immediately applied themselves to the task of organizing."[40] A 1937 article in the ACWA's bimonthly publication, *The Advance*, explained that organization of these "viciously exploited" workers was made possible only because the garment union afforded the workers the opportunity to join the ACWA and utilize its prestige. On their own the laundry workers "lacked leadership" and experience.[41]

Historian Karen Pastorello frames the ACWA's decision to bring in the laundry workers as one of social justice and credits ACWA leader Bessie Hillman with convincing the union to extend a charter. Pastorello points to Hillman's strong record in support of women's and civil rights and her desire to support a predominantly low-wage Black and female workforce. Taking in the laundry workers, Pastorello argues, enabled the ACWA to actualize its commitment to a broad civil rights platform and "brought the union closer to industrial democracy."[42]

Garment leaders' portrayal of the birth of Local 300 cast the ACWA in the role of savior, obscuring the decades of activism by Black and radical workers that preceded the garment union's intervention. Such portrayals also minimized the practical considerations at play. Between 1929 and 1932 the ACWA lost fifty thousand members as the industry functioned at 30 percent of its previous capacity.[43] Bringing in the laundry workers would bolster the garment union's sagging membership and allow garment officials to extend their jurisdiction over an industry closely related to that of the white duck workers.

Rose Schneiderman's interpretation of affiliation mirrored that of the ACWA, although with the industrial feminist playing a more central role. In her autobiography, published in 1967, Schneiderman recounted that a young man named Abraham Brickman (likely Herman Brickman) approached her with the plan of "getting the laundry industry into a single organization." Schneiderman was thrilled, since she feared that the lack of "promising leaders" among the workers would enable the "few Communist members to immediately take over." Schneiderman visited her friend Sidney Hillman, who was president of the ACWA, and Local 300 was born.[44] In Schneiderman's account, thirty years of hard work paid off when she convinced Hillman and the ACWA to bring in the laundry workers.

Black workers had a different understanding of the birth of Local 300, one that placed Adelmond at the center of affiliation. Civil rights leader Anna Arnold Hedgeman described Adelmond as the "founder" of the ACWA union, and garment activist Maida Springer called her the "mainspring" of the union, a leader who "gave life, gave reason to an industry that people felt degraded and hopeless in."[45] According to Robinson, as organization proceeded in the mid-1930s the Trinidadian activist approached all of the large international unions in New York City, including the ILGWU, to find a home for the laundry workers. The ACWA was the only union that responded to her overtures.[46] The recollections of Robinson and other Black female activists stand in stark contrast to the ACWA's account, in which mostly white male trade unionists founded the union through a series of negotiations with the employers' associations and high-ranking union officials. In Robinson's telling, a militant Black national-ist and trade unionist led a mostly Black workforce into the Amalgamated, an analysis that underscores the significance of feminist scholarship which calls us to expand our traditional conceptions of leadership to include those who influenced and inspired the loyalty of participants, as well as those who held formal leadership titles.[47]

Communist laundry workers Jessie Smith and Beatrice Lumpkin provided yet another interpretation of affiliation. Both Smith and Lumpkin believed that the employers orchestrated affiliation because they believed they could secure more business-friendly contracts from the ACWA. The garment union in turn brought in the workers because they needed new dues-paying members. Lump-kin argued that the ACWA was "just greedy enough, powerful enough, with enough clout in the CIO to swallow up the LWIU." Lumpkin described affilia-tion as an "unfriendly acquisition," while Smith described it as a "coup d'état" forced on a group of workers who had little understanding of union politics, an interpretation that minimized Black workers' demonstrated capacity for independent political thought.[48] Smith's and Lumpkin's views also reflect the early skepticism with which some communists approached the CIO, especially in industries where they were already active.[49]

Although not at all ideologically aligned, the Chinese Hand Laundry Alliance (CHLA), which represented the city's Chinese hand laundry owners, shared the communists' interpretation of affiliation. Chinese laundry owners insisted that the ACWA took in the laundry workers so that it could "collect more fees to increase the union's revenue so that the bureaucrats can get more income." The CHLA shrewdly noted that although Black workers comprised a majority of the membership, the ACWA laundry union was run entirely by white male officials.[50] The different interpretations and criticisms reveal that in 1937 a confluence of interactions and motivations among laundry owners, laundry workers, ACWA officials, WTUL leaders, and Black worker activists helped steer the laundry union into the ACWA.

The Laundry Workers' Declaration of Independence: The First Contract

With headquarters at 1133 Broadway, Local 300 opened branch offices in Man-hattan and the boroughs in the summer of 1937 and began negotiating with the employers' associations in the linen supply branch.[51] Led by Myer Bernstein,

Samuel Berland, Noah Walter, and Louis Simon, the committee announced a month later a two-year agreement for the ten thousand linen supply laundry workers, the majority of whom were women and people of color. Only after the contract was written was the membership consulted, and only then for a yes or no vote. The workers ratified the agreement at a large membership meeting held August 3, 1937, at the Hippodrome.[52]

The agreement, which would become the master contract for the different branches of the laundry industry, saw inside workers win a minimum wage of $15.75 for a forty-five-hour workweek and a guaranteed eleven months of work per year earning at least $15.00 per week. At the time, women laundry workers earned median weekly earnings of $14.57, and one woman in six received less than $12.00 a week.[53] In contrast, washers won the significantly higher minimum wage of $20.00 per week. Drivers won minimum wages of $30.00 to $35.00 per week, and drivers' helpers won $25.00 per week and a maximum of fifty hours per week. All workers won overtime pay of time and a half, double time for holidays, a fifteen-minute rest period during the hot summer months of July and August, and seven paid holidays, and the employers accepted the principle of the five-day workweek for all workers, to be established through a joint employer-worker commission. Workers employed for more than one year received one week of paid vacation and three to five sick days. All workers won a 10 percent increase not exceeding two or three dollars, depending on the position. Employers were to distribute work as equally as possible during slack periods, and workers could not be fired and replaced with new workers without cause. The agreement called for the establishment of impartial arbitration machinery to resolve grievances and included a no-strike clause for the duration of the agreements. The union and employers appointed Herman Brickman, the long-standing representative of the employers' association, as the first impartial chair. Most significantly, the agreement prohibited the employers from hiring nonunion workers. The union agreed to supply the employers with union workers within a reasonable time period. If no such workers were available, then the employers could hire a nonunion worker, provided that she or he immediately joined the union. ACWA officials described the agreement as the workers' "Declaration of Independence," explicitly casting themselves in the role of liberator.[54]

After a period of costly and bitter labor disputes, the employers entered into bargaining and accepted the agreement as a means to achieve stability through the establishment and rigorous enforcement of uniform labor costs and the elimination of spontaneous workplace stoppages. The union and employees established the jointly led Stabilization Commission to ensure individual laundries complied with the standardized wages, hours, and grievance procedures outlined in the contract. Employers were prohibited from operating below the

FIGURE 7. Laundry strike, New York City, undated. Credit: Sam Reiss. Folder 4, box 46, 5743 P, ACWA Photographs, Kheel Center, Cornell University, Ithaca, NY.

cost of production or taking laundry from nonunion drivers or hand laundries that had not signed union agreements (organization would soon spread to the hand laundries). Certificates would be provided to compliant laundries, and noncompliant laundries could be fined by the impartial chair at a rate of between $100 and $1,000.[55] The employers' and union representatives' shared background—nearly all of the leaders on the two sides were white men—contributed to the cooperative spirit emerging among the former adversaries. An article in *The Advance* entitled "Union and Management Get Together to Talk It Over" featured a group of sixteen white and one Black man in suits and ties sitting around a conference table laughing. In an industry with a predominantly female and Black workforce, it was impossible to distinguish the union representatives from the employers, with the exception of the single Black worker.[56]

"Hey, CIO Girl! We Want a Union Too!": Organizing under the ACWA

With the first master agreement signed in the linen supply laundries, in the fall of 1937 the ACWA established the Laundry Workers Organizing Committee (LWOC) to organize workers in the other branches of the industry. The ACWA assigned Bernstein and garment official Vincent Messina to lead the committee and provided funds to hire thirty organizers. Half of those hired were communists.[57] Unlike the AFL, the CIO embraced, at least initially, communist participation and leadership in its unions; recognition of the radicals' valuable organizational, administrative, and bureaucratic experience; and shared commitment to the success of the Second New Deal. At the same time, as historian Steven Fraser notes, CIO leaders sought to control the radicals by establishing highly centralized organizing committees in industries such as steel and textiles and in the laundries.[58] Lumpkin, one of the fifteen radicals hired by the ACWA, was excited to organize for the LWOC and appreciated that her pay doubled from ten dollars a week to twenty dollars a week, a raise that enabled her to buy her first suit. But she also complained that garment officials used money to control the organizers. Lumpkin interpreted the directive that organizers comply with all instructions from the head office as the ACWA's first attempt to control the radicals and workers and shift the locus of power from the shop floor to staff who were financially dependent on the garment union.[59]

Consistent with the broader goals and commitments of the industrial union movement, the LWOC hired African American organizers. The Black press, which was watching the campaign closely, reported that the committee included three Black women, including Adelmond, and three Black men and that a Black worker, Walter, served on the negotiating committee. The *New York Amsterdam News* reported that three of the sixteen office assistants were Black.[60] Adelmond quickly emerged as one of the campaign's most effective and popular organizers. Robinson described the things that Adelmond would do to organize a shop as "sheer guts and grit." In particular, the five-foot-two Trinidadian organizer became known for using head butts to slam abusive bosses to the ground. Robinson explained that because she was from the West Indies, Adelmond knew how to butt by using the back of her head to throw the boss on the floor, all without ever lifting a finger.[61] African American Cecil Toppin, the future manager of the laundry union, recalled that Adelmond would "get out there and fight with the man and I've seen her spit in many a man's face. . . . Charlotte was a tough lady."[62] Adelmond's public and sometimes violent acts of resistance encouraged the workers to recognize their individual and collective power. Robinson insisted that Adelmond influenced a "lot of people. Even her enemies respected her. They had to."[63]

Smith and Lumpkin remembered that in 1937 workers flooded into the union. The two women approached the workers with union cards at lunch, visited them at night in their homes, and took them to the local tavern for beer and trade-union talk. Lumpkin recalled that the African American workers were "very militant and among the first to sign union cards." She remembered knocking on doors in Harlem and recalled that once she explained that she was with the Laundry Workers Union and not a collection agency "there'd be a big smile, 'Come in.'"[64] As word spread that Lumpkin and her fellow organizers were on their way to the plants, workers would run out to shout at them: "Hey, CIO girl! We want a union, too!"[65] Instead of waiting for organizers to come to their shops, Walter reported that the workers marched into union headquarters demanding union cards. Lester Granger, assistant executive secretary of the National Urban League, remembered the "furious intensity" of 1937, with the laundry workers "signing up for memberships themselves and hustling out to sign up others."[66] Smith likened the uprising to a bubble bursting and Lumpkin to a prairie fire. Once they had signed up a plant, Smith and Lumpkin established shop committees and recruited one worker from each department. Rank-and-file worker leaders then took over "the work inside," recruiting their coworkers to the union. During an interview in 2007, Lumpkin explained, "That hasn't particularly changed that I know of."[67] The rank-and-file intensive organizing employed by Lumpkin, Smith, Adelmond, and Walter brought thousands of workers into the union.

As the LWOC continued its work, union leaders began negotiations on behalf of the fifteen thousand workers employed in the family and wholesale laundries. After failed negotiations, the impartial chair, Dr. George Taylor, awarded the inside workers a minimum wage of thirty-five cents an hour and a forty-four-hour workweek for the women and forty-eight for the men. The drivers won wages of between thirty and thirty-five dollars a week, and all of the workers won a 10 percent wage increase. The rest of the agreement was modeled after the linen supply contract and brought the total number of laundry workers under union contract up to twenty-five thousand. The union established branch offices to serve its growing membership in Harlem, the Bronx, Brooklyn, Queens, and Long Island.[68] With the support of allies including the New Jersey Urban League and the Yonkers-based Citizens Committee, they also organized workers in Westchester, Newark, and Yonkers.[69] In April 1939 the union chartered New Jersey laundry Local 355.[70] The ACWA would also extend its activities into Massachusetts and Connecticut and by the end of the 1940s had laundry members in Ohio, Tennessee, Michigan, Maryland, and Utah.[71] New York's laundry workers had indeed started the ball rolling.

The Creation of the Laundry Workers Joint Board (LWJB)

With a membership of close to thirty thousand workers, in October 1937 the ACWA divided Local 300 into nine separate locals, each with an executive board united under the LWJB. Six of the locals were comprised of family service laundry workers in New York City, Westchester, and Long Island (Locals 300, 326, 327, 328, 329, and 330); Local 331 represented linen supply workers; Local 332 represented wholesale laundry workers; and Local 333 represented hand laundry workers.[72] Members elected delegates to serve on the twenty-three-member LWJB (later expanded to forty members), which in turn elected the full-time officers of the board, including the manager and assistant manager, secretary treasurer, president, vice president, and board of directors (each local was allowed one delegate on the board of directors). The LWJB negotiated contracts for all branches of the industry, collected union dues, coordinated activities between locals, oversaw the LWOC, directed activities, and paid for the local's expenses, including the salaries of business agents and other union officers. In the coming months, the LWJB established the Compliance Department to settle complaints unresolved by business agents, the Control Department to ensure that agreements were properly executed, the Employment Office to place union members in jobs, the Education Department, and a grievance committee. The LWJB was accountable to the ACWA's general executive board and paid per capita taxes to the Amalgamated.[73]

The reorganization of Local 300 enabled union officials to deal with the distinct needs of their locale or sector, but it also distanced rank-and-file workers from the union's central operations, where full-time officials accountable to the ACWA would set the union's agenda. Even the creation of the LWJB was made with little input from the workers. Only after union leaders had drawn up a set of bylaws for the LWJB was the matter taken to the membership for a vote. The reorganized union moved from 1133 Broadway to a modern office building at 160 Fifth Avenue.[74]

In its final organizational push, the union turned its attention to the six thousand to seven thousand workers employed in the city's hand laundries. An army of paid organizers canvassed the shops, and in December 1937 the union secured an agreement with the Queensboro Hand Laundry Employers Association, which represented 250 hand laundries employing one thousand workers. The agreement included a closed shop, impartial arbitration, equal division of work, a general 10 percent wage increase, overtime pay of time and a half, and a wage scale that included $3.25 for an eight-and-a-half-hour day for mangle workers and $3.60 for an eight-and-a-half-hour day for family ironers. Shirt ironers were to be paid ten cents for each plain shirt ironed and twelve cents for fancy shirts, thus preserving the male shirt ironers' higher wage-earning status. Drivers won twenty-eight dollars a week, and general workers won twenty-one dollars a week.[75] Organizing in the hand laundries continued for the next year, with strikes being called on a daily basis and often lasting only a few hours. In his history of the union, Louis Nestel noted that after a union official took the hand laundry worker for a short walk, a settlement would be reached upon their return.[76] In December 1938 the union won a second agreement with the New York Hand Laundrymen's Association modeled after the Queensboro contract, which covered eight hundred hand laundries in Manhattan and the Bronx. The second hand laundry agreement brought the total number of unionized laundry workers in New York City up to thirty thousand.[77]

Among those who remained outside the union fold were the independent drivers, who solicited laundry from customers and took it to whichever plant offered the lowest price. The bob-tails, as they were called, depressed profits and wages by inciting price wars between plants. To eliminate the competitive bidding structure and regularize the flow of work, the union convinced the independent drivers to register with employers who had signed union contracts. In exchange for relinquishing their autonomy, the drivers won union protection against arbitrary dismissal. By December 1937 one thousand of the approximately two thousand to three thousand bob-tails had joined the union (estimates of the number of bob-tails varied widely).[78] In March 1938 the men chartered Local 324, Independent Laundry Drivers Agents Union, affiliated with but not under the jurisdiction of the LWJB. The men's insistence on a separate local belied their continued commitment to craft unionism and desire to preserve the traditional race- and gender-based boundaries in the laundries. The ACWA rationalized their acceptance of the craft local on the grounds that the agents had "special problems of their own that require individual attention." Local 324 sent flying squads to plants where employers refused to sign agreements, and the LWJB convinced laundries under its jurisdiction to refuse work from bob-tails.[79] By August 1938 Local 324 had close to two thousand members and over one hundred agreements with employers representing 95 percent of agent shops.[80]

In 1938 the union started organizing the five hundred to eight hundred mostly white women and Black men in the city's ten Chinese-owned power laundries, as well as workers employed in the Chinese-owned hand laundries. The union reported that white, Black, and Chinese men worked alongside white and Black women in the hand laundries. Union leaders described conditions in the Chinese hand laundries, where the workers earned as little as six dollars or seven dollars a week, as comparable to "medieval labor slavery."[81] Organization in the Chinese-owned laundries proceeded slowly over the next few years. A pivotal strike at the New Sunlight Power Laundry was won only after the Chinese consul general, Lu Hain-Yu, intervened. With the support of the consul, in January 1941 the workers won a contract that included the closed shop, minimum weekly wages of $15.20 for the female workers for a forty-two-hour workweek, a $2.00 wage increase for the drivers, six paid holidays and vacation, and the settlement of future disputes through arbitration. The consul's intervention underlined the laundry's economic importance within the Chinese community. Strikes continued at the rest of the Chinese power laundries. Through a combination of strikes and negotiations, the union had organized five of the ten Chinese-owned power laundries by the end of 1941. It would take until the end of the 1940s to bring the remaining five into the union.[82]

The union was less successful organizing the Chinese-owned hand laundries, where many of the employees were Chinese workers, often relatives or friends of the owner. The close relationships between the employers and workers, intensified by their shared background, as well as the workers' entrepreneurial ambitions (most Chinese hand laundry workers expected to one day open their own shop), made organization of the Chinese hand laundry workers all but impossible. And of course Chinese workers had good reasons to be distrustful of the labor movement, given its long history of anti-Asian racism and support for restrictive immigration legislation. The Chinese Hand Laundry Alliance, founded in 1933 by Chinese hand laundry owners, insisted that the union's real intention was to drive the Chinese laundries out of the trade altogether.[83]

The AFL-affiliated Laundry Workers International Union sporadically challenged the ACWA laundry union. In 1937 Walter reported that the AFL had given whisky to the men and ice cream to the women to convince them to return to the LWIU.[84] A longtime supporter of the ACWA, Mayor La Guardia forbade the AFL from setting up counterpickets where CIO workers were on strike and scolded AFL officials for trying to undermine the new union. When elections for union representation were held at the State Labor Relations Board, New York City's laundry workers voted for the CIO. In 1939 Walter reported that the AFL laundry union was on the verge of disintegration as laundry workers across the city repudiated the "degenerate" union.[85] Walter was not exaggerating: by 1940 the ACWA had established unparalleled dominance in the laundry industry, claiming close to thirty thousand power and hand laundry workers and drivers, an accomplishment that had eluded the workers and their allies for decades.

The Bubble Burst: Understanding the Organization of New York's Laundry Workers

The work of resource mobilization theorists and collective identity theorists can help illuminate how, after decades of failed attempts, New York's laundry workers were finally able to organize in the late 1930s. Resource mobilization theorists argue that social movements are most successful when adequate resources, in particular, money and labor, are strategically deployed to facilitate collective action and when the movement develops links with other groups and enjoys external support.[86] Studies on union organizing similarly illuminate the importance of organizational resources and union strategy to collective action and worker mobilization. Labor scholars Kate Bronfenbrenner, Tom Juravich, and Robert Hickey argue that unions that enjoy adequate staff and financial resources and run aggressive grassroots campaigns that develop rank-and-file leadership are those most likely to succeed.[87]

Resources and strategy are critical to a campaign's success, but so too are the presence of worker solidarities at the shop floor level. Collective identity theorists have demonstrated that the development of a "sense of groupness and a common interpretive framework" inspires individuals to take collective action, especially when such activism entails significant risks and is necessary to sustain solidarity on a long-term basis.[88] Union campaigns are most likely to succeed when they can tap into preexisting worker networks and solidarities forged through workers' shared experiences of oppression, social attachments, and shop floor activism.[89]

The laundry workers were able to organize in 1937 and 1938 because of the simultaneous presence of adequate union resources and internal activist solidarities. In the late 1930s the ACWA provided the external resources that enabled the laundry workers to transform their grassroots activism into lasting gains. The garment union lent the laundry workers $150,000 to conduct an organizing campaign and provided professional staff with administrative and organizational experience. The ACWA furnished the laundry workers with twenty-four office workers, ten trunk telephones, a main office with seven branches, and the most up-to-date office equipment.[90] Most importantly, the ACWA provided the funds to hire thirty organizers, workers like Adelmond and Smith whose deep knowledge of the industry and broad networks among the workers facilitated the campaign's success. A well-funded campaign led by experienced union leaders and skilled organizers using a rank-and-file intensive approach helped secure the thousands of union cards that brought the employers to the bargaining table.

Affiliation with the established ACWA also made unionization palatable to the employers' associations. Brickman insisted that the employers would not have signed the agreements had the workers not joined the Amalgamated, a union they trusted.[91] While the impartial chair perhaps overestimated the ACWA's role, New York's laundry employers had indeed refused to negotiate with what they perceived as a rebellious, militant union led by radical workers.

The garment union's success in turn depended on the deep-rooted internal activist solidarities among the workers, nurtured by years of shared oppression, grassroots organizing, and collective action. In 1940 ACWA general executive board member Hyman Blumberg, a future manager of the laundry union, admitted that organization "could not have been possible unless there was a deep rooted revolt among the rank and file in the shops."[92] Substandard working conditions, sweatshop wages, and abusive and often racist and sexist treatment formed the basis for this collective revolt. Lumpkin attributed the upsurge to the "miserable wages, long hours, hot, heavy work, sexism, and racism [that] had ground the laundry workers down." Robinson explained that in 1937 the laundry workers had "just reached the peak that they had to do something. . . . [T]hey just couldn't exist on the wages and the treatment." After being enslaved for years, the laundry workers "were willing to make the sacrifice" Robinson insisted. They were willing to risk their jobs and livelihoods by joining the union.[93]

The ACWA's success depended on the willingness of rank-and-file workers to take extraordinary economic risks and, in the case of Black workers, to challenge Jim Crow. The campaign drew from and contributed to the culture of protest, transforming Depression era Harlem. Encouraged by the promises of the New Deal but frustrated by continuing patterns of racial discrimination, African Americans in New York (and elsewhere) led highly public and visible campaigns for economic and racial justice in the 1930s. Black Harlemites held sit-ins at local relief offices that discriminated against Black recipients, marched to city hall to demand equal access to New Deal programs, organized jobs campaigns and antieviction movements, and boycotted stores that refused to hire African American workers. As historian Cheryl Greenberg argues, the responsiveness of the government to Black demands and African Americans' understanding of their relative deprivation when compared to white workers, who disproportionately benefited from New Deal programs, inspired mass-based political actions focused on winning equitable treatment.[94] Part of this dynamic culture of protest animating the urban North, New York's laundry workers engaged in a grassroots revolt that helped forge the activist solidarities that fueled the campaign's success.

The prounion climate created by the Wagner Act also contributed to the campaign's success. Lumpkin recalled that the organizers opened each meeting with a reading of the Wagner Act and insisted that "the reason we were so successful that summer is the climate had been created in which the workers wanted to join the union, they knew they had that right." With the state supporting the workers' activism, Lumpkin argued that in 1937 "joining the union had become the popular thing to do."[95] New Deal legislation, including the Wagner Act, was particularly significant for African Americans, who in the 1930s finally saw what a responsive government could do and shifted their political loyalties to the Democratic Party. The New Deal, Greenberg argues, acted as a "psychological boost" that "energized Black urban protest."[96]

Finally, the CIO's interracial social unionism contributed to the workers' success. Even longtime AFL laundry unionist Joseph Mackey grudgingly admitted that the CIO had sparked the laundry workers' "imagination" and encouraged them to aspire to "some hoped for ideals."[97] These ideals, long held by the workers themselves but now finally articulated by organized labor, contributed to the dramatic union victory. Traditional racial and gender divisions did not disappear overnight, but the conditions were abysmal enough and the CIO and New Deal promising enough to convince the workers to organize industrially across racial and gender lines.

African American laundry worker Florence Rice described unionization as "the salvation." Rice explained, "We got better wages, worked a certain amount of hours." In a 1938 radio broadcast, African American laundry worker and union activist Dorothy Bailey told listeners that with unionization the workers no longer had to work in water up to their knees while handling acids that made their nails fall off.[98] Wages rose from as little as five dollars a week to fifteen dollars, and workers were guaranteed eleven months of employment, as well as sick days and paid holidays. These were important protections, given that laundry workers, like domestic and agricultural workers, were excluded from the 1938 Fair Labor Standards Act—evidence, historian Gabriel Winant argues, of the New Deal's valorization of industrial (male) labor over work traditionally performed by women and people of color, who would continue to be excluded from the benefits of social citizenship.[99]

Just as important as the bread-and-butter gains won by laundry workers, those same workers won dignity and respect with union membership. Sabina Martinez explained that because of the union, bosses who had once subjected the workers to their "whims and fancies" now treated them with respect. Unemployed workers no longer had to wait outside the plant trying to curry favor with the foreman to get hired but rather got placed through the Employment Office. Lumpkin insisted that "dignity on the job came with the union" and argued that the modest wage gains were "small next to the gain in dignity and the right to be a human being." Most importantly, with the union the foreman was no longer "king," free to abuse the workers at will. While sexual harassment was not eliminated altogether, Lumpkin argued that "the worst abuses were stopped."[100]

With Robinson and Adelmond leading the way, the workers won dignity and respect with unionization. Springer described her two friends as "fierce about workers' dignity. Fierce! These people who stand over big steam tubs and ironing tables and big machines with dirty clothes going around inside had a right to personal dignity and decent wages."[101] Hyman Blumberg of the ACWA argued that the union restored to the workers the "dignity of first-class citizenship." Turnover rates in the industry declined by 50 percent as conditions improved and as workers used the new arbitration machinery rather than their feet to contest abusive conditions.[102]

In 1937, then, a confluence of factors brought the laundry workers into the union, including the support of the ACWA. But even before the CIO was born, Black and white laundry workers in Harlem, the Bronx, and Brooklyn had been mobilizing at the shop floor level, supported by their radical, feminist, and Black labor allies. The deep-rooted revolt described by ACWA leaders was led and sustained by militant workers like Adelmond and Lumpkin, who in the 1940s would try to build a union committed to both economic justice and racial equality.

CHAPTER EIGHT

The "Democratic Initiative"

Fighting for Control of the Laundry Workers Joint Board

The late 1930s and early 1940s formed an exciting and challenging period for the Laundry Workers Joint Board (LWJB). As the war lifted the country out of the Depression, Charlotte Adelmond and her coworkers fought to maintain and extend the gains they had secured in the first collective agreements. Top union officials from the Amalgamated Clothing Workers of America (ACWA) established the Education Department for the workers, led initially by Bessie Hillman and later by Dollie Robinson. Individual locals organized activities to promote union consciousness and build solidarity. Many of the activities delivered through the Education Department and at the local level were led and sustained by women.

The first three years of the union's life were marked by both conflict and growth as African Americans, communists, and white male garment officials vied to set the union's agenda. Replicating patterns in their own organization, ACWA leaders appointed a cadre of white male garment officials to run the laundry union. Inspired by the CIO's commitment to racial equality and by their own activism, Black workers had a different vision for the union, one that saw women and people of color leading the battle for racial justice and economic dignity. Under the leadership of Adelmond, a Black activist faction emerged, dubbed the "democratic initiative" by her good friend and ally Dollie Robinson. Robinson explained that "the only thing that we had in the Laundry, that probably the old unions didn't have, was that we were very vocal in our Joint Board meetings. And the fights were very good." Robinson believes that the workers' insistence on democratic control and their willingness to challenge top union bureaucrats were "one of the reasons why they [the ACWA] didn't understand us too well." The laundry workers were the "rebels" who brought new energy and ideas into the "seasoned" garment union.[1]

Alongside Black workers, communists in Brooklyn laundry Local 328 led their own battle for local autonomy and union democracy. Blacklisted by the employers in the Bronx, Beatrice Lumpkin moved in 1940 to Brooklyn, where she obtained work in a laundry under the jurisdiction of the Left-led Local 328. From her position on the local's executive board, Lumpkin organized social events for the workers and represented the local at the 1940 CIO state convention. The conflict that erupted at that convention between Lumpkin and ACWA officials set the stage for the expulsion of the radicals from the laundry union in 1941. The battles that took place in the late 1930s and early 1940s between white male garment officials, Black laundry workers, and communists both animated the union and highlighted the different interests and agendas within the industrial union movement.

Setting Up Shop under the ACWA

Laundry workers greeted the first union election under the ACWA, held in the spring of 1938 at the Harlem Labor Center, with great enthusiasm. An estimated twenty-five thousand African American women voted during the five-day election period. The *New York Amsterdam News* reported that the workers were "anxious to demonstrate more fully the Negro's capacity to lead" and described the election as the union's "first test of genuine democracy." The election did in fact bring significant numbers of Black people into office, although mostly at the shop and local levels rather than at the LWJB level.[2] Workers elected twenty-one-year-old Robinson shop steward of Brooklyn Local 332, representing wholesale laundries. Robinson's effective handling of grievances convinced her coworkers to elect her secretary of Local 332's executive board. Louis Simon, the future manager of the LWJB, described Robinson as the "person in the shop who everyone looked up to."[3]

Adelmond won the position of business agent of Local 327, the only female business agent in the union, overseeing twenty family service laundries in Brownsville. Half of Local 327's membership was Black. The *New York Amsterdam News* described Adelmond as an activist who had "worked in all the jobs that women hold in the laundries." The ACWA's *The Advance* reported that the new business agent already had a huge popular following.[4] Other Black workers elected to positions included Odell Clark, who served on the executive board of Local 326, representing family laundries in Westchester; Hexton Harden, business agent of Local 332, representing wholesale laundry workers; and Bert Jemmott, business agent in Local 331, representing workers in linen supply laundries. From 1938 to 1950 Adelmond served as the sole Black female business agent in the union.[5]

In 1938 the twenty-three elected delegates of the LWJB elected Samuel Berland manager and Noah Walter assistant manager of the LWJB.[6] The *Amsterdam News* celebrated the election of the thirty-year-old Walter but in the same article noted that in an organization where more than half of the membership was Black, only eight African American men served on the twenty-three-member LWJB. The Black newspaper also reported that despite the urging of his coworkers, Walter had decided not to run for the top position of manager, telling his friends that he was of "greater service" to the union as assistant manager. Walter likely understood that given that more than half of the twenty-three delegates on the LWJB were white, he was unlikely to have been elected manager of the union. Six months later the *New York Amsterdam News* announced that "we think that Mr. Walter should be advanced to a higher position and that other Negroes be placed in the executive set-up."[7]

Except for Berland and the officers of Brooklyn Local 328, communists did not fare well in the 1938 elections. Smith and Lumpkin accused the ACWA of removing the leftists from their organizing positions immediately before the election so as to isolate them from the workers, a tactic used by CIO leaders who wanted to minimize the influence of communists in the emerging industrial unions, including in the Steelworkers' Union. According to Smith and Lumpkin, ACWA officials handpicked a slate of popular inside workers to run in the first election and co-opted them with money.[8]

Despite these alleged maneuverings, Berland, the former head of the communist-led laundry union, won the top position of Manager of the LWJB. Berland's ascension reflected the union's radical roots and the support the communists enjoyed among at least some of the workers. But it also threatened top garment officials who were intent on consolidating control over their new jurisdiction. In August 1938, only a few months after the election, eighteen of the twenty-three LWJB officials voted in favor of removing Berland. ACWA officials who spoke on the LWJB's behalf explained that while Berland had been effective in the early stages of organizing, when "devotion to the cause" was needed to unite the "small groups of struggling and often discouraged union members," his lack of experience rendered him incapable of running a large union with complicated problems. ACWA leaders described Berland's attempts to contest the decision as undemocratic, disruptive, and indecent.[9] Berland's ousting marked the beginning of the long and tumultuous process through which ACWA and LWJB officials would eject the communist founders of the union.

At the time of Berland's removal, a group of LWJB officials informed the ACWA's general executive board that the LWJB was "split wide open with partisan politics of a deep rooted character." A faction led by Secretary Treasurer Louis Simon accused Berland and his communist supporters of trying to hijack the union. It is unclear whether the Hungarian-born driver and union official was ideologically opposed to communism or whether he saw the communists as competition for control of the union, or a combination of the two. Simon had immigrated with his parents to New York City as a child. He returned to Europe to serve during World War I and was taken as a prisoner. Upon his return to the United States in 1922, Simon worked as a busboy, factory worker, insurance agent, and cab driver and then finally, beginning in 1931, he worked as a laundry driver at the Bronx's Superfine Laundry. His fellow drivers elected him secretary treasurer of Teamsters Local 810 in 1933. Simon helped orchestrate the merger of the inside workers and drivers in 1937, as well as their affiliation with the CIO and ACWA. A staunch anticommunist, he would quickly emerge as a leading force in the union, slowly but methodically building what Black workers would later come to describe as a "Trade Union Empire." In 1938, with Simon taking the lead, the LWBJ's board of directors asked the ACWA to appoint a manager to run the fractured organization, a request with which garment officials speedily complied.[10]

In August 1938 the ACWA appointed Walter Cook, a public accountant and auditor who owned a small Brooklyn accounting firm, to replace Berland, by-passing the eminently qualified Walter. ACWA officials explained that the union did not possess the "material from which to pick the right kind of manager."[11] Laundry workers and Cook quickly clashed. Laundry officials claimed that Cook tried to intimidate the workers and isolate Walter and demanded that the ACWA replace him with "a *man* who comes from the laundry industry" (italics added) and appoint a full-time general officer to work with the troubled union.[12]

Cook in turn reported that inexperienced laundry officials, whom he accused of lacking in "moral tone and idealism and without ethical standards," of a range of misdeeds, including selectively enforcing arbitration decisions and playing favorites with the employers. Cook criticized LWJB officials for allowing shop chairmen to engage in "petty pilferings" and singled out Simon for requesting money for shady purposes and for his association with Mafia-type characters. Finally, Cook claimed that a recent burglary had been an inside job and accused unidentified union officers of engaging in "orgies with women and liquor parties."[13] The latter allegation suggests that laundry officials were taking advantage of women laundry workers—likely Black women, given their significant numbers in the industry and history of abuse by both the employers and organizers.

Ultimately, the ACWA sided with Simon, Walter, and the rest of the LWJB and removed Cook. Rather than choosing a laundry worker to replace Cook, however, in May 1939 the ACWA appointed veteran garment official Gustave A. Strebel. When Strebel became ill four months later, ACWA president Sidney Hillman appointed GEB member and ACWA vice president Hyman Blumberg as manager.[14]

Consistent with patterns in their own union, where only a handful of female activists held leadership positions, in the 1940s the ACWA would appoint a series of white men to run the LWJB, usually choosing a high-ranking white male official from the garment union. Men held most of the paid staff positions in the LWJB, and when the union launched a new organizing campaign in the mid-1940s, all of the organizers were men.[15] During an interview in 1976, Robinson reported that Adelmond "was the only woman in that organization and the others were men," an assessment that minimized Robinson's own role in the union. Robinson remembered that the men would hold meetings late at night so that they could "get their action through, when women had to go home to children and to husbands and things of this sort." Robinson became a "night owl" so that the men could not "put anything over" on her. She remembers that there "were a few women like that. We were giving all our time." Robinson was annoyed by women who were not willing to make similar sacrifices, a reluctance she found most pervasive among women who had not been trained in the labor movement. In 1976 she told interviewer Bette Craig that she preferred to work with men because they were more willing to take action and move faster.[16] Robinson, who attributed her own activism and determination to her trade union background, recognized that the exclusionary tactics that normally minimized women's participation in movements (e.g., holding meetings late night) had in fact contributed to her own politicization and refusal to concede power to men or to delay her demands for justice.

In the 1940s the ACWA continued to employ some of the union's organizers, and ACWA officials remained actively involved in the hiring and firing of union staff. The garment union's legal counsel represented the laundry union. The laundry workers did not have their own publication but instead were given a section, usually one or two pages in *The Advance*, edited by staunch anticommunist J. B. S. Hardman. The workers did not hold their own convention, often a site of political debate, but instead attended the ACWA biennial conventions, where the garment union set the agenda. The parent union required that the LWJB send monthly financial reports to its General Office for approval, and once a year the ACWA audited the union. The ACWA's Research Department conducted all investigations and surveys into conditions in the industry and prepared materials for negotiations. Under the union's highly centralized bargaining structure (all laundries in the same branch of the industry negotiated simultaneously with the employers' associations), ACWA officials partook in contract negotiations and signed the agreements, and the LWJB had to secure ACWA authorization before calling a strike.[17] As the workers would quickly learn, affiliation with the ACWA left little space for local autonomy or organic leadership.

From the Picket Line to the Boardroom:
Industry-Conscious Unionism

In March 1938 New York State's Laundry Minimum Wage Board, on which Adelmond served, issued a directory order establishing a minimum wage of thirty-five cents per hour for women and minors in New York City, Westchester, and Nassau and thirty-two cents an hour for workers in the rest of the state, to be incrementally increased to thirty-five cents, or $15.75 for a forty-five-hour work-week.[18] Workers and their allies, including representatives from the League of Women Voters, the Consumers' League, and the Women's Trade Union League (WTUL), urged the board to establish a higher rate, citing the $23.40 a week cost of living for a single woman. Sympathetic board officials countered that any attempt to bring wages up to subsistence level in one jump would be disastrous to the industry, and they set the minimum wage at thirty-five cents an hour.[19] The new legislation meant the union wage was now the minimum wage. It was against this backdrop that bargaining began in the autumn of 1939 to renew the contract in the family and wholesale laundry divisions.

In September 1939 Blumberg, Walter, Simon, LWJB president Roger Douglas, and a rank-and-file committee chosen by the locals began negotiations. In a picture in *The Advance* of the close to forty officials and "active workers" engaged in negotiations, not a single woman appeared, and only a handful of the men were Black.[20] In the new agreement, signed in Mayor La Guardia's office on November 14, 1939 (a nod to the mayor's early support for the union), the workers won a five-day workweek, and the employers agreed to a survey of prevailing wages to establish minimum rates per position and department. The establishment of rates by classification would, union officials celebrated, prevent the employers from hiring all new workers at thirty-five cents an hour, regardless of position. ACWA vice president and LWJB manager Hyman Blumberg rejoiced that the absurd practice of allowing an employer to hire a "man in the wash kitchen for 35 cents an hour," the same rate applied to flat-work ironers (most of whom were Black women), would now be eliminated.[21] Blumberg's comment made clear what was left unsaid: the classification system would do little to help the most disadvantaged workers, who, because of occupational race- and sex-typing, were assigned the least valued and lowest-paying jobs in the laundries.

The survey of prevailing wages that followed, covering thirteen thousand workers in 171 laundries and conducted by ACWA research director Gladys Dickason, confirmed what the workers already knew. Men's jobs (washing and driving) paid twice as much as women's jobs (ironing, shaking, sorting, hand washing, marking, and folding). Head washers, who were always white men, earned on average $32.08 a week, while flat-work ironers, who were always women and often Black, averaged $14.00 for a forty-hour workweek. The investigation found that even when doing the same job women earned less than men. In 1939 male markers earned on average $24.75 a week, while female markers earned $16.00.[22]

When the employers and union were unable to agree on a rate system, in July 1940 arbitrators Herman Brickman and Max Meyer intervened and assigned rates of between thirty-six and forty-one cents for 165 job classifications.[23] Flatwork ironers received the lowest wage of thirty-six cents an hour (only one cent more than the minimum wage), while washroom workers, excluding the head washer, whose wage was negotiated separately, received minimum weekly wages of twenty dollars. Engineers, who were always white men, won a minimum wage of forty dollars a week. The arbitrators conceded that the rates would not provide an adequate standard of living or protect the health of the lowest-paid workers but insisted that competitive pressures such as home washing machines made it impossible to provide more.[24] As a result, in 1940 unionized laundry workers remained among the lowest-paid workers in New York City. Of fifty-three industries in New York State, only ten paid less than the laundry. Average weekly wages of all industrial workers in New York State was $27.72, compared to $20.84 for the laundry workers. Dickason pointed out that most of the workers who sent their clothes to a power laundry earned more than the workers who washed their garments. Lumpkin remembers that in 1940 her union wage barely covered rent, food, and essential clothing.[25]

The rate system of course disadvantaged women and people of color, since the union acknowledged but did not challenge their exclusion from the "skilled" jobs assigned the highest wage rates. In a 1939 series of articles in *The Advance* on the economics of the industry, labor economist and educator Jack Barbash insisted that the wage differentials between white and Black workers were not "justified by any difference in skill." Black workers, Barbash argued, "are apt to get less wages only because there are fewer job opportunities for them, and usually, in the final count, they are forced to 'take what they can get.'" In the same series Barbash argued that tradition, prejudice, and exploitation accounted for Black workers' concentration in the laundries.[26] Adelmond insisted that the union's failure to challenge the discriminatory hiring practices and wage scales revealed that its leaders were concerned only with getting more money for the highest-paid white male workers.[27]

The laundry contracts would serve in much the same way as the Protocols of Peace had been intended to serve for the garment workers in the wake of the 1909 uprising. The protocols, which Sidney Hillman had been trying to enforce when the garment workers recruited him to lead the recently formed ACWA in 1914, were an experiment in industrial democracy pioneered in the 1910s by progressive legal jurist and future Supreme Court justice Louis Brandeis. A series

of trade agreements signed by a number of manufacturers' associations and the
ILGWU, the protocols established marginally better wages, shorter hours, holidays, and grievance arbitration by the Joint Board of Sanitary Control, composed
of union, employer, and government representatives. Annelise Orleck describes
the protocols as a "mixed blessing." The agreements facilitated unionization in
the low-wage decentralized garment industry and secured minimum wages and
safer working conditions—at least for workers employed in plants operated by
the large manufacturers that abided by the rulings—but also institutionalized the
gender-based occupational structure in which men monopolized the highest-
paying jobs. The protocols would also have the intended effect of diminishing
the influence of radicalized rank-and-file immigrant women on the shop floor.[28]

Under the laundry agreements, women and people of color similarly won
small wage improvements and a modicum of job security, but they would continue to toil in the lowest-paid and least desirable positions, with little prospect
of moving up the occupational ladder. The workers' capacity to contest these
discriminatory hiring and employment practices shrank in the 1940s under the
increasingly bureaucratic and hierarchical unionism promoted by the ACWA
and enacted by white male laundry officials.[29] Articles in *The Advance* lectured
the workers on the need to respect the collective agreement and to take direc-
tions from their leaders. Workers were informed that improvements could be
achieved only if they did not "go haywire" from their early successes and expect
the employers to give more than they reasonably could. Laundry workers were
instructed to eschew direct action for impartial arbitration, the "civilized" and
"peaceful substitute" to the brute force of the shop floor. A picture in *The Advance*
showed a white male worker with bulging muscles and a big grin standing on
top of his prostrated employer. The caption beside it read: "This is not arbitration." In contrast, the picture below featured three white men in suits sitting
around a boardroom table reading documents. The caption beside it read: "This
is arbitration."[30] The images valorized negotiation led by white professional and
rational men who were in control of their emotions over the kinds of militant
direct-action tactics used by workers like Adelmond, who, quite literally, threw
the boss to the ground with her head butts.

Laundry workers were certainly not averse to using the new arbitration machinery. Between August and November 1937 workers filed 572 complaints with
the impartial chair. Complaints included unjust discharge, failure to pay the
agreed-upon wage, failure to provide vacation or sick leave, and improper classification of workers. The most common grievances, Robinson reported, involved
employers who arbitrarily moved workers into different positions and foremen
who mistreated or intimidated the workers. The employers, Robinson explained,
rewarded favored workers with perks like better job assignments and assigned
less favored workers to jobs like shaking. When workers complained the bosses

forced them to stay home because of small infractions of the rules, "or what they considered their rules."[31] The union was most vigilant about defending workers who had been fired for engaging in union activities. By 1940 the impartial chair had ruled in over twenty-five hundred cases, mostly in favor of the union.[32]

Integral to the union's stabilization program was the implementation of the checkoff system of dues, under which the union automatically deducted union dues from the workers' paychecks.[33] Beginning in 1940, the union contracts included a provision mandating the checkoff, a development that streamlined the operation of the union's finances but that also, as scholar Nell Geiser argues, reflected the union's preference for efficiency over rank-and-file participation. In contrast, some other CIO locals, including those in the auto, rubber, and steel industries, rejected the checkoff system to allow for greater rank-and-file participation in contract negotiations and in the operation of the union.[34]

Laundry workers who had been organizing since at least the early 1930s resented the tight control exercised by the garment union. Robinson argued: "We were shut out! . . . Because in the Amalgamated, decisions were made by the president and vice presidents. It didn't include us. We got the decision after it was made." She insisted that the heavy-handed oversight of the ACWA and the implementation of a bureaucratic, workplace-oriented unionism shut rank-and-file workers out of the "decision-making process" and channeled power upward into the union hierarchy.[35] Smith and Lumpkin similarly complained that the ACWA ran the LWJB "from the top down, sometimes with an iron fist." Smith opined that the ACWA was able to manipulate the workers because few of them had formal trade union experience before joining the union. The ACWA, Smith argued, "told everybody what to do."[36]

In 1939 a group of drivers complained that their locals were not adequately addressing their issues and proposed the creation of a separate local composed exclusively of drivers. Walter immediately denounced this resurgence of craft unionism and warned the LWJB that if the drivers were allowed to form their own local, other groups would similarly demand separate charters.[37] The union had succeeded in 1937 because it was an industrial union that united women and men, Black and white, and inside workers and drivers. The LWJB denied the drivers' request, but the men's hasty return to craft unionism was a disappointing development that reflected the fragility of the CIO's "culture of unity" at the shop floor level.[38]

The Making of the Laundry Workers' Education Department

In 1937 the ACWA established the LWJB's Education Department and appointed Bessie Abramowitz Hillman as director. Abramowitz Hillman had helped launch the 1910 walkout at Chicago's Hart, Schaffner & Marx, which paved the way for the formation of the ACWA. Although qualified herself for the position, she helped convince her future husband, Sidney Hillman, to take on the presidency of the new union because she understood that only a man would be accepted to lead the fledgling organization. After her marriage in 1916 she continued to organize workers in New York City. As a leader with a demonstrated commitment to women's unionism and as someone whose loyalty to the ACWA was unquestioned, Hillman was a natural choice to lead the new department. But the ACWA's decision to appoint Hillman was both cost effective as well as strategic. In contrast to most unions, in which paid staffers held the position of education director, Hillman performed the job as an unpaid volunteer, a reflection of the devaluation of her labor as Sidney Hillman's wife.[39] Robinson, who became Hillman's close friend, described the director as warm and "honest to a fault." Although Hillman had a strong Yiddish accent that could have made people "antagonistic" toward her, Robinson recalled that everyone loved her.[40]

Berthe Daniel of the WTUL helped Hillman establish the first classes for the laundry workers, but then the WTUL retreated into the background. Consistent with its longtime commitment to support the most marginalized workers, the WTUL in the 1940s would devote its increasingly limited resources to domestic, beauty parlor, restaurant, and other nonunion workers, many of whom fell outside the scope of federal labor protections.[41]

Like fellow social unionist Fannia Cohn, who was the ILGWU's education director, Hillman saw education as an opportunity to introduce new workers to the labor movement while also providing them with social and cultural activities, the roses that Schneiderman insisted workers deserved.[42] In the winter of 1937, with the aid of the WTUL and the Negro Labor Committee, Hillman set up classes on trade union tactics, parliamentary law, and public speaking in Harlem, the Bronx, Brooklyn, and Manhattan (later expanded to Westchester, Queens, and Long Island), but she spent just as much time setting up cultural and athletic programs at the union's six recreation centers.[43] With their newly acquired shortened workweek, laundry workers and their children could attend dances, join the Dramatic Group or baseball team, take tap or ballroom dancing or swimming lessons, or watch labor movies such as *Millions of Us* and *Work Pays in America*. Enrollment in the union's social activities doubled between 1937 and 1939. In May 1939 Hillman reported that more than eight thousand laundry workers had participated in the department's activities. Under the direction of well-known vocalist Anna Ward, the popular Laundry Workers' Chorus held weekly rehearsals and performed in uniforms purchased with money the workers had raised. Such activities, Hillman understood, not only eased the drudgery of hot days in the laundries but also helped build solidarities among the workers. Singing and playing together, Hillman argued, helped "promote a better understanding among the members" and cemented friendships.[44]

Conferences, retreats, and day trips were among the Education Department's most popular activities. In the summer of 1938, 150 delegates attended the first educational conference at Camp Three Arrows, eighty miles outside of New York City. Interspersed between performances by the choir and impromptu softball games, Walter, Bessie Hillman, Dorothy Bellanca, and other ACWA officials gave talks to the workers.[45] Also popular were the yearly Spring Festivals, grand affairs attended by thousands of workers. The 1939 festival opened with a large procession of workers carrying banners and pennants representing the different musical, sports, and study groups. In her opening speech Hillman celebrated the sixteen thousand laundry workers who had participated in the department's programming and emphasized the ACWA's commitment to "bring our members closer together, regardless of color, creed or nationality." After a performance by the chorus, Rose Schneiderman presented a trophy, named in her honor, to Adelmond's Local 327, that year's reigning basketball champions. Each player received a gold pin. The union awarded education certificates to participants of the study groups. The one-day festival concluded with the chorus leading in the singing of "Glory Glory Amalgamated."[46] Through the Spring Festival, regular picnics, hikes, an annual dance, and performances of the Joint Board Chorus, including a rendition of "We Shall Be Free," the Education Department helped create what historian Lizabeth Cohen has described as a "family-oriented union culture."[47]

As a longtime advocate of racial justice, Hillman ensured that the Education Department operated on an interracial basis. In 1944 Black economist Herbert Northrup reported that the department's activities were conducted "without any discrimination" and noted that Black workers participated "at least as well as whites." He also lauded the ACWA for providing much-needed cultural and recreational opportunities to Black workers.[48] Articles in *The Advance* show white and Black children playing together at Christmas parties and a Joint Board Chorus in which white and Black men sang alongside Black and white women. The union regularly promoted dances and other social activities at the Harlem Labor Center. Lumpkin remembered attending dances there alongside her fellow African American laundry workers, including Noah Walter, who informed Lumpkin that she did not have "the real feel for this African American dance."[49] It is unclear, however, whether white and Black laundry workers regularly socialized outside of seasonal parties and the Joint Board Chorus. Given that the union conducted many of its activities in neighborhood and local union centers and public schools, residential segregation likely limited opportunities to socialize on an interracial basis, despite Hillman's efforts.[50]

The Education Department's interracialism reflected the CIO's commitment to organizing across racial lines, but its roots sprang from the pioneering programs developed in the early 1900s by labor women such as Fannia Cohn. Under Cohn the ILGWU's Education Department offered cultural and social activities that celebrated workers' diverse ethnic, racial, and cultural traditions and histories. Classes on Russian literature and parties that included Spanish dances and African American spirituals drew workers from diverse backgrounds into the union, fostered cross-cultural exchange, and nurtured interethnic and interracial friendships. Historian Daniel Katz describes the ILGWU's particular brand of multiculturalism as "mutual culturalism" and argues that it emerged out of the immigrant Jewish socialist labor movement.[51]

As the head of the LWJB's Education Department Hillman embraced aspects of Cohn's educational philosophy. Like Cohn she used social and cultural programming to unite workers from diverse backgrounds and enrich the women's lives—an estimated three-quarters of those who participated in the social and cultural activities were women. Hillman mentored women laundry unionists, including Robinson.[52] But she would not use the Education Department as a space to promote rank-and-file activism or to encourage the workers to organize around race and gender. Under Cohn the Education Department became an oppositional space from which immigrant women garment workers challenged the male leadership and developed their own agenda and vision for the union. With Hillman at the helm, the LWJB's Education Department did not become a space where women and people of color could develop their own agenda or demand accountability from the predominantly white male union leadership.[53]

Despite the popularity of many of the Education Department's activities, in June 1939 Hillman reported that only 5 percent of the total membership had enrolled in its programs. She attributed the disappointing turnout to the union's youth. To nurture the workers' leadership skills and more regular involvement with the department, she set up a special class on public speaking and encouraged workers from each plant to choose a member to promote the department's activities.[54]

It is possible that the low enrollment rates were the result of the workers' preference for attending activities organized by their own locals where they could socialize with workers from the shop floor. Equally possible is that the workers remained tied to social and kin networks based in their neighborhoods.[55] Many of the women also had domestic responsibilities that left little time for social activities. In his history of the union, Louis Nestel argued that the Education Department's reach was limited by the fact that most of the workers were poor Black middle-aged women who had domestic responsibilities at night.[56]

Another explanation for the low enrollment levels exists. It is possible that with a membership that was at least 60 percent Black, the Education Department would have attracted more workers if it had regularly addressed issues of race, as did the ILGWU. ILGWU Local 22, with its large Black contingent, including Maida Springer and Frank Crosswaith, worked closely with the Negro Labor Committee (NLC) to offer courses and lectures on race relations. Many of

FIGURE 8. Dollie Lowther Robinson (*second from right*) with a group of laundry workers, New York City, undated. Credit: Sam Reiss. Folder 16, box 8, 5743 P, ACWA Photographs, Kheel Center, Cornell University, Ithaca, NY.

these talks and activities were initiated by NLC chairman and socialist garment unionist Frank Crosswaith.[57] Black laundry workers, in contrast, did not benefit from their union's ongoing collaboration with the NLC. In the early 1940s the LWJB severed ties with the Black trade union organization without, according to the NLC, "giving cause."[58] While the union records are silent about the reasons for disaffiliation, it is possible that white garment and laundry officials saw the NLC as competition for the workers' loyalty. An article in *The Advance* reported that in 1939 two thousand laundry workers crowded into Harlem's Park Palace Hall and one thousand more were turned away to hear Crosswaith discuss his candidacy for New York City councilman. The NLC certainly had the support of New York City's Black laundry workers.[59]

It is also possible that white laundry officials did not want to draw special attention to race, which, after all, would have necessitated a reckoning with the racist hiring and employment practices that relegated Black workers to the most difficult jobs in the laundries, where they earned the lowest wages. Robert Zieger notes that even as they organized Black workers, industrial union leaders tried to "minimize the racial character of the CIO enterprise," insisting that the movement "held out equal rights for all, special treatment for none." The CIO's color-blind analysis ignored the systemic racism that undermined the attainment of equality for Black workers everywhere.[60] White laundry unionists who saw their record on race as beyond reproach—and pointed to their large Black membership as proof—felt little inclination to affiliate with an organization committed to promoting Black leadership and equal rights. As a result, the laundry union would not develop courses in tandem with the NLC in the 1940s, a missed opportunity for the workers, the union, and the Education Department.

"From the Cradle to the Grave": Dollie Robinson and the Education Department

In 1941, when the ACWA appointed Bessie Hillman to direct the union's War Activities Division, she appointed Robinson to the post of assistant education director. Robinson took over the top job in 1943 at the age of twenty-six.[61] Robinson's meteoric rise in the union owed much to her ability to act as a mediator between different groups. Gardner C. Taylor, pastor of Brooklyn's historic Concord Baptist Church, which Robinson attended, described Robinson as a liaison between the African American and labor communities. Taylor explained that Robinson entered the union movement at a time when labor needed someone "who understood the posture, the determination of Black people in this country, to interpret that position . . . to really get through to the labor movement the aspirations of underprivileged people."[62] Her political skills and perseverance made her well-suited to these tasks. Donna Shalala, the president of Hunter College, where Robinson worked in the 1970s, insisted that Robinson had a "sophistication . . . an instinctive brilliance for how to work the political system." Even though she often lost, "she kept moving, and her enthusiasm for helping people and making the process work for poor people was infectious." If there was a "brick wall," Shalala explained, Robinson would "turn in another direction and just keep moving."[63] Springer, who met Robinson through the WTUL in the 1930s, described Robinson as an "absolute political animal." Even though Robinson was younger, she moved in the same social and political circles as Springer. Robinson, Springer argued, was "big, [and] she moved around with an older crowd," including the Hillmans.[64]

By the time Robinson began working with the Education Department, she had amassed considerable experience in the field of worker education. In June 1940, in recognition of her talents as an organizer and shop floor leader, the LWJB awarded Robinson one of two annual awards to attend the seven-week summer course at the Hudson Shore Labor School, the successor of the Bryn

Mawr Summer School for Women Workers. Robinson explained that "Hudson Shore was where, really, I learned about workers' education." It was "unbelievable," she argued, how much workers learned there.[65] With unions paying for courses and living expenses, Robinson and her coworkers took classes in history and economics, participated in the school's social and cultural activities, and forged new friendships. Reta Oddi from Boston wrote in *The Advance* that all of the students came to "love and respect" Robinson because of her sincerity. Workers elected Robinson to the school's board of directors, where she served as the first Black female representative.[66] In 1941, on the recommendation of Mabel Leslie of the WTUL and Hudson Shore staff, Robinson won a full scholarship from the American Labor Education Service to attend the Summer Institute for Social Progress at Wellesley College. Like thousands of other women who completed these programs, Robinson brought the knowledge and skills she amassed there back to her union.[67]

In describing her emergence as a labor leader and educator, Robinson cited the influence of the WTUL. Robinson first learned about the WTUL in the mid-1930s, when the organization sent Helen Blanchard to Brooklyn to support the laundry workers. Impressed by the practical support the WTUL provided and its commitment to worker education, Robinson joined the organization. During an interview in 1976, she explained that the WTUL was the "only way we could learn about unions, because we knew nothing about unions, we knew that we were oppressed and wanted to do something about it." Robinson recalled that before attending classes at the WTUL's Lexington Avenue headquarters in the 1930s she did not know how to conduct a union meeting, take minutes, or call elections. Robinson argued that the WTUL filled a vacuum, given the reluctance of male union leaders to provide educational training out of fear that an educated rank and file would challenge their leadership, a belief shared by Lumpkin.[68] Education, Robinson explained, made male leaders nervous because "they weren't sure whether they were teaching you how to take over from them or what." The activist noted that the ACWA and ILGWU were a "little further advanced" than other unions where "some of the girls had quite a hard time," but she still believes they could have done more. By arming women unionists with practical knowledge and skills, the WTUL "performed a very real function for young trade unionist women who were active but needed to know how to be active and what to do."[69]

Robinson equally appreciated the mentorship opportunities provided by longtime activists such as ILGWU leader Pauline Newman and Rose Schneiderman. When Robinson faced challenges in the union she would head to the WTUL office to "vent" and get the advice and "guidance of an older woman who had been through it."[70] The young laundry worker deepened her commitment to the WTUL by becoming a delegate, alongside Adelmond, representing the laundry union. In 1943 Robinson was elected to the WTUL's executive board, where she served on the education and legislative committees.[71]

Through her involvement in the LWJB's Education Department Robinson developed a warm and enduring friendship with Bessie Hillman, who, Robinson pointed out, "was great before even Sidney Hillman was great among workers." Hillman not only offered advice to Robinson but also went "out in the field" with her to solve a problem.[72] When Robinson gave birth to her daughter, Jan, in 1952 she named Hillman godmother. Hillman pushed Robinson, who described herself as not "a religious churchgoer," to have Jan baptized. Hillman stood next to Robinson and her daughter during the ceremony, held at Pastor Gardner Taylor's Concord Baptist Church in Brooklyn. Springer, Jan's second godmother, was in Europe during the christening but sent a dress from Denmark for Jan to wear. Jan would spend part of every summer at Hillman's summer cottage, and Hillman attended many of Jan's school functions. Hillman, Robinson recalled, "took the role of godmother very seriously."[73] Philoine Fried, Bessie Hillman's daughter, remembered Jan bringing her friends to their summer cottage. Fried also recalled having to go down to the beach to make sure that they could get into the all-white private enclave.[74]

What Nestel saw in the laundry workers' age and maternal status as an impediment to participation, Robinson saw an opportunity to provide educational programing to Black children who did not normally enjoy access to social and cultural activities. As education director, Robinson, who explained that the department wanted to "touch the worker from the cradle to the grave," organized weekly dancing, drama, and music classes for the workers and their children. With Robinson's support, the children published their own newspaper. In the early 1940s Robinson, who had taken piano lessons as a young girl in the South, spearheaded the purchase of musical instruments and secured free piano lessons for the children at the union's Fifth Avenue headquarters and in Brownsville, Brooklyn. In 1943 she proudly reported that the Brownsville recreation center had a twenty-one-piece orchestra "composed of the children of laundry workers" who were learning to play under the tutelage of professional musicians.[75] Robinson's commitment to children's programming reflected and drew inspiration from the African American tradition of "othermothering," described by Black feminist scholar Patricia Hill Collins as a "generalized ethic of caring and personal accountability" that recognized the care of all Black children as a community responsibility.[76] By providing Black workers and their children with access to social and cultural opportunities usually reserved for the middle class, Robinson's programming contributed to the broader goals of racial empowerment and uplift.

As part of her agenda to empower Black laundry workers, Robinson recruited Black activists to work for the Education Department, including leftist author

Ann Petry. The daughter of a pharmacist from Saybrook, Connecticut, Petry moved to Harlem in 1938, where she became a voice for progressive causes. Petry first wrote for the *New York Amsterdam News* and then in the 1940s for the left-wing Harlem weekly the *People's Voice*, copublished by Adam Clayton Powell Jr. Robinson and Petry met in 1938 when Petry wrote an article about the laundry workers. As assistant education director, Robinson recruited Petry to work for the union organizing skits and other children's programs. While working out of Robinson's office, Petry continued to write for the leftist *People's Voice* and completed her first novel, the critically acclaimed *The Street*, published in 1946. *The Street*'s main character, Lutie Johnson, was a single mother living in Harlem and working in a power laundry to support herself and her young son. Like so many other Black women, Johnson had begun her wage-earning career as a live-in domestic servant for a wealthy white family in Connecticut. The father, who owned a manufacturing company, drank heavily, and the family's friends made hushed comments around Johnson about Black women's propensity to make "passes" at white men, leading Johnson to wonder "why they all had the idea that colored girls were whores." Eager to reunite with her son, Bub, and escape the sexually charged work environment, Johnson quit her job and moved to Harlem, where she rented a dingy overpriced tenement apartment and got a job as a presser in a power laundry. The laundry provided a welcome escape from domestic service, but Johnson described the conditions as hot, difficult, and sometimes unbearable. Eager to leave the laundry, Johnson attended night classes at a business school on 125th Street, where she learned shorthand and typing. Even though her "back ached and her arms felt as though they had been pulled out of their sockets" from long days in the laundry, she still attended night classes for four long years, determined not to have to "wash clothes or work in a laundry" forever. Yet although she passed her civil service examinations, as a Black woman Johnson was unable to secure an office job.[77] Lack of economic opportunities, racism, overpriced housing and food, and the ever-constant threat of sexual violence eventually led Johnson to murder the man who was trying to force her into prostitution. The book's main themes—poverty, racism, exploitation, and sexual violence—were no doubt informed by Petry's interactions with the laundry workers, many of whom, like Johnson, supported children and lived on the edge of poverty. That *The Street* was so full of despair and violence suggests that the laundry workers Petry interacted with lived difficult lives.[78]

In recognition of the fact that many laundry workers were mothers combining wage earning with domestic responsibilities, Robinson held classes for mothers on topics such as nutrition and first aid and "how to handle their children." When Robinson discovered during the 1944 presidential campaign that seventy-three members were unable to read or write, she spearheaded literacy classes and convinced the New York Public Library to lend the union

Local 327

CHARLOTTE ADELMOND
Business Agent

Charlotte Adelmond began work in the laundry industry in 1925. Soon began to feel the need for an organization. 1933 she was told of Local 810. Went to them seeking information, was told to get people in shop. She spoke to 20 people, planned a meeting and 7 people showed up. Those 7 formed nucleus for the organization that began in Brownsville and set the ball rolling, later to stage the famous Brownsville strike. She was an active leader in that drive. 1937 after CIO organization, was sent to Bryn Mawr Labor School. Upon her return she became paid organizer. Appointed by Industrial Commissioner as one of 3 employee members of 2nd Laundry Minimum Wage Board. 1938 elected Business Agent in Local 327, which position she holds at the present time. Only women Business Agent in the Joint Board.

MAX SCHIFF
Business Agent

Max Schiff, a driver in the industry since 1930 was an active member in Local 810. In 1937 when present organization was formed he was working in the Erasmus Laundry. One of first to offer financial aid to new organization. The drivers of Erasmus Laundry through him contributed funds to help Joint Board in the early days. He then was appointed organizer in Westchester. Later transferred to Brooklyn. 1938 he was elected Business Agent in Local 327. He holds that position today having been re-elected in past election for another 2 year term.

Tenth Anniversary Celebration

FIGURE 9. Charlotte Adelmond, business agent, Local 327, Laundry Workers Joint Board (LWJB) of Greater New York, 1947. Credit: "The Journal of the LWJB: Tenth Anniversary Celebration," 1947. Box 139, 5619, ACWA Records, Kheel Center, Cornell University, Ithaca, NY.

two hundred books every month to be used in a library housed in the Education Department.[79] Robinson's literacy work mirrored that of longtime civil rights activist and educator Septima Clark, who would become the Southern Christian Leadership Conference's (SCLC) director of education. The southern-born Clark led the Citizenship Education Program, which led to the creation of Citizenship Schools in the South. The schools taught literacy as a means to empower southern African Americans and connect them to the civil rights movement. Like Clark, who was the daughter of a laundry worker, Robinson understood literacy and education as critical to the goals of racial and political empowerment and movement building.[80] Throughout her long career as a labor activist, Robinson would promote worker education as a vehicle to empower Black workers and enrich their daily lives, an opportunity she understood as particularly valuable for Black and female unionists. Robinson's commitment to education drew from and contributed to the specific tradition among Black women activists who promoted education to foster self-reliance, leadership capacity, and a knowledge of one's rights.[81]

"Sheer Guts and Grit":
Charlotte Adelmond in Action

Robinson had a good friend and staunch supporter in Charlotte Adelmond. The two women worked well as a team, a function of their divergent but complementary organizing and leadership styles. Springer described Robinson as a "highly educated, soft-spoken, both physical and mental giant" and Adelmond as a militant trade unionist and Black nationalist who was "outspoken and outrageous." Both women were zealous in their defense of worker rights, but the southern-born Robinson adopted a less confrontational approach that relied on worker education, building alliances with labor and progressive allies, and mentoring young trade unionists. Robinson theorized that it required both "revolution and evolution to gain progress, and you have to decide which one you're with."[82] Robinson preferred the evolutionary approach, working incrementally and sometimes behind the scenes to effect social change, while Adelmond chose the revolutionary route, using highly visible and confrontational tactics to demand immediate reform.

When Adelmond's contemporaries talked about her, the first thing they mentioned was how she dressed. Robinson explained that "to prove she was strong," Adelmond wore a shirt and tie, cut her hair short before the Afro was popular, and wore a felt hat. Springer remembered that Adelmond put her hair in an Afro and wore a "man-tailored" suit, comfortable walking shoes, and a felt hat pulled down tightly over one eye. Springer insisted that "you could not miss Charlotte with her fedoras and her tweed skirts." Springer described Adelmond and Robinson as powerfully built, tall, and "not thin" women who exuded strength.

Alongside her strength, Adelmond's friends recalled her "sweet Trinidadian sing-song voice" and ability to cook up a storm.[83] Cecil Toppin recalled that Adelmond wore a black suit, a wide-brim hat, and comfortable walking shoes, a mannish style adopted by Black lesbians such as Harlem performer Gladys Bentley, whom contemporaries described as a "bulldagger."[84] Adelmond was in fact a lesbian and in the 1940s was raising a daughter she had adopted as an infant from Trinidad with a female partner.[85]

A business agent for Local 327, Adelmond was regularly featured in the union newspaper for her "energetic alertness" on behalf of the workers. Articles lauded Adelmond for being the first and last person at the union office and for leading "quickie" strikes when the employers refused to comply with the contract. A work stoppage led by Adelmond in 1938 at the Household Laundry saw the workers win $400 in back wages.[86] In February 1939 workers at the Weaverly Laundry expressed their "enthusiastic thanks" to Adelmond for "using every pressure available" to get the employer to pay back wages. The workers insisted that "it was all but a lost cause" until Adelmond intervened and secured a victory.[87]

As a leader committed to rank-and-file empowerment, Adelmond understood the importance of maintaining an active membership. Springer recalled that Adelmond always reminded the workers to keep fighting "lest we relax our vigil."[88] Adelmond understood that the union would thrive only if the workers remained active in the day-to-day functioning of the organization and only if they were willing to defend their rights. The Trinidadian activist's commitment to participatory democracy mirrored the civil rights organizing of Ella Baker of the SCLC, who similarly promoted grassroots activism, decentralized leadership, and radical democracy.[89] Adelmond's passion and commitment won her the love and respect of her coworkers. Accounts in *The Advance* describe the business agent as having a "huge personal following." When a 1939 notice in the union newspaper informed the workers that "Charlotte was ill," her coworkers responded by sending her flowers, fruit, and Valentine's Day cards.[90]

In 1938 Adelmond was among a large contingent of Black workers to attend New York State's first CIO convention. Adelmond was no doubt thrilled when the CIO adopted a "Negro Rights" resolution affirming its commitment to racial justice and demanding that the state ban the discriminatory real estate practices that led to overcrowding, poor health, and lack of housing for Black people. Laundry workers celebrated when convention delegates chose fellow laundry worker Noah Walter to serve as one of fourteen vice presidents of the newly organized New York State CIO Industrial Union Council and as a member of the CIO state executive board.[91] Walter used his growing stature to promote labor and civil rights. In 1939 he spoke at the memorial, organized by the leftist Workers' Defense League, for Joseph Shoemaker, the labor organizer who had been tarred and feathered and then flogged to death by Tampa City police and members of the Ku Klux Klan.[92]

It was Adelmond, though, and not Walter who led the first charge against the ACWA and LWJB leadership over what Black workers described as racist treatment. In 1940 Black workers reported to the *Amsterdam News* that top ACWA officials had arbitrarily removed African Americans from elected positions and replaced them with whites, a practice that had led to a "sharp decline in Negro office-holders." The workers accused white union officials of giving staff jobs to white workers who had been voted out of office and of appointing white men to fill vacancies in hand laundry Local 333 instead of holding elections.[93] Black laundry workers insisted that at least four of the six Employment Offices discriminated against Black workers in job placements. In one of the six offices, Black workers were the "last to be considered," even after "refugee whites." Only two of the offices—the Harlem office and the Central Office on East 17th Street, which was run by African American Odell Clark—did not discriminate against workers of color. Rumor had it, though, that Clark would soon be removed on the grounds of "inefficiency." (Clark would in fact remain in the union for twenty more years, at which point he was finally ousted.) Two large plants, the Cascade Laundry in Brooklyn and the National Laundry in the Bronx, employed only white workers, a charge confirmed by economist and contemporary Herbert Northrup. Northrup reported that a minority of white workers complained if they were not given preference over African Americans in hiring. When Walter raised the issue of racial discrimination at an LWJB meeting, LWJB manager Hyman Blumberg and African American business agent Roy Soden accused him of "attempting to disrupt the union."[94]

Given her history of worker militancy, it should come as no surprise to learn that Adelmond led the charge against the ACWA-appointed manager. In 1940 Adelmond publicly accused Blumberg of racism. Angered and embarrassed that Adelmond had challenged him in public, the ACWA vice president and laundry manager suspended her for three months. Adelmond's coworkers described the suspension as part of a "well laid plan to eliminate Negroes from offices of the union." A delegation of thirty-five Black workers led by George Wakefield protested the suspension and presented formal charges of discrimination and prejudice against Blumberg to the ACWA's general executive board. The delegation demanded that Adelmond be immediately reinstated and that Blumberg apologize to all Black members in writing and be suspended for six months without pay.[95]

Adelmond's behavior shocked and enraged Blumberg because it challenged the racial status quo, which held that all Black people were subordinate to all white people. It also contradicted the "politics of respectability" adopted by some Black women as a strategy to challenge racist stereotypes. The politics of respectability, historian Evelyn Brooks Higginbotham argues, saw Black women adopt a pleasing and well-mannered demeanor that denoted their cultural superiority and right to be treated with dignity and respect. Adelmond was among a vanguard of Black female activists described by historians LaShawn Harris, Dayo Gore, and Erik McDuffie as rejecting this strategy and employing militant liberationist tactics in their struggles for economic and civil rights.[96] Like the Black communist women described by LaShawn Harris, Adelmond eschewed traditionally feminine behavior, dress, and public etiquette and pursued racial and economic justice through protest, agitation, and public acts of resistance that included discursive confrontations and head butts. The Trinidadian activist used her body and public spaces to stage racial confrontations that exposed the union's shortcomings and demonstrated her own and, by extension, the workers' power. Respectability for Adelmond meant being treated equally and not waiting to be given what was rightfully hers.[97]

Ultimately, it was Walter's rather than the workers' intervention that resulted in Adelmond's reinstatement. Walter explained that Adelmond had just recently "barely warded off a nervous breakdown" and might justifiably be excused for an "irritable mood." The assistant manager admitted that while in an organization with so many nationalities "it would be foolish to deny the existence of all prejudice," he insisted that the union did not discriminate and resorted to gendered language to "excuse" Adelmond's hysterical behavior. Walter's intervention ended the standoff, and Adelmond was back in the union, at least for the time being.[98]

While Robinson surely supported her outspoken friend, she did so in a covert manner. As education director, Robinson automatically won a spot on the LWJB, where she used her diplomatic skills and connections to influential whites like Bessie Hillman to support Adelmond and other outspoken unionists. Robinson explained that one of the reasons she served on the LWJB was so that she could protect "those elected officials who were really serving us best." She explained that "we were always threatened, thinking that the people who had really served us well were going to be ganged up on and removed." Robinson's colleagues insisted she was well suited to play the role of intermediary. Labor feminist Esther Peterson remembered that Robinson was the one person who was able to "get us to really sit down and analyze as whites what this all meant."[99] With Adelmond taking on the role of public provocateur, Robinson worked behind the scenes to create the space for her friend to continue her advocacy.

In 1940, the same year that Blumberg suspended Adelmond from the union, the thirty-six-year-old business agent became a naturalized US citizen.[100] There is no record to explain why, after sixteen years in the United States, Adelmond decided to naturalize, but it is possible that the turmoil in the union influenced her decision. Equally likely she was inspired by the gains Black workers had made under the New Deal and in the CIO and wanted to protect those gains at the voting booth, especially as Europe fell under fascist rule. Either way, her decision to naturalize distinguished her from many of her fellow migrants who did not apply for citizenship either because of the racism they encountered in the United States or because they believed they enjoyed more rights and status as foreigners than as Black Americans.[101]

There is no record of the ACWA's response to the charges of racism levied against the union and Blumberg. At a 1942 banquet honoring Blumberg for his two years of service to the laundry union, LWJB secretary treasurer Louis Simon thanked him for helping to unite the workers across racial lines. Simon insisted that the "understanding developed between the white workers and the Negro workers" constituted the union's "most remarkable achievement." Blumberg welcomed the praise, only casually alluding to tensions in the union. In gendered language that framed solidarity in masculine terms, Blumberg insisted that it was "impossible to have every soldier in a great army satisfied."[102] Garment and laundry officials' public framing of Blumberg and the ACWA as incubators of interracial solidarity and manly unionism contradicted the lived experiences of African Americans and women and highlighted a gap between white industrial union leaders' public commitments to racial justice and their practices.

The ACWA and Its Communist Laundry Workers: The Case of Local 328

While the democratic initiative under Adelmond's leadership challenged the racist practices of top union officials, communist laundry workers in Brooklyn led their own movement for union democracy. Despite their shared opposition to the leadership, the two movements appear not to have intersected. By the time Samuel Berland was removed from the position of manager in the summer of 1938, most of the communist founders of the union had already left, including Jessie Smith.[103] An exception was Beatrice Lumpkin, who in 1938 decided to take a leave from college, explaining that "union work was too important and too exciting" for her to be in school. Lumpkin was able to find work in a laundry through the union's new Employment Office, but, much to her chagrin, she never made it past the two-week trial period in any one laundry. In three weeks she worked in five different laundries. Lumpkin had no idea why she was fired and wondered if the employers and union had colluded to keep her out of the industry, seeing her as an unwanted agitator. Out of work, she returned to Hunter College, thankful for the public college's free tuition. She finished her degree in February 1939, the same year her mother died of cancer and her father suffered a series of debilitating strokes, which Lumpkin attributed to the stress of the Depression and long years working in the hand laundry (her father never fully recovered). When her father gave up the family apartment in 1939 and moved into a furnished room, Lumpkin moved to an apartment with her first boyfriend, Butch, a commercial artist and fellow communist who came from an Irish German Catholic family.[104] Unemployed and with rent to pay, Lumpkin needed to find work quickly in 1939, so when her comrades in Brooklyn Local 328 invited her to apply for a job in Brooklyn, she did. Just in case she was on a "don't hire list," she used her mother's maiden name of Chernin (at the time she was Beatrice Shapiro) to obtain work at Brooklyn's Spartan Laundry. Lumpkin described the trip from the Bronx to Brooklyn as traumatic and joked that she needed a passport. After working briefly at the Spartan she moved to the Brighton Laundry, which, with its five hundred mostly Black and Puerto Rican women workers, was one of the largest plants in Brooklyn. (By 1938 some plants employed as many as a thousand workers, though most employed no more than one hundred.) Lumpkin quickly won a spot on Local 328's executive board. A 1939 article in *The Advance* described her as a "live wire."[105]

Local 328, the only local under leftist control, appeared regularly in the pages of *The Advance* for organizing new laundries, for securing back pay for the workers, and for defending the workers against antiunion bosses. In September 1939, when Joe Trepaldo of Brooklyn's Imperial Laundry replaced his regular workers with strikebreakers and signed a contract with the AFL laundry union, *The Advance* reported that Local 328 organized "one of the strongest picket lines that Brooklyn has seen in recent years." The picketing lasted for more than three months and ended with the reinstatement of all the discharged workers.[106] The Left-led local hosted regular social events, including celebrations for engaged laundry workers, and supported prolabor candidates. An article in *The Advance* recognized communist business agent Mike Coleman for his "untiring" work in support of ACWA leader Dorothy Bellanca's 1938 candidacy for New York State's American Labor Party.[107]

Much of Local 328's activism was led and sustained by women workers who organized social events such as spaghetti parties. White and Black women served as organizers, shop committee members, and local officers, and in 1939 they established a women's boxing team, where they learned to shout as loudly as their bosses. Women workers from the Brighton Laundry where Lumpkin worked organized the Tiny Women's Club, although it is unclear what the group did.[108]

In February 1939, under Simon's oversight, the LWJB called for an election of Local 328's executive board. Lumpkin recalls that as the counting continued into the wee hours of the night the local decided to lock the ballot box in a warehouse and continue counting the next day. When the workers returned the following morning they discovered that someone had added an additional name to the hundreds of ballots cast for the communist slate. Because the pro-Left ballots now included too many names, the LWJB invalidated them, and the radicals lost the election. Lumpkin and her comrades believe that someone from the LWJB had entered the warehouse during the night and tampered with the ballots. Shortly after the election, then manager Walter Cook wrote to Sidney

Hillman complaining that Simon had asked him to authorize fifty dollars for the warehouseman for services too shocking to commit to paper. In the same letter Cook accused Simon of meddling in the election.[109]

Lumpkin and her comrades demanded a hearing with Hillman. The radicals accused Simon of election tampering and of appointing business agents instead of holding elections, an accusation also levied by the democratic initiative.[110] In July 1939 the ACWA agreed to hold new elections. Lumpkin and her communist slate were overwhelmingly reelected. Lumpkin won the position of education director. As a member of the local's executive board she was invited to lavish functions hosted by the ACWA and was irked to attend a dinner at a fancy hotel where her meal cost more than the workers earned in a week.[111]

Less than six months after the new election, conflict erupted once again between the Left-led local and the LWJB. In 1940 the communists accused the LWJB of handpicking a group of delegates to represent their local at the upcoming CIO state convention in Rochester, New York, in violation of the bylaws, which called for the election of delegates. Lumpkin and her comrades called an emergency meeting of Local 328, where the membership elected Lumpkin and three others to represent them in Rochester. Lumpkin and her comrades drove all night through the foggy Adirondack Mountains to arrive at the convention on time. When the credentials committee reported the next morning Lumpkin screamed at the top of her lungs that as the democratically elected representatives she and her comrades should be seated in place of the hand-picked delegates. She remembered being shocked when a few minutes later pandemonium broke out when communist leader Mike Quill of the Transport Workers Union tried unsuccessfully to defeat Sidney Hillman's resolution in support of President Roosevelt. ACWA official and credentials committee member Abe Chatman called for the immediate expulsion of the Left-led National Maritime Union, the Newspaper Guild, the United Office and Professional Workers, the State, County, and Municipal Workers, and the Furriers' Union and summoned the police to remove the leftists.[112] Lumpkin quickly gleaned that the laundry workers' struggle was playing out against the backdrop of a much broader battle within organized labor, one that had intensified as a result of the Soviet Union's signing of the 1939 Non-Aggression Pact with Hitler. In line with directives from the Comintern, in 1940 American communists denounced President Roosevelt's program of domestic mobilization, a position that angered Hillman and other CIO leaders who were working closely on the New Deal president's reelection campaign. In June 1940 Congress passed the Smith Act—the intended targets being communists—which made it a crime to advocate, advise, or teach the violent destruction of the US government. It was under the Smith Act that in 1949 eleven national Communist Party leaders were found guilty of conspiring to destroy the US government.[113] In 1940 the communists' embrace of left-wing isolationism and their attacks on the Roosevelt administration increased their vulnerability within the CIO and beyond.

In early 1941, not long after the convention battle, the LWJB suspended Local 328 business agents Mike Coleman and African American George McGriff for "conduct unbecoming union officers." The LWJB accused the communists of bringing armed guards to a membership meeting, of slandering the ACWA, and of trying to influence laundry workers to join the party. An article in *The Advance* reported that rank-and-file laundry workers disapproved of how the communist "clique" ran Local 328, noting specifically the leftists' use of stalling tactics at union meetings and their propensity to fast-track comrades into jobs, circumventing the union Employment Office (tactics the communists were in fact well known for). The communists in turn accused LWJB officials of resorting to dictatorial and undemocratic methods to control the union.[114] A *New York Times* article entitled "Ban on Reds Voted by Laundry Union" described the suspensions as the "first step in the organization's internal housecleaning." The second step, the *Times* reported, was the adoption by the LWJB of a resolution prohibiting Communists, Nazis, and fascists from holding union office. When Julius Halprin, the lone communist member of the LWJB, protested he was swiftly removed by his fellow LWJB members.[115]

The LWJB launched an investigation that ended with charges being filed with the ACWA against all of the executive members of Local 328. ACWA officials put the local under the receivership of Louis Stark and Franz Daniel from the ACWA's General Office. ACWA vice president and staunch anticommunist Jacob Potofsky and Frank Rosenblum headed a committee of ACWA officials tasked with deciding the communists' fate. Lumpkin's coworkers elected her to represent them before the committee.[116]

In a prelude to how the CIO would operate in 1949 and 1950 when it ejected its eleven Left-led unions, the ACWA-led committee acted as investigator, prosecutor, and judge in the trial. After a ten-day investigation the committee produced a two-hundred-page report based on interviews with forty-five workers. Dozens of witnesses were brought in to testify against the leftists, including a former comrade. The panel found the communists guilty of ignoring ACWA policy, of pressuring workers to join the party, and of refusing to hand over minutes and financial records. Concluding that the local was under the complete domination of the Communist Party, the ACWA expelled the entire group. The deposed leaders briefly considered establishing an independent union but decided that they did not want to jeopardize the existing contracts.[117] By 1941 the communists were permanently out of the laundry union. As in the automobile workers' and steelworkers' unions, CIO leaders harnessed the communists' expertise and dedication in the early stages of organizing when "devotion to the cause was necessary" but ejected the radicals once they had fulfilled the task of helping to organize large numbers of workers and had become disruptive to the administration of the union.[118]

Interviewed more than half a century after her expulsion, Lumpkin, who in 2020 turned 102, believed that the "clothing workers got tired of us and decided they could just pull us out, take us out, as the gangster expression goes." Despite this assessment, Lumpkin, who is still a member of the Communist Party, nonetheless spoke of the ACWA in largely positive terms. In 2006 she pointed out that the ACWA had made "outstanding contributions to many progressive causes," not least of which was to help stem the rise of fascism, which gripped the world in the 1930s and 1940s. Lumpkin explained that personally "she got over their horrible breach of democracy" but insisted that there was one comment that she could neither forget nor forgive. At the end of the trial ACWA vice president Frank Rosenblum asked her, "Why are you so involved with politics? At your age, you should be thinking of getting married." (Lumpkin was twenty-two at the time.) Although Lumpkin had been targeted for her radicalism and affiliation with the Communist Party, it was Rosenblum's comment about gender that continued to rankle the activist.[119]

Understanding the Anti-Left Crusade in New York's Laundries

As Lumpkin came to understand, the conflict between the communists and nonradical laundry and garment officials was part of a much broader struggle for control of the labor movement, one that was shaped by the shifting imperatives of the Comintern and the domestic Red Scare. The signing of the Nazi-Soviet Pact and American communists' attacks on Roosevelt provoked anger and mistrust among industrial union leaders who had embraced the president and his New Deal program and saw his reelection as critical to the continued growth of organized labor.[120] The tensions were also fueled by substantive differences in political vision: Were unions vehicles for social mobility or revolutionary transformation? Robert Zieger argues that CIO leaders would ultimately and rather quickly embrace the "traditional agenda of collective bargaining, centralized and authoritative leadership, and fundamental support for basic American institutions." For the CIO's founders, Zieger argues, the real challenge was how to bring the grassroots militancy of workers—inspired in some cases by communist organizing—"into the ambit of a revitalized and assertive American labor movement." The ejection of the communists was part of this larger conflict, which ended with the expulsion of the eleven Left-led unions and the consolidation of the labor movement's support for corporate capitalism, social Keynesianism, and the Democratic Party's Cold War liberalism. With the intensification of the Cold War and the 1947 Taft-Hartley Act's anticommunist provisions, there would be no more space in the CIO for radical trade unionists who challenged the capitalist system at home or American imperialism and Cold War politics abroad.[121]

While it is impossible to know conclusively how the expulsions affected the laundry union, numerous studies have shown that Left-led unions enjoyed higher levels of union democracy. One such study by sociologists Judith Stepan-Norris and Maurice Zeitlin looked at thirty-five CIO international unions in the late 1940s and saw this increased level of union democracy reflected in the presence of democratic constitutions, in institutionalized opposition, and in active memberships.[122] Zieger argues that the "overall record of communist-influenced unions with respect to collective bargaining, contract content and administration, internal democracy, and honest and effective government was good."[123] It is possible that the communists would have nurtured a more democratic union culture than the one that developed in the laundry union in the 1940s.

It is also possible and even likely that communist participation and leadership would have nurtured a more socially progressive unionism, evident in Left-led unions such as the United Packinghouse Workers (UPWA); the International Union of Mine, Mill, and Smelter Workers; and the Food, Tobacco, and Agricultural Workers Union. The UPWA established the Women's Activities Committee and Anti-Discrimination Department and pursued the placement of Black women in higher-paying jobs traditionally assigned to white workers. In postwar New York the unions with the strongest civil rights records were those led by Black leaders and those with leftist bases, including the United Electrical, Radio & Machine Workers of America and National Maritime Union. The anticommunism of the late 1940s, historian Martha Biondi argues, "undermined the dynamic Black-labor-left nexus" at the heart of New York City's postwar civil rights movement.[124] Taking heed of historian Eric Arnesen's call not to romanticize the Communist Party's civil rights work after the Popular Front, when the party pursued a "modified civil rights agenda," it still seems probable that communist laundry workers would have helped foster a more vigorous commitment to racial justice.[125] Under the LWJB's predominantly white male leadership, shorn of its communist founders, women and people of color would make only marginal gains in the 1940s, and both groups would encounter both overt and covert discrimination on the shop floor and in the union hall as they pursued their civil rights agenda.

CHAPTER NINE

"Putting Democracy into Action"

The Laundry Workers' Double V Campaign

In the summer of 1942, alongside Anna Arnold Hedgeman, who was executive director of the National Committee for a Permanent Fair Employment Practices Commission, Pauli Murray of the Workers' Defense League, and Bessie Bearden of the Housewives' League, Dollie Robinson organized the Silent Parade under the auspices of the New York Division of the March on Washington Movement (MOWM) to protest the execution of Virginia sharecropper Odell Waller by an all-white jury. The verdict, handed down after a routine disagreement between Waller and his landlord, Oscar Davis, resulted in Davis's death, garnered national attention as civil rights activists denounced a sharecropping system that locked southern African Americans into a cycle of poverty and debt, a political system that excluded Black southerners from electoral politics altogether, and a racial double standard that allowed a white man to kill a Black person with impunity. The leftist *People's Voice* reported that nearly five hundred African Americans marched in "ominous, grim silence" down the streets of Harlem to the throb of muffled drums in a nonviolent demonstration against the "violent mob acts of southerners."[1] The widespread coverage of Waller's execution owed much to the advocacy of the socialist Workers' Defense League (WDL) but was also a function of the civil rights activism of Black northerners who linked the defeat of fascism abroad with the defeat of racism at home, the goals of the Double V Campaign.

Inspired by wartime mobilizations against fascism and by the activism of Black trade union and civil rights leaders such as A. Philip Randolph, African American laundry workers would pursue their own civil rights agenda, demanding racial justice at work, in their union, and in their communities. Their civil rights unionism found expression in their support for political parties committed to economic empowerment and Black representation, in their determination to challenge the Jim Crow practices of private organizations, in their demands for a nondiscrimination clause in the union contracts, and in their insistence for the promotion of Black men into driving positions. Black workers understood that the advancement of these goals depended on their ability to win leadership positions in their union, so they continued their struggle to secure Black representation on the Laundry Workers Joint Board (LWJB). With the leaders of the "democratic initiative" at the helm, the laundry workers' wartime activism contributed to what historian Jacquelyn Dowd Hall describes as the first phase of the modern civil rights movement.[2] For Robinson and her coworkers, the war was a period of both hope and agitation as they pursued their agenda through the union, through new political parties, and through their own civil rights organizations.

Wartime Bargaining and Arbitration

The economic mobilization sparked by World War II lifted the country out of the Depression, but it would take years for Black workers to reap some of the benefits of war-induced labor shortages. This was particularly true in New York City, which was not initially home to many defense industries. In 1940 40 percent of Black New Yorkers still received some sort of relief. When defense jobs finally did become available employers hired white workers first, leaving African Americans concentrated in traditionally racialized fields such as service work and unskilled factory work. Throughout the war Black families in New York City continued to earn less than white families while being forced to pay more for inferior housing, attend the worst schools in the city, and receive the least adequate medical care. The economic boom of the war years, Cheryl Greenberg argues, did "not substantially alter Harlem's economic or social life." Nor did it lead to significant improvements in conditions in the laundries.[3]

In 1942, with wages lagging behind inflation, the union requested a cost-of-living increase. After a series of negotiations, the inside workers won a five-cent hourly increase, bringing their minimum hourly wage up to forty-one cents, or $18.45 for a forty-five-hour workweek. In contrast, drivers won an extra $5.00 a week and a minimum wage of $41.50 a week, the same as the head washers. As in the past, the arbitrators awarded the highest wage gains to the positions held by white men, who earned more than double that of their female coworkers.[4] Even when they held the same position, women continued to earn less than men. In 1942 the arbitrators awarded female shirt ironers 45.5 cents an hour and male shirt ironers 52.5 cents. Male flat-work packers won wages of 65 cents per hour, while the women were paid 52 cents. The union leadership did not contest the sex-based wage differentials, even though, as Alice Kessler-Harris points out, the equalization of wages for the same job would not have threatened the patterns of occupational segregation that protected men's higher wage-earning power.[5] In 1964 Louis Simon, by then manager of the union, complained that one of the "undesirable effects" of the National War Labor Board's (NWLB) wartime control over wages was that the gap between the highest-paid shirt finishers, a position held by both men and women, and the lowest-paid flat-work ironers, a position held by Black women, had shrunk during the war from four to two cents an hour. Simon was especially aggrieved that the reduced differentials had become permanent.[6]

Laundry workers responded to the paltry wage gains by leaving the industry altogether. Florence Rice, who had described unionization as the "salvation," seized the opportunity to work as an internal grinder at Wright Aeronautical, where she earned between eighty-five and ninety-five dollars a week.[7] Joining Rice, who described her new job as "utopia," between July 1942 and July 1943, five thousand of her coworkers left the laundries for higher-paying jobs in the manufacturing and defense sectors. An employer representative from one of the large laundry associations reported that in some plants only 20 percent of workers had been employed for more than a year. In June 1943 the United States Employment Service reported that it could fill only 18 percent of its one thousand openings in hospital laundries and firms with war contracts. Applicants refused jobs in laundries because of the "unpleasant working conditions, heavy work, [and] low rates of pay."[8]

Evidence suggests that despite their higher wage-earning power, men, who enjoyed greater employment opportunities, left the laundries first. The proportion of New York State's laundry workers who were women rose during the war from 57 percent to 62 percent. The proportion of workers who were Black also increased as African American women eager to escape domestic service replaced white laundry workers as they moved into higher-paying manufacturing or defense jobs.[9] The high turnover rates and labor shortages came at a particularly inconvenient moment for the employers, as the influx of married women into the workforce increased the demand for laundry services. In New York City the exodus also led to a sharp decrease in union membership from close to thirty thousand at the war's start to twenty thousand by the war's end.[10]

In January 1943 the NWLB approved an arbitration decision to raise the laundry workers' wages by 3.5 cents. The NWLB ruled that the national wage freeze order did not apply to the "low-paid" laundry industry and its mostly Black workers, a ruling that explicitly linked the laundry's low wages to its racialized workforce. Union leaders, who urged the workers to respect the no-strike pledge, organized labor's voluntary agreement to forgo work stoppages during the war in exchange for government support and maintenance of membership clauses that compelled workers in unionized workplaces to automatically become dues-paying members, conceded that wartime wage gains did not "permit some of our members to live as they would like to live, or as we would like them to live."[11] Even tobacco workers, a traditionally low-wage group of workers, earned more than the laundry workers.[12]

Following in the path of its parent organization and eager to stem the exodus from the industry, in 1942 the LWJB established a benefit fund, which was administered jointly through the union and employers' associations and financed through employer payroll contributions, set originally at 1 percent to rise to 2 percent in 1946. Workers who were ill received up to six dollars a week for twelve weeks, and new mothers received maternity benefits of twenty-five dollars. Laundry workers eagerly availed themselves of the new benefits. In the first year of the fund's operation, one thousand workers filed claims, mostly for sick benefits. An additional thirty-eight workers filed for maternity benefits and thirty-two for death benefits. Three out of every four of the claimants were female, and the average age of disabled and ill claimants was forty-one. By 1945 the fund had paid out $200,000 in benefits.[13]

The Laundry Workers Launch Their Double V Campaign

The laundry workers' battle for equitable treatment and fair wages took on new meaning during the war as Black men joined a racially segregated armed forces and as Black people everywhere contributed to the domestic efforts to defeat fascism. Laundry workers were inspired by and would contribute to the civil rights organizing sparked by the glaring contradiction between the nation's antifascist commitments and its treatment of Black people at home. In 1941 A. Philip Randolph, president of the Brotherhood of Sleeping Car Porters, organized the MOWM to protest the exclusion of Black workers from defense jobs and racial segregation in the armed forces. The prospect of one hundred thousand African Americans marching on Washington convinced President Roosevelt to issue Executive Order 8802, which banned discrimination in companies with defense contracts and established the Fair Employment Practice Committee (FEPC) to enforce its mandate. As a result of the order, the percentage of war workers who were Black jumped from 3 percent in 1942 to 8 percent in 1944. At the municipal level, New York City councilman and Black civil rights activist Adam Clayton Powell Jr. convinced Mayor La Guardia to order private companies with city contracts to hire Black workers.[14]

Laundry workers who had long been fighting racist treatment harnessed the wartime rhetoric of democracy to demand equal treatment for all African Americans. At a flag ceremony at Harlem's Carolyn Laundry in honor of the one thousand laundry workers serving in the armed forces, Noah Walter insisted that "part of the fight on the home front is to see to it that democracy is put into action." Laundry workers cheered when Walter, who served on the MOWM's

National Committee, demanded that the FEPC be made permanent so that the "returning soldier must know that his fight has not been in vain." Trinidadian-born laundry activist Roy Soden, a rising star in the union, urged the workers "to dedicate themselves to the creation of a greater degree of freedom, equality and democracy for these boys to come back home to."[15]

Soden had been working in laundries since moving to New York City in 1927. He worked as a packer, assistant washer, and classifier at the National Laundry in Harlem, where Jessie Taft Smith worked in the early 1930s. Soden helped organize the National, and in 1938 the union appointed him head of the recently founded LWJB employment office. In 1940 members of his Local 300 elected him business agent and in 1942 trade manager of the local. During the war Soden advocated for the equal treatment of Black workers in the union and joined the left-wing American Labor Party, where he represented Black aspirations for political and civil rights.[16]

Laundry workers' civil rights unionism could be seen most clearly in their response to the American Red Cross's blood drive. In 1941 the LWJB organized a blood drive for the American Red Cross that, under orders from the War Department, excluded the blood of Black donors. Protests from labor and civil rights organizations convinced the American Red Cross to begin taking blood from African Americans in January 1942, but only on a segregated basis. Robinson, who alongside Bessie Hillman and Amalgamated Clothing Workers of America (ACWA) leader Esther Peterson served on a national committee to promote the drive, argued that it was "one of the hardest assignments" she ever got because of the workers' reluctance to donate under the racist policy. Black laundry workers were not alone in their reluctance to give blood under the segregated policy. As historian Thomas Guglielmo argues, opposition to the racist policy went beyond civil rights organizations and leaders to include prominent physicians and scientists, African American actors, screenwriters and poets, interracial neighborhood councils and Black sororities and fraternities, among others.[17] It was Adelmond, though, and not Robinson, who led the public charge against the policy. Anna Hedgeman vividly remembered that in the middle of a meeting of labor and civil defense leaders, "suddenly, Charlotte Adelmond, the founder of the Laundry Workers Union in New York, a sturdy, thoughtful and dedicated unionist, rose and said: 'I will give no blood to the war effort and will not appeal to my workers to give until the practice of the segregation of Negro blood is stopped.'" After a moment of dead silence a white trade unionist asked Adelmond what she would say to an army brother in North Africa dying from lack of blood. Adelmond stood up, raised her head high, and responded: "If that happens, at least I will know that he died for democracy." Hedgeman recalled that the "meeting ended on that note. What could anyone say?"[18] Adelmond, who argued that the blood policy rested on the "same line of thinking that had given rise to Hitler," insisted that the "political power of the entire labor movement should have been brought to bear to correct this injustice to some of their members." The activist leader understood that racism and Nazism sprang from the same insidious roots (the Nazis had in fact consulted American race laws on segregation, racial purity, and interracial marriage to draft the Nuremberg Laws) and was shocked and dismayed when her fellow laborites failed to oppose a policy that undermined the dignity of Black Americans everywhere.[19] Defeating Hitler required eradicating the racist American jurisprudence and practices that had inspired the drafters of the Nuremberg Laws and that maintained white supremacy at home.

Anticipating the sociological arguments used by the NAACP to challenge segregation in public schools, Adelmond also emphasized the psychological damage the blood policy inflicted on Black children, pointing out that blood segregation placed a "stigma of inferiority . . . on an unborn generation of Negroes." "No self-respecting group," Adelmond concluded, "could be expected to accept such a policy, regardless of the cost or consequence."[20] A militant Garveyite and Black nationalist, Adelmond insisted that Black Americans would not subordinate their demands for equal treatment and dignity to the larger imperative of winning the war.

While Adelmond led the public charge against the racist blood policy, Robinson used her relationships with influential whites to work behind the scenes to effect change. Robinson asked Bessie Hillman, who was heading the drive, to take up the policy with the American Red Cross's national office in Washington. Hillman at first declined, but Robinson held her ground, telling Hillman that if she took on the cause, she would be considered a "martyr." When Hillman left for Washington Robinson did not know if she was going to raise the issue. It was only later when she read the minutes from the meeting that she discovered that Hillman had indeed challenged the policy, a testament to Robinson's persuasiveness and Hillman's commitment to racial justice.[21] The interaction between the two women illuminates the role of interracial friendships and liberal whites in the battle against Jim Crow.

In 1942 Robinson responded to a call from her friend Pauli Murray, who was working for the socialist WDL to organize the Silent Parade for Odell Waller. By 1942 Waller had been executed, found guilty of murder by an all-white jury selected from poll tax rolls. The march, organized out of WDL founder A. Philip Randolph's office, was intended to highlight the hypocrisy of asking Black people to support a war for democracy when they were denied basic political rights at home.[22] Murray, who organized the march, put Robinson in charge of recruiting Black workers. According to Maida Springer, it was Robinson who recognized the importance of including "young people and trade union people" in the march. With Robinson and Murray at the helm, hundreds of protestors marched down 14th Street chanting "Jim Crow has got to go." Springer recalls that during the parade the "tall and strapping" Robinson held the center of a large white banner that read "Jim Crow Has Got to Go," while she and the slightly built Murray, sporting her trademark cropped hair and white sailor pants, held the ends of the banner. The march highlighted New York's emergence as an early locus of the civil rights movement and solidified the bonds between Robinson, Adelmond, Springer, and Murray, bonds that helped sustain their activism.[23] Robinson and Adelmond would turn to this Black female activist network in 1949 when they faced the most serious threat to their leadership.

In 1944 at the workers' urging, the LWJB passed a resolution calling on the federal government to make the FEPC permanent and to provide adequate funds so that it could continue its important work. Not content to wait for government action, the workers demanded that the LWJB enact the principles of fair employment by negotiating the inclusion of a nondiscrimination clause in the laundry contracts and by securing the removal of the requirement that the workers include their race and color on employment registration cards, a practice that the workers argued made it easy for employers to maintain "lily white workforces." The union secured the elimination of the racial ID question but failed to secure a nondiscrimination clause in the agreements.[24]

Acutely aware of the need to protect and advance their economic and civil rights through electoral politics as well as union activism, laundry workers were among the earliest and most vocal supporters of New York State's American Labor Party (ALP), founded in 1936 by garment unionists, including Sidney Hillman and Rose Schneiderman, as well as liberal Democrats and socialists. (The party would also gain the support of the communist party, which in 1941 under Stalin officially joined the Allies in the war.) As well as supporting Roosevelt and prolabor candidates, the ALP served as a vehicle for Black workers determined to increase their political power.[25] Robinson, who served as treasurer of the ALP's Brooklyn wing, explained that she became politically active "because of the organization of the American Labor Party." While criticizing the party for not having more Black people in leadership positions, Adam Clayton Powell Jr. nonetheless insisted that the ALP offered "the Negro his last chance to come into his own in the political life of America."[26] A 1940 article in the ACWA newspaper, *The Advance,* reported that "with deep conviction of what the New Deal had meant to them," hundreds of laundry workers canvassed for Roosevelt and joined local ALP clubs, where they served as officers and rang doorbells for prolabor candidates.[27]

Determined to represent their own interests, Black laundry workers ran for office as ALP candidates. In 1940 Noah Walter ran as an ALP candidate from the Twenty-First District in Harlem for the New York State Assembly. The *New York Amsterdam News* reported that the laundry workers "pledged their whole-hearted support" for the popular union leader.[28] Six years later, Roy Soden, described by the leftist *People's Voice* as "destined to become the Adam Powell of the Bronx," ran on an ALP ticket as the Bronx's first Black congressional candidate. Although Soden lost the election, he polled an impressive twenty-four thousand votes, a turnout that Louis Simon attributed to the laundry workers who had actively supported his campaign. (Soden also enjoyed the support of a group of Black ministers, who organized churchgoers to vote for Soden and Black veteran Chester Addison.) As Martha Biondi argued, the inroads made by Black ALP candidates increased the influence of African Americans in the Democratic Party and revealed the fluidity and independence of Black political thought and activism in the mid-twentieth century. Far from being politically disengaged or unsophisticated, overwhelmed by the burdens of wage labor, African American laundry workers made careful political decisions about where and how to expend their precious time and resources.[29]

Black Patriotism and Self-Determination

While Black laundry workers challenged the American Red Cross's racist blood policy and demanded equal opportunities at work, white laundry and garment leaders downplayed the severity of racial discrimination on the home front and within the segregated armed forces. A 1943 article in *The Advance* entitled "The Negro's Stake in American Victory" instructed Black workers to support the war in order to preserve the "undeniable progress" they had enjoyed since emancipation. The article contrasted Hitler's abhorrent racial policies to the protection Black Americans enjoyed under the US government, a contrast that pointedly omitted the widespread racial violence that Black Americans experienced, including both lynchings and police brutality.[30] Only six months after the article's publication, a white police officer in Harlem shot Black soldier Robert Bandy after he intervened in the arrest of a Black woman. The shooting sparked a race riot that resulted in six deaths and injuries and arrests of close to a thousand mostly African American people. The 1943 Harlem riot came on the heels of a race riot in Detroit that left thirty-four dead, twenty-five of whom were African American, the consequence of the racial tensions exploding across the country over housing and job competition, continued anti-Black police brutality, and the pervasive mistreatment of Black soldiers.[31] White union officials' portrayal of racism as a minor inconvenience that would be eliminated with the passage of time belied the experiences of Black Americans and underlined the distance between a leadership that prioritized winning the war over securing equality at home and activist Black laundry workers demanding immediate action.

Even as they criticized racist practices like the blood drive, African American laundry workers actively supported the war effort. In 1942 the workers assessed themselves 10 percent of one week's pay and in 1943 10 percent of eight hours' pay for the war effort. (Lackluster wage gains likely contributed to the workers' decision to donate less in 1943.) The LWJB conducted a Buy a Bomber drive to raise money for the construction of a bomber plane. The War Savings Staff of the US Treasury Department allowed the laundry workers to name the aircraft they helped fund, since the LWJB was the only union to raise money on an industry-wide basis. Laundry workers raised a stunning $548,000, surpassing their original goal of $300,000. The union recognized Adelmond, a member of the Bomber Committee, where she served alongside other Black workers, including Odell Clark and Myrtle Toppin, as one of the top fundraisers for the plane.[32]

As education director, Robinson launched a book drive for the armed forces. Laundry workers canvassed Harlem housewives, and drivers picked up and delivered the donated books to the New York Public Library. By April 1943 the union had collected four thousand books for the troops.[33] The workers' participation and leadership in home front mobilizations such as the book drive reignited their demands for greater representation on the LWJB.

In 1943 the democratic initiative demanded that the ACWA appoint a Black person to head the union. ACWA leaders acquiesced. It is probable that white garment officials feared the potential for unrest should they deny the workers' request, given the recent activism of worker leaders, including Adelmond and Soden. It is also possible that the 1943 Harlem race riot, which saw Black people of all ages and social classes attack white property and symbols of white power and privilege, prompted the garment leaders' cooperation.[34] To accommodate the workers' demands, the ACWA chose Walter, by then a married man with a seven-year-old child, as manager. Instead of allowing Walter to independently lead the union, however, for the first time ever the ACWA appointed a comanager, garment official William Baron, the sitting manager of the LWJB, to serve alongside Walter.[35] We know little of what transpired next between the two men except that Walter's tenure as comanager was short-lived. Barely six months into his appointment, Walter accepted a position with the New York State Industrial Board. The *New York Amsterdam News* reported that the position came with an annual salary of $8,500, making Walter the highest-paid Black person to ever serve under a New York State administration. Walter told the newspaper that he had originally intended to decline the offer, despite the handsome wage, explaining that after twenty-five years of active service in organized labor he could not imagine leaving the movement, but leave he did. ACWA officials and to a lesser extent Walter framed the move as a promotion, but Black workers asked: "Why did they kick Noah Walter out and upstairs when he was demanding justice for all?" A group of workers reported to the *New York Amsterdam News* that Walter had been pushed out of the union because the leadership did not want to see a Black person poised to become the sole head of the union.[36] Three years later, in his greeting to the union on its tenth anniversary, Walter, who was by then commissioner of the state's Compensation Board, was more sanguine, praising the union for its achievements while noting that our victory "has not always been smooth. Nor is the way of life!"[37] Walter's philosophical greeting masked what must have been deep disappointment that he was never able to lead the union he helped found.

With Walter gone, there was no one at the very top to defend the principles of interracial unionism. In 1944 the engineers and maintenance workers requested permission to form a separate local. The men—all of whom were white—explained that as "highly skilled craftsmen" who were the "heart of the union" and the "life-blood" of the industry their needs were not being served by an organization that included the "mangle girl" and the "wringer man"—a thinly veiled racist and sexist attack on the women and people of color in the laundries. The men expressed their outrage that unskilled and presumably Black workers served as business agents negotiating on the men's behalf. ACWA leaders quickly complied, and Laundry Maintenance Men's Local 446, representing one thousand white engineers and maintenance men, was born.[38] The formation of the engineers' local demonstrated that at least some white workers remained unconvinced of the benefits of industrial unionism and were unwilling to organize with workers they considered occupationally and socially inferior. It also reveals that top union leaders were no longer willing to intervene in defense of the industrial union project and in defense of racial and gender solidarity as they had in 1939, when Walter convinced the leadership to deny the drivers' request to form a separate local.

A Rank-and-File Upsurge?

By 1945 laundry workers who had once greeted unionization as the salvation were angry and disappointed that their activism had not resulted in better working conditions or the elimination of the racist practices that kept Black workers confined to the lowest-paying positions in the industry. In 1945, when the contracts came up for negotiation, the workers demanded a ten-cent cost-of-living increase and the promotion of Black men into the top position of head driver. Soden lambasted the employers for refusing to "part with the excess profit" they had made during the war or to promote Black men to the highest-paid jobs. The laundry activist also warned that the workers' "patience had reached the limit."[39] Black unionists described a deep-rooted "restlessness in the shops" and predicted that the workers would soon join the seven million other American workers who had struck between 1942 and 1945 in defiance of the no-strike pledge and the directives of their union leaders.[40]

In the face of an impending rank-and-file upsurge, the ACWA brought in Vice President Frank Rosenblum to take over negotiations and pleaded with the workers to give the union an additional two weeks to secure an agreement. Adelmond was one of four women to serve on the thirty-five-member negotiating committee. The workers reluctantly agreed to wait but in the meantime formed "vacation committees" to coordinate "extended vacations" in the event that their demands were not met.[41]

Alarmed by the grassroots mobilization, in December 1945 the employers agreed to a new contract. Inside workers won a minimum hourly wage of 60.5 cents and a 10 percent wage increase up to a maximum of 10 cents an hour, and the drivers and their helpers (all men) won a $4.00 wage increase. The contract included a provision to create a joint committee to consider the drivers' "problems" and to "take such action as is mutually agreed on."[42] ACWA officials described the agreement as a "miracle," although of course it was far less than that. Not only had Rosenblum failed to secure the minimum hourly wage of sixty-five cents he had formerly described as the "absolute minimum," but the contract did not include seniority rights that would have enabled Black men to ascend to the highest-paying positions in the industry. As in the past, the largest wage gains applied to the positions held exclusively by white men, whose monopoly over those positions remained unchallenged.[43] And in fact in 1945 the union leadership would actively work with management to maintain these traditional gender-based wage differentials. A 1945 internal union memo requested that the employers give all new male hires an additional five cents so that "the relationship between male and female workers remain substantially unchanged."[44]

World War II represented a period of both opportunity and frustration for the laundry workers, who took inspiration from and contributed to the dynamic civil rights unionism animating the urban North a decade before Rosa Parks launched an uprising that toppled Jim Crow. The laundry workers' civil rights unionism found expression in their support for the American Labor Party, in their determination to challenge the Jim Crow practices of organizations such as the American Red Cross, in their demand that Black men be promoted to the position of driver, and in their insistence that the government promote equality of opportunity through the continuation of the FEPC. Black workers understood that advancing these goals depended on winning leadership positions on the LWJB, and both during and after the war they would continue their battle for self-determination.

CHAPTER TEN

"Everybody's Libber"

The Laundry Workers' Postwar Civil Rights Unionism

The immediate postwar years saw significant turmoil in the Laundry Workers Joint Board, the result of competitive pressures in the industry, an employer offensive, and internal conflict between the leadership and members of the "democratic initiative," the Black activist faction. The racial tensions that had animated the union since its birth exploded in the late 1940s as work contracted and as Louis Simon, the secretary treasurer of the LWJB, consolidated his power over the union. Rank-and-file workers accused the ACWA-appointed managers and Simon of failing to enforce the contracts and of engaging in dictatorial and racist practices toward the majority Black and Puerto Rican workforce. Frustrated by the union's failure to win meaningful gains at the bargaining table or pursue a civil rights agenda, Black laundry workers intensified their battle for racial justice and union democracy. Charlotte Adelmond pursued her civil rights agenda by demanding that the employers comply with the agreements and that the union enforce the workers' rights through arbitration; by publicly confronting the leadership for engaging in racist and sexist practices; and by organizing through her local, where the workers demanded racial justice at home and for people of color abroad fighting colonialism. Dollie Robinson supported and nurtured the workers' activism through educational initiatives; by building alliances with labor and civil rights activists, including the indomitable congressman Adam Clayton Powell Jr.; by mentoring workers of color; and by founding and supporting organizations that enabled Black women to advance their race, class, and gender interests.

An examination of Adelmond's and Robinson's postwar organizing illuminates the complex ways in which Black working-class women organized at the intersection of multiple positionalities, a reflection of the simultaneity of race, class, and gender oppression in their lives, as well as their location within and commitment to diverse goals and movements. As activists, Robinson and Adelmond employed an intersectional and fluid approach to organizing, which Robinson articulated as a refusal to identify with one ideology or one movement to the exclusion of all others. Robinson explained that "I never was one 'ism' or the other. . . . Since sometimes that 'ism' was saying what I wanted to have said, and sometimes the other 'ism' said what I had to say."[1] The women's multifaceted activism and commitment to eradicating all forms of discrimination contributed to the burgeoning civil rights movement; to the mid-twentieth-century working-class women's movement; and to organized labor, which was quickly approaching its zenith.

Postwar Pains in the Laundry Industry

While many sectors of the economy soared in the postwar period, the result in part of unprecedented levels of peacetime military spending, the laundry industry faced serious challenges as a result of the proliferation of home washing machines and laundrettes. Large companies such as Maytag launched aggressive advertising campaigns that portrayed power laundries as the repositories of other people's dirt—"other people" meaning both customers and workers. Home washing machines had come on the market as early as the 1920s, and significant numbers of Americans owned them, often purchased on credit, by the 1940s. The decision to bring the work back into the home, Arwen Mohun argues, reflected American consumers' preference for privacy and a "clearer delineation of public and private." It also meant that laundry work was one of the few domestic chores to leave the home only to return there less than fifty years later. In New York City, competition came primarily in the form of launderettes and coin-operated washing machines installed in the apartment houses where most city residents lived.[2]

On the heels of Noah Walter's hasty 1944 departure from the union, in 1946 Black workers demanded that the ACWA appoint a Black person to head the union. Garment officials acquiesced and chose Trinidadian Roy Soden and Joe Gentile (who was white) as comanagers of the union. Like Soden, Gentile was part of the 1937 group that had helped found the union. After serving as a shop chairman for Local 327, Gentile joined the LWJB as sergeant-at-arms, and in 1942 he was elected president. The ACWA placed the two laundry workers under the supervision of Frank Rosenblum, the general secretary treasurer of the ACWA, thus maintaining the practice of having a white male garment official at the head of the union.[3]

Under Soden and Gentile, the union initiated an organizing campaign among workers employed in the Chinese-owned power laundries not yet under union contracts. Within seven months, the managers reported that the organizers—all men—had brought most of the workers into the union. Soden and Gentile revived the Stabilization Committee to ensure the vigorous enforcement of contracts and promised to provide the workers with "maximum protection" by sending cases to arbitration and by continuing to organize new laundries.[4] The comanagers oversaw the negotiation of a cost-of-living increase that saw the minimum wage for inside female workers rise from 60.5 cents per hour to 66.6 cents. The union heralded the new agreement as a victory, but in the same year the New York Labor Department reported that 78 percent of women laundry workers earned less than what was required to maintain an adequate standard of living.[5]

Despite the managers' active organizing program, after Soden and Gentile had spent only a year in office, the ACWA removed them from their positions, citing corruption allegations made by the Chinese Hand Laundry Alliance (CHLA). In the spring of 1947 CHLA officials accused the managers and other top laundry officials of taking bribes from an unspecified group of Chinese power laundry owners. According to the CHLA, the laundry unionists had collaborated with the Chinese power laundry owners to prevent the CHLA from opening its own power laundry, which would have competed with the existing Chinese-owned power laundries for business. The ACWA intervened and dismissed five lower-ranking union officials and at the same time removed Soden and Gentile from office.[6] Reports of the comanagers' removal in *The Advance* offered few details, noting only and rather paternalistically that the discovery of "irregularities" had led the ACWA to remove Soden and Gentile for the "protection and welfare of the members." The garment union appointed Sander Genis, ACWA vice president and manager of the ACWA Minnesota Joint Board, to head the union.[7]

Genis quickly provoked the ire of the workers when in 1947 he extended the existing contract by three years through a supplemental agreement. The workers won an additional day of paid holidays and a minimum wage increase, from $24.20 a week to $25.25 for family service workers and $25.80 for linen supply workers. Instead of taking the agreement to the membership for a vote, Genis allowed a handful of delegates and LWJB officers to vote on it. The group, all men, unanimously approved the agreement. An article in *The Advance* reported that in the meeting where LWJB officials announced the new agreement, only one business agent complained. Genis dismissed the sole critic, likely Adelmond, and reminded the workers that "directions must come from the manager," explicit acknowledgment of the union's hierarchical structure.[8]

In the same meeting during which Genis announced the new agreement, he also promised to open an office in Harlem so that the union could more effectively handle employer requests for workers. It took too long, Genis explained, for employment requests to be processed through the union's downtown headquarters on Fifth Avenue.[9] The announcement begs the question, Why, in a union with a majority Black membership, was there not already an office in Harlem, where many of the city's laundries were located and where many of the workers lived? The opening of a Harlem office also reveals that top union leaders accepted as natural and inevitable the recruitment of Black workers to fill the mostly low-wage and difficult jobs in the laundries.

A Postwar Social Accord?

As business declined in the late 1940s, the result of competition from laundrettes and to a lesser extent home washing machines, some of New York's laundry owners refused to abide by the existing contracts, and many new plants refused to sign agreements at all. In 1947 the union reported that the Compliance Department had received a total of 7,804 complaints about contract violations since the union's founding. While most of the early complaints involved cases of unfair discharge, often as a result of union activity, later complaints indicated a growing refusal among employers to pay the agreed-upon rate or give the workers the holiday pay to which they were entitled. Sixty percent of the cases went to the impartial chairs after mediation through the Compliance Department failed.[10] In 1948, when the union reopened contract negotiations, citing an increase in the cost of living, the employers balked at the union's request for a fifteen-cent hourly wage increase and for the first time ever disputed the impartial chair's right to make a ruling. The impartial chairs rejected the challenge and awarded the workers a 10 percent wage increase, a very modest victory for the union.[11]

In the face of new competitive pressures, laundry owners revived old defenses, insisting that they would be bankrupted if they were forced to pay the workers the union rate, overtime, or holiday pay. Some employers refused to pay the drivers the minimum wage on the grounds that the men received tips, which they did not share with the firm. Foremen reintroduced the speedups of the preunion days, and some of the workers became ill from the unreasonable production quotas. When the workers in one laundry complained the boss called in the police.[12]

In the mid- and late 1940s laundry workers complained that the impartial chair, Herman Brickman, the former representative of one of the large employers' associations, took months to hand down decisions, if at all. Even the union's top leaders, perpetual cheerleaders of impartial arbitration, admitted that there were significant delays in decisions and that the arbitration machinery was not functioning as it should.[13]

In 1947 Adelmond, with the help of civil rights lawyer Pauli Murray (the two women most likely met through Robinson and Maida Springer, friends of Murray), compiled a list of rulings that demonstrated Brickman's proemployer bias, a bias that dated back to at least 1942. The fifty-page report revealed that Brickman refused to award complainants back pay in cases where the employer had failed to pay the union wage, a practice that encouraged employers to violate the agreements so that they could save money while the union filed a grievance. The memo included letters to the managers from workers irate over what they perceived as the union's inability or unwillingness to compel the impartial chair to uphold their union rights.[14] The letters suggest that the laundry workers saw up close some of the shortcomings of grievance arbitration. As labor scholars such as Dan Clawson and Robert Zieger argue, grievance arbitration enabled workers to express their discontent and demand accountability from their employers, but in a legalistic way that left them dependent on professional staff and arbitrators. The locus of conflict, Zieger and Gilbert Gall argue, shifted from the shop floor to hearing rooms, where lawyers and bureaucrats determined the outcome. The 1947 passage of the Taft-Hartley Act, which narrowed the range of permissible union tactics, hastened this legal turn.[15] In the laundry industry, grievance arbitration left the workers dangerously dependent on staff and union leaders who proved unable or unwilling to effectively address delays in arbitration and, even more problematically, a potentially biased impartial chair.

As the workers' frustration grew, ACWA and LWJB officials urged patience, telling the workers that any disagreements or misunderstandings with the employers or arbitrators would be resolved in a matter of time. Genis noted that it had taken the garment workers twenty-five years to establish a mutually beneficial relationship with their employers. "What is possible in the garment trade," Genis explained, "is not yet possible in the laundry trade."[16] Top union officials pointed to the benefit fund as a shining example of what the workers gained through union membership. But the workers complained that it took months to receive the insurance payments, if at all. Adelmond pointed out that babies were walking before the plan paid out maternity benefits. She was particularly critical of the union's refusal to take dues from members who were laid off for more than four months (in 1948 the union reported 132 unemployed workers), a practice that rendered them ineligible for sick or death benefits and deprived them of the rights and privileges of union membership.[17]

Union leaders tried to shore up the LWJB's dwindling membership by launching new organizing drives and targeting new groups, including office workers and employees in laundrettes. In 1948 the LWJB chartered Laundry Office and Clerical Workers Local 548. The decision to charter a separate local for the all-white female office staff represented a stunning rejection of the industrial unionism that had brought the organization into existence in 1937. In 1950 the union launched a second campaign to organize "laundry store girls" and employees of launderettes and in October established Local 596 for these workers.[18] The organizing campaigns, which did little to address shop floor conditions, elicited the wrath of the employers. In November 1950 the LWJB reported that some of the employers had used "terrorist methods" to hamper the union's organizing drive in South Brooklyn and noted that LWJB member and engineer Gerald Peters had been attacked near his home by the "hirelings of some non-union firms."[19]

The virulent antiunionism of at least some of New York's laundrymen reveals that the laundry workers did not benefit from a postwar labor-management accord or "social contract" under which the employers accepted the union and bargained in good faith in exchange for labor stability and industrial peace. While historians such as Nelson Lichtenstein debate whether such an accord ever existed, noting the high postwar levels of employer antiunionism and worker militancy (strike levels in the 1940s and 1950s, for example, remained high), New York's laundry owners were certainly not operating under the assumptions of an accord when they challenged basic union rights like arbitration.[20] Yet, confronted with the employers' increasingly aggressive antiunion tactics, industry-conscious garment and laundry officials urged the workers to respect the collective agreement and resolve disputes through an admittedly flawed arbitration system. For laundry and some other low-wage service and industrial service workers, many of whom were female and workers of color, employer antiunionism and the conciliatory tactics of union leaders (often white and male) meant that the 1950s and 1960s were not a "fabled golden age" when union membership catapulted them into the growing middle class. In the laundry industry, with its deeply entrenched gender- and race-based occupational hierarchies and wage scales, women and people of color, who constituted more than two-thirds of the workforce, bore the brunt of the postwar employer offensive.[21]

The Fight for Equality

In the postwar era, top garment and laundry leaders accepted and in fact actively worked to maintain the laundry's traditional occupational divisions and wage disparities. In 1949 the union and several employers' associations signed a memo regarding minimum wage rates that stipulated that "the traditional male-female wage differentials are to be maintained but not *publicized*" (italics added). The emphasis on discretion was likely the result of the 1944 passage of New York State's Equal Pay Law. The law, secured through the advocacy of workers, the WTUL, and the CIO, among others, banned wage differentials based on sex. (It allowed, however, differentials based on seniority, experience, skill, ability, and a number of other broad and often subjective criteria.) When the Equal Pay Bureau, tasked with enforcing the law, discovered in 1948 that at least two-thirds of employers were unaware of the law, the bureau launched a public education campaign, promoting the Equal Pay Law through radio programs and lectures to women's clubs and civic groups.[22] It was perhaps because of this campaign that in 1949 an internal LWJB document labeled "Discussion Points" for the upcoming contract negotiations included as a goal the elimination of sex-based rate differentials. Yet despite this stated objective, the 1950 contract included sex-based wage differentials in every single job classification in which both women and men worked, ranging from 5 to 7.5 cents an hour. Female folders were to be paid 75 cents an hour, and male folders 82 cents an hour. To bypass the Equal Pay Law, the union and management inserted the clause that men and women employed in the same classification did not perform the "same quantity and/or quality of work." Adelmond angrily concluded that "discrimination because of sex has persisted in the industry because the Management of the Joint Board has been lax in insisting upon compliance by employers with the Equal Pay Law."[23]

The benefit fund, administered by Louis Simon, also included differentials based on sex. In 1946 the union secured sick and accident benefits of twelve dollars a week for men and eight dollars a week for women. Knowing that the majority female workforce would never support such a differential, union leaders instructed the business agents not to call attention to the gap at the upcoming ratification meeting. Self-described as "a woman, knowing the facts," Adelmond was so incensed that she wrote to ACWA vice president Frank Rosenblum about the hardship that the differential imposed on women laundry workers, many of whom were the sole supporters of their families. As Adelmond well understood, the ideal of the male breadwinner model upon which such differentials rested—an ideal that enjoyed a resurgence in postwar America as women were urged to return to the home—had never been an unattainable if desirable goal for Black families. Adelmond noted, moreover, that the employer paid the 2 percent contribution to the fund regardless of the recipient's sex and informed Rosenblum of a recent Women's Bureau study that found that only 3 of the 168 unions in New York with benefit funds differentiated on the basis of sex. Must our union, Adelmond asked Rosenblum, be one of the minority? The issue, Adelmond insisted, was a question of "moral justice to our women unionists."[24] Like the union feminists in the Steelworkers' Union about whom sociologist Mary Fonow writes, Adelmond refused to deploy strategic arguments about lower-paid women workers replacing men, an argument that appealed to men's economic interests; instead, she insisted that women be paid the same as men as a matter of equity, fairness, and justice.[25]

Adelmond understood that equity arguments alone would not sway the leadership. At a moment when the nation was moving to the right—by 1946 the Republican Party had gained control of both Houses of Congress, the first time since 1930—Adelmond argued that labor needed women's support—half of the electorate—as a "bulwark against the fascist and nazi hoards that are beginning to sweep the country."[26] The activist business agent argued that racism and sexism undermined the moral legitimacy of the union movement and gave the "demagogues and rabble rousers material to knife us with." But despite Adelmond's careful framing of the issue, Rosenblum refused to intervene. When the workers discovered the differential the union instructed the business agents to advise members that they had voted for the contract. In 1950 the union continued to pay women four dollars less than men for sick benefits.[27]

With Adelmond's support, in 1948 a group of Black men led by the aptly named Langston Rivers applied to become drivers. Adelmond demanded that the manager, Sander Genis, arrange a conference with the employers to discuss the men's request. At the same time she informed Genis that the employers' refusal to hire Black men as drivers violated New York State's 1945 Law against Discrimination in Employment. The Fair Employment Practice Committee (FEPC) state law, won through the grassroots advocacy and mobilization of more than fifty labor, civic, religious, political, and civil rights groups, demonstrated Black workers' success in "linking racial fairness with winning the war." The first major legal success of the postwar civil rights struggle, the antidiscrimination law was also the first US law prohibiting racial and religious discrimination in private employment, a testament, Martha Biondi argues, to African Americans' determination to build a social democratic state in New York City. The law armed militant Black workers like Adelmond with legal ammunition in their battle to secure equality in the workplace.[28] But despite the state law and despite Adelmond's advocacy, Genis refused to raise the issue with the employers. In 1950 Adelmond concluded that there was an "unwritten code" in the union that Black men were not to be hired as drivers, engineers, or maintenance men. The leadership's failure to challenge the racist hiring practices was particularly disappointing, Adelmond argued, given that garment officials had convinced the laundry workers to join the ACWA by emphasizing officials' commitment to racial justice. The CIO's egalitarian rhetoric attracted Black workers to the labor movement but provoked anger and resentment when such commitments proved superficial.[29]

While Adelmond led the charge for Black men to be promoted to the position of driver and for equal pay for equal work, what labor feminists would come to refer to as the "rate for job," she does not appear to have challenged women's exclusion from the relatively high-paying driving and machine washing positions; nor did her good friend Dollie Robinson or radical organizer Jessie Smith.[30] When asked in 2006 why only men operated the washing machines, Smith explained, "Even though I was radical, I never thought about that aspect. . . . It wasn't something I was dealing with that way." A communist organizer who fought for better working conditions for all laundry workers and racial justice for Black workers, Smith admits that she never questioned the organization of laundry work into men's and women's jobs or the devaluation of the jobs assigned to women.[31] Karen Pastorello notes a similar response among female activists in the ACWA and argues that women garment leaders accepted the sexual division of labor "because they perceived it in terms of craft divisions where women's competition with men was minimal." The sex-segregated labor force, Alice Kessler-Harris elaborates, "encouraged women to compare their wages to those of other women . . . a process that tended to limit aspirations for higher wages to what appeared possible." Like the labor feminists described by Dorothy Sue Cobble, women laundry activists "imagined ending gender hierarchies without necessarily ending all gender differences."[32] As part of the democratic initiative, Robinson and Adelmond pursued women's advancement as part of a broader and more visible civil rights agenda centered on racial justice and union democracy. The women's gendered imaginations, the institutional constraints of the industrial union movement, and the perhaps greater salience of race in their lives shaped the form and content of their activism.[33]

It is possible, however, that had there been a more robust women's movement or feminist culture in the LWJB, as there was in some other CIO unions, Adelmond and other women unionists might have challenged the sex-segregated occupational structure. In some industries, wartime disruptions provided opportunities for union women to challenge long-standing patterns of gender segregation and discrimination.[34] Opportunities for women's activism were especially abundant, Ruth Milkman argues, in the United Auto Workers (UAW) and United Electrical (UE) Union, where the leadership hired women staffers, encouraged women unionists to pursue leadership roles, and developed educational programming focused on "women's issues."[35] In 1942 the UE, in collaboration with the UAW, won a critical case against General Motors that established the principle of equal pay as government policy. The UE, historian Lisa Kannenberg argues, went a step further by challenging the structure of job segregation. Male unionists supported these equality challenges, Milkman argues, because they needed women's support and because of the CIO's ideological commitment to egalitarianism.[36] In contrast, no such space existed during or after the war for women unionists in the LWJB, where they confronted a male leadership determined to preserve white male privilege in all its manifestations.

Louis Simon's Rise to Power and the "Democratic Initiative"

In the postwar era laundry workers attributed their poor working conditions to the leadership's willingness to "play ball" with the employers. Workers directed such complaints at ACWA-appointed officials such as Sander Genis and Frank Rosenblum, but even before Simon's ascension to the position of manager in 1950, workers targeted him, for they understood his central role in the administration of the union. Simon's rise to power was controversial. The maintenance workers described the secretary treasurer as power hungry and accused him of using underhanded and "sinister" methods to undermine the ACWA-appointed managers. Simon, the men argued, surrounded himself with "power crazed paid officers" who did his bidding.[37] In a series of articles on the laundry union, Carl Lawrence of the *New York Amsterdam News* reported that Simon's power came from his tightfisted control of the union's $2 million benefit fund and from his propensity to ensure the loyalty of handpicked officials by rewarding them with jobs and perks like access to a car, accusations also levied against Simon by the communists, whom Simon had helped eject in 1941.[38] Adelmond accused Simon of raising dues so that he could increase the number of staff jobs that could be handed out as patronage positions. She also noted that officials on the board of directors held paid union jobs in violation of an amendment adopted by the membership to prohibit such practices. Workers complained that through such practices Simon ensured that he always had a "bootsie" to support his leadership, a position that was filled by his loyal aide and future assistant manager, African American Odell Clark.[39]

Originally from Statesville, North Carolina, Clark moved with his family to New York City during the Great Depression. In 1937, while still a teenager, he took a job in a hand laundry running errands and delivering laundry for eight dollars a week. (Clark would not have been hired as a driver in a power laundry.) Because the boss expected him to be on call "anytime day or night," Clark attended high school at night as a part-time student.[40] He eventually got a job as a packer in a power laundry, where he worked seventy hours a week. A 1950 article in *The Advance* described Clark, who was part of the original 1937 group that joined the CIO and ACWA, as "just a little shaver" (colloquial for young lad) who went along with "Simon and the other sturdy leaders in their determined quest" to form a union.[41] A profile of Clark that appeared in the *New York Amsterdam News* under the more dignified title "Labor Pioneer" reported that Clark joined the union because he was "revolted" watching the women "break their backs" day and night for starvation wages and then be fired without cause by their tyrannical bosses. Laundry workers elected Clark shop chairman of Local 300 in 1938 and business agent in 1945, and in 1950 Simon would handpick him to become assistant manager.[42] Clark's allegiance to Simon gave him power in the union, but articles like the one in *The Advance* reveal his racial infantilization as just a "little shaver" who joined a group of sturdy white men in the formation of the union.

Simon consolidated his power in the 1940s by surrounding himself with supporters such as Clark and by eliminating internal opposition. Workers accused Simon of arbitrarily removing popular Black business agents and replacing them with "machine men" who were easily controlled with money. Lawrence of the

New York Amsterdam News reported that if a worker was not a "Simon man," they were going nowhere fast. To minimize rank-and-file participation in the union, Simon refused to furnish the workers with a complete set of the bylaws or to hold regular membership meetings, despite Adelmond's and the workers' repeated requests.[43] Decisions were made by the LWJB and announced to the workers. Robinson believed that this lack of democracy and transparency started with the parent union. She insisted that the laundry workers were "receivers of decisions" made by ACWA presidents and vice presidents.[44] When an unpopular decision was about to be forced on the workers, the LWJB invited the organizers and business agents to a cocktail party, where they were pressured to toe the line. Only through the secret ballot "in the true sense," Adelmond argued, would the workers be protected from such coercive tactics, tactics that were particularly effective, Adelmond also noted, because of the high labor turnover during the war, which had brought many workers inexperienced with union politics into the laundries.[45]

In response to this consolidation of power and the removal of Black officials, activist laundry workers renewed their battle to secure a top position in the union. In 1947 the LWJB's nine paid Black officials—including Adelmond, Robinson, and Clark—demanded that the ACWA allow them to elect a Black comanager or assistant manager of the union. It is likely that the group understood from experience that the ACWA would never allow a Black person to independently lead the union. The group underlined the urgency of their request by noting that the workers had for some time been expecting a high-level appointment of a representative from the "racial strain of half, or more than half, of the members" of the union. The group asked that they be allowed to choose their own representative, given that the ACWA had chosen so poorly in the past (a reference to Roy Soden). The workers explained that Soden's fall had caused them great shame, since we "share a greater disgrace when one of ours fails." Genis reluctantly agreed and told the group to choose a representative. The group chose Adelmond, the "pioneer member," but she declined, citing personal reasons.[46]

There is no explanation for Adelmond's decision, but it is likely that she understood that the garment union would refuse her appointment, and she was willing to subordinate any leadership aspirations of her own to the larger imperative of securing the top position for a Black person. White male union officials who were unlikely to have supported a Black woman for manager would certainly not have supported a known agitator who had already been suspended from the union (1940). It is also possible that Adelmond felt pressure to support a Black man, who, because of racial discrimination, did not enjoy the same patriarchal privileges and access to leadership positions as a white man.[47] Seven of the nine officials, including Robinson and Adelmond, voted for Hexton Harden, the popular business agent of Local 332; two, including Clark, voted for Clark.[48]

Harden had been working in laundries since 1927, when he arrived in New York City. He helped organize the short-lived AFL-affiliated laundry Local 135 in Brooklyn in 1935 and was a founding member of Local 300, for which he became a paid organizer. Beginning in 1938, workers elected Harden for four consecutive terms as a business agent of Local 332, and in 1943 he became trade manager of the local, a position he held in 1947, when the democratic initiative selected him to represent them on the LWJB.[49] The group reported the results to Genis, who nonetheless supported Clark. The democratic initiative accused Genis of exploiting intraracial tensions to "deprive the 85% Negro membership of the unity of action that is required to achieve their aspirations."[50] Internal power struggles, exacerbated by white union officials, compromised Black workers' capacity to achieve self-determination.

Stymied in their efforts to win representation on the LWJB, leaders of the democratic initiative pursued their civil rights agenda within their own locals. The workers' activism reflected the increasingly international outlook of Black Americans who in the 1940s linked their struggles against white supremacy at home with the independence movements being launched by people of color abroad.[51] In 1948 Adelmond's Local 327 drafted a resolution demanding that Ethiopia be recognized as one of the first victims of fascism and be given compensation from its former colonial aggressors. The resolution expressed support for Ethiopia's claim to Eritrea, without which, the workers argued, the country would remain "backward, as so often described by the Western powers." The 1935 fascist invasion of Ethiopia by Italy had produced outrage and, as African American studies scholar Eric McDuffie argues, prompted Black Americans "to see black struggles in global terms like never before." A proud Garveyite and Black nationalist, Adelmond considered pan-Africanism and international solidarity to be critical components of the global struggle against racism. Intent on publicly supporting the anticolonial struggles of their brothers and sisters abroad, Black laundry workers demanded that the Ethiopia resolution be submitted to the upcoming ACWA Biennial Convention in Atlantic City.[52]

The framing of the Ethiopia resolution underlined the workers' familiarity with the new rights discourse generated during the war. The resolution included a reference to the Atlantic Charter, the declaration of principles signed by President Roosevelt and British prime minister Winston Churchill in 1941, outlining their vision for the postwar world. Adelmond and her coworkers noted that points 3 through 7 of the charter asserted the rights of people everywhere to self-determination and freedom from fear and want, provisions the workers interpreted through their own experiences in a union that failed to secure subsistence-level wages or support Black workers' aspirations for self-determination. As historian Keisha N. Blain argues, the charter became a mobilizing tool for activists across the African diaspora, including Amy Jacques Garvey, especially after Churchill declared before British Parliament that the rights contained in the charter would not apply to people of color, evidence Blain argues of the "persistence of the twentieth-century global color line." But despite the workers' thoughtful arguments, the LWJB refused to adopt the resolution or submit it to the upcoming ACWA convention. Genis told Adelmond to "forget the Ethiopian question in New York City." At the same time, garment officials allowed resolutions in support of the Jewish victims of the Holocaust and the Italian victims of Mussolini to be read onto the convention floor and approved $1 million in donations for the United Jewish Appeal and Italian rehabilitation. Adelmond expressed her disappointment that an organization whose leadership was predominantly Jewish was unwilling to support the civil rights demands of another oppressed group. She chastised the leadership for their "selfish and narrow attitude" and utter disregard for Black workers who had asked only for an expression of support for Ethiopia and not money.[53]

Dollie Robinson's Postwar Activism

Robinson supported Adelmond and the democratic initiative's civil rights agenda through educational initiatives and political advocacy, by mentoring workers of color, and through her leadership and participation in civil rights organizations. On the heels of the organizing drive launched by Soden and Gentile in 1946, close to one thousand new workers joined the union, many of whom had little or no union experience. Robinson responded by launching a series of new classes to explain how the union functioned, including a mandatory new members' course. To make the courses more appealing she purchased a movie projector and ended each class with a movie.[54] The educational initiatives reflected Robinson's long-standing belief that an educated workforce provided the best defense against an undemocratic leadership.

The growing complexity of the collective agreements contributed to Robinson's decision to enroll part time in law school at the age of twenty-six. Robinson explained that she was so "teed off" with the lawyers for making it "hard for workers to understand" their rights that she went to law school so that she could "put those contracts into words that workers could understand." While still working for the union, she started law school at New York University in September 1943, specializing in labor law. Robinson understood that a law degree would enable her to represent the interests of the laundry workers and African Americans more broadly. She explained that "I may never earn my living as a lawyer, but we as Negroes have a great need for free legal advice." Alongside Pauli Murray, who had just finished law school at Howard University, Robinson was among a pioneering group of African American women who would put their legal skills to the service of labor, civil, and women's rights.[55]

While attending law school, Robinson married James Robinson, a fellow labor activist who worked for the Board of Education. Robinson met her future husband in the early 1940s through the union, where he worked as the Education Department's sports director. She described her husband as a "rebel" who unconditionally supported her career, including her unconventional decision to attend law school.[56] Robinson was one of only three or four women in her class, and when she graduated in 1952 she was eight months pregnant with her daughter, Jan, a condition she admits was "unusual" for a law student in those days. As Robinson did the bulk of her education work at night, the union supported her decision and took advantage of her new skills by having her fill out income tax forms for the members. Using Robinson's growing legal expertise, the union boasted that it saved members thousands of dollars in accounting fees. From 9:00 a.m. to noon Robinson went to law school and then headed to the union office to begin preparing for evening classes.[57]

Robinson attributed her ability to work full time, to attend school, and later to raise a daughter to her mother's support. The labor activist realized one day that her mother had been part of nearly every major decision Robinson had made. After her divorce from James Robinson in the early 1950s (Robinson explained that as devoted activists, she and her ex-husband were simply "too much alike"), she once again lived with her mother. Dora Lowther took Jan to her private Quaker school every morning. The two women eventually bought a brownstone on Agate Court, off of Atlantic Avenue in Bedford-Stuyvesant, where Jan Robinson lives today with her own family. Even though the trade unionist paid for the house, she insists that her mother was the "ruler of that roost." Although not a social activist herself, Lowther supported her daughter and approved of her activism, although she worried that the long hours and "hectic" pace took a toll on her daughter's health.[58]

Despite Robinson's busy schedule, the union continued to send her out on organizing jobs. When in the mid-1940s a strike broke out at a Brooklyn laundry controlled by known gangster Anthony Carfano the union dispatched Robinson to Brooklyn, where she opened the picket line every morning at 4:30 before going to school at 9:00. During the strike Robinson became friendly with some of the Italians living in the area, in particular, with a well-known storeowner known as Mama. Robinson and Mama worked out a deal whereby Robinson filled out the Italians' income tax and immigration forms, and in return the Italians opened the picket line at Carfano's laundry and collected union cards. Although she was never able to organize the plant (Robinson explained that it was a "controlled shop"), the degree of cooperation that emerged between the mostly Black women and Italians is a testament to Robinson's commitment to interracial organizing and coalition-building at the community level.[59]

In 1947 Robinson attended the CIO National Education Conference in Columbus, Ohio, where she and a group of 150 Black and white delegates staged a daylong sit-in at a coffee shop that refused to serve Robinson and three other Black delegates. Sit-ins, used by the recently formed interracial Congress of Racial Equality as a tool to desegregate public spaces, supplemented the NAACP's legal approach to dismantling Jim Crow.[60] A year later, in 1948, Robinson attended the Civil Rights Congress (CRC) in Cleveland, Ohio. Formed in 1946, the Left-led CRC continued the antiracist and legal work of the erstwhile communist-led National Negro Congress and International Labor Defense. In 1951 CRC executive director William Patterson would present the petition "We Charge Genocide" to the UN, a searing account of the racial abuses Black Americans experienced and an indictment of the US government's failure to enforce their constitutional rights.[61] Robinson reported on the CRC meeting to the LWJB, which subsequently authorized her to draft a civil rights and women's resolution committing the laundry union to supporting equality of opportunity regardless of sex, race, creed, or color.[62]

Robinson of course understood how superficial the leadership's commitment to these principles was, and so she spent much of her time mentoring workers of color, including Cecil Toppin, the future manager of the LWJB. At the urging of his mother, Myrtle Toppin, a laundry worker and union official, Cecil Toppin began working for the LWJB at the age of twenty-one. He would rise from office worker to the top position of manager in 1982, becoming the first and much-beloved Black head of the union. Toppin recalled that on his way up Robinson always had words of encouragement for him: "I remember when I was moving up the ladder and how Dollie everytime I saw her she kept telling me to hang in don't give up, it's gotta come your way. I mean Dollie encouraged people like that." Toppin distinctly recalled Robinson's determination to see a Black person leading the union. He recounted that "Dollie felt very strongly that this union shoulda been led by a Black, back in the days of 1948, 1950. And I know she had made that a part of her agenda."[63]

Robinson recalled in her 1976 oral history interview that she was particularly committed to mentoring women, who, she explained, "have a lot of confidence in me. Because I become a mother figure. I don't care if I am fifteen years old or what. I mean, because I encourage women, always."[64] Elisabeth Petry, the daughter of Robinson's close friend, activist, and author Ann Petry, insisted that Robinson's friendship and support buoyed her mother and many other women of color. Elisabeth Petry described Robinson as a role model and insisted that despite her mother's accomplished group of friends, "none of them rivaled Aunt Dollie in wielding power."[65] In 1976 the Soroptimist Club, an international organization committed to empowering women, formally recognized Robinson's lifetime commitment to mentoring women with the Women Helping Other Women Award. Robinson's mentorship of women of color was central to her civil rights unionism and reflected and drew on Afrocentric conceptions of mothering, captured in the National Association of Colored Women's motto, "Lifting as we climb."[66]

As part of her commitment to empower Black women, Robinson, alongside Petry, helped found in 1942 the Negro Women, Incorporated (NWI), an auxiliary of Congressman Adam Clayton Powell Jr.'s political action committee, the People's Committee. Organized in 1941, the People's Committee helped launch Powell's career, beginning with his 1941 election to the New York City Council, where he became the first Black councillor to ever serve.[67] In the 1940s the People's Committee organized Freedom rallies, gala pageants in Madison Square Garden, and in 1946 a Save the FEPC rally. Steeped in her own battle to win self-determination and racial justice for Black laundry workers, Robinson embraced Powell's message of Black empowerment and his rejection of the language and politics of assimilation, a position that Biondi argues presaged the Black power critique of racial liberalism. Robinson worked closely with Powell on his platform to secure better jobs and higher wages for Black workers, to eliminate police brutality, to desegregate schools, and to win support at the national level for antilynching and anti–poll tax bills. Springer recalled that Powell had great respect for Robinson and that the two activists became very close friends and allies.[68]

In the 1940s Robinson served as vice president of the NWI, based out of Powell's Abyssinian Church. Petry served as executive secretary. The organization provided space for women of color to discuss common concerns and attracted Black women from diverse socioeconomic backgrounds and ideological affiliations. The NWI hosted talks with well-known activists, including Springer, who addressed the group in 1945 about her trip to England as a US labor delegate. Robinson had arranged the talk. Future Civil Rights Congress leader Ada B. Jackson spoke to the group about the importance of voting. As scholar Katrina Caldwell notes, the NWI was the culmination of the activist work being carried out by African American women such as Robinson and Petry, race leaders committed to empowering Black women and nurturing their participation in diverse social movements.[69]

Robinson remained convinced of the importance of the political sphere to the attainment of civil and economic rights. Like Sidney Hillman, she abandoned the American Labor Party in the mid-1940s, citing the increased influence of radicals such as Vito Marcantonio, the socialist congressman from East Harlem. Robinson had long criticized the communists for their harsh tactics and "techniques of elimination," but it is also possible that she left the ALP out of fear of being associated with radical groups and activists. As the Cold War intensified, conservative and racist forces determined to stop the expansion of the New Deal and maintain white supremacy linked organized labor and civil rights with communism, a strategy that would silence many progressive activists who feared prosecution by the state or unemployment as a result of their labor and civil rights activism.[70]

As a Democrat, Robinson helped register new voters and develop the party's emerging civil rights platform. She worked closely on the campaign to secure the reappointment of Myles A. Paige to the New York Court of Special Sessions. Paige, a former officer in the renowned infantry unit known as Harlem's Hell-fighters and founder of the Harlem Lawyers' Association, had been appointed to the court by Mayor La Guardia. Robinson convinced ACWA vice president Hyman Blumberg to help coordinate labor's support for Paige's reappointment. Robinson insisted that it was Blumberg's intervention that secured a second term for the Black judge. The reappointment also, Robinson argued, demonstrated that "the labor movement was having its impact in communities [of color] because they were supporting and working there."[71] The successful campaign strengthened Robinson's commitment to forging interracial alliances between white trade union leaders and Black communities.

Black Women's Organizing at the Intersection of Race, Class, and Gender

Except for Bessie Hillman, Robinson's closest relationships were with other Black women who simultaneously organized at the intersection of race, class, and gender, demanding economic justice for all workers, racial justice for Black workers, and better treatment for women workers. Although Springer belonged to the ILGWU, and Robinson and Adelmond were members of the ACWA, the women formed a tight clique that sometimes annoyed their colleagues. In the 1940s, when ILGWU president David Dubinsky and ACWA head Sidney Hill-man were engaged in fierce ideological and jurisdictional disputes and vying for President Roosevelt's favor, Robinson, Adelmond, and Springer's close relationship made them the "curiosity of sections of the labor movement." Springer remembered that Bessie Hillman was always asking Robinson, "Diyah, you still with that Dubinskynic?" Despite the expectation that the women would be "enemies," Springer insisted, "Nothing or no one broke the relationship between the three of us." Springer served as the godmother to Robinson's daughter, Jan, and would similarly adopt Jan's husband, Melvyn McCray, a journalist, documentarian, and former producer at ABC, as her "big godson."[72]

Historian and Springer biographer Yevette Richards maintains that the relationship between the three women was based on "gender and race issues" rather than the ideological debates that were consuming the union leadership. Robinson, Adelmond, and Springer's tight friendship transcended interunion disputes and centered on their shared experiences as Black women navigating a labor movement led by white men. Springer explained, "Our base was narrow in terms of the number of Negroes who were working as staff people. We all knew one another. We attended conferences together. We attended all kinds of events together."[73] When they encountered racism or sexism on the job or in the union they turned to one another, taking solace in their shared experiences and working together to develop strategies of resistance.

The women's advocacy on behalf of women and workers of color and their participation in labor and civil rights struggles reveal the complex ways in which race, class, and gender discrimination shaped Black women's activism. In 1969 Robinson told a journalist from the *New York Times* that Black women were treated like "second-class citizens" in every movement in which they participated, including civil rights.[74] Articulating what scholars call the triple oppression or triple jeopardy of racism, classism, and sexism, Robinson explained to the *Times* that as a Black working-class woman fighting for social change she had had to "conquer a lot of territories. I always felt I represented every minority on the face of the earth. I was a black, female, low-income working person."[75] Describing herself as "everybody's libber" who refused to identify with one "ism" over the other, Robinson mused that while "that's not good for personal aggrandizement . . . it's excellent for the soul."[76] Her good friend Pauli Murray similarly insisted that she could not be "fragmented into Negro at one time, woman at another, or worker at another."[77] Black women's lived experiences at the intersection of multiple systems of oppression negated the value or possibility of organizing around a single identity or single oppression.

As women who experienced simultaneous forms of discrimination, Robinson's and Murray's battles for justice and equality were necessarily fluid and intersectional, incorporating the goals and strategies of diverse movements or "isms," in Robinson's words. But for all their similarities Murray and Robinson departed on the use of labels. While Murray called herself a feminist, Robinson adamantly rejected the label. In 1969 Robinson insisted that "I was always one woman with a lot of men in the labor movement, and I made it a point not to be a feminist. I just want equal treatment. Whatever the men get, I want."[78] Her refusal to identify with or use the term "feminist"—not uncommon among Black women—may have been strategic. As a female labor leader operating in a man's world, she may have rejected the label so as not to alienate her male colleagues.[79] It is also possible that Robinson's rejection of feminism as a descriptor of her ideology and activism may have been the result of a lack of affinity with the 1960s and 1970s women's movement, which prioritized the experiences, voices, and agenda of white middle-class women. During two interviews, one in 1969 and one in 1976, she expressed a certain alienation from a movement that, while enjoying critical working-class antecedents, did not speak to the experiences of poor women, working-class women, or women of color, among others.[80] In 1970 Black women were arguably less concerned with securing the rights of married and older women to work in industries like the airlines and Wall Street or to eat lunch at New York City's exclusive Oak Room than they were with tackling the legacy of slavery and Jim Crow, including but not limited to issues relating to poverty and economic exploitation, sexual abuse, racist policing, and lack of health care and educational opportunities. The second wave feminist analysis of employment as inherently liberating and the home and family as a site of oppression did not resonate with the lived experiences of most women of color.[81] Like the welfare rights activists, including Johnnie Tillmon, who, historian Premilla Nadasen argues, brought a race and class critique to women's oppression, Robinson "formulated a distinctive and broadly based analysis of women's liberation that spoke to the needs of many women who were not traditionally considered a part of the feminist movement."[82]

The middle-class focus of the 1960s and 1970s women's movement stood in stark contrast to what Dorothy Sue Cobble and Dennis Deslippe demonstrate came before it when women unionists were at the forefront of the battles to eradicate sex discrimination. In the 1940s and 1950s labor women led the battle to secure women's right to work in occupations of their own choosing, to end wage differentials based on sex, and to win social supports for mothers so that they could combine wage earning with domestic responsibilities. Labor feminists also advocated, with varying levels of commitment and success, for an end to racial discrimination. Cobble identifies Robinson as part of this robust working-class feminist movement, which was more ethnically and racially diverse than its Progressive Era predecessor (including the WTUL), the result in part of the CIO's more inclusive organizing.[83]

Robinson certainly had the credentials to be considered a labor feminist. She was a leader of her union and later employee of the Women's Bureau and the New York Department of Labor, as well as a critic of the Equal Rights Amendment (ERA), a position most labor feminists held. In her 1976 oral history interview Robinson criticized ERA leaders such as National Woman's Party chair Emma Guffey Miller for not understanding labor women's opposition to the ERA. Robinson sympathized with the former leaders of the WTUL, whom she described as the "first women's righters." Robinson explained that she "had been brought up" on the view that protective labor legislation ought to be extended to men. "We used to have a famous saying," Robinson recalled. "Well, sure, we don't want women to lift fifty pounds. But there are some men who can't lift fifty pounds, too. We don't want them excluded. We want the law extended to them." Robinson's view on wage justice explicitly challenged the assumption that all men were stronger than all women—a common justification for paying men more than women—and rested on the belief that all workers needed protection from dangerous working conditions. If ERA supporters had tried to extend labor protections to men, they would have won the support of labor women, Robinson insisted. Deeply enmeshed in the Women's Bureau circle and union movement, Robinson contributed to the arguments being developed to eradicate sex-based wage discrimination while also critiquing the ERA for undermining protective labor laws.[84]

Robinson's interviews suggest that she believed that by defining herself as a feminist she would minimize the other identities around which she organized, tying her to an ideology and movement that alone did not explain or promise to eliminate her oppression. Rejecting labels gave her the autonomy to move between movements committed to economic justice and women's and civil rights, an autonomy that mirrored Black feminist demands for self-definition and self-determination.

Central to Black feminism, Black feminist sociologist Deborah K. King argues, is the right to "decide for ourselves the relative salience of any and all identities and oppressions, and how and the extent to which those features inform our politics." Robinson refused to allow others to define her activism and political thought. Her autonomous, self-defined standpoint reflected her lived experiences as a Black working-class woman who was organizing at the intersection of multiple systems of domination and was committed to building diverse coalitions in her pursuit of social justice.[85] Such a posture, Patricia Hill Collins argues, was not uncommon among African American women, who were more likely to engage in strategic affiliations and "reject ideology as the overarching framework." The diverse forms of discrimination that Black women experienced, Collins argues, fostered an activism based on "negotiation and a higher degree of attention to context."[86] It also enabled Robinson to retain a critical stance toward the organizations and movements in which she participated and to employ a coalitional approach in her activism.

Adelmond similarly described her activism broadly, defining her philosophy as based "upon courage, tolerance, liberty, independence, faith, love and charity for all." Springer explained that Adelmond opposed all forms of discrimination and oppression, "regardless of the person against whom it is directed." In her 1950 resignation letter from the union, Adelmond insisted that she was unwilling to compromise her fundamental beliefs and principles by remaining in an organization that was not committed to stamping out any and all forms of discrimination "against any race or class of workers, based upon color, religion or sex." Springer insisted that Adelmond's activism was not only about "color" but also about securing dignity and respect for all workers.[87] This humanist vision, Collins argues, was common among Black women whose organizing promoted the liberty and empowerment of all people.[88] Like Pauli Murray, who situated Black women at the "forefront of the struggle for human rights," rights that were indivisible, Robinson and Adelmond held a humanist vision that sought the eradication of all forms of discrimination and the empowerment of all people struggling against injustice.[89]

As women who were acutely aware of the interconnectedness of race, class, and gender oppression, Robinson and Adelmond simultaneously pursued economic dignity, civil rights, and women's empowerment. They made contributions not only to the labor movement but also to the burgeoning civil rights movement and, despite an unwillingness to adopt the label of feminism, to the women's movement. Both women critiqued workplace and union sexism, and in the 1960s Robinson applied a gender critique to the civil rights movement, which she noted also relegated women to secondary roles. Women's marginalization in other social movements led Robinson to argue for the need for an organization focused on women. The United Auto Workers' Dorothy Haener, one of the founders of the National Organization for Women (NOW), credits Robinson for helping to develop the idea for NOW. "What we need," Robinson told Haener, "[is] an NAACP for women." Robinson, who argued that women were marginalized in every movement in which they participated, raised the idea with Haener in early 1966 at a talk the auto unionist gave at a conference in Milwaukee.[90]

As the challenges of the immediate postwar years reveal, despite the women's multifaceted activism and the continued advocacy of the "democratic initiative," the laundry union delivered far less than it had promised. Through collective bargaining the workers won regular but very modest wage gains. Under the benefit fund, workers received sickness and accident benefits, but men received more than women. Grievance arbitration proved inadequate to address the escalating contract violations, and union leaders failed to support the workers' efforts to challenge discriminatory hiring and promotion practices. The union's failure to nurture a leadership that represented the diversity of the workforce or that challenged the long-standing patterns of race and gender discrimination meant that the LWJB would not function as a vehicle for racial justice like the Brotherhood of Sleeping Car Porters and other Black railroad unions did or as Left-led unions such as the United Packinghouse Workers did.[91] Adelmond's and Robinson's continued efforts to build a democratic union that was accountable to women and people of color put them on a collision course with the leadership that would finally explode in 1950.

CHAPTER ELEVEN

"We're Just Not Ready Yet"

The Ousting of Charlotte Adelmond
and Dollie Robinson from the
Laundry Workers Joint Board

In 1949 the long-standing conflict between the democratic initiative and the ACWA culminated in an all-out battle that pitted Black trade unionists against the ACWA and LWJB secretary treasurer Louis Simon. The battle, described by the workers as a shop floor revolt against "dictatorial rule, shady practices, Negro discrimination and union-sanctioned intolerable working conditions," was led by Charlotte Adelmond.[1] The insurgency was precipitated by events taking place in the union but was also inspired by the successes of the postwar civil rights struggle. By the end of the 1940s, Black civil rights activists and their allies in New York City had helped secure the passage of landmark antidiscrimination legislation, including the 1945 Law against Discrimination; had sent Black politicians, including the formidable Adam Clayton Powell Jr., to Washington; and had contributed to the movement that resulted in the permanent Fair Employment Practice Committee. Black urban activists had helped break down the color line in major league baseball, taken their protests against lynching to the doors of the White House, and petitioned the United Nations to investigate the domestic status of US racial minorities. Black Americans' demands for racial justice convinced President Truman to create the President's Committee on Civil Rights in 1946. The commission's final report, *To Secure These Rights*, released a year later, described racial inequality as a moral problem and its eradication as a Cold War imperative. Calling for the abolition of all forms of racial and religious segregation and discrimination, antilynching and anti–poll tax legislation, equality of opportunity in housing, education, and public services, and additional support for the Justice Department to prosecute civil rights abuses, the presidential report, Martha Biondi argues, both "endorsed and legitimized the legislative agenda of the grassroots African American struggle for racial justice."[2]

While civil rights activists won key battles at the national and state levels, the stunning defeat of Republican presidential candidate New York governor Thomas E. Dewey in 1948 represented a major victory for labor. The labor vote helped return President Truman to power and the Democrats regain control of both houses of Congress. In 1948, nationally, nearly fifty African Americans ran as candidates on the Progressive Party ticket. The political mobilizations taking place in New York and other northern cities and the challenge from the left-wing Progressive Party convinced the Democratic Party to adopt its most progressive civil rights platform yet.[3] In 1949 it seemed like the country was on the verge of taking a huge step forward in the battle to end discrimination, and Black laundry workers expected to see these gains reflected in their union. When they encountered familiar patterns of union racism and discrimination they launched their most militant challenge to date.

The Reassignment of Charlotte Adelmond

In 1949 rank-and-file anger over racist treatment and substandard working conditions precipitated an all-out war for control of the LWJB. Black workers reported to the *New York Amsterdam News* that they felt betrayed by the modest and in some cases negligible wage gains secured through collective bargaining. In 1949 women laundry workers earned on average thirty-one dollars a week, far less than what was required to maintain a minimum standard of living. Workers pointed out that the minimum wage had become the maximum wage, at least for women and workers of color.[4] They also accused union officials of refusing to press discrimination cases and of raising dues to add "more machine men to the payroll." With the aid of Simon's efficiency-minded staffers, speedups for inside workers, 80 percent of whom were Black and Puerto Rican, had reached the "highest pitch in the history of the industry."[5]

At a staff meeting in December 1949, Adelmond accused the ACWA-appointed manager, Sander Genis, and the secretary treasurer, Louis Simon, of failing to hold the employers accountable to arbitration decisions, in particular, those in which workers had won back pay for overtime work; of failing to ensure the workers received the minimum union wage and their sick and pension benefits; and finally, of prohibiting members from transferring their membership between locals, a practice that rendered longtime union members ineligible to vote in elections.[6] Angered that Adelmond had publicly challenged him, Genis removed her from her position as business agent of Local 327 and reassigned her to do organizing work under the supervision of Louis Simon. When Adelmond demanded an explanation, Genis accused her of "harassing" him and of raising issues that were "gimmicks." Adelmond, who at the time had a fractured ankle from a recent fall, as well as chronic back pain, was physically unable to organize, so Genis put her on vacation leave and told her to report back to work February 1, 1950.[7]

All longtime laundry workers eventually developed work-related health issues. In 1933 Adelmond had burned her arm on an uncovered steam pipe, a relatively common injury. But in the 1940s she had two accidents that led to long-term health problems.[8] On April 4, 1945, Adelmond fell down eight stairs at the union headquarters at 160 Fifth Avenue when she slipped on a wet cigarette butt. The business agent injured her left ankle and lower back and missed over a week of work. The Workmen's Compensation Board put Adelmond on a reduced workload of "light work" for three days a week and awarded her $308 for disability benefits over a period of ten weeks. For the rest of her time at the union Adelmond suffered from back and ankle pain related to the 1945 injury. At times she had difficulty bending down and walking, and her left ankle was prone to giving out, causing her on one occasion to fall off a ladder while washing her windows. While she was being treated for injuries related to the fall, a physician diagnosed Adelmond with a heart condition (respiratory problems were common among laundry workers), which sometimes left her bedridden. During one of Adelmond's medical visits, a Dr. Arkin of Park Avenue unceremoniously discharged her for being overweight and refused to see her until she dropped 45 of her 195 pounds of body weight. In 1947, when the Workmen's Compensation Board refused to approve further treatments for her ankle, Adelmond wrote to the board that the pain she suffered was sometimes "unbearable," especially when she had to work more than three days a week. She noted, though, that the workers were very kind and covered her absences.[9]

On October 24, 1949, a month and a half before the December staff meeting where Genis reassigned Adelmond, the activist's left ankle gave way as she was getting off a city bus, causing her to fall and fracture her right ankle. The cast she had to wear made it difficult to get around and left her feeling, according to one doctor, "nervous and uneasy." The doctor commented on Adelmond's weight and recommended physical therapy and the use of an elastic bandage for her ankle to provide support and "value as psychotherapy."[10] The now medically described hysterical Adelmond purchased a brace from M. Braverman and Sons Custom and Orthopedic Shoe Specialists for forty-four dollars, which the insurance carrier refused to cover. As late as 1952 she was still trying to get compensation for her injuries, with Pauli Murray, listed as "Paul Murray" in one of the claims, as her legal representative. In April 1952 the board denied her claim.[11]

Evidence suggests that Genis's December 1949 reassignment of Adelmond to organizing work (while she was wearing a cast!) was a response to both her ongoing advocacy and her insistence that the union intervene in a work-related sexual assault she suffered a few months prior at the hands of Mr. Eddie Chinanki of the Alabama Laundry. According to Adelmond, after numerous failed attempts to get Chinanki to pay one of his workers back pay (as per an arbitration award), Adelmond and the union accountant visited his shop, where Chinanki physically assaulted Adelmond, striking her on her left breast and ripping her clothing. Adelmond immediately went to the union office to report the assault to Simon, who told her to tell the union lawyer, which she did. A week later, when the union had still done nothing, Adelmond reported the attack to Genis, who was by then back in the office. Genis told Adelmond to file a civil suit against Chinanki or take up the matter with the Employers' Association. Adelmond pushed back, insisting that the attack was a union matter. When at a staff meeting other officials reported being attacked in a similar manner by some of the employers, Genis finally relented and agreed to pursue the matter. At a subsequent LWJB meeting Genis reported that he had won a financial settlement from Chinanki of fifty dollars to replace Adelmond's torn suit and one hundred dollars for a donation to the National Urban League, the latter of which was Adelmond's suggestion. As grossly inadequate as it was, the business agent never received the paltry settlement, for she would soon be out of the union. Adelmond believed that her insistence that the union recognize and pursue the sexual assault as a union matter contributed to her reassignment and ultimate ousting from the union.[12]

Given Adelmond's injuries, Genis's reassignment of her to organizational work effectively removed her from the union. Referring to Adelmond's 1940 suspension by ACWA vice president Hyman Blumberg, Simon crowed to a group of workers that "the first time Charlotte Adelmond was suspended," and "this time she is fired and is going to stay fired."[13] As they had in 1940, the workers rallied to Adelmond's defense, sending petitions to Genis demanding that she be reinstated. Genis accused Adelmond of riling up the workers and reassigned her to work under Hexton Harden of Local 332. Adelmond reluctantly agreed, noting that the reassignment violated the ACWA's Constitution and bylaws and conveying her anger and pain at having to leave her post and abandon the workers. Adelmond, who noted that the union had begun in her Thatford Avenue home in 1933 with seven workers, threatened to complain to the ACWA's general executive board if she were not given her old job back.[14]

A "Knock-Down-Drag-Out Floor Fight": The Final Battle between the Democratic Initiative and the LWJB

The final showdown between Adelmond and Genis coincided with the upcoming ACWA biennial convention to be held in May of 1950 in Cleveland, Ohio. Former driver Max Schiff, a Genis and Simon loyalist and business agent in Adelmond's Local 327, nominated four proadministration delegates to attend the convention. Citing the bylaws, Adelmond insisted that the membership and not Schiff ought to nominate the delegates.[15] Reminiscent of the leftists' 1941 battle with the union leadership over representation at the ACWA convention, eight hundred Black workers from Adelmond's Local 327 met a week later and elected their own convention delegates to a parallel "anti-administration ticket." Carl Lawrence of the *New York Amsterdam News* predicted that there would be a "knock-down-drag-out floor fight" at the convention between white union leaders and Black organizers and business agents, who were tired of being "pushed around in lily-white fashion." Adelmond, whom Lawrence described as the "spunky little veteran of 13 years," was elected as a delegate, as was Langston Rivers, the Black worker who had demanded that the union challenge the racist hiring practices that prevented Black men from becoming drivers.[16] ACWA officials accused Adelmond of disrupting the election and suspended her without pay. At the same time, they brought in ACWA national secretary Frank Rosenblum to replace Genis.[17]

The *New York Amsterdam News*, which was following the battle closely, reported that Adelmond had been suspended for "daring to oppose top officers of her unit." The newspaper also noted that some ACWA officials doubted the legality of her suspension.[18] Doubts aside, the garment union upheld the suspension. The opposition group pooled their resources and sent their own candidates to the convention, which Adelmond did not attend. Although the opposition slate reported speaking at the convention and the *Daily Worker* reported that the workers filed discrimination charges against Simon, the convention record does not include the workers' testimony or the charges. Bernard Burton of the *Daily Worker* accused ACWA officials of acting in typical Amalgamated fashion by hashing out the issues behind closed doors in hotel rooms. The racial conflict taking place in the union had no place in the official record.[19] During the crisis Adelmond turned to her good friend Maida Springer for support. Springer helped Adelmond print out mimeographs at the ILGWU headquarters that explained to the workers what was happening.[20]

On April 17, during the convention crisis, workers at Brooklyn's Cascade Laundry launched a wildcat strike. Cascade workers belonged to Adelmond's Local 327 but were handled by fellow business agent Max Schiff. The *Daily Worker* and the *New York Amsterdam News* reported that twelve hundred mostly Black and Puerto Rican workers walked off the job after being denied the right to vote on a no-raise agreement negotiated by Simon. The disgruntled workers signed membership applications with John L. Lewis's United Mine Workers' (UMW) District 50. The UMW had chartered District 50 in 1936 to organize workers outside of mining. No doubt aware of the unrest in the CIO laundry union (under Lewis the UMW left the CIO in 1942), only two weeks earlier the UMW had hired former laundry officials Roy Soden and Joe Gentile and assigned six other experienced organizers from their Washington headquarters to organize New York's laundry workers.[21] LWJB officials, including Odell Clark, rushed to the scene and urged the workers to honor the contract and return to work. Clark blasted the *New York Amsterdam News* for its "cockeyed" criticism of the LWJB and defied "anyone to mention any union with a better record for good race relations." Despite her suspension from the union, Adelmond offered to talk to the workers on behalf of the LWJB.[22]

The accounts of what happened next vary. The *New York Amsterdam News* reported that the workers refused to go back to work and that a group of a thousand laundry workers marched into the auditorium of the Brooklyn Labor Lyceum, where they denounced the LWJB. A group of women strikers chanted, "We're through with you." A spokesperson for the workers described the walkout as a strike against both the union and the employer.[23] In contrast, articles in the ACWA's *The Advance* claimed that once the "duped" workers who were "inexperienced in raiding tactics" realized that the LWJB was not leading the walkout, they dutifully returned to work, an interpretation that cast the women as unsophisticated and easily manipulated.[24] Given the long-standing tensions between women laundry workers of color and their union leaders, the *New York Amsterdam News*' analysis likely presented the more accurate portrayal of the workers' position.

The Cascade strike and worker discontent made the LWJB vulnerable to raids from other organizations. In 1950 organizers from District 50 promised to provide the laundry workers with a democratic "bonafide trade union" that would hold regular elections and get rid of the "hacks of the union bosses." Denouncing the laundry's "virtual slave conditions," District 50 promised to win a minimum hourly wage of one dollar and provide the workers with a union that would "not only give lip service to [the] FEPC in Washington" but also "establish the principles within its own house."[25] Over a thousand mostly Black and Puerto Rican workers signed membership applications with Lewis's union.[26]

Amalgamated laundry officials went on the defensive, claiming that District 50 was led by racketeers and outsiders intent on destroying the union, a narrative that echoed Cold War propaganda that attributed unrest of any kind, especially labor and civil rights, to external agitators. The LWJB produced a series of pamphlets urging the workers not to jeopardize the gains they had secured under the ACWA and filed injunction proceedings against District 50.[27] UMW officials accused Mayor William O'Dwyer, a Democratic machine politician with ties to the ACWA (Robinson remembered the union assigning her to work on O'Dwyer's 1945 mayoral campaign), of siding with the garment union and of sending in the police to intimidate the strikers.[28] Although the laundry workers would ultimately stay with the LWJB, the wildcat strike and workers' interest in the UMW reveal the existence of widespread rank-and-file discontent with the ACWA laundry union.

Simon's Ascension: Taking Over the LWJB

Simon understood the turmoil in the laundry union as an opportunity to consolidate his power. The secretary treasurer framed the conflict as a power struggle between ACWA leaders intent on maintaining control over the LWJB and laundry workers seeking greater autonomy from the parent union, an interpretation that purposefully obscured the racialized and gendered roots of the struggle. At the May 1950 ACWA convention, Simon demanded that the garment union allow the laundry workers to elect their own manager. Rather than risk losing the workers altogether (Simon threatened to take the LWJB out of the ACWA if the garment leaders denied his request), ACWA leaders acquiesced and called for an election.[29]

At Simon's urging, the ACWA held the election in June rather than October, the original date. According to Bernard Burton of the *Daily Worker*, Simon demanded an earlier election so as to prevent the opposition group from having time to mobilize. Black workers accused Simon and his supporters of conducting nominations at "quickie meetings" that were held on short notice and advertised as unimportant. With only days to respond, Black workers assembled a "New Deal" slate to run against Simon's slate.[30] In the week leading up to the election, the democratic initiative, including Myrtle Toppin and George Locker, accused the election committee, under Simon's control, of forcing several New Deal candidates to withdraw. They also accused the secretary treasurer of violating election rules by pressuring LWJB officials to vote for his slate and of using race to drive a wedge between the drivers and largely Black opposition forces. As a former driver, Simon understood all too well how racial animosities could be harnessed to defeat the insurgent movement.[31]

In the days leading up to the election, the New Deal slate requested that the Honest Ballot Association be allowed to conduct the election. The association was founded in 1909 by civic reformers determined to bring fairness and accountability to elections held hostage by machine politics. The ACWA refused the workers' request for external oversight and quietly supported Simon's candidacy. Simon's maneuvering, the ACWA's support for Simon, and the hasty election ensured a Simon victory. Of the twenty thousand members of the union, eighty-four hundred voted, the highest turnout in the history of the union.[32] The arguably low voter turnout—both in 1950 and previously—suggests that nonactivist workers had become disengaged from the union. In her 1950 resignation letter, Adelmond explained that many of the workers felt that the union was "so powerful and complex" and so impersonal that it was impossible to have their "voices heard where union policies are concerned."[33] In 1950 many laundry workers did not believe that their participation in the union would have any real impact. The mandatory new members' course, conducted by Robinson, was an attempt to draw the workers into the union and provide training that would empower rank-and-file workers to participate in the administration of the union.

The low turnout was also likely related to fears of retaliation as the leadership removed progressive unionists from the organization in the late 1940s. Adelmond explained that "the shops are small, workers are easily put on the stop and afraid to vote their convictions." Economic fears loomed large. The embattled business agent recognized that "the security of his family and his economic welfare are perhaps more vital and immediate to him than his right to voice his opinions."[34]

The 1950 LWJB election returned most of the Simon loyalists to power. The forty-member LWJB in turn elected Simon as manager, and Simon chose Odell Clark as assistant manager, much to the anger of Black workers, who argued that the LWJB and not Simon ought to select the assistant manager. The LWJB reelected Roger Daniels as president and African American Philip Cox as vice president and allowed Simon to retain his position as secretary treasurer. Adelmond described the consolidation of power as a threat to union democracy and an "invitation to political power struggles," which would subordinate the interests of the membership. The LWJB elected only two women to sit on the ten-member board of directors, and there were no women members of the finance, grievance, and membership committees.[35] All of the top positions were held by men, most of whom were white. Instead of providing for greater local democracy, the election had enabled Simon to consolidate his control and eliminate workers demanding racial justice and union democracy.

A second set of elections took place in 1950, this time for representation on the eighteen-member ACWA executive board. Popular Black business agent Hexton Harden, described by the *New York Amsterdam News* as a "militant spokesman for equality of opportunity," ran for the board, as did Simon.[36] Hexton had been chosen by the democratic initiative in 1947 to represent them as assistant manager (although Genis never appointed him). In 1950 Lawrence of the *New York Amsterdam News* noted that several ACWA "big shots" looked with favor on Harden's candidacy, since no Black worker had ever run for the position, but another article in the same newspaper suggested that Harden had run against the wishes of the CIO administration. Black workers framed the election as a test of the ACWA's commitment to racial justice, since no African American had ever served on the garment union's executive board. In contrast, two women, Bessie Hillman and Gladys Dickason, served on the board.[37]

In the weeks leading up to the election, Black workers accused Simon of visiting the plants with ballot boxes during work hours and of pressuring workers to vote for him, in violation of election rules. They also noted that Harden's name appeared last on the ballot behind Simon's name, even though all of the other candidates' names appeared in alphabetical order. A copy of the ballot that appears in *The Advance* confirms that Harden's name was inexplicably last on the ballot of nineteen names, the only name not listed in alphabetical order.[38] With only eighteen spots available, Harden's supporters accused Simon of encouraging the workers to vote for the first eighteen candidates.

Once again, Black workers lost their bid for representation. Both Simon and Harden received the fewest number of votes of the nineteen candidates (in Simon's case, 13,000 fewer than any other candidate), but Simon received 101,676 votes compared to Harden's 24,201 votes. The single Black candidate was the only candidate not voted onto the ACWA's executive board. Laundry workers argued that the outcome proved that "even in unions some white people are determined to keep Negro members in a special place. We're just not ready yet." They also noted that while Jewish and Italian workers were well represented on the executive board, a Black person had never served.[39]

Shortly after the 1950 elections Simon fired Harden from his position as business agent of Local 332, citing the workers' support for District 50. But given that Simon loyalist Max Schiff, the business agent who oversaw the Cascade Laundry, where workers had signed cards with District 50, was allowed to keep his post, it is clear that Simon removed Harden for challenging him. Workers from twelve shops threatened to quit if Harden were not reinstated and accused the LWJB of "following the white supremacy attitude." The workers angrily noted that of the fifty paid officers in the union, only thirteen were Black, and only one, Adelmond, was a Black woman, and she was on her way out. Harden declined to comment to the *New York Amsterdam News*, stating only that the union should respect the members' wishes. Despite the workers' protests, Harden was permanently out of the union.[40]

The Banishment of Charlotte Adelmond

Adelmond faced a similar fate as Harden. Although Simon had forbidden her from going into the shops in the weeks leading up to the 1950 election, Adelmond easily won reelection as business agent of Local 327. Robinson recalled that no matter whom the union ran against her or what methods they used, Adelmond always won by "an overpowering number of votes." Simon, however, made it impossible for her to continue in her job. When Adelmond called shop meetings Odell Clark turned up to contradict everything she said. Adelmond reported that at membership meetings Simon sent officers to act as "mental pressure groups" to undermine her authority and to intimidate her.[41]

On December 6, 1950, Adelmond resigned from the LWJB, explaining that she could no longer work for individuals who "give lip service to high sounding principles of trade union democracy and equality and at the same time do everything in their power to suppress and oppose any one who wants to make these principles a living reality." She insisted that to be a successful business agent in the LWJB and to win the "favor" of certain ACWA officials, one had to surrender "one's rights, principles and self-respect and become what is commonly called a 'handkerchief head,' 'boot licker,' or 'stoolpigeon.'" Unwilling to assume these stereotypical roles, Adelmond was thus driven out of the union. She concluded that under the current leadership, "there is no hope for the attainment of the better things of life."[42] The last time Adelmond appears in the union records is in April 1951, when an article in *The Advance* notes that the former business agent tried, unsuccessfully, to convince a group of Colonial Laundry workers who had walked off the job when their employer refused to contribute to the benefit fund to leave the Amalgamated and join a different and unspecified union. The *New York Amsterdam News* tried, without success, to reach Adelmond for comment.[43]

Adelmond's resignation letter included a forty-three-page memorandum prepared by Pauli Murray outlining the discrimination and harassment that she and other Black workers had faced in the union. The memorandum outlined the union's failure to challenge the racist and sexist hiring practices that confined women and people of color to the lowest-paying positions in the laundries and the pervasive mistreatment of the workers by the employers and, most shockingly to Adelmond, by the union leaders themselves. Adelmond explained that while she understood that it would take time for the union to develop a "spirit of brotherhood and equality," she was nonetheless shocked by the persistent mistreatment of Black workers and by the union's unwillingness to root out racial discrimination. She accused union leaders of patronizing Black workers and of failing to understand that the "issue of Civil Rights must be worked upon continuously by all labor and liberal organizations." She denounced white union officials for treating the workers with "callousness," of playing "divide in order to rule" by pitting Black workers against one another, and by supporting only those Black officials who acted as "lackeys and mouthpieces."[44] Adelmond also condemned ACWA officials, expressing her disappointment that a union that represented workers from another oppressed group (Jewish workers) had not used its influence to abolish discrimination but instead had allowed white laundry officials to do "pretty much as they please." She criticized garment officials for getting involved in "petty political squabbles" and for tolerating unethical behavior. Despite the ACWA's public posturing and progressive resolutions on racial issues, Adelmond noted that not a single Black worker had ever served on its executive board to interpret the "needs and aspirations" of Black workers.[45]

Adelmond's determination to secure racial justice for Black workers and the widespread support she enjoyed among the rank and file precipitated her downfall in a union that relegated Black people to second-class citizenship. Springer describes Adelmond's refusal to compromise as "part of her undoing." During an interview conducted in the 1980s, Springer explained that "this was so long ago and people couldn't accommodate that. And whether anyone said anything about it or not this made people angry who couldn't accept her vigilance, her forthrightness. She was too much for them." Adelmond's behavior challenged the racial status quo at a moment when Black Americans were delivering petitions to the UN, challenging racial discrimination in the courts, and refusing to leave white-only designated spaces. Her behavior also challenged the postwar emphasis on traditional gender roles, a domestic ideal that had long eluded Black women, whose history of wage earning and activism cast them as disruptive, deviant, and even dangerous.[46] Adelmond's refusal to accommodate union racism and union sexism terrified and angered a leadership determined to preserve white male privilege in all its forms. Like the communist workers who challenged conservative garment and laundry leaders in the early 1940s, Adelmond posed a threat that had to be contained and, when that proved impossible, eliminated.

Like Springer, Robinson believed that Adelmond's militancy and refusal to compromise led to her ousting. Robinson explained that "some people seeing strength, the weaklings hang on and tear down the strength." But she also wondered whether if "with proper guidance" Adelmond might have been able to navigate the politics and perhaps "never would have been out of the union."[47] It is possible that the guidance Robinson alluded to might have come from the WTUL had the organization remained involved in the laundry union. Rose Schneiderman attended the odd reception of the LWJB in the 1940s, but for the most part the WTUL redirected its increasingly limited resources to workers without unions and received few calls for support. Robinson explained that by the 1940s most unions had their own educational programs and were no longer willing to provide financial or moral support to the WTUL. She further hypothesized that working women who had not gone through the struggles of the 1910s and 1920s did not appreciate the WTUL as much as they should have. Robinson regretted the WTUL's 1949 closing and wished that she and others who had understood its value had tried harder to prevent its demise.[48] One wonders too where Bessie Hillman stood on Adelmond's ousting and whether she could have prevented her departure. Karen Pastorello argues that despite Hillman's important role in the founding of the ACWA and her position as vice president, Hillman, like other women garment leaders, wielded little actual power in a union that relegated women to secondary roles.[49]

Robinson understood that Adelmond's militant defense of the workers' rights and refusal to compromise her principles—the qualities that made her such an effective organizer and advocate of workers of color—also prevented her from making the compromises necessary to maintain a position of leadership in a "strong company union" run by men. In 1976, reflecting on her forty years of experience in the labor movement, Robinson theorized that "the real person who organized may never be the person that can conform to the crushing of the top leadership."[50] Adelmond's ousting by the union leadership and her refusal to conform mirrored the marginalization of female civil rights leaders such as Ella Baker of the Southern Christian Leadership Conference (SCLC), who, despite her critical leadership in the movement, was never able to secure a permanent position in the male-led SCLC. Sociologist Bernice McNair Barnett argues that Baker's experience reflects a larger pattern—in which we can also locate Adelmond—where women initiate movements and serve as leaders in the early phases, when a movement is "unstructured, emergent, and dangerous," only to be displaced in later phases by men who win public recognition and status as movement leaders.[51] Adelmond's refusal to subordinate her principles to the demands of the leadership, her outspoken opposition to "second-class treatment of union workers," and her refusal to play the "part of 'handkerchief' head Negro" precipitated her removal from the LWJB.[52]

Adelmond was devastated by the ousting. Robinson recalled that Adelmond became a hermit after leaving the union, a pioneer who was not able to "reap the benefits" of what she had sowed. Springer remembered that when Adelmond died in 1976 in Jamaica, New York, at the age of seventy-two she was a very "sick" and "broken" woman.[53] Robinson wondered whether if she and Adelmond had developed interests outside of the labor movement, they might have better been able to withstand the crushing disappointments. Robinson explained that "there was nothing that I did that wasn't connected with the union. My whole life was in it."[54] Robinson and Adelmond worked tirelessly to transform the LWJB into a vehicle of racial and economic justice and were devastated when they could not.

Another Blast:
The Reassignment of Dollie Robinson

Robinson faced a similar although somewhat less brutal fate than Adelmond. As conflict wracked the union Robinson tried to bolster the Education Department by introducing a new class on labor law and a series of popular bowling outings. Somewhat more surprisingly but consistent with the 1950s emphasis on traditional womanhood, the Education Department also introduced a "charm class," conducted by Kara Nelson, that covered topics such as makeup and wardrobe planning.[55] Despite these new initiatives, in late 1950 the ACWA removed Robinson from her position of education director and reassigned her to organize in the South, part of the CIO's doomed Operation Dixie. Lawrence of the *New York Amsterdam News* described Robinson's removal as one of the "first blasts concerning discriminatory tactics," while Burton of the *Daily Worker* described Robinson and Adelmond as "ousted Negro leaders." Burton also noted, perhaps with some slight satisfaction, that in the past the women had joined the Simon clique in their anticommunist witch hunts but were now "given the ax themselves, as soon as the most militant leaders were eliminated."[56]

The board assigned African American Bert Jemmott to lead the Education Department, a position he held while retaining his job as business agent for Local 331. A department that had at one time enjoyed two dedicated staff members now had less than one full-time person. Jemmott had worked in the industry since 1929, when he got a job as a checker in a linen supply laundry. In 1937 he helped organize his plant, and the workers subsequently elected him business agent and trade manager of linen supply Local 331. As Robinson's replacement, Jemmott spearheaded a new initiative to provide sales training courses to help family drivers "increase their earnings and protect their jobs." The union arranged for the courses to be taught by instructors from City College's Baruck School of Business.[57] The new initiative represented a significant departure from Hillman's and Robinson's programming, which had provided social, cultural, and athletic opportunities to the workers and their children, as well as courses in union procedure. One wonders how Jemmott, a Black man whose race barred him from obtaining a driving position, felt about overseeing a program that would benefit white men alone. The union replaced Jemmott in the early 1960s with Jacob Schlitt, a Jewish labor and civil rights activist with a degree in education from City College.[58]

Letters that Robinson wrote to Hillman from Florida suggest that she understood the reassignment as a punishment. Robinson compared the ACWA's machinations to President Truman's firing of General MacArthur, arguing that "sometimes I think that Mr. Truman got his lessons in diplomacy from some of our present day Union leaders."[59] Robinson's reassignment was most likely a consequence of her continued support for Adelmond and her determination to see people of color assume leadership positions in the union. Her close relationship with ACWA leaders Bessie Hillman, Hyman Blumberg, and Esther Peterson likely saved her from being removed from the union altogether. Robinson acknowledged that her friendship with Hillman and Blumberg gave her a wider berth than many of her friends had, but she also recalled that there were times when she was in "deep trouble." Robinson recognized that it must have been hard on Hillman to always champion her and insisted that her friend's support "helped me survive." By 1951 the *New York Amsterdam News* reported that the efforts to penalize Robinson had ended.[60]

Adelmond's and Robinson's distinct organizing and leadership styles, shaped by their different personal histories, migration paths, and activist trajectories, among other factors, help explain why Adelmond was ousted from the union and Robinson reassigned. Robinson spent her formative years in the Jim Crow South. Although she does not report any childhood memories of racial violence or discrimination, she could hardly have been unaware of the racial codes that relegated Black children to underfunded segregated schools and kept most African Americans away from the voting booth.[61] Her mother, Dora Lowther, ultimately abandoned the South, leaving behind a dense network of family and friends and a good job cutting hair for teachers at the State Normal School because of the lack of educational opportunities for Black children there. When Robinson later considered becoming a teacher in the South, she recalled that her mother was "hell bent" against it "because she knew the South."[62] While Robinson's childhood was by all accounts idyllic, her life's trajectory was shaped by a fiercely protective mother's attempts to shield her daughter from the insidious racism that undermined opportunities for Black people everywhere.

Adelmond, on the other hand, spent her formative years in Trinidad, where Black people were in the majority and had a long history of resisting the white power structure. In the nineteenth and early twentieth centuries, Black Trinidadians established radical political, nationalist, and trade union movements, including the Trinidad Workingmen's Association, one of the leading labor organizations in the Caribbean.[63] Building on this tradition of radical resistance, Caribbean migrants brought with them militant tactics, including, in Adelmond's case, the head butt. Springer explained that, exposed to radical organizations at home, "many of the people from the Caribbean arrived here very politicized." Jessie Smith remembered that some of the foreign-born Black laundry workers had come to the United States with "socialistic ideas" and were among the earliest supporters of the laundry campaign.[64]

The extreme racism that Caribbean migrants encountered in the United States and their inability to obtain work commensurate with their education and skill levels contributed to their radicalization. Overnight, Caribbean migrants moved from majority to despised minority status. For some migrants, it was their first experience of racism not rooted in class differences. Many of the migrants were highly skilled workers whose dreams of occupational mobility were dashed on the shoals of American racism. Underemployment contributed to their politicization and would lead them to the forefront of movements to fight racial discrimination in industries such as the garment trades and laundries. Historian James Winston argues that with their history of "frontal resistance to oppression," many Caribbean migrants found it difficult or impossible to master the "etiquette of race" that Black Americans, especially those in the Jim Crow South, were forced to adopt as a matter of survival.[65]

Adelmond moved to New York City in 1924, when the "New Negro" and nationalist Garvey movements were at their zenith. Like so many other young Caribbean migrants, including Springer, she was drawn to the defiant posture and tactics of Garvey's Universal Negro Improvement Association. Garvey's message of Black pride and leadership, Pan-Africanism, and insistence that Black people be treated with dignity and respect resonated deeply with Adelmond and shaped her own activism, including her refusal to compromise in the face of injustice.[66]

Robinson moved to New York City in 1930, when the Garvey movement was in decline. As the Great Depression decimated African Americans' already limited wage-earning potential, many Black workers turned to the organized labor movement, especially after the emergence of the CIO. Robinson became politically active at the moment when the labor movement was becoming a more inclusive space committed, at least in principle, to racial equality. Inspired by the CIO's egalitarian rhetoric and its willingness to organize workers of all backgrounds and skill levels, Robinson opted to work within the labor movement, forging alliances with progressive white unionists and workers of color to pursue social change through organizing, educational work, and mentoring. This approach and the support she enjoyed from influential white unionists such as Hillman and Blumberg saved Robinson from suffering the same fate as Adelmond.

Although Robinson understood her reassignment as a banishment, she embraced the opportunity to work with African Americans in the South, where she encountered a different but related set of challenges. In Chattanooga, Tennessee, where she was organizing laundry workers, the owner of the restaurant beneath her rental apartment played the jukebox all night to drive her out of town. She recalled that some towns, such as Miami Beach, Montgomery, and Athens, Georgia, among other places, would "get us out rather quickly." While fending off such challenges, Robinson found herself in the uncomfortable position of having to explain the racial mores of the South to white union officials back in New York City. In Miami Beach Robinson worked with a white organizer named Pete Zuba. While Zuba rented a bungalow with a bedroom and kitchen in a white neighborhood, Robinson rented a tiny one-room apartment in the "Black section" of town and cooked her meals on a hotplate. Despite her inferior accommodations, Robinson's expenses were higher than Zuba's. When the ACWA Finance Office sent her a letter questioning the discrepancy, Robinson wrote back in red pencil: "It takes more for Black America to live in the South than it does for white America." The union never questioned Robinson's expenses again. In May 1951 she wrote to Hillman that she hoped to continue working for the Amalgamated but confessed that recent events had "not done much to stimulate that resolve." She also urged her good friend to visit her in the South, where Black people faced "open animosities rather than hypocritical relationships."[67]

Organizing in 1951 was complicated for Robinson by the fact that she was pregnant with her daughter, Jan. Robinson wrote to Hillman that the ACWA ought to set up a "Husband's Traveling Fund." Later in her life she reflected on the toll that organizing and travel had taken on her marriage, which ended shortly after Jan's birth in July 1952, a month after she finished law school. Despite the challenges she faced in the segregated South, Robinson recalled the period as rewarding and argued that working with Black southern workers had "been good for my soul," letting her forget, even if only briefly, that "there was ever anything unpleasant about the 'cause.'"[68]

After Jan's birth Robinson was ill for two years, too exhausted to even open a book. Her friends believed that she was worn down by the struggles and compromises she had had to make. Springer remembered that Robinson "cried out of frustration very often. . . . What she was frustrated and cried about was the compromise that she couldn't get it all at once. And by her standards it was do all at once." When a woman Robinson was mentoring in New York City's District 65 was mistreated by the leadership, she lamented, "It hurts you; it crushes your heart."[69] Activism and political leadership came with a cost for leaders such as Robinson and Adelmond who had high expectations of themselves and of the movement and who bore witness to the workers' suffering and disappointment.

"We Want Our Fair Share":
Dollie Robinson's Postlaundry Organizing

Disappointed by her experiences in the LWJB and ACWA, Robinson nonetheless remained committed to the labor movement, pursuing workers' rights through posts in the government and union movement while also continuing to organize politically at the community level. Alongside a group of African American men, in 1953, Robinson helped found the influential Brooklyn-based Pioneer Civic Association. The group was led by Myles Paige, the Black judge whom Robinson had helped win reelection in the mid-1940s. When Robinson first approached the men about joining the Association, they informed her that "we can't have you coming to a meeting of all men," but Robinson showed up anyway, criticizing the men for their propensity to talk but not take action and informing them that if she had six sons she would be ruling the world. As a new mother, Robinson offered to do the "leg work" organizing people in the community while she took Jan out on her daily walks.[70] Robinson's activism, described by women's studies scholar Kimberly Springer as "interstitial politics," enabled her to combine her commitment to mothering and politics by organizing "in the cracks" of her daily life. Robinson served briefly as a coleader of Brooklyn's Democratic Club, representing the Pioneer Civic Association.[71]

Robinson would follow the path of Rose Schneiderman, moving between positions in the labor movement and government. From 1956 to 1958 she served as New York State's secretary of labor, a position for which Bessie Hillman had recommended her. During her time as secretary she worked undercover at a migrant labor camp, using a little Minox camera to document the workers' con-

FIGURE 10. Dollie Lowther Robinson, the new secretary of the New York State Department of Labor (*far left*), meets with state industrial commissioner Isador Lubin, ACWA vice president Bessie Hillman, and ACWA vice president Gladys Dickason (*far right*), undated. Credit: Sam Reiss. Folder 16, box 8, 5743 P, ACWA Photographs, Kheel Center, Cornell University, Ithaca, NY.

ditions. Robinson described the change she and her staff were able to secure as incremental and expressed her frustration at how long it took to secure progressive labor reform, even from her perch as head of the Department of Labor.[72]

In 1961 Robinson's good friend Congressman Adam Clayton Powell Jr. tapped her for a job in Washington to work as a special assistant in the Women's Department of the Bureau of Labor under Director Esther Peterson. Robinson, who at the time was organizing hospital workers for AFSCME District Council 37, distinctly remembered Powell calling her to tell her that "I've just left the White House and the President tells me to tell you to come on down."[73] In her 1995 memoir, longtime labor and consumer activist Esther Peterson insisted that it was she and not Powell who was behind Robinson's appointment. Peterson explained that she appointed Robinson because she wanted to see the Labor Department "take the lead in minority hiring by bringing Black women into the Kennedy administration."[74]

Robinson and Peterson's relationship extended back to the 1930s, when the two women met through the WTUL. Peterson remembered that in the 1930s she recruited Robinson to attend the Bryn Mawr Summer School and that the two women became fast friends. Robinson served with Peterson and about fifteen other women in the Labor Advisory Committee, established in 1945 by the Women's Bureau to function as a policy think tank for women labor leaders. Robinson was part of a small but influential group that helped Peterson draft the proposal that convinced President Kennedy to establish the President's Commission on the Status of Women (PCSW).[75]

Whether it was Powell or Peterson who suggested Robinson for the position of special assistant is unclear, although perhaps both did. The Black community celebrated Robinson's appointment as evidence of their growing political power in Washington and feted her with fancy receptions attended by African American luminaries.[76] The former laundry activist worked on high-profile files, including the committee on the status of minority women, chaired by National Council of Negro Women head Dorothy Height. Regrettably, we do not have a record of Robinson's response to Height's final report, "Problems of Negro Women," which hypothesized that Black women's wage-earning prowess had created a matriarchal family structure that destabilized the Black family and emasculated Black men, a reiteration of sociologist and future US Senator Patrick Moynihan's matriarchy thesis.[77] Shortly after the publication of the report, and perhaps not entirely unrelated, Robinson resigned from the Women's Bureau.

Robinson did not directly discuss her departure from the Women's Bureau in her 1976 oral history interview or in the video documentary her son-in-law, Melvin McCray, produced in 2006. In the interview Robinson alluded to interpersonal tensions between Peterson and herself. Robinson explained that she "got awfully angry" with Peterson because she would always talk about her own children but never ask Robinson about Jan. Robinson finally told Peterson that "until you ask me about Jan, I'm not interested in hearing anything about yours." She also reported that she had left jobs where coworkers had failed to express an interest in her daughter.[78] In brief statements to the Black press, Robinson denied that her "resignation" had anything to do with "problems in the agency." She reported that she had been offered a promotion in Washington but preferred to return to her "first love," the labor movement, and to her family in Brooklyn.[79] Peterson publicly lamented Robinson's departure, telling the press that "my sadness over losing a friend and colleague is softened only by the fact she is returning to trade unionism, a field we both love." Peterson honored Robinson at her farewell party with gifts and accolades.[80]

In her memoir, published thirty years later, Peterson told a very different story about Robinson's departure. Peterson insisted that she been forced to fire Robinson when she refused to hand over data she had collected for the Women's Bureau, a violation of her duties as a public official. Peterson complained that

Robinson did not "appreciate that she was now a government employee; [and] we had a program to carry out." Referencing their twenty-five-year friendship, Peterson described herself as a victim of Robinson's unprofessional behavior and lamented that firing her had been one of the hardest decisions she had ever had to make. "I loved that woman," Peterson recalled. "I did everything I could to put her forward, but she made it impossible."[81]

Peterson attributed Robinson's act of insubordination to both personal failings and radical influences. Peterson reported that Robinson "had such a huge chip on her shoulder that weighed her down." Such resentments, Peterson argued, led Robinson to act unprofessionally, leaving Peterson no choice but to fire her. Yet, somewhat inconsistently, Peterson also attributed Robinson's transgression to external influences. The director explained that Robinson had become "very close to some of the more radically activist Blacks in Washington," who instilled in her a "bitterness and a claim that came out as 'We want our fair share.'" Recognizing that Robinson was under the influence of radical forces, Peterson magnanimously concluded that "I don't blame her, I want to blame what was an almost evil influence over her. I think of Dollie as a victim of the times." Unwilling or unable to believe that her friend and subordinate would challenge her (and, by extension, the unwritten rules of a crumbling Jim Crow system), Peterson blamed the evil Black activists in Washington, who had misled Robinson.[82] In this telling Robinson is both an angry Black woman, a familiar trope, especially at a moment when Moynihan's matriarchy thesis was in ascendance, and a victim who was easily manipulated by radical Black activists, who were being unreasonable and even evil in their demands for racial justice.[83] No mention is made of the fact that Robinson was explicitly challenging racist workplace and social hierarchies when she refused to allow Peterson to patronize her by monopolizing their personal conversations and by micromanaging her work.

Both of Peterson's interpretations erased Robinson's lifetime of commitment to civil rights and record of activism and political leadership. It is clear that by 1963 the usually diplomatic Robinson had reached her limit. She was perhaps, like Pauli Murray, who served on the President's Commission on the Status of Women, also dismayed by Height's report, which blamed Black wage-earning women for many of the systemic problems afflicting the Black community.[84] Robinson, moreover, surely knew that she was overqualified for the position she held under Peterson. Her friend the esteemed African American journalist Ethel Payne of the *Chicago Defender*, known as the "First Lady of the Black Press" (Payne was only the second Black woman to be admitted to the White House press corps), criticized Robinson's appointment, arguing that the Kennedy administration "puffed up that appointment as far as they could go. . . . But so many of us felt that that was just so much tokenism. That she really had all the qualities to be at least an Assistant Secretary of Labor, not just to the Women's Bureau." (In the same year, 1963, Payne, the daughter of a sleeping car porter, would publicly criticize A. Philip Randolph for not inviting any women to speak at the March for Jobs and Freedom in Washington, DC, at which Martin Luther King Jr. delivered his historic "I Have a Dream" speech.)[85] Robinson, who by this time had more than two decades' experience in organized labor and government, as well as a law degree, surely resented being appointed to a position for which she was overqualified.

It is also likely that Robinson was indeed inspired by the more militant demands being made by Black nationalists, civil rights activists such as Rosa Parks, Jo Ann Robinson, and Ella Baker and by longtime supporters of organized labor. In 1959 Randolph challenged George Meany at the AFL-CIO conference about the shocking persistence of racially segregated locals. A few months later Black trade union leaders founded the Negro American Labor Council (NALC). Operating as a pressure group on organized labor, the NALC drew on Black separatist traditions that rejected white paternalism for Black self-determination, the goals and posture of the nascent Black Power movement.[86] In the South, Black Americans had put their bodies on the front lines of bloody battles to desegregate public spaces and exercise their right to vote. Young people, whom Robinson had always understood to be at the vanguard of social change, were no longer willing to defer to white allies to set the agenda and timeline for the freedom struggle. While we do not know for certain what happened between Peterson and Robinson, the falling out represents the tenuousness of interracial friendships in the twilight of Jim Crow as Black Americans refused to acquiesce to the patronizing practices of white liberal allies, no matter how well meaning.

After the turmoil in Washington, Robinson once again returned to the labor movement, taking a position as assistant (yet again) to the president of the Hotel and Allied Service Employees Union. Robinson coordinated the union's drive to organize hospital, hotel, and other low-income service workers.[87] It was while she was leading this drive that Elisabeth Petry, Ann Petry's daughter, first saw a Black woman in charge. When Elisabeth visited Robinson's Manhattan office in 1964 she was shocked to find a group of "small white men circling her desk and taking orders" while her mother's friend knitted a pink angora sweater for a friend's baby. Petry remembers how small the men appeared as they scurried around the tall, imposing Robinson, who sat behind an enormous desk holding the tiniest knitting needles Petry had ever seen. Petry wondered if Robinson had staged the incident so that Petry could see a Black woman exercising power, but either way: in 2009 she still vividly remembered her first experience seeing a Black woman in charge.[88]

In 1965 Robinson went to Africa as part of the Department of Commerce's East African Trade Fair to promote American products abroad. In the evenings she snuck off to attend clandestine union meetings in the hills organized by the hotel workers. She described the unions there, which were still in their infancy, as the "greatest in the world." "The people serving us in the hotels," Robinson explained, "in the daytime—these people who were so meek and humble. At night, when they'd scratch on your door to come to a meeting, they were the leaders." Masses of people, Robinson argued, attended union meetings on the hill.[89] In 1968 Robinson ran in the Democratic primary in Bedford-Stuyvesant for the seat for the newly created Twelfth Congressional District in the US House of Representatives, losing to state assemblywoman Shirley Chisholm.[90]

In the final period of Robinson's life, she moved into the educational sphere, serving on the board of the Small College, a unit of Brooklyn College that provided adult education. Robinson had helped convince the city to provide funds for the program. Springer insisted that "there are masses of people who graduated from college as adults as a result of her efforts." Her final job (she died in August 1983 after a series of strokes) reflected her lifelong commitment to education.[91]

In 1976 Robinson framed her removal from the LWJB in philosophical terms, explaining that "it was better for me to have a free soul, I mean being a free operator," than to have built up the resentments that destroyed so many others, no doubt an allusion to her good friend Adelmond. Robinson moved "in and out of the [labor] movement" and appreciated that her approach gave her the autonomy to speak candidly about the movement. She admitted, though, with a hint of regret, that had she been older and more experienced when the racial upheavals erupted in the laundry union, she might have chosen to stay and fight.[92] In the 1940s Robinson fought hard for the laundry workers while also maintaining her personal and professional autonomy and dignity. The fact that she survived is a testament to her perseverance and to the keen political skills with which she was so widely credited.

The LWJB under Louis Simon: Colonial Unionism

The 1950 ousting of the leaders of the democratic initiative all but guaranteed the continued marginalization of women and people of color in the laundry union. George Morris of the *Daily Worker* described Simon and the union's mostly white officers as behaving "like colonial agents" toward the Black and Puerto Rican workers. The workers noted that 75 percent of the membership was controlled by the two thousand drivers and four hundred engineers, all of whom were white men. Rank-and-file workers told the *New York Amsterdam News* that union leaders followed the "white supremacy attitude" and reported that Simon and his ACWA supporters insisted on having a white manager and white president of the LWJB and a white chairman of the board of directors. Simon's wife, Irene Simon, led the retired members program, established in 1957, on a voluntary basis.[93]

With the leaders of the democratic initiative ejected from the union, Simon launched a campaign to rebuild the organization. As part of his initiative, in

July 1950 he announced that the union would intensify the organizing drive begun in the mid-1940s and establish a new Stabilization Committee (once a permanent office) to ensure the observance of all provisions of the collective agreement. In July 1952 Simon reported that against "great odds" the union had managed to organize fifty-three new laundries. The manager insisted that union officials would zealously enforce the collective agreement and lectured the business agents on their duty to police the employers and to provide the workers with excellent service.[94]

In a departure from past practice, Simon announced in 1950 that the sex-based differentials in sickness and accident benefits had been eliminated, a longtime demand of Adelmond's. Simon explained that because of the benefit fund's excellent condition, the union would now be able to pay all union members fifteen dollars, instead of ten dollars for women and fifteen dollars for men. The elimination of the differential was framed not as an issue of equity but rather as one of financial circumstance. No mention was made of New York State's Equal Pay Law or of Adelmond's advocacy.[95] In 1954 the union opened the Amalgamated Laundry Workers Health Center to provide laundry workers with out-patient care, as well as diagnostic, preventive, and therapeutic services. A year later the center extended its services to the "nonworking dependent wives of members" but not husbands, an extension that benefited only the minority male membership.[96]

Simon addressed the workers' long-standing complaints about union democracy by promising to hold regular shop meetings and LWJB meetings. Members were assured that they would enjoy "complete freedom" to discuss union matters and offer constructive criticism. He also promised to expedite complaints against the Amalgamated Insurance Company about the slow payment of benefits, another one of Adelmond's demands.[97]

In March 1951, after returning from a short and "much needed rest," Simon announced that the efforts to rebuild the union had succeeded. The former driver declared that the deserters had been beaten and their misguided followers had returned to the union fold. He reported with satisfaction that workers in seven locals had agreed to an assessment of one dollar a month to strengthen the union. The manager rejoiced when in January 1952 at a State Labor Relations Board representation election, requested by the AFL-affiliated Laundry Workers International Union, workers voted to stay with the LWJB. Of the 11,202 votes cast, only 1,573 were for the AFL, evidence, Simon argued, of the workers' support for the CIO union.[98] The manager warned against any future acts of disloyalty and singled out potential disrupters who might try to inject racial politics into the union to advance their agenda. Simon and Clark described the rebuilding of the union as a "golden chapter" in the LWJB's history, and ACWA vice president Jacob Potofsky praised Simon for running a "clean and honest organization."[99]

In order to prevent the emergence of another Charlotte Adelmond, Simon revised the procedures for business agents in 1952. Since the union's inception, locals had elected their own business agents. Following the practices used in the New York joint boards in the clothing and shirt industries, beginning in 1952 the locals would be allowed to nominate business agents, but the elections would be held at the membership rather than at the local level. The LWJB in turn would assign successful candidates to a district. Simon explained that the new process would empower the manager to move business agents around to where they were most needed. It would also enable the manager to dilute the ties between popular business agents and rank-and-file workers while also exerting tighter control over local staff.[100]

A "Special Place" for Black Workers:
The LWJB in the 1960s

Throughout the turmoil, African American leader Odell Clark supported Simon, denouncing the disrupters for "artificially creating racial issues which have not existed and do not exist." Clark insisted that Simon was committed to racial equality and pointed to the manager's highly visible financial support of the National Urban League and NAACP and his own position as assistant manager as proof. Yet when Simon was out of town on business trips a white organizer was put in charge of the union rather than Clark.[101] Clark nonetheless supported Simon and trumpeted the union's longtime commitment to labor-management cooperation. In 1953 he told a group of Yale University students that "harmony between labor and management is conducive to productivity" and proudly noted that since the union's formation in 1937 the laundry workers had never had to resort to a major strike.[102]

Despite his loyalty, Clark would suffer a similar fate as Adelmond. In 1959, after twenty years with the union and ten years as assistant manager, Clark was removed by the forty-member LWJB in what workers described as a "surprise move." The LWJB chose African American Burt Jemmott, trade manager of Local 331, to replace Clark, keeping the practice of having a Black person under a white head. Black workers, who accused Simon of orchestrating the ousting, told the *New York Amsterdam News* that Clark had been removed because the "controlling whites" feared that he was in line to assume the position of manager should Simon retire. The move angered Black workers, who sent letters of protest to the union, demanding a review of the process.[103]

The ousting must have been incredibly painful for Clark, who, unlike Adelmond, probably never saw it coming. In 1960 Clark finally denounced Simon, accusing the manager of using sneaky tactics to control union elections and to build a "Trade Union Empire." Clark accused Simon of fomenting racial tensions between white and Black workers and of discriminating against Black union candidates and officials. He also accused the ACWA of collaborating with Simon to keep Black workers in a "special place" in the union.[104] Unable to secure a new job, Clark volunteered with the NAACP, work he ruefully noted was rewarding but did not pay the bills. In 1961 Congressman Powell appointed Clark assistant chief investigator for the House of Representatives Committee on Labor and Education. The *New York Amsterdam News* reported on the appointment with the title "Paging Laundry Workers!"[105]

In October 1960 Black laundry worker Sylvia Cullman wrote an editorial thanking the *New York Amsterdam News* for taking an interest in the "deplorable conditions" in the laundry union. She accused Simon of making a $2,500 donation to the Urban League, where he served on the national board, to offset Clark's charges of racism.[106] As Cullman understood, Simon's suppression of Black leaders went hand in hand with his public support of civil rights. Simon served as a trustee of the National Urban League, as a member of the executive board of the New York Urban League, and on the labor committee of the United Negro College Fund. Social reform organizations such as the Urban League provided window dressing for Simon. Cullman, who reported that she was nearly sick to her stomach after hearing Simon give a speech at the Urban League on civil rights, argued that the donations revealed that Simon believed that Black people could be bought. She also accused Jemmott, Clark's replacement, of being a "real Uncle Tom." Her coworkers, Cullman insisted, needed to "wake up and get wise" to these tactics, and the *New York Amsterdam News* needed to "keep right on knocking this hypocrite."[107]

In 1960, a year after Clark's ousting, the AFL-CIO appointed Simon chairman of the New York City Central Labor Council's recently created Civil Rights Committee. The appointment, AFL-CIO officials explained, was in recognition of Simon's "many years of activity in the civil rights movement." Simon also won a spot on the National AFL-CIO Civil Rights Committee, founded to head off criticism from the left-wing National Negro Labor Council (NNLC). Simon's appointment as a civil rights watchdog left the *New York Amsterdam News* asking, "Who Watches Simon?"[108]

In 1961 the Harlem-based United African Nationalist Movement (UANM) picketed a dinner at the Waldorf-Astoria where Simon was being awarded a distinguished service award by the New York City Central Labor Council. Led by former Garveyite street orator James R. Lawson, the UANM saw itself as the rival of the Urban League, which the UANM accused of being "in the pay of white folks" and rejected the social welfare policies of urban liberalism. Five hundred people, including National Urban League head Lester Granger, paid twenty-five dollars a ticket to hear testimonials to Simon. Sitting two seats over from Simon was civil rights activist Bayard Rustin. Most galling to the UANM, Simon's award came with a round-the-world trip to visit top union

FIGURE 11. Louis Simon (*standing on the left of the image*) receiving a distinguished service award from the New York City Central Labor Council at the Waldorf Astoria. Standing to his direct left is ACWA vice president Frank Rosenblum. At the far right of the image and seated is civil rights leader Bayard Rustin. Ca. 1961. Credit: Sam Reiss. Folder 1, box 33, 5743 P, ACWA Photographs, Kheel Center, Cornell University, Ithaca, NY.

and government leaders, including in Africa.[109] UANM picketers demanded congressional hearings into the "sweatshop wages" of the city's twenty thousand Black and Puerto Rican laundry workers and into Simon's activities, as well as an immediate union election conducted on a "democratic basis" to ensure a more representative leadership. They also protested Simon's upcoming trip to Africa, arguing that the union should send a Black laundry official instead.[110]

Despite the efforts of Black workers in the 1940s and 1950s and Black nationalist organizations in the 1960s, Simon remained head of the laundry union until 1982, when he finally retired and was replaced by the popular Black union leader Cecil Toppin, a man whom Robinson had mentored. In the 1960s scholars Nathan Glazer and Daniel Patrick Moynihan described the laundry as a low-wage industry with a "Negro and Puerto Rican working force . . . represented by a union whose top leadership is Jewish." They also noted that this was something the Black worker was apt to resent.[111]

Carmen Western, a Puerto Rican laundry worker who organized under Simon in the 1960s and 1970s, explained that Simon controlled the union by handpicking officials he could control. She described Simon as a "very, very dry person" who was "very particular with his people. He was friendly with the people that he liked." Western had to be careful about what she said, because Simon had stool pigeons who reported back to him. She also remembered that Simon was not a good listener or public speaker, something she attributed to the fact that "he was not a laundry worker, let me put it that way. He never was." By the 1960s Simon had become so disconnected from the rank and file that organizers like Western did not believe he had ever worked in the industry, even as a driver.[112]

African American Joan Boyce, whose mother worked in a laundry, began working in the union office in 1969. She remembered that Simon would come into the office at around seven in the morning and leave by two in the afternoon, spending most of his time behind a closed door. In 2008 she described him as "alright" but remembered that he "didn't do a lot of talking to the girls in the office," something she attributed in part to his age. "You have to understand," Boyce explained, that "when Simon retired in '82, he was already in his eighties."[113]

Under Simon, the LWJB offered little space for rank-and-file participation in the union. The pages of *The Advance*, once filled with stories about the social and organizational activities taking place at the local level and through the Education Department, celebrated the accomplishments of the union's leaders. Stories about individual workers were rare, and the Education Department appears to have all but disappeared. Articles admonished the workers to appreciate the wage gains secured through collective bargaining, as modest as they were, and the insurance benefits.

Steven Fraser, Kim Moody, Elizabeth Faue, and other labor scholars argue that as early as the 1940s some CIO unions embraced the bureaucratic, business unionism associated with their former nemesis, the American Federation of Labor. In unions such as the United Auto Workers and LWJB, this evolution was carried out through the suppression of internal opposition, the routinization of collective bargaining, the expansion of the administrative apparatus, and the rejection of the social unionism that had animated the CIO in its formative years. In the LWJB the removal of the communists in the early 1940s and the ousting of the leaders of the democratic initiative in the late 1940s hastened this process.[114] The deliberate suppression of Black and radical workers' activism illustrates some of the limitations of the mid-twentieth-century labor movement for women and people of color and highlights the tensions between union democracy and union bureaucracy that played out in some industrial unions in the postwar era.[115] The ejection of the founding leaders of the union and the business unionism that flourished in the 1950s put serious limits on what the LWJB would achieve for its members. In 1966, after thirty years of no strikes, close to half of the union membership—approximately eighty-five hundred workers—earned less than $1.50 an hour, the new minimum wage, set to go into effect in January 1967, and women and people of color continued to earn the lowest wages and perform the most difficult jobs. In response to these conditions, in 1967, on the cusp of the rise of the Black Power movement, the laundry workers finally went out on strike for the first time in thirty years.[116]

Epilogue

Building a Democratic Initiative in the Twenty-First Century

By the early 1970s the Laundry Workers Joint Board had become a shell of its former self. The medical center, which had served thousands of laundry workers and their families in the 1950s and 1960s, was all but abandoned. By 1964 the union's membership had dropped from its high point of thirty thousand in 1939 to under fifteen thousand.[1] When African American laundry worker Joan Boyce moved from the shop to the union office in 1969, beginning her career as a bookkeeper for the LWJB's successor, the Laundry, Dry Cleaning and Allied Workers Joint Board (now the Laundry, Distribution and Food Service Joint Board, Workers United, affiliated with the Service Employees' International Union), the union had eight thousand members. By 2008 the membership had dropped to forty-five hundred members. When she was interviewed in 2008, Boyce, whose mother worked for the union during its heyday, reported that the workers no longer participated in union activities except around negotiation time. While Boyce recognized that the contraction of the industry and subsequent decline in membership had contributed to the low levels of worker engagement, she also wondered if "the problem is, today—maybe it's that the membership doesn't see what the union does for them . . . or how they can help the union. Which is a shame."[2] Boyce, who attended LWJB Christmas parties with her mother and sisters in the 1950s, lamented that the Education Department, which had given the laundry workers "someplace to go, someplace that they gathered," was no longer active. She wondered if the organization's failure to maintain its social programs had contributed to the worker apathy she saw all around her.[3]

The traditional explanation for the decline of the laundry union is that the postwar proliferation of self-serve Laundromats, affordable home washing and drying machines, and new fabrics that required little or no ironing decimated the industry and thus the union. And these developments certainly did diminish the industry and contribute to the union's shrinking numbers, but power laundries did not disappear, as some postwar narratives suggest. In 2018 the laundry and dry cleaning sector employed 213,350 people nationwide, not much less than in 1930.[4] Laundries survived by doing what they had always done: they adapted to the changing needs of their customers. Laundries that had offered family service returned to the industry's roots by branching out into industrial and institutional work and offering new services such as dry cleaning, carpet cleaning, and alterations. By the 1960s most laundries did some cleaning and dyeing, and most dry-cleaning plants did some laundry work. Some power laundries opted to confront the competition head-on, building and operating their own coin-operated laundries or Laundromats.[5]

Linen supply laundries have been particularly well situated to capitalize on the expansion of hospitals and long-term care homes, institutions that produce large amounts of laundry and, consistent with neoliberal practices, have been outsourcing their work. In the early 2000s the majority of power laundry workers labored for corporations such as Cintas and Aramark, companies that provide and launder linen, uniforms, and other products for hospitals, hotels, restaurants, and other businesses. Cintas alone employs more than thirty thousand workers in its five hundred facilities across the United States and Canada and controls about one-third of the US uniform market.[6]

The hand laundries of the early and mid-1900s are the retail laundries of today, small storefront shops that provide wash and fold services and that are owned and operated mainly by immigrant families, many of whom are Chinese. In 2019 New York City was home to four thousand retail laundries. As in the early 1900s, retail laundry shops employ vulnerable workers, including significant numbers of Latinx and undocumented workers. Much like their predecessors reported, the workers describe hot and dangerous working conditions, abusive treatment, and wages as low as seven dollars an hour, about half of the city's minimum wage for small businesses. In a 2019 investigative report produced by Fabrice Robinet for the *New York Times*, Megan Chambers, comanager of the SEIU-affiliated Laundry, Distribution and Food Services Joint Board, explained that with thousands of shops competing for the same customers, the retail laundry sector was engaged in a "race to the bottom."[7]

In contrast to retail laundries, the power or industrial laundries of the twenty-first century are highly mechanized and mostly corporate-owned establishments. Washing machines now automatically feed the detergent into the machines and unload the laundered garments. A machine washer can now operate multiple machines simultaneously using a computer program. Robotic conveyer systems transfer linens and uniforms between the large cylindrical tunnel washers, industrial driers, and flat-work machines, the latter of which now automatically unfold tangled pieces, eliminating the much despised position of shaking.[8]

From the outside, the industrial laundries of the early 2000s give the illusion of being safer and cleaner than the crowded dingy laundries of the early 1900s. In 2008 Katie Unger, a union research strategist and coordinator of Uniform Justice, a campaign to organize Cintas workers, pointed out that while "a newer laundry certainly looks like a nicer place to work—it's cooler, it's cleaner, it has less visible, sort of, visible hot and sweatiness," laundries in fact remain extremely dangerous workplaces, a result of both automation and the fact that many employers do not install adequate safety guards. Industrial accidents remain common, especially at companies like Cintas, where high production quotas encourage workers to sacrifice safety for job security.[9] Lax safety standards and high production quotas contributed to the 2007 death of Cintas worker Eleazar Torres Gomez of Tulsa, Oklahoma. Torres Gomez was burned to death after a robotic arm swept him into an industrial drier while he stood on an unguarded conveyer belt trying to dislodge a jam. The Occupational Safety and Health Administration (OSHA) fined Cintas $2.78 million for safety and health violations that contributed to the man's death, the highest fine ever levied against a service sector employer. Four years later, in 2011, Kevin Burgess, a Cintas worker in Louisville, Kentucky, died in a similar accident when he was pulled into an industrial drier while trying to dislodge a jam.[10]

Poor environmental conditions remain among the most serious problems in the laundry industry. Workers at plants servicing hospitals handle linen covered in blood, feces, and dangerous biohazards and report finding needles and body parts in the bags. Workers washing linen and uniforms from restaurants find rotten food, broken glass, and cockroaches in the bundles. Despite such conditions, many employers fail to provide basic protective equipment or vaccinations for their workers.[11] Edgar Gonzalez-Cierra, an immigrant from the Dominican Republic who worked in a Bronx laundry between 2006 and 2011, reported that the employer failed to provide the workers with soap to wash the vomit, blood, and feces from their hands.[12]

Much like the power laundry owners discussed in this book, in the early 2000s laundry employers hired workers who were structurally disadvantaged by their race, ethnicity, gender, immigration status, and other social variables. In 2020 two-thirds of laundry workers are women, and many are Latin American immigrants and African Americans. In the early 2000s Cintas, one of the nation's largest industrial launderers, reported that close to three-quarters of its production or inside workers were minorities, compared to less than one-tenth of its managers and officials. In New York City immigrant women who have lost their jobs in the garment industry as factories relocate to the nonunion South or abroad have moved into laundries where employers exploit their lack of employment options, much like their employers did in the 1920s, when they hired Black women escaping domestic service.[13] The composition of today's laundry workforce reveals the remarkable historical continuity in the gendering and racialization of care and service work such as cleaning. As historian Gabriel Winant notes, in the twenty-first century women of color overwhelmingly perform the welfare state's tasks of caring for the old, sick, disabled, and other "surplus populations," work that is located in the low-wage and often unregulated service and care sectors, which, with the decline of manufacturing, have moved to the center of the economy.[14] With the structural collapse of manufacturing, laundry workers have the dubious distinction of working in an industry that cannot be outsourced. Their gendered and racialized labor forms the heart of the postindustrial economy.

As in the past, minimum wage and overtime violations are common in the laundry industry. In 2007 a staff member with a government regulatory agency in New York explained, "There's an industry-wide problem about failure to pay the minimum wage, and these workers are almost never paid time and a half. When we ask owners why they're paying so little, they say, 'That's what everybody else pays.'" In 2018 laundry workers nationwide took home median hourly earnings of $11.16, and 25 percent earned less than $10.00 an hour.[15] Sexual harassment, common in the early 1900s, persists today. At Cintas, racialized workers and women report being the targets of crude sexual and racist jokes and comments. At a Cintas plant in North Irvington, New Jersey, the general manager called the women "sluts" and "bitches" and used the N-word to refer to African Americans.[16] Even after the passage of antidiscrimination laws, women and people of color continue to face overt racial and sexual abuse in the laundries.

The gender-based occupational divisions implemented at the turn of the twentieth century have for the most part remained intact today. In the early 2000s laundry employers excluded women from the higher-paying washing and driving jobs, a testament to the resilience of the sexual division of labor that took root during the industry's formative years. As the durability of the laundry's occupational structure reveals, once a job is defined as male or female, the demand to fill that job becomes sex-specific.[17] In a 2004 Equal Employment Opportunity Commission complaint, Cintas worker Robert Ramirez reported that when the women asked to work in the wash room, the manager "just laughed." In 2009 UNITE HERE organizer Doria Barrera explained that when women applied for driving jobs they were told that those were "men's jobs." Lawsuits filed by workers and their union allies have led to the employment of some female drivers, but in most laundries, driving jobs, which pay more and provide the greatest opportunities for occupational advancement, continue to be held by men.[18]

With a few exceptions, the race-based occupational divisions that so angered Charlotte Adelmond have remained intact in the twenty-first century. Black and Latinx men have gained access to driving and washing jobs only because the exodus of white men from the industry in the second half of the twentieth century necessitated their hiring. But in places where white men continue to work in laundries, the racial division of labor remains in place. Cintas workers report that the employers refuse to hire African Americans and Latinx workers for higher-paying jobs as drivers, salespeople, and managers and instead assign them the dirtiest and lowest-paying jobs on the production floor. When African American Robert Harris tried to get a job as a driver at Cintas's Rochester, New York, location in 2004, his white supervisor frankly admitted that the company was not going to hire Black men as drivers.[19]

Racist hiring practices have encouraged the drivers to see themselves as a higher class of workers, much like they did in the early 1900s. In many cities, drivers are represented by the Teamsters rather than the unions that represent the production workers. Even in cities like New York, where drivers belong to the same union, Boyce admits that organizers have trouble convincing the men to support the inside workers because of the perks they enjoy, such as higher wages. In some campaigns, the union has been able to organize the inside workers but failed to get the drivers until the union had secured the first contract.[20] The deeply entrenched gender- and race-based occupational hierarchies in the laundry continue to impede unionization.

Laundry Worker Mobilizing in the Twenty-First Century

Substandard working conditions have spurred laundry worker organizing and elicited allied support both in New York and beyond. In 2011, with the support of community allies, laundry workers in New York City founded the Laundry Workers Center. The grassroots, worker-led nonprofit aims to build solidarity and empower the mostly women of color who work in the city's retail laundries. Like the WTUL did in the 1910s and 1920s, the Laundry Workers Center provides educational training for the workers and helps forge alliances between worker activists and sympathetic community allies.[21] To raise public awareness about conditions in the laundries, in 2018 the Laundry Workers Center published the results of a survey, conducted by members who posed as customers, that uncovered that one in five retail laundry workers earned less than the minimum wage and 36 percent did not receive overtime pay. In June 2018 a group of laundry workers who participated in the survey began holding protests in front of some of the city's most exploitative laundries.[22]

As in the 1930s, when Mayor La Guardia supported the laundry campaign, New York's laundry workers have benefited from political support at the municipal level. Appalled by the abysmal conditions in New York City laundries that serviced restaurants, hotels, and hospitals, in 2015 New York City councilmembers African Latino Ritchie Torres, the first openly gay candidate elected to legislative office in the Bronx and as of the November 2020 election the first openly gay Black man to serve in Congress as the representative of New York's Fifteenth Congressional District, and Dan Garodnick introduced the City Laundry Equity and Accountability (CLEAN) Act. Framing the passage of the act as a necessity for both the workers and public health, the CLEAN Act sought to improve standards in the industry through licensing and regulation requirements. Torres announced the legislation on the steps of city hall flanked by members of CLEAN NYC, a coalition of labor, public health, community, and immigrant organizations determined to improve conditions in the laundries. The City Council unanimously passed the CLEAN Act in July 2016, and shortly thereafter Mayor Bill de Blasio signed the bill into law.[23]

As in the 1930s, low wages and poor working conditions have inspired union campaigns, including at Cintas, which, as the nation's largest industrial launderer and uniform provider, sets the standards in the industry. In the fall of 2002 UNITE (which had not yet merged with HERE) launched a nationwide campaign entitled Uniform Justice to organize Cintas's seventeen thousand laundry workers and drivers through card-check and neutrality agreements.[24] What transpired next was a campaign that in many ways resembled the campaign fought and won in the 1930s by Dollie Robinson, Charlotte Adelmond, Beatrice Lumpkin, and Jessie Smith.

In the early 2000s a core group of worker leaders from Cintas, many of them women of color, emerged from the shop floor to lead a campaign to win economic and racial justice. Backed by a large international union, they built a movement focused on eradicating the racist and sexist work culture at Cintas, as well as winning economic dignity for the workers, a strategy that mirrored the social and civil rights unionism employed by Black workers and their allies in the early and mid-twentieth century. Uniform Justice's expansive and intersectional approach attracted key allies, including the NAACP, the Congressional Hispanic Caucus, Jobs with Justice, and faith-based organizations such as Interfaith Community for Worker Justice, alliances that resembled those formed one hundred years earlier with the Women's Trade Union League, the Negro Labor Committee, the League of Women Shoppers, local ministers, and community leaders.[25]

Yet the Cintas campaign did not produce the internal activist solidarities that were critical to the workers' success in the 1930s. In the early 2000s a core group of worker leaders, mostly women of color, engaged in significant activism: conducting home visits and talking to their coworkers about their rights; sending petitions to management; forming organizing committees; educating community and business leaders and local politicians about the conditions at Cintas; and, finally, participating in marches in their hometowns, in Cincinnati (the site of Cintas's headquarters), and in Washington. But despite the leadership and activism of these worker leaders, the vast majority of Cintas workers did not participate in the campaign. One worker leader explained that "there's no collegiality amongst coworkers, there's no group spirit, no union, we're not united." Most of the workers were not mobilized to publicly support the campaign or to engage in collective action.[26]

Fears of employer retaliation loomed large during the Cintas campaign and suppressed worker participation, which is unsurprising, given Cintas's well-documented history of antiunionism. Cintas has a long record of engaging in unlawful surveillance and harassment of union organizers and disrupting organizing meetings. In an extraordinary move, in 2008 the company filed a RICO (Racketeer Influenced and Corrupt Organizations Act) suit against UNITE HERE, the Teamsters, and Change to Win alleging that the unions had used negative and false attacks in an "extortion" campaign to damage the company's reputation and force it to enter into card-check neutrality agreements. The company-led union attacks sowed doubt in the workers' minds about organized labor's capacity to protect workers. A Mexican American washer explained that "all the people are afraid, they are few who support the union because they're afraid they'll fire them."[27]

Employers used similarly aggressive tactics in the 1930s, but laundry workers today face increasingly sophisticated antiunion tactics in the form of well-paid antiunion consultants and industrial psychologists. One worker described the company men sent from Cintas's Ohio headquarters to hold captive audience meetings as "brainwashers." Labor legislation that once protected workers now protects employers. Captive audience and one-on-one meetings where workers are interrogated and told not to unionize were unfair labor practices in 1935. Today they are both legal and standard practice at companies like Cintas.[28] The well-funded antiunion campaigns launched by companies like Cintas and Walmart and the retrograde decisions made by the National Labor Relations Board have created a vastly more hostile organizing climate than in 1937, when the US president encouraged American workers to join a union. Beatrice Lumpkin remembered that with the signing of the Wagner Act "fear of joining a union was not a big factor then. Workers were not afraid because the U.S. government backed their legal right to join a union."[29]

Worker antiunionism, in part a response to the business unionism that took root in some unions in the postwar years, also undermined the Cintas campaign. Many of the Cintas worker leaders attributed the campaign's difficulties to their coworkers' distrust of unions because of their past membership in an ineffective union. Worker leaders explained that some of their coworkers believed that unions existed only to take money from workers, a belief that sociologist Steven Lopez refers to as "do-nothing unionism."[30] The seeds of these attitudes were planted by leaders like Louis Simon, who ran the LWJB like his own personal fiefdom.

Like the employers discussed in this book, Cintas management has also fomented tensions among workers by pitting African Americans against Latinx workers and inside workers against drivers. In the rabidly anti-immigrant climate of the early 2000s, the company also uses fears of deportation to intimidate workers. In 2006, as the union campaign was beginning to gain some steam, Cintas fired some of the most militant union supporters when they received "no-match" letters from the Social Security Administration; these letters indicate that a worker's Social Security number does not match a number on record with the government. Although no-match letters are sometimes the result of clerical error or change in marital status and are not to be used to fire employees, Cintas went ahead and fired four hundred workers nationwide, including some of the most militant prounion supporters.[31] Uniform Justice's lack of organizing success, then, underlines both the hostile organizing climate of the twenty-first century and the important interplay between organizational resources and internal activist solidarities. In the mid- and late 1930s laundry workers enjoyed the support of an international union that was able to tap into the deeply rooted internal solidarities forged by worker leaders such as Smith and Adelmond, who, alongside their coworkers, had mobilized against Depression-era conditions and racist treatment. The relatively favorable political and legal climate of the 1930s, the radical organizing of communists, and the militancy of Black workers who were part of the broader culture of protest in Harlem produced a vibrant worker-led campaign.

Learning from the Past:
The Case of the LWJB

As workers and their union allies look to the future, what can they learn from Dollie Robinson, Charlotte Adelmond, Beatrice Lumpkin, and Jessie Smith? During an interview in 1976, Robinson attributed organized labor's difficulties in general and the LWJB's in particular to the movement's failure to build coalitions with community allies and to nurture young trade unionists. Robinson explained that she did not see any labor people "doing anything in any churches, in any community rooms. They're all doing great things, big things, but on that local level, they're not doing it." Robinson argued that the movement had more "control when we were coming up, because we were really trying to convince communities that we were respectable people." The LWJB succeeded in the 1930s because Robinson, Smith, and others understood the value of rooting the union in the community and of forging alliances with local leaders and community organizations. In the 1970s, Robinson argued, unions used money to win workers' support without doing the hard work of building support at the community level. Unions, she lamented, no longer had the community ties.[32]

FIGURE 12. Beatrice Lumpkin speaking in front of Veracare Nursing Home on behalf of the Steelworkers Organization of Active Retirees, United Steel Workers, January 17, 2018, Chicago. Standing behind and to Lumpkin's right is Illinois governor J. B. Pritzker. Courtesy of Beatrice Lumpkin.

In 2006 Smith similarly worried that unions no longer organized in communities or enjoyed the support of rank-and-file workers, circumstances she attributed to the undemocratic and hierarchical practices of some union leaders. Critical to labor's revitalization, Smith argued, was organizing from the "bottom-up." The nonagenarian lamented that "everything is from the top-down now. There couldn't have been a movement if it wasn't from the bottom-up." Elaborating further, Smith explained, "I notice a lot of people have that attitude, that they know more than someone else. They want to let you know that. They try to be leaders and they're not good leaders. . . . the idea is to bring someone up to your level if you're a leader, an organizer, and train other people to be good leaders." Like Robinson and Adelmond, Smith understood that the centralization of power and the sometimes patronizing approach of top union leaders alienated workers and contributed to the movement's decline. In this context in 2006, she was hopeful that worker centers, with their community-based

approach to organizing and emphasis on worker empowerment, might fill the
vacuum created by organized labor's shrinking numbers.[33]

In 1976 Robinson was particularly critical of labor's failure to reach out to
Black communities, which she described as "so open for help that it's not even
funny." She wondered if perhaps labor was afraid to work with marginalized
Black communities, scared that their mobilization could spark a movement that
union leaders could not control. She pondered, "You see, you have to think of
what's the long-range program. And if you wake up sleeping dogs, you're going to have to deal with them. But if you let them sleep, you can just go ahead
and forget about them."[34] Union leaders perhaps feared the determination and
idealism of activist workers like Adelmond who refused to accept anything less
than equality at work and within the union. Deeply saddened by the LWJB's
demise, Robinson believed that the leaders let their "egos" and fear get in the
way and refused to develop "young-blood thinking."[35]

Lumpkin hypothesized that union leaders feared educating workers, since an
"informed, mobilized membership . . . may not re-elect you." Instead of nurturing the next generation of laundry workers to take over the union, Simon consolidated his power in the 1950s by surrounding himself with loyal supporters,
mostly white men who benefited from the status quo. Such practices meant that
despite the efforts of activist workers, such as those in the democratic initiative,
Black workers remained relegated to second-class citizenship or were ejected
from the union they had helped build. Robinson aptly noted that such leadership "perpetuated itself and nothing else."[36]

In the 1930s radical and African American workers used civil disobedience,
impromptu walkouts and strikes, community alliances, and social and educational activities to build solidarities and challenge the employers. Similarly
disruptive and innovative tactics might be used effectively today against corporations like Cintas that are extremely averse to negative publicity and that
require a quick turnaround of their product. Dan Clawson insists that to spark
the massive upsurge necessary to revitalize labor, unions will have to be willing to act aggressively, to break the rules, to engage in high-risk activism, and
to support worker-led mobilizations. Consistent with Robinson's and Smith's
observations, Clawson argues that the labor movement must connect with
its members in their communities and forge alliances with the organizations
and movements that represent other aspects of a worker's identity—the intersectional organizing so effectively employed by Robinson and Adelmond. Of
course, workers at antiunion corporations like Cintas and Walmart are un-
derstandably reluctant to risk their jobs, especially given the evisceration of
labor law protections. In this regard, labor law reform that allows workers to
unionize through card-check certification processes and includes mandates
for first contract arbitration is essential.[37] The history of laundry organizing
suggests that, just like the Wagner Act, labor law reform that protects instead

of hinders a worker's right to unionize would serve as a catalyst for organizing in the laundry and other low-wage industries.

Despite their sometimes bumpy road with the labor movement, Robinson, Smith, and Lumpkin remained convinced that the attainment of a more just society depends on the success of organized labor. In 2020, at the age of 102, Lumpkin, who is still a member of the Communist Party (in 1949 Bea married fellow comrade and African American steel worker Frank Lumpkin, whose epic struggle against Chicago's Wisconsin Steel in the 1980s and 1990s is chronicled in her book *"Always Bring a Crowd!": The Story of Frank Lumpkin, Steelworker*), continues to walk picket lines in her hometown of Chicago, most recently for Chicago teachers (wearing a hazmat suit constructed by her grandson Soren Kyale to protect her from the coronavirus!).[38] She campaigns for prolabor candidates in traditionally Republican states such as Indiana. Lumpkin believes that women's rights and civil rights can "best advance when labor's rights advance." For this reason, Lumpkin, a founding member of the Coalition of Labor Union Women, supported Barack Obama over Hillary Clinton in the 2008 race for the Democratic Party's presidential nomination, citing Obama's superior record in support of worker rights. In 2020 she supported Democratic presidential candidate Joe Biden and was pleased to see a woman of color, California senator Kamala Harris, win the position of vice president of the United States. (Bea voted by absentee ballot at a mailbox in her Chicago neighborhood wearing her hazmat-style suit.)[39] In 2017 Lumpkin helped found INTERGEN, a coalition of retirees from the Illinois Alliance for Retired Americans, young activists from the labor movement, the United Steelworkers, Chicago Young Workers, and Chicago Student Action. Lumpkin serves as corresponding secretary. The intergenerational and multiracial group supports initiatives such as the Fight for $15 minimum wage, Free Tuition Illinois, and broader struggles to win affordable health care and preserve Social Security.[40] Robinson, who understood firsthand that the transfer of knowledge and skills to young people was critical to maintaining a robust labor movement, would no doubt approve.

In 2006 Smith, who lived until the age of one hundred, predicted that people were finally waking up and realizing that "many of the things we struggled for, that people take for granted, are now being threatened. People are beginning to think again." She left the world in 2015 optimistic that young people and workers would rise to the challenges wrought by late capitalism.[41] Despite their mistreatment by the LWJB, Smith, Lumpkin, and Robinson remained convinced of organized labor's capacity to build a more just and equitable society for workers, women, and people of color. (It is not clear, given her ousting from the union and subsequent retreat from public life, if Adelmond felt the same way.) Robinson perhaps expressed it best when she explained, "I still love that movement. You can't get away from the fact that this is the best beginning ground for people. It really is, where their livelihood is."[42]

Notes

Introduction

1. "The Journal of the Laundry Workers Joint Board: 10th Anniversary Celebration," box 139, Amalgamated Clothing Workers of America Records, 1914–76, collection no. 5619, Kheel Center, Cornell University, Ithaca, NY (hereafter ACWA Records); Louis Paul Nestel, *Labor Relations in the Laundry Industry in Greater New York* (New York: Claridge Publishing, 1950), 37–40.

2. Dollie Lowther Robinson, interview by Bette Craig, July 1976, 3, 58–59, Twentieth Century Trade Union Woman: Vehicle for Social Change Oral History Project, Institute of Labor and Industrial Relations, Michigan Historical Collections, Bentley Historical Library, University of Michigan (hereafter Robinson, interview by Craig, TCTUW).

3. "Report of Organization," June–September 1937, 1, reel 4, New York Women Trade Union League Records, Arthur and Elizabeth Schlesinger Library on the History of Women in America, Radcliffe College, Cambridge, Massachusetts, microfilm version, *Papers of the Women's Trade Union League and Its Principal Leaders*, by Nancy Schrom Dye, Robin Miller Jacoby, and Edward T. James (Woodbridge, CT: Research Publications, [1985]) (hereafter NY WTUL Records); "Ten Thousand Laundry Workers Get ACWA Contract," *The Advance* 23, no. 9 (September 1937): 19; Nestel, *Labor Relations*, 38–40.

4. "The Journal of the LWJB," box 139, collection no. 5619, ACWA Records; Nestel, *Labor Relations*, 37–43; George S. Schuyler, "Harlem Boasts 42,000 Negro Labor Unionists," *Pittsburgh Courier*, August 21, 1937, 14.

5. US Department of Commerce, Bureau of the Census, *Fifteenth Census, Volume V: General Report on Occupations* (Washington, DC: Government Printing Office, 1933), 85.

6. Marilyn Bender, "Black Woman in Civil Rights: Is She a Second-Class Citizen?," *New York Times*, September 2, 1969, 42. This book uses Dollie Lowther Robinson's married name (she married in the middle of this story) to maintain consistency with other scholarly works.

7. Patricia Hill Collins, *Black Feminist Thought: Knowledge, Consciousness, and the Politics of Empowerment* (New York: Routledge, 1990), 225; Keona K. Ervin, *Gateway*

to Equality: Black Women and the Struggle for Economic Justice in St. Louis (Lexington: University Press of Kentucky, 2017), 3–4.

8. An exception is Arwen P. Mohun's *Steam Laundries: Gender, Technology, and Work in the United States and Great Britain, 1880–1940* (Baltimore, MD: Johns Hopkins Press, 1999).

9. Jacqueline Jones, *Labor of Love, Labor of Sorrow: Black Women, Work and the Family from Slavery to Present* (New York: Vintage Books, 1985), 177–78; Paula Giddings, *When and Where I Enter: The Impact of Black Women on Race and Sex in America* (Toronto: Bantam Books, 1988), 142–44.

10. Joe William Trotter, *Black Milwaukee: The Making of an Industrial Proletariat* (Urbana: University of Illinois Press, 2007), xii–xiii; Robinson, interview by Craig, 59, TCTUW.

11. Jane Filley and Therese Mitchell, *Consider the Laundry Workers* (New York: League of Women Shoppers, 1937); Ethel L. Best and Ethel Erickson, *A Survey of Laundries and Their Women Workers in 23 Cities*, United States Department of Labor, Women's Bureau Bulletin No. 78 (Washington, DC: Government Printing Office, 1930), 5, 17–36.

12. Alice Kessler-Harris, *A Woman's Wage: Historical Meanings and Social Consequences* (Lexington: University Press of Kentucky, 2014), 112.

13. Nancy Schrom Dye, *As Equals and as Sisters: Feminism, the Labor Movement, and the Women's Trade Union League of New York* (Columbia: University of Missouri Press, 1980).

14. "Annual Report of the WTUL," March 1, 1923–February 29, 1924, 2, reel 22, NY WTUL Records.

15. Trade Union Unity League, *Trade Union Unity League: Its Programs, Structures, Methods and History* (New York: Trade Union Unity League, 1930), 25–46; Mark Solomon, *The Cry Was Unity: Communists and African Americans, 1917–1936* (Jackson: University Press of Mississippi, 1998), 66. This book refers to Jessie Taft Smith by her married name, as she spent most of her one hundred years as Smith.

16. "Laundry Workers Strike: 1,200 Quit in Lower Bronx," *New York Times*, June 27, 1933, 15; Jessie Taft Smith, interview by the author, December 24, 26, 2006, New York. During the Third Period (1928–34), when capitalism was under crisis, the Communist International (Moscow) instructed communists everywhere to reject alliances with social democrats and to organize independent, communist-led "red unions."

17. Nestel, *Labor Relations*, 58; New York State Department of Labor, "Minimum Wage for Laundry Workers," box 2, folder 60, 62, National Consumers League Records, collection no. 5235, Kheel Center, Cornell University, Ithaca, NY.

18. Karen Pastorello, *A Power among Them: Bessie Abramowitz Hillman and the Making of the Amalgamated Clothing Workers of America* (Urbana: University of Illinois Press, 2008), 111–12; Nestel, *Labor Relations*, 37–43.

19. Anthony Oberschall, *Social Conflict and Social Movements* (Englewood Cliffs, NJ: Prentice Hall, 1973); Oberschall, *Social Movements: Ideologies, Interests, and Identities* (New Brunswick, NJ: Transaction Publishing, 1993); Andrew Martin, "Resources for Success: Social Movements, Strategic Resource Allocation, and Union Organizing Outcomes," *Social Problems* 55 (2008): 501–24.

20. Marc Dixon, Vincent J. Roscigno, and Randy Hodson, "Unions, Solidarity, and Striking," *Social Forces* 83, no. 3 (2004): 3–33; Marc Dixon and Vincent J. Roscigno, "Status, Networks, and Social Movement Participation: The Case of Striking Workers," *American Journal of Sociology* 108 (2003): 1292–1327.

21. "Ten Thousand Laundry Workers Get ACWA Contract," *The Advance* 23, no. 9 (September 1937): 19.

22. David M. Lewis-Colman, *Race against Liberalism: Black Workers and the UAW in Detroit* (Urbana: University of Illinois Press, 2008), 1; Marshall F. Stevenson, *Challenging the Roadblocks to Equality: Race Relations and Civil Rights in the CIO, 1935–1955*, Center for Labor Research, Working Papers Series, Ohio State University, 1991, 5–7; Lizabeth Cohen, *Making a New Deal: Industrial Workers in Chicago, 1919–1939* (Cambridge: Cambridge University Press, 1990); Rick Halpern, *Down on the Killing Floor: Black and White Workers in Chicago's Packinghouses, 1904–1954* (Urbana: University of Illinois Press, 1997).

23. Marshall F. Stevenson, "Beyond Theoretical Models: The Limited Possibilities of Racial Egalitarianism," *ILWCH* 44 (Fall 1993): 5, 36–37, 45–51; Stevenson, *Challenging the Roadblocks*, 13, 24–25; Herbert Hill, "The Problem of Race in American Labor History," *Reviews in American History* 24, no. 2 (June 1996): 196–208; Michael Goldfield, "Race and the CIO: The Possibilities for Racial Egalitarianism during the 1930s and 1940s," *ILWCH* 44 (Fall 1993): 1–32; Martha Biondi, *To Stand and Fight: The Struggle for Civil Rights in Postwar New York City* (Cambridge, MA: Harvard University Press, 2003), 26–28; Robert Zieger, *The CIO 1935–1955* (Chapel Hill: University of North Carolina Press, 1995), 84; Robin D. G. Kelley, *Hammer and Hoe: Alabama Communists during the Great Depression* (Chapel Hill: University of North Carolina Press, 1990).

24. Ruth Milkman, "New Research in Women's Labor History," *Signs* 18, no. 2 (Winter 1993): 383; Milkman, "Redefining 'Women's Work': The Sexual Division of Labor in the Auto Industry during World War II," *Feminist Studies* 8, no. 2 (Summer 1982): 337–72; Milkman, *Gender at Work: The Dynamics of Job Segregation by Sex during World War II* (Urbana: University of Illinois Press, 1987), 65–77, 84–98, 104, 96 (quote); Nancy F. Gabin, *Feminism in the Labor Movement: Women Workers and the United Auto Workers, 1935–1975* (Ithaca, NY: Cornell University Press, 1990), 1–28, 31–46; Dennis A. Deslippe, *Rights Not Roses: Unions and the Rise of Working-Class Feminism, 1945–80* (Urbana: University of Illinois Press, 2000); Dorothy Sue Cobble, *The Other Women's Movement: Workplace Justice and Social Rights in Modern America* (Princeton, NJ: Princeton University Press, 2004), 15–17; Lisa Kannenberg, "The Impact of the Cold War on Women's Trade Union Activism: The UE Experience," *Labor History* 34, no. 2–3 (1993): 309–23; Mary Margaret Fonow, *Union Women: Forging Feminism in the United Steelworkers of America* (Minneapolis: University of Minnesota Press, 2003), 6, 16–19; Heidi Hartman Strom, "Challenging Women's Place: Feminism, the Left, and Industrial Unionism in the 1930s," *Feminist Studies* 9, no. 2 (1983): 368; Elizabeth Faue, *Community of Suffering and Struggle: Women, Men, and the Labor Movement in Minneapolis, 1915–1945* (Chapel Hill: University of North Carolina Press, 1991).

25. Robinson, interview by Craig, 46–47, TCTUW.

26. Biondi, *To Stand and Fight*, 1–6; Robert Rodgers Korstad, *Civil Rights Unionism: Tobacco Workers and the Struggle for Democracy in the Mid-Twentieth Century South*

(Chapel Hill: University of North Carolina Press, 2003); Nelson Litchtenstein, *State of the Union: A Century of American Labor* (Princeton, NJ: Princeton University Press, 2002).

27. Jacquelyn Dowd Hall, "The Long Civil Rights Movement and the Political Uses of the Past," *Journal of American History* 91, no. 4 (March 2005): 1245–46, 1254; Robert Korstad, "Civil Rights Unionism and the Black Freedom Struggle," *American Communist History* 7, no. 2 (2008): 255–57.

28. I thank Professor Premilla Nadasen for helping me frame this struggle.

29. Dayo F. Gore, *Radicalism at the Crossroads: African American Women Activists in the Cold War* (New York: New York University Press, 2011), 6; Belinda Robnett, "African-American Women in the Civil Rights Movement, 1954–1965: Gender, Leadership and Micromobilization," *American Journal of Sociology* 101, no. 6 (1996): 1661–93.

30. Charlotte Adelmond to Members of the Board of Directors, LWJB, "Reasons for Resignation of Charlotte Adelmond from the LWJB," December 6, 1950, folder 559, Pauli Murray Papers, Schlesinger Library on the History of Women in America, Radcliffe Institute for Advanced Study, Harvard University, Cambridge, MA.

Chapter One. "We Win a Place in Industry"

1. Isabel Wilkerson, *The Warmth of Other Sons: The Epic Story of America's Great Migration* (New York: Random House, 2010), 8–11.

2. Sylvia Woods, "If I Had Known What I Know Now," in *Black Women in the Middle West Project: A Comprehensive Resource Guide, Illinois and Indiana*, ed. Darlene Clark Hine et al. (Indianapolis: Purdue Research Foundation, 1986), 20–29.

3. Best and Erickson, *A Survey of Laundries*, 17–36.

4. Jean Collier Brown, *The Negro Woman Worker*, United States Department of Labor, Women's Bureau Bulletin No. 165 (Washington, DC: Government Printing Office, 1938), 2–9; Trotter, *Black Milwaukee*, xi–xii, 227–30.

5. Mohun, *Steam Laundries*, 16–40, 48.

6. Ibid., 15 (quote), 22, 27; Carole Turbin, *Working Women of Collar City: Gender, Class, and Community in Troy, New York, 1864–86* (Urbana: University of Illinois Press, 1992), 21.

7. Turbin, *Working Women*, 21, 24–28, 43–46, 177.

8. Ibid., 107–13, 155–66, 172–90.

9. Ibid., 36, 46–60, 113–28, 155–68, 172–90.

10. Mohun, *Steam Laundries*, 51–54, 62.

11. US Department of Commerce and Labor, Bureau of the Census, *Special Reports: Occupations at the Twelfth Census* (Washington, DC: Government Printing Office, 1904), cvii, cix–cxiii, cxv; US Bureau of the Census, Bulletin 8, *Negroes in the United States* (Washington, DC: Government Printing Office, 1904), 8, 59; US Department of Commerce and Labor, Bureau of the Census, *Statistics of Women at Work* (Washington, DC: Government Printing Office, 1907), cvii–cx, 57.

12. Ibid.

13. Mary White Ovington, *Half a Man: The Status of the Negro in New York* (1911; repr., New York: Hill and Wang, 1969), 34, 78, 82.

14. Tera Hunter, *To 'Joy My Freedom: Southern Black Women's Lives and Labors after*

the Civil War (Cambridge, MA: Harvard University Press, 1997), 56–57; Mohun, *Steam Laundries*, 39–42, 139–49.

15. Mohun, *Steam Laundries*, 16, 19–21, 39–44.

16. "Day of Public Laundries: Terrors of Washday in Apartment Houses Overcome," *New York Times*, November 19, 1899, 12.

17. Mohun, *Steam Laundries*, 51–52.

18. US Department of Commerce, Bureau of the Census, *Fifteenth Census of the United States, Manufactures: 1929, Volume II, Reports by Industries* (Washington, DC: Government Printing Office, 1933), 1392–96; Mohun, *Steam Laundries*, 50; Hunter, *To 'Joy My Freedom*, 207–8.

19. US Department of Commerce, Bureau of the Census, *Thirteenth Census of the United States, Volume X, Manufactures 1909: Reports for Principal Industries* (Washington, DC: Government Printing Office, 1913), 887–89, 898; Turbin, *Working Women*, 21–29, 36, 44–59, 111, 127–28.

20. Nancy Tomes, *The Gospel of Germs: Men, Women, and the Microbe in American Life* (Cambridge, MA: Harvard University Press, 1998), xv, 2–20, 33, 64–65, 113–15, 145; Mohun, *Steam Laundries*, 29–42.

21. Turbin, *Working Women*, 19–21; Fred DeArmond, *The Laundry Industry* (New York: Harper and Brothers, 1950), 32; Jack Barbash, "Economics and Organization of the Laundry Industry," *The Advance* 25, no. 2 (February 1939): 10.

22. Mohun, *Steam Laundries*, 39–42.

23. DeArmond, *The Laundry Industry*, 32–40; Sylvia Rosenberg Weissbrodt, *Women Workers in Power Laundries*, Women's Bureau Bulletin No. 215 (Washington, DC: Government Printing Office, 1947), 2, 30; Mohun, *Steam Laundries*, 159–61.

24. Product Use and Development Division, Good Housekeeping, *Home Laundering* (New York: Heart Magazines, 1944), 16–17; Jesse Thompson, "Why Laundry Sales Will Grow," *Laundry Age*, April 1940, 34, box 53, collection no. 5619, ACWA Records; US Bureau of the Census, *Fifteenth Census of the United States, Manufactures*, 1397.

25. US Department of Commerce, Bureau of the Census, *Thirteenth Census of the United States, Volume IV, Population: Occupation Statistics* (Washington, DC: Government Printing Office, 1914), 94, 574; US Department of Commerce, US Bureau of the Census, *Fifteenth Census, Volume V: General Report on Occupations* (Washington, DC: Government Printing Office, 1933), 49.

26. US Department of Commerce and Labor, *Statistics of Women at Work* (Washington, DC: Government Printing Office, 1907), 56.

27. US Bureau of the Census, *Thirteenth Census of the United States, Volume X*, 889; Bureau of the Census, *Fifteenth Census, Volume V*, 49, 85.

28. US Bureau of the Census, *Thirteenth Census, Volume IV*, 94, 432–33; Mohun, *Steam Laundries*, 111.

29. Sue Ainslie Clark and Edith Wyatt, "Women Laundry Workers in New York," *McClure's Magazine* 36 (February 1911): 404, 407–8 (quotes); Clark and Wyatt, *Making Both Ends Meet: The Income and Outlay of New York Working Girls* (New York: Macmillan, 1911), 188–89, 191, 195; Dorothy Richardson, "The Long Day: The Story of a New York Working Girl," in *Women at Work*, ed. William L. O'Neill (Chicago: Quadrangle Books, 1972), v–vi, 277–79.

30. Chicago Commission on Race Relations, *The Negro in Chicago: A Study of Race Relations and a Race Riot in 1919* (New York: Arno Press and the New York Times, 1968), 383.

31. US Department of Commerce, Bureau of the Census, *Fourteenth Census, Volume IV, Population: Occupations* (Washington, DC: Government Printing Office, 1923), 358–59; Mohun, *Steam Laundries*, 172–73. Of the forty thousand men who worked in laundries in 1920, 41 percent were native-born white, 30 percent were Chinese, 18 percent were foreign-born, and 11 percent were Black.

32. Emma Shields, *Negro Women in Industry,* Bulletin of the Women's Bureau Bulletin No. 20 (Washington, DC: Government Printing Office, 1922), 5, 11–12, 15.

33. Brown, *The Negro Woman Worker*, 8; Lois Rita Helmbold, "Downward Occupational Mobility during the Great Depression: Urban Black and White Working-Class Women," *Labor History* 29 (1988): 135–72.

34. US Bureau of the Census, *Fifteenth Census, Volume V*, 85. Of the eighty thousand men working in power laundries, 58 percent were native-born white, 18 percent were white immigrants, 13 percent were Black, and 11 percent were Chinese.

35. Best and Erickson, *A Survey of Laundries*, 8–12.

36. Brown, *The Negro Woman Worker,* 8.

37. US Bureau of the Census, *Fifteenth Census, Volume V,* 49, 85; L. Baynard Whitney, "Negro Power Laundries Employ 100 Workers in Harlem Section," *New York Amsterdam News*, October 24, 1928, 9.

38. George Haynes, *The Negro at Work during the World War and during Reconstruction* (New York: Negro Universities Press, 1921), 127.

39. US Department of Commerce and Labor, *Statistics of Women at Work,* 56–58; Jacqueline Jones, *Labor of Love, Labor of Sorrow: Black Women, Work and the Family from Slavery to the Present* (New York: Vintage Books, 1985), 30, 125–26.

40. Quoted in Hunter, *To 'Joy My Freedom*, 56–58, 109–10.

41. DeArmond, *The Laundry Industry,* 23–24; Hunter, *To 'Joy My Freedom*, 57–58; Grace Elizabeth Hale, *Making Whiteness: The Culture of Segregation in the South, 1890–1940* (New York: Vintage Books, 1998), 98–104, 151–52, 160–61.

42. Elizabeth Beardsley Butler, *Women and the Trades* (1909; repr., New York: Arno and the New York Times, 1969), 203.

43. Jessie Smith, interview by Nell Geiser, February 26, 2006, New York; Smith, interview by the author, June 24, 2007, New York.

44. Bertha M. Nienburg and Bertha Blair, *Factors Affecting Wages in Power Laundries,* United States Department of Labor, Women's Bureau Bulletin No. 143 (Washington, DC: Government Printing Office, 1936), 5, 68; Mohun, *Steam Laundries*, 149.

45. Frank Crosswaith, "Around and Beyond," *New York Amsterdam News*, February 21, 1942, 7.

46. New York Department of Labor, *A Study of Hygienic Conditions in Steam Laundries*, Special Bulletin No. 130 (Albany, NY: Division of Industrial Hygiene, 1924), 10.

47. US Bureau of the Census, *Fourteenth Census, Volume IV*, 394–95, 1162; Best and Erickson, *A Survey of Laundries*, 12, 88–89, 92–94.

48. Richardson, "The Laundry Day," in O'Neill, *Women at Work*, 279–80.

49. Jane Filley and Therese Mitchell, *Consider the Laundry Workers* (New York: League of Women Shoppers, 1937), 11, 36.

50. Alice Kessler-Harris, *Out to Work: A History of Wage-Earning Women in the United States* (New York: Oxford University Press, 1982), 128–41; Evelyn Brooks Higginbotham, "African-American Women and the Metalanguage of Race," *Signs* 17, no. 2 (Winter 1992): 260–61.

51. US Bureau of the Census, *Fourteenth Census, Volume IV*, 699; US Bureau of the Census, *Fifteenth Census, Volume V*, 290.

52. Anna Arnold Hedgeman, *The Trumpet Sounds: A Memoir of Negro Leadership* (New York: Holt, Rinehart and Winston, 1964), 36.

53. US Senate, *Report on Condition of Woman and Child Wage-Earners in the United States, Vol. XII: Employment of Women in Laundries* (Washington, DC: Government Printing Office, 1911), 42, 48, 71, 75–76, 104, 115; Katharine Anthony, *Mothers Who Must Earn* (New York: Survey Associates, 1914), 78–79; Best, *A Survey of Laundries*, 90–96; New York Department of Labor, *A Study of Hygienic Conditions*, 12–13, 58.

54. Mohun, *Steam Laundries*, 250–51.

55. Evelyn Nakano Glenn, "From Servitude to Service Work: Historical Continuities in the Racial Division of Paid Reproductive Labor," *Signs* 18, no. 1 (Autumn 1992): 8, 20, 32; Jones, *Labor of Love*, 177.

56. US Bureau of the Census, *Fifteenth Census, Volume V*, 74–87; Brown, *The Negro Woman Worker*, 2.

57. Elizabeth Clark-Lewis, *Living In, Living Out: African American Domestics and the Great Migration* (New York: Kodansha, 1996), 48–49; Premilla Nadasen, *Household Workers Unite: The Untold Story of African American Women Who Built a Labor Movement* (Boston: Beacon Press, 2015), 10–11.

58. Florence Rice, "It Takes a While to Realize That It Is Discrimination," in *Black Women in White America: A Documentary History*, ed. Gerda Lerner (New York: Pantheon Books, 1972), 275–76.

59. Yevette Richards, *Maida Springer: Pan Africanist and International Labor Leader* (Pittsburgh: University of Pittsburgh Press, 2000), 31; Hedgeman, *The Trumpet Sounds*, 37.

60. David M. Katzman, *Seven Days a Week: Women and Domestic Service in Industrializing America* (Urbana: University of Illinois Press, 1981), 48–78, 93; Brown, *The Negro Woman Worker*, 2; Nadasen, *Household Workers Unite*, 11.

61. Chicago Commission on Race Relations, *The Negro in Chicago*, 383–84.

62. Best and Erickson, *A Survey of Laundries*, 97–98, 155; Patricia E. Malcolmson, *English Laundresses: A Social History, 1850–1930* (Urbana: University of Illinois Press, 1986), 147–49.

63. Clark-Lewis, *Living In, Living Out*, 121–22.

64. Claude A. Barnett, "We Win a Place in Industry," *Opportunity* 7, no. 3 (March 1929): 83–84.

65. Trotter, *Black Milwaukee*, xi–xii, 227–30, 236–38.

Chapter Two. A Miniature Hell

1. Vivian Morris, "Laundry Workers," in *A Renaissance in Harlem: Lost Voices of an American Community*, ed. Lionel C. Bascom (New York: Avon Books, 1999), 76–81.

2. Bureau of the Census, *Fifteenth Census, Volume V*, 85.

3. Beatrice Lumpkin, e-mail message to the author, August 7, 2006, August 9, 2006; Filley and Mitchell, *Consider the Laundry Workers*, 43; DeArmond, *The Laundry Industry*, 178–89; US Department of Labor, *Job Descriptions for the Laundry Industry* (Washington, DC: Government Printing Office, 1937), xxviii, 249, 253. This book uses Beatrice Shapiro Lumpkin's married name, as she has spent most of her more than one hundred years as Lumpkin and has published widely under the name Lumpkin.

4. Rose Schneiderman with Lucy Goldthwaite, *All for One* (New York: Paul S. Erikson, 1967), 211–12.

5. Mohun, *Steam Laundries*, 51–53, 60–62, 106–7, 114.

6. Filley and Mitchell, *Consider the Laundry Workers*, 26, 38; Mohun, *Steam Laundries*, 234–44.

7. Nienburg and Blair, *Factors Affecting Wages*, 32–33.

8. DeArmond, *The Laundry Industry*, 184–85.

9. Ibid.; Collins, *Black Feminist Thought*, 177–78.

10. Herbert R. Northrup, *Organized Labor and the Negro* (New York: Harper and Brothers, 1944), 132–33; Jessie Smith, phone conversation with the author, August 31, 2006; Smith, interview by the author, December 24, 2006, New York.

11. Nienburg and Blair, *Factors Affecting Wages*, 26–27, 37; US Department of Labor, *Women Workers in Power Laundries*, 9–11; Glenn, "From Servitude to Service Work," 8, 20, 32.

12. New York State Department of Labor, *Hours and Earnings of Women Employed in Power Laundries in New York State*, Special Bulletin No. 153 (New York: Bureau of Women in Industry, 1927), 5–9; Bureau of the Census, *Fifteenth Census, Volume II*, 1400–1401; Mohun, *Steam Laundries*, 51.

13. New York Department of Labor, *A Study of Hygienic Conditions*, 10–28; Filley and Mitchell, *Consider the Laundry Workers*, 16, 45–46; Mohun, *Steam Laundries*, 51–53, 60–62, 106–7, 114.

14. Beatrice Lumpkin, interview by the author, May 23, 2007, Chicago.

15. Robinson, interview, TCTUW, 53 (quote); Louis I. Harris and Nellie Swartz, *The Cost of Clean Clothes in Terms of Health: A Study of Laundries and Laundry Workers in New York City*, (New York: New York Department of Health, 1917), 44–59.

16. Elizabeth B. Butler, *Women and the Trades: Pittsburgh, 1907–1908* (New York: Charities Publication Committee, 1909), 167, 200 (quote); Best and Erickson, *A Survey of Laundries*, 4; Harris and Swartz, *The Cost of Clean Clothes*, 26.

17. New York State Department of Labor, *Hours and Earnings of Women in Five Industries*, Bureau of Women in Industry Bulletin No. 121 (Albany: J. B. Lyon Company, 1923), 9–19.

18. Filley and Mitchell, *Consider the Laundry Workers*, 47; Best and Erickson, *A Survey of Laundries*, 5, 37–60.

19. Evelyn Macon, interview, in *First Person America,* ed. Ann Banks (New York: Knopf, 1980), 126.

20. Smith, interview by the author, December 26, 2006, New York; Jessie Taft Smith, interview by Bea Lemisch, November 19, 1981, in *The Oral History of the American Left: Radical Histories, 1920–1980,* eds. Jonathan Bloom and Paul Buhle, Tamiment Library and Robert F. Wagner Archives at New York University, New York, 1984.

21. Beatrice Lumpkin, "I Helped Organize the CIO," *People's Weekly World,* March 15, 2003.

22. Filley and Mitchell, *Consider the Laundry Workers,* 24 (quote); A. Thomas, "Negro Laundry Workers Are Organizing," *The Liberator,* October 20, 1932 3 (quote).

23. Emma Cosby, "Conditions in Laundries," *New York Amsterdam News,* April 4, 1936, 12; Collins, *Black Feminist Thought,* 77.

24. US Department of Labor, *Job Descriptions,* xiii–xv, 21–29; US Department of Labor, *Employment of Women in Power Laundries in Milwaukee* (Washington, DC: Government Printing Office, 1913), 38–40.

25. US Department of Labor, *Job Descriptions,* xiii–xv, 21–29; Best and Erickson, *A Survey of Laundries,* 10, 71–75, 84–85.

26. Best and Erickson, *A Survey of Laundries,* 71–75, 84–85; US Department of Labor, *Job Descriptions,* xiii–xv, 21–22.

27. Lumpkin, e-mail message to the author, August 9, 25, 2006; "Misery in Cleveland Laundries Exposed," *Working Woman* 1, no. 12 (1930): 3.

28. "Misery," 3; US Department of Labor, *Employment of Women,* 11–14, 38–39; Mae Massie Eberhardt, interview by Marcia Greenlee, November 5, 1979, in *The Black Woman Oral History Project,* ed. Ruth Edmonds Hill (Westport: Meckler, 1991), 3:234–36.

29. Lumpkin, e-mail message to the author, July 31, August 9, 2006; US Department of Labor, *Job Descriptions,* xv–xvii, 41, 53–54, 235; New York Department of Labor, *A Study of Hygienic Conditions,* 18–27; Sterling D. Spero and Abram L. Harris, *The Black Worker: The Negro and the Labor Movement* (New York: Columbia University Press, 1931), 177.

30. US Department of Labor, *Employment of Women,* 40–49; Filley and Mitchell, *Consider the Laundry Workers,* 31–32 (quote); US Department of Labor, *Job Descriptions,* xvii, 53–54.

31. US Department of Labor, *Job Descriptions,* 9, 53; Filley and Mitchell, *Consider the Laundry Workers,* 20, 31 (quote).

32. Filley and Mitchell, *Consider the Laundry Workers,* 9–10 (quote); Spero and Harris, *The Black Worker,* 177; US Department of Labor, *Women Workers in Power Laundries,* 10.

33. DeArmond, *The Laundry Industry,* 236.

34. New York Department of Labor, *A Study of Hygienic Conditions,* 18–27; US Department of Labor, *Employment of Women,* 40–48.

35. Lumpkin, e-mail message to the author, July 31, August 9, 2006.

36. Robinson, interview by Craig, TCTUW, 53.

37. New York Department of Labor, *A Study of Hygienic Conditions,* 20.

38. Lillian Matthews, "Women in Trade Unions in San Francisco," in *University of California Publications in Economics,* ed. Adolph C. Miller (Berkeley: University of California Press, 1913), 3: 20–21.

39. DeArmond, *The Laundry Industry,* 89.

40. "Award of Arbitrators," case no. 2612, July 19, 1940, 7–9, folder 21, box 54, collection no. 5619, ACWA Records.

41. US Department of Labor, *Job Descriptions,* xvii, 35–36; New York Department of Labor, *A Study of Hygienic Conditions,* 20, 26; Best and Erickson, *A Survey of Laundries,* 5, 11.

42. Smith, interview, in *Oral History of the American Left*; Harris and Swartz, *The Cost of Clean Clothes,* 32.

43. "A Job in a Laundry," in *I Am a Woman Worker,* ed. Andria Taylor Hourwich and Gladys L. Palmer (New York: Arno Press, 1974), 42–43.

44. Caroline Manning, *The Immigrant Woman and Her Job* (New York: Arno Press, 1970), 120; Harris and Swartz, *The Cost of Clean Clothes,* 14, 37–38.

45. Smith, interview by the author, December 26, 2006, New York; Smith, interview by Geiser, February 26, 2006, New York.

46. US Department of Labor, *Job Descriptions,* xxv, 61–62, 167, 179; Filley and Mitchell, *Consider the Laundry Workers,* 11–12 (quotes); Mohun, *Steam Laundries,* 88.

47. Macon, interview, in Banks, *First Person America,* 126–27; Filley and Mitchell, *Consider the Laundry Workers,* 11–12; New York Department of Labor, *A Study of Hygienic Conditions,* 61.

48. Best and Erickson, *A Survey of Laundries,* 84–85.

49. DeArmond, *The Laundry Industry,* 239, 245; US Department of Labor, *Employment of Women,* 59; Mohun, *Steam Laundries,* 88–89, 159.

50. Butler, *Women and the Trades,* 173 (quote); Clark and Wyatt, "Women Laundry Workers," 407; James R. Barrett and David Roediger, "Inbetween Peoples: Race, Nationality and the New Immigrant Working Class," *Journal of American Ethnic History* 16, no. 3 (1997): 4–9.

51. Best and Erickson, *A Survey of Laundries,* 5–6, 10, 73–75; Smith, interview by the author, December 26, 2006, New York.

52. DeArmond, *The Laundry Industry,* 238; Filley and Mitchell, *Consider the Laundry Workers,* 10, 16–24; US Department of Labor, *Employment of Women,* 50–53.

53. Hedgeman, *The Trumpet Sounds,* 36–38.

54. Robinson, interview by Craig, TCTUW, 52.

55. Hedgeman, *The Trumpet Sounds,* 35–36; DeArmond, *The Laundry Industry,* 237–39.

56. Best and Erickson, *A Survey of Laundries,* 10, 73.

57. Butler, *Women and the Trades,* 178; DeArmond, *The Laundry Industry,* 240–42; Smith, interview by the author, December 26, 2006, New York; Mohun, *Steam Laundries,* 106.

58. Butler, *Women and the Trades,* 182 (quote); US Senate, *Report on Condition of Woman and Child Wage-Earners in the United States, Vol. XII: Employment of Women in Laundries* (Washington, DC: Government Printing Office, 1911), 23, 42 (quote); US Department of Labor, *Employment of Women,* 6, 19–22, 62–69; Barrett and Roediger, "Inbetween Peoples," 16–18.

59. Collins, *Black Feminist Thought,* 43.

60. Lumpkin, e-mail message to the author, July 31, August 9, 23, 25, 2006; Lumpkin, "I Helped Organize"; John Jung, *Chinese Laundries: Tickets to Survival on Gold Mountain* (New York: Yin & Yang Press, 2007), 90; Turbin, *Working Women*, 26–29, 51–52.

61. US Department of Labor, *Job Descriptions*, 143–91; Carole Turbin, "Collars and Consumers: Changing Images of American Manliness and Business," *Enterprise and Society* 1 (September 2000): 507–35.

62. Filley and Mitchell, *Consider the Laundry Workers*, 12 (quote); Best and Erickson, *A Survey of Laundries*, 5–6, 10.

63. Best and Erickson, *A Survey of Laundries*, 73–75; US Department of Labor, *Job Descriptions*, 37; Butler, *Women and the Trades*, 168, 186–87.

64. US Department of Labor, *Job Descriptions*, xxvii.

65. Butler, *Women and the Trades*, 188–90.

66. US Department of Labor, *Job Descriptions*, xxvii–xxviii, 219, 231–37; Best and Erickson, *A Survey of Laundries*, 6, 73.

67. "Wanted, Family Ironers," *New York Amsterdam News*, October 24, 1923, 11.

68. Manning, *The Immigrant Woman*, 13, 107, 130–31.

69. Best and Erickson, *A Survey of Laundries*, 30; US Department of Labor, *Job Descriptions*, 267.

70. Bureau of the Census, *Fifteenth Census, Volume V*, 85.

71. Woods, "If I Had Known," 22.

72. Nienburg and Blair, *Factors Affecting Wages*, 26, 33–34; Northrup, *Organized Labor*, 132.

73. DeArmond, *The Laundry Industry*, 161; Nienburg and Blair, *Factors Affecting Wages*, 26, 33–34.

74. Nienburg and Blair, *Factors Affecting Wages*, 35.

75. L. Baynard Whitney, "Negro Power Laundries Employ 100 Workers in Harlem Section," *New York Amsterdam News*, October 24, 1928, 9.

76. Smith, interview by the author, December 24 and 26, 2006, May 27 and 28, 2008, New York; Smith, interview by Geiser, February 26, 2006, New York; Smith, interview by Lemish, in *Oral History of the American Left*.

77. "Bosses Divide Negro and White Workers," *Working Woman* 1, no. 12 (1930): 6; Robinson, interview by Craig, TCTUW, 52.

78. Milkman, *Gender at Work*, 3 (quote).

79. DeArmond, *The Laundry Industry*, 245; Milkman, *Gender at Work*, 8.

80. Smith, interview by Geiser, February 26, 2006, New York; Smith, interview by the author, December 24, 2006, New York; Beatrice Lumpkin, *Joy in the Struggle: My Life and Love* (New York: International Publishers, 2013), 85–86.

81. Nancy A. Hewitt, "'The Voice of Virile Labor': Labor Militancy, Community Solidarity, and Gender Identity among Tampa's Latin Workers, 1880–1921," in *Work Engendered: Toward a New History of American Labor*, ed. Ava Baron (Ithaca, NY: Cornell University Press, 1991), 147.

Chapter Three. The 1912 Uprising of New York City's Laundry Workers

1. "Laundry Trust Plan Revealed by Strike," *New York Times*, January 2, 1912, 1; "Arbitration Truce in Laundry Strike," *New York Times*, January 4, 1912, 3 (quote).

2. Margaret Hinchey, "Thirty Days," *Life and Labor* 3, no. 9 (September 1913): 264 (quote), reel 5, Women's Trade Union League Publications, Arthur and Elizabeth Schlesinger Library on the History of Women in America, Radcliffe College, Cambridge, Massachusetts, microfilm version, *Papers of the Women's Trade Union League and Its Principal Leaders*, by Nancy Schrom Dye, Robin Miller Jacoby, and Edward T. James (Woodbridge, CT: Research Publications, [1985]) (hereafter WTUL Publications); Lara Vapnek, "Margaret Hinchey," *American National Biography Online*, http://www.anb.org/articles/15/15-01325.html.

3. "Laundry Strikers Get Many Recruits," *New York Times*, January 3, 1912, 4 (quotes); Mary E. Dreier, "To Wash or Not to Wash: Ay, There's the Rub; The New York Laundry Strike," *Life and Labor* 2, no. 3 (March 1912): 71–72, reel 5, WTUL Publications.

4. Dreier, "To Wash," 71–72; Annelise Orleck, *Common Sense and a Little Fire: Women and Working-Class Politics in the United States, 1900–1965* (Chapel Hill: University of North Carolina Press, 1995), 53–80.

5. M. C. Schroeder and S. G. Southerland, *Laundries and the Public Health: A Sanitary Study Including Bacteriologic Tests*, United States Department of Public Health Service (Washington, DC: Government Printing Office, 1917), 4.

6. Beatrice Lumpkin, e-mail message to the author, July 29, August 9, 10, 12, 21, 2006; US Senate, *Report on Conditions of Woman and Child Wage-Earners in the United States, Vol. 12, Employment of Women in Laundries* (Washington, DC: Government Printing Office, 1911), 9–14; Jung, *Chinese Laundries*, 52.

7. Jung, *Chinese Laundries*, 1–12, 29–42, 58–65; Renqui Yu, *To Save China, to Save Ourselves: The Chinese Hand Laundry Alliance of New York* (Philadelphia: Temple University Press, 1992), 1–12, 20–42, 58–65, 130–37.

8. Bureau of the Census, *Fifteenth Census, Volume V*, 85; Yu, *To Save China*, 9, 35 (quote).

9. Beatrice Lumpkin, e-mail message to author, August 10, 21, 2006; Schroeder and Southerland, *Laundries and the Public Health*, 4–9.

10. Jung, *Chinese Laundries*, 75–103; Yu, *To Save China*, 23–24.

11. US Department of Commerce, Bureau of the Census, *Fourteenth Census of the US, Volume IV: Population, 1920, Occupations* (Washington, DC: Government Printing Office, 1922), 43.

12. Bureau of the Census, *Thirteenth Census, Volume X*, 895; Schroeder and Southerland, *Laundries and the Public Health*, 4.

13. Bureau of the Census, *Thirteenth Census, Volume IV*, 574.

14. "Laundry Trust Plan Revealed by Strike," *New York Times*, January 2, 1912, 1; Mohun, *Steam Laundries*, 53–61, 137–38.

15. Turbin, *Working Women*, 3, 71, 108–29; Philip S. Foner, *Women and the American Labor Movement: From Colonial Times to the Eve of World War I* (New York: Free Press, 1979), 244–45.

16. Harry L. Morrison to Frank Morrison, April 22, 1914, 1–2, reel 39, *American Federation of Labor Records: The Samuel Gompers Era* (Sanford, NC: Microfilming Corporation of America, 1979); Lillian Matthews, *Women in Trade Unions in San Francisco* (Berkeley: University of California Press, 1913), 10–19, 34–36; Mohun, *Steam Laundries*, 134–36.

17. "Laundry Trust Plan Revealed by Strike," *New York Times*, January 2, 1912, 1; "Laundry Strikers Get Many Recruits," *New York Times*, January 3, 1912, 4; "Laundry Workers," undated notes, 2, reel 25, NY WTUL Records; Dreier, "To Wash."

18. "The Journal of the Laundry Workers Joint Board: 10th Anniversary Celebration," box 139, collection no. 5619, ACWA Records.

19. Jung, *Chinese Laundries*, 90–91, 130.

20. Ibid.; "Laundry Workers Ask More Wages," *New York Times*, April 4, 1901, 9; "Laundry Strikers Get Many Recruits," *New York Times*, January 3, 1912, 4; Smith, interview by the author, December 26, 2006, New York.

21. "Laundry Workers Ask More Wages," *New York Times*, April 4, 1901, 9; "Laundry Strikers Get Many Recruits," *New York Times*, January 3, 1912, 4; "The Journal of the Laundry Workers Joint Board."

22. Dreier, "To Wash," 68–70; Helen Marot, "New York: Laundry Workers' Strike," *Life and Labor* 2, no. 2 (February 1912): 55–56, reel 5, WTUL Publications; "Young Girls Tell of Laundry Hardships," *New York Times*, January 20, 1912, 14.

23. Dreier, "To Wash," 68–71; "Laundry Trust Plan Revealed by Strike," *New York Times*, January 2, 1912, 1; "Laundry Strikers Get Many Recruits," *New York Times*, January 3, 1912, 4.

24. "Arbitration Truce in Laundry Strike," *New York Times*, January 4, 1912, 3; "Laundries to Open, Defying Strikers," *New York Times*, January 5, 1912, 8.

25. Orleck, *Common Sense*, 53–63.

26. Ibid., 3–7, 54–63, 88–89, 129–30; Nancy Schrom Dye, *As Equals and as Sisters: Feminism, the Labor Movement, and the Women's Trade Union League of New York* (Columbia: University of Missouri Press, 1980); Alice Kessler-Harris, "Where Are the Organized Women Workers?," in *Gendering Labor History*, by Alice Kessler-Harris (Urbana: University of Illinois Press, 2007), 25–33.

27. "Both Sides 'Victors'; Laundry Piles Up," *New York Times*, January 6, 1912, 24; Kessler-Harris, "Where Are the Organized Women Workers?," 29–30.

28. Dreier, "To Wash," 72 (quote).

29. Marot, "New York," 55; "Laws Help Men, Not Girls, Declares Miss Hinchey," *Washington Post*, December 2, 1913, 5l; Lara Vapnek, *Breadwinners: Working Women and Economic Independence, 1865–1920* (Urbana: University of Illinois Press, 2009), 133.

30. "Parade for Girl Strikers," *New York Times*, January 13, 1912, 7; Dreier, "To Wash," 72 (quotes).

31. "Secretary's Report to Executive Board," January 25, 1912, 1; Dreier, "To Wash," 72 (quote); Marot, "New York," 55; "Laundries to Open, Defying Strikers," *New York Times*, January 5, 1912, 8.

32. Dreier, "To Wash," 71-72; Orleck, *Common Sense*, 80.

33. "Actors to Aid Laundry Folk," *New York Times*, January 18, 1912, 10; Orleck, *Common Sense*, 177.

34. "Church Folk Hear Strikers," *New York Times,* January 15, 1912, 2 (quote); "Parade for Girl Strikers," *New York Times,* January 13, 1912, 7; "Actors Aid Laundry Folk," *New York Times,* January 28, 1912.

35. "Parade for Girl Strikers," *New York Times,* January 13, 1912, 7 (quote); Vapnek, "Margaret Hinchey"; Meredith Tax, *The Rising of the Women: Feminist Solidarity and Class Conflict, 1880–1917* (Urbana: University of Illinois Press, 2001), 170–77.

36. "Votes for Women," *Life and Labor,* 215 (quote), reel 5, WTUL Publications; "Suffrage Demanded by Working Women," *New York Times,* April 23, 1912, 24 (quote); Vapnek, *Breadwinners,* 147.

37. Tax, *The Rising of the Women,* 170–74.

38. "Long Hours in Laundries," *New York Times,* January 17, 1912, 4; Orleck, *Common Sense,* 62.

39. "Long Hours in Laundries," *New York Times,* January 17, 1912, 4.

40. "Young Girls Tell of Laundry Hardships," *New York Times,* January 20, 1912, 14 (quote); "Laundry Strike Justified," *New York Times,* January 30, 1912, 5; Paul Kennaday, "Verdict on the Laundries," *New York Times,* February 6, 1912, 10.

41. "Votes for Women," 215; Dreier, "To Wash," 72 (quote).

42. Charles Bailey to Frank Morrison, January 30, 1912, 1 (quote), reel 39, AFL Records; "Notes: Laundry Workers," 2, reel 25, NY WTUL Records; Foner, *Women,* 305–6.

43. Hinchey, "Thirty Days," 264; "New York," *Life and Labor* 4, no. 3 (March 1914): 92, reel 5, WTUL Publications; Schneiderman with Goldthwaite, *All for One,* 211–12.

44. "The Journal of the Laundry Workers Joint Board"; "Reject Laundry Strike," *New York Times,* February 3, 1924, 5.

45. "Ground Work Laid for Laundry Trust," *New York Times,* April 3, 1912, 6.

46. "Annual Report, 1918–1919," 4 (quote), reel 22, NY WTUL Records.

47. Bureau of the Census, *Fourteenth Census, Volume IV,* 841.

48. "Laws Help Men, Not Girls, Declares Miss Hinchey," *Washington Post,* December 2, 1913, 51.

49. "Minutes of WTUL Board Meeting," July 27, 1916, 1, reel 2, NY WTUL Records.

50. "Ballot Plea Fails," *New York Times,* February 3, 1914, 2; Vapnek, *Breadwinners,* 154–55.

51. "Margaret Hinchey Tells of Wilson," *New York Times,* February 5, 1914, 9; Vapnek, *Breadwinners,* 155.

52. "Laws Help Men, Not Girls, Declares Miss Hinchey," *Washington Post,* December 2, 1913, 5.

53. Maggie Hinchey to Leonora O'Reilly, December 1913, reel 6, Leonora O'Reilly Papers, Arthur and Elizabeth Schlesinger Library on the History of Women in America, Radcliffe College, Cambridge, Massachusetts, microfilm version, *Papers of the Women's Trade Union League and Its Principal Leaders,* eds. Nancy Schrom Dye, Robin Miller Jacoby, and Edward T. James (Woodbridge, CT: Research Publications, [1985]).

54. Tax, *The Rising of the Women,* 170–71; Orleck, *Common Sense,* 92–93.

55. "Laws Help Men, Not Girls, Declares Miss Hinchey," *Washington Post,* December 2, 1913, 5.

56. Ibid.; Vapnek, *Breadwinners,* 132; Vapnek, "Margaret Hinchey."

57. Quoted in Tax, *The Rising of the Women*, 176.

58. Turbin, *Working Women*, 116–22.

59. Mohun, *Steam Laundries*, 110.

Chapter Four. The Rise and Fall of Local 284

1. "Passengers for Voyage of Vandyk, May 16, 1924," Statue of Liberty–Ellis Island Foundation, Inc., https://www.libertyellisfoundation.org/passenger-result; Irma Watkins-Owens, *Blood Relations: Caribbean Immigrants and the Harlem Community, 1900–1930* (Bloomington: Indiana University Press, 1996), 1, 92–111; Richards, *Maida Springer*, 67–68.

2. Wilkerson, *The Warmth of Other Sons*, 8–11; Cheryl Lynn Greenberg, *Or Does It Explode? Black Harlem in the Great Depression* (New York: Oxford University Press, 1991), 13–17, 94–95; Winston James, *Holding Aloft the Banner of Ethiopia: Caribbean Radicalism in Early Twentieth Century America* (London: Verso, 1998), 13–30.

3. Virginia E. Sanchez Korrol, *From Colonia to Community: The History of Puerto Ricans in New York City* (Berkeley: University of California Press, 1983), 20–31, 44–45; James, *Holding Aloft*, 197.

4. James, *Holding Aloft*, 42–43.

5. "Passengers for Voyage of Vandyk, May 16, 1924"; Watkins-Owens, *Blood Relations*, 19.

6. Watkins-Owens, *Blood Relations*, 3, 19–27, 22 (quote).

7. James, *Holding Aloft*, 83–84 (quote); Richards, *Maida Springer*, 30–33; Daniel Katz, *All Together Different: Yiddish Socialists, Garment Workers, and the Labor Roots of Multiculturalism* (New York: New York University Press, 2011), 82, 110.

8. Greenberg, *Or Does It Explode?*, 19.

9. Federal Writers' Project, *New York Panorama* (Michigan: Scholarly Press, 1972), 132; Federal Writers' Project, *The WPA Guide to New York City* (New York: New Press, 1992), 461.

10. Orleck, *Common Sense*, 215–40.

11. Robinson, interview by Craig, 1, 45, 56, TCTUW.

12. Bureau of the Census, *Fifteenth Census, Volume IV*, 1132–33; Bureau of the Census, *Fifteenth Census, Volume II*, 1396, 1400–1401.

13. "Blames Laundries," *New York Times*, April 1, 1928, 13 (quote).

14. Elizabeth Porter Wyckoff, "Washless Wash Days," *New York Times*, November 27, 1921, XX7.

15. Bureau of the Census, *Fourteenth Census, Volume IV*, 841, 1162.

16. Elizabeth Porter Wyckoff, "Washless Wash Days," *New York Times*, November 27, 1921, XX7 (quotes).

17. Bureau of the Census, *Fifteenth Census, Volume IV*, 1132–34; Bureau of the Census, *Fifteenth Census, Volume V*, 85.

18. "Minutes of the Organization Committee," December 1, 1925, reel 3, NY WTUL Records; Barrett and Roediger, "Inbetween Peoples," 4–9.

19. A. Thomas, "Negro Laundry Workers Are Organizing," *The Liberator*, October 20, 1932, 3.

20. Filley and Mitchell, *Consider the Laundry Workers*, 26, 28–30, 48, 57–58, 57 (quote).

21. "Fight a Laundry Trust," *New York Times*, July 15, 1912, 3; "To Buy Rough Dry Plants," *New York Times*, October 19, 1919, 5; Yu, *To Save China*, 8–9.

22. Beatrice Lumpkin, e-mail message to the author, July 29, August 9, 10, 12, 21, 2006 (quotes); "Convention of Laundry Men," *New York Times*, November 11, 1900, 12.

23. Jung, *Chinese Laundries*, 75–103; Yu, *To Save China*; Schroeder and Southerland, *Laundries and the Public Health*, 4–9; Smith, interview by the author, December 26, 2006, New York.

24. "Report of the Work of the WTUL," November 23, 1, reel 2, NY WTUL Records; Smith, interview by the author, December 26, 2006, New York.

25. Turbin, *Working Women*, 27, 51–52.

26. Hugh Frayne to Samuel Gompers, January 10, 1923, 1, reel 39, *American Federation of Labor Records*; Mabel Leslie, "New York Laundry Workers," *Life and Labor* 2, no. 8 (April 1924): 1 (quote), reel 7, WTUL Publications.

27. "The Role of Local 280 in the Laundry Industry," *Harlem Liberator*, July 22, 1933, 5; Leslie, "New York Laundry Workers," reel 7, WTUL Publications; "From March 1924 to February 1925," 1925, 1, reel 3, NY WTUL Records.

28. Orleck, *Common Sense*, 16–30; Katz, *All Together Different*, 36–39.

29. Alice Kessler-Harris, "Rose Schneiderman and the Limits of Women's Trade Unionism," in Kessler-Harris, *Gendering Labor History*, 71–76; John Thomas McGuire, "From Socialism to Social Justice Feminism: Rose Schneiderman and the Quest for Urban Equity, 1911–1933," *Journal of Urban History* 35, no. 7 (2009): 1001.

30. Orleck, *Common Sense*, 42–44; Kessler-Harris, "Rose Schneiderman," 74–82.

31. Orleck, *Common Sense*, 90–91.

32. A. Philip Randolph to Mrs. Gerel Rubien, June 3, 1949, reel 1, Rose Schneiderman Papers, Tamiment Library and Robert F. Wagner Archives, New York University, New York, microfilm version, *Papers of the Women's Trade Union League and Its Principal Leaders*, by Nancy Schrom Dye, Robin Miller Jacoby, and Edward T. James (Woodbridge, CT: Research Publications, [1985]).

33. "From March 1924 to February 1925," reel 3, NY WTUL Records; Rose Schneiderman to Mrs. Albert Erdman, February 14, 1924; Rose Schneiderman to Mrs. Kenneth Walser, reel 11, NY WTUL Records.

34. "Report of Work of WTUL," September 1923, 1 (quote); "Report of the Work of the WTUL," November 1923; "Report of the Work of the WTUL," February 1924, reel 2 (quote), NY WTUL Records.

35. Ray Marshall, *The Negro Worker* (New York: Random House, 1967), 17–20, 57–81; Ira De A. Reid, *Negro Membership in American Labor Unions* (New York: Negro Universities Press, 1969), 90–99; Greenberg, *Or Does It Explode?*, 110.

36. "Negro and White Laundry Workers Prepare Strike," *Harlem Liberator*, December 23, 1933, 1 (quote).

37. Leslie, "Organizing Laundry Workers in New York," undated, ca. 1924, 2, reel 11, NY WTUL Records; "Annual Report of the WTUL," March 1, 1923 to February 29, 1924, 2, reel 22, NY WTUL Records.

38. Jessie Smith, phone conversation with the author, July 23, August 31, 2006; Smith, interview by the author, December 24, 2006, New York.

39. Collins, *Black Feminist Thought*, 77.

40. "Report of Work of the WTUL," November 1923, 1; "Report of the Work of the WTUL for December 1923," January 3, 1924, 1, reel 2, NY WTUL Records; "Untitled Report," ca. 1924, 2 (quotes), reel 21, NY WTUL Records; "Monthly Bulletin," April 1923, 1; "Monthly Bulletin," December 3, 1923, 1, reel 8, WTUL Publications.

41. "Annual Report of the WTUL," March 1, 1923 to February 29, 1924, 2, reel 22, NY WTUL Records; "Untitled Report," ca. 1924, 2 (quotes), reel 21, NY WTUL Records; "Report of the Work of the WTUL for December 1923," January 3, 1924, 1; "Minutes of the Executive Board Meeting of the WTUL," January 31, 1924, 3; "Report of the Work of the WTUL," January 31, 1924, 1 (quote); "Report of the Work of the WTUL," February 1924, 1; "Report of Work," March 1924, 1; "Minutes of the Special Meeting of the Strike Council," August 8, 1924, 1, reel 2, NY WTUL Records.

42. Rose Schneiderman to Mrs. Albert Erdman, February 14, 1924, 1; Rose Schneiderman to Mrs. Kenneth Walser, February 14, 1924, 1; Rose Schneiderman to Mrs. George Seligman, February 20, 1924, 1, reel 11, NY WTUL Records.

43. "Report of the Work of the WTUL," April 1924, 1; "Report of the Work of the WTUL," May 1924, 1; "Minutes of the Special Meeting of the Strike Council," August 18, 1924, 1; "Report of Work of WTUL," November 1924, 1; "Report of Work of WTUL," December 1924, 1, reel 2, NY WTUL Records; Schneiderman with Goldthwaite, *All for One*, 212–13.

44. Arthur C. Holden to Rose Schneiderman, March 26, 1924, 1 (quotes), reel 11, NY WTUL Records; New York Urban League, *The Negro in New York* (New York: Urban League, 1931), 12.

45. Charles Lionel Franklin, *The Negro Labor Unionist of New York* (New York: Columbia University Press, 1936), 87–93, 95–97.

46. Greenberg, *Or Does It Explode?*, 110.

47. "Report of the Work of the WTUL," April 1924, 1; "Report of the Work of the WTUL," January 1924, 1, reel 2, NY WTUL Records; "Annual Report," March 1, 1926, to March 1, 1927, 4–5 (quote), reel 3, NY WTUL Records.

48. "Report of the Work of the WTUL," March 1924, reel 2, NY WTUL Records; Greenberg, *Or Does It Explode?*, 110.

49. "Report of Work of New York WTUL," February 26, 1925, 1 (quote); "From March 1924 to February 1925," 1; "Minutes of the Organization Committee," December 1, 1925, 1, reel 3, NY WTUL Records; "Annual Report," March 1924 to March 1925, 3–4, reel 22, NY WTUL Records; "WTUL Bulletin," January 1920, reel 8, WTUL Publications.

50. "The Role of Local 280 in the Laundry Industry," *Harlem Liberator*, July 22, 1933, 5 (quotes).

51. "From March 1924 to February 1925," reel 3, NY WTUL Records; Orleck, *Common Sense*, 118, 127–28, 149–55.

52. "From March 1924 to February 1925," 1, reel 3, NY WTUL Records.

53. Franklin, *The Negro Labor Unionist*, 100–102; Shannon King, *Whose Harlem Is This, Anyway? Community Politics and Grassroots Activism during the New Negro Era* (New York: New York University Press, 2015), 77–79; Watkins-Owens, *Blood Relations*, 106–7; Greenberg, *Or Does It Explode?*, 110.

54. Cornelius L. Bynam, *A. Philip Randolph and the Struggle for Civil Rights* (Urbana: University of Illinois Press, 2010), 70–73; Katz, *All Together Different*, 182.

55. Maida Springer Kemp, interview by Elizabeth Balanoff, June 27, 1977, 72, TCTUW.

56. Franklin, *The Negro Labor Unionist*, 88–93, 107–9; Bynum, *A. Philip Randolph*, 47–62.

57. James, *Holding Aloft*, 136–38 (quote); Larry Alfonso Greene, "Harlem in the Great Depression: 1928–1936" (PhD diss., Columbia University, 1979), 15–16, 31–34.

58. Watkins-Owens, *Blood Relations*, 112–25.

59. Greene, "Harlem in the Great Depression," 31–38; Richards, *Maida Springer*, 22; Karen S. Adler, "'Always Leading Our Men in Service and Sacrifice': Amy Jacques Garvey, Feminist Black Nationalist," *Gender and Society* 6, no. 3 (September 1992): 346–75.

60. Robinson, interview by Craig, 1–3, TCTUW.

61. Yevette Richards, *Conversations with Maida Springer: A Personal History of Labor, Race, and International Relations* (Pittsburgh: University of Pittsburgh Press, 2004), 121–22 (quotes); Richards, *Maida Springer*, 20–22; 67–68; Springer Kemp, interview by Elizabeth Balanoff, 70–73 (quotes), TCTUW; Robinson, interview by Craig, 1–3, TCTUW.

62. "Executive Secretary's Report," October 1925, 1; "Report to Executive Committee," November 14, 1925, 1; "Report of June 1–December 31, 1925," 5, reel 1, Negro Labor Committee Records, Schomburg Center for Research in Black Culture, New York (hereafter cited as NLC Records); "Annual Report," March 1, 1926 to March 1, 1927, 3, reel 8, NY WTUL Records; Greenberg, *Or Does It Explode?*, 109.

63. "Organization Report 1925," March 27, 1925, 3–6; "Report of Work from Sept. 17–Oct. 29, 1925," 1, reel 3, NY WTUL Records.

64. "Monthly Bulletin," June 7, 1926, 1, reel 8, WTUL Publications; "Organization Report 1925," March 27, 1926, 3–6; "Minutes of Organization Committee," December 1, 1925, 2; "Minutes of the Executive Board Meeting of the WTUL," April 29, 1926, 1, reel 3, NY WTUL Records; "Report to Executive Committee," November 14, 1925, reel 1, NLC Records.

65. Lauri Johnson, "A Generation of Women Activists: African American Female Educators in Harlem, 1930–1950," *Journal of African American History* 89, no. 3 (Summer 2004): 229–30.

66. "Organization Report 1925," March 27, 1926, 3–5; "Organization Report of the Laundry Workers for May," 1926, 1, reel 3, NY WTUL Records; "Only 20 at Labor Rally," *New York Times*, March 15, 1926, 6.

67. "Organization Report for November of WTUL," 1926, 1, reel 3, NY WTUL Records.

68. "United Laundry Workers," *New York Amsterdam News*, March 24, 1926, 1 (quotes); Greenberg, *Or Does It Explode?*, 110–11.

69. Frank Crosswaith to Morris Ernst, June 5, 1926, 1, reel 1, NLC Records; Franklin, *The Negro Labor Unionist*, 110; "Organization Report 1925," March 27, 1925, 5, reel 3, NY WTUL Records.

70. Greenberg, *Or Does It Explode?*, 21–22.

71. Kessler-Harris, *A Woman's Wage*, 122–23; Collins, *Black Feminist Thought*, 186.

72. "Organization Report for January," 1928, 1 (quote), reel 3, NY WTUL Records; "Annual Report," March 1, 1927, to February 29, 1928, 2; "Convention Report," June 1, 1926, to April 30, 1929, 7, reel 8, WTUL Publications.

73. "Women Join Laundry Strike," *New York Times*, February 28, 1928, 18; "Report of Organization Work," February 1928, 1; "Report of Organization Work," March and April

1928, 1, reel 3, NY WTUL Records; "Annual Report," March 1, 1927, to February 29, 1928, 3, reel 22, NY WTUL Records; Schneiderman with Goldthwaite, *All for One*, 214.

74. "Report of Organization Work," February 1928, 1; "Report of Organization Work," March and April 1928, 1, reel 3, NY WTUL Records.

75. "Report of Organization Work," March and April 1928, 1–2, reel 3, NY WTUL Records; Schneiderman with Goldthwaite, *All for One*, 212–15.

76. Hyman H. Bookbinder, *To Promote the General Welfare: The Story of the Amalgamated* (New York: Amalgamated Clothing Workers of America, 1950), 28, 38–39.

77. Alice Kessler-Harris, "Problems of Coalition-Building: Women and Trade Unions in the 1920s," in Kessler, *Gendering Labor History*, 53–54.

78. Dye, *As Equals*, 139, 162.

79. Katz, *All Together Different*, 1–16, 24–29, 44–47.

80. Ibid., 1–15, 24–29; Rose Schneiderman, "Speech to the National Conference of Christians and Jews," February 1944, 1 (quote), reel 21, NY WTUL Records.

81. Orleck, *Common Sense*, 16–30; Katz, *All Together Different*, 46–71.

82. Schneiderman with Goldthwaite, *All for One*, 214–15; "Report of Organization Work," March and April 1928, 1–2, reel 3, NY WTUL Records; Franklin, *The Negro Labor Unionist*, 180.

Chapter Five. "It Was Up to All of Us to Fight"

1. Smith, interview by the author, December 24, 2006, New York.

2. Smith, interview by Bea Lemisch, November 19, 1981, in *The Oral History of the American Left*; Leo Wolman, *Ebb and Flow in Trade Unionism* (New York: National Bureau of Economic Research, 1936), 144.

3. New York Department of Labor, *Industrial Bulletin: Minimum Wage Regulations to Help the State's Laundry Industry*, November 1950, 13, folder 1, box 54, collection no. 5619, ACWA Records; Jack Barbash, "Economics and Organization of the Laundry Industry," *The Advance* 25, no. 3 (March 1939): 18.

4. Beatrice Lumpkin, interviews by the author, 2007–9, Chicago; Mohun, *Steam Laundries*, 194; Greenberg, *Or Does It Explode?*, 79.

5. Ella Baker and Marvel Cooke, "The Bronx Slave Market," *The Crisis* 42 (November 1935): 330–40.

6. New York Department of Labor, *Industrial Bulletin*, 13–14; "Wages Are Cut in Laundry Industry," *Young Worker* 7, no. 12 (December 1929): 8.

7. Franklin, *Negro Labor Unionist*, 106 (quote).

8. Greene, "Harlem in the Great Depression," 64–67, 85; Greenberg, *Or Does It Explode?*, 44–45, 53–56, 78–79, 145.

9. "Replaced by White Workers after 3 Years in Laundry," *The Liberator*, October 31, 1931, 3 (quotes); "L.S.N.R. Reports on Discrimination in Laundry," *The Liberator*, November 7, 1931, 3.

10. Filley and Mitchell, *Consider the Laundry Workers*, 15–16, 21, 36, 40, 47, 55; "Laundry Worker Tells of Speed Up," *Working Woman* 1, no. 9 (June 1930): 5.

11. New York Department of Labor, "Report of the Laundry Minimum Wage Board to

the Industrial Commissioner of New York State," August 11, 1933, folder 60, box 2, 5235, National Consumers League Records, Kheel Center, Cornell University, Ithaca, NY.

12. "Survey Shows Cuts in Wages of Women," *New York Times*, April 24, 1931, 18; Robinson, interview by Craig, 1, 45, 51–52, 59, TCTUW.

13. "The Truth about the Case against Local 324," *The Advance*, August 1, 1943, 6.

14. Barbash, "Economics and Organization," 18; Nestel, *Labor Relations*, 25–28. By 1945 national business sales had increased beyond pre-Depression levels to $650 million.

15. Filley and Mitchell, *Consider the Laundry Workers*, 17, 35.

16. Morris, "Laundry Workers," 76–77; Macon, interview, in Banks, *First Person America*, 127; Lawrence W. Levine, *Black Culture, Black Consciousness: Afro-American Folk Thought from Slavery to Freedom* (Oxford: Oxford University Press, 1977), 5–19, 30–40, 161, 208–17.

17. Mark Naison, *Communists in Harlem* (Urbana: University of Illinois Press, 1983), 3–11; Biondi, *To Stand and Fight*, 4–25.

18. Naison, *Communists in Harlem*, 18; Kelley, *Hammer and Hoe*, 14–30; Biondi, *To Stand and Fight*, 4–5, 45; Edward P. Johanningsmeier, "The Trade Union Unity League: American Communists and the Transition to Industrial Unionism, 1928–1934," *Labor History* 42, no. 2 (May 2001): 170–74.

19. Quoted in Erik S. McDuffie, *Sojourning for Freedom: Black Women, American Communism, and the Making of Black Left Feminism* (Durham, NC: Duke University Press, 2011), 43–44; LaShawn Harris, "Running with the Reds: African American Women and the Communist Party during the Great Depression," *Journal of African American History* 94, no. 1 (Winter 2009): 24; Naison, *Communists in Harlem*, 18–19, 34–35; Gore, *Radicalism at the Crossroads*, 29, 48, 68–73.

20. Naison, *Communists in Harlem*, xvii, 10–11, 34–35, 43–49.

21. Ibid.; Erin Royston Battat, *Ain't Got No Home: America's Great Migrations and the Making of an Interracial Left* (Chapel Hill: University of North Carolina Press, 2014), 35–36; Smith, interview by the author, June 28, 2007, New York.

22. Naison, *Communists in Harlem*, 3–11; Biondi, *To Stand and Fight*, 4–6.

23. Naison, *Communists in Harlem*, 35, 49 (quote).

24. Carole Boyce Davies, *Left of Karl Marx: The Political Life of Black Communist Claudia Jones* (Durham, NC: Duke University Press, 2007), 51, 57–59; Mary E. Triece, *On the Picket Line: Strategies of Working-Class Women during the Depression* (Urbana: University of Illinois Press, 2007), 22–25; McDuffie, *Sojourning Freedom*, 21, 88–89.

25. Quoted in Robert Shaffer, "Women and the Communist Party," *Socialist Review*, May–June 1979, 78–83.

26. Gore, *Radicalism at the Crossroads*, 29, 48, 68–73; Boyce Davies, *Left of Karl Marx*, 37–44, 51–52; McDuffie, *Sojourning Freedom*, 89; Claudia Jones, "An End to the Neglect of the Problems of the Negro Woman!," reprinted from *Political Affairs*, June 1949, https://palmm.digital.flvc.org/islandora/object/ucf%3A4865.

27. Trade Union Unity League, *Trade Union Unity League: Its Programs, Structures, Methods and History* (New York: Trade Union Unity League, 1930s), 25–46; Solomon, *The Cry Was Unity*, 66.

28. Johanningsmeier, "The Trade Union Unity League," 157–62, 168–71; Wolman, *Ebb and Flow*, 143–145.

29. Smith, interview by the author, December 24, 2006, New York; Smith, interview by Lemisch, in *Oral History of the American Left*; Orleck, *Common Sense*, 172.

30. Smith, interview by the author, December 24, 26, 2006, June 24, 28, 2007, New York; "Six Held as Reds in Bronx," *New York Times*, March 7, 1930, 2.

31. "Reds Assail Trotsky at Convention Here," *New York Times*, March 2, 1929, 6 (quotes); "Communists Clash with Police Parade," *New York Times*, May 19, 1929, 1; Smith, interview by the author, December 24, 2006, New York.

32. "J. P. Morgan Sails on the Mauretania," *New York Times*, July 25, 1929, 24; Smith, interview by the author, June 28, 2007, New York; Smith, interview by Lemisch, in *Oral History of the American Left*.

33. Smith, interview by the author, December 24, 26, 2006, June 24, 28, 2007, New York; "Soviet Grows Angry on Chinese Clashes," *New York Times*, August 20, 1929, 5.

34. Naison, *Communists in Harlem*, xvii, 10–11, 34–35, 43–49; Battat, *Ain't Got No Home*, 35–36; Smith, interview by the author, December 25, 2006, June 24, 28 (quote), 2007, New York.

35. Smith, interview by the author, December 24, 26, 2006, June 24, 28, 2007, New York; "Soviet Grows Angry on Chinese Clashes," *New York Times*, August 20, 1929, 5.

36. Smith, interview by the author, June 24, 2007, May 27, 2008, New York.

37. Peggy Dennis, *The Autobiography of an American Communist: A Personal View of a Political Life, 1925–1975* (Westport, CT: Lawrence Hill & Co., 1977), 55–57, 77, 128–31, 190–91, 294.

38. Beatrice Lumpkin, *Joy in the Struggle: My Life and Love* (New York: International Publishers, 2013), 1, 14–16, 46–48.

39. Ibid., 48 (quote), 50; Lumpkin, interview by the author, June 2, 2008, Chicago; Katz, *All Together Different*, 101.

40. Lumpkin, interview by the author, June 2, 2008, Chicago.

41. Lumpkin, *Joy in the Struggle*, 1 (quote), 3, 15, 52–55; Lumpkin, interview by the author, June 2, 2008, May 3, 2009, (quote) Chicago.

42. Lumpkin, interview by the author, May 3, 2009, Chicago; Lumpkin, *Joy in the Struggle*, 14–16, 36–45.

43. Lumpkin, interview by the author, May 3, 2009 (quote), June 2, 2008, Chicago; Lumpkin, *Joy in the Struggle*, 15–16, 50–51 (quotes).

44. Lumpkin, *Joy in the Struggle*, 17–35, 52–54, 78; Lumpkin, interview by the author, May 3, 2008, Chicago.

45. Lumpkin, *Joy in the Struggle*, 21–24, 24 (quote).

46. Lumpkin, interview by the author, June 2, 2008, May 3, 2009, Chicago; Lumpkin, *Joy in the Struggle*, 29, 44–51, 65–67, 44, 65 (quotes).

47. Lumpkin, interview by the author, May 3, 2009, Chicago.

48. Boyce Davies, *Left of Karl Marx*, xxiii–xxiv, 29–44; McDuffie, *Sojourning for Freedom*, 96–99.

49. McDuffie, *Sojourning for Freedom*, 4, 4 (quote), 8, 13, 97–99; Harris, "Running with the Reds," 21–23, 30; Gore, *Radicalism at the Crossroads*, 68–71.

50. Boyce Davies, *Left of Karl Marx*, 2, 30–31, 38, 48.

51. Lumpkin, *Joy in the Struggle*, 18–23, 28–33, 40–41, 57–61.

52. Lumpkin, interview by the author, May 3, 2009, Chicago (quotes).

53. Ibid.; Solomon, *The Cry Was Unity*, 22–29, 33–37, 172–73.

54. Lumpkin, interview by the author, May 23, 2007, Chicago; Lumpkin, *Joy in the Struggle*, 80–81.

55. "Laundry Workers to Meet Sunday," *The Liberator*, November 21, 1931, 4; Smith, interview by the author, December 24, 2006, New York.

56. "Unorganized Laundry Workers Support Fight on NRA Slave Code," *Harlem Liberator*, October 7, 1933, 3 (quotes); A. Thomas, "Negro Laundry Workers Are Organizing," *Harlem Liberator*, October 20, 1932, 3; "Nat. Laundry Has Low Wages," *Young Worker*, June 19, 1930, 3; Smith, interview by author, December 24, 2006, New York.

57. Smith, interview by the author, December 24, 2006, June 24, 2007, New York.

58. "Report of New York TUUC," July 13, 1932, 2–3, reel 230, Files of the Communist Party of the USA in the Comintern Archives, Tamiment Library and Robert F. Wagner Labor Archives at New York University, New York; Smith, interview by the author, May 27, 2008, New York.

59. Smith, interview by the author, December 24, 2006, New York; Smith, interview by Lemisch, in *The Oral History of the American Left*.

60. "Laundry Union Calls a Strike in Active Shops," *Daily Worker*, August 22, 1931, 6; "Active Laundry Co. Strike Called Off," *Daily Worker*, January 7, 1932, 2; "Laundry Workers Strike in N.Y.," *Daily Worker*, February 29, 1932, 2.

61. "Chiefs of AFL Local 810 Help Laundry Bosses," *Daily Worker*, March 1, 1933, 4; Leon Blum, "How the Late Larry Fay Built Laundry Racket," *Daily Worker*, March 8, 1933, 4; David Witwer, *Corruption and Reform in the Teamsters Union* (Urbana: University of Illinois Press, 2003), 84–92.

62. "Laundry Union Born in Fight on Racketeers," *Daily Worker*, June 7, 1933, 3; Blum, "How the Late Larry Fay," 4; Smith, interview by the author, June 24, 2007, New York; Smith, interview by Geiser, February 26, 2006, 13–15, New York.

63. Smith, interview by the author, December 24, 26, 2006, June 24, 2007, New York; Smith, interview by Lemisch, in *The Oral History of the American Left*; "Negro Women Workers—Organize," *Working Woman* 1, no. 5 (February 1930): 6; "Laundry Worker Tells of Speed Up," *Working Woman* 1, no. 9 (June 1930): 5; "Parole Officer Gets $500 to Railroad Leon Blum," *Daily Worker*, June 22, 1933, 3.

64. Smith, interview by the author, December 24, 2006, New York.

65. Smith, interview by the author, December 24, 26, 27, 2006, New York.

66. Smith, interview by the author, July 23, December 24, 2006, New York; Franklin, *The Negro Labor Unionist*, 208; "Laundry Union Born in Fight on Racketeers," *Daily Worker*, June 7, 1933, 3; "Unit Page—Section 4," February 13, 1933, 1, folder 9, box 1, Clarina Michelson Papers, Tamiment Library and Robert F. Wagner Labor Archives at New York University, New York.

67. Maud White, "Laundry Workers and the Fight against Low Pay, Long Hours," *Daily Worker*, May 13, 1933, 5; "Harlem Laundry Workers Strike against Wage Cuts," *Harlem Liberator*, July 1, 1933, 1; Smith, interview by the author, December 24, 26, 2006, New York.

68. Smith, interview by the author, December 24, 26, 2006, New York; "Unit Page—Section 4," February 13, 1933, 1, folder 9, box 1, Michelson Papers; "Scottsboro Case

Debated," *New York Amsterdam News*, December 2, 1931, 11; "Communists behind the Hunger March Moving on Capital," *New York Times*, November 29, 1931, 1.

69. "Laundry Strike Still Going Strong," *Daily Worker*, March 21, 1932, 2; "Strike at the Fairway Laundry Solid," *Daily Worker*, December 14, 1932, 2; "Laundry Workers Meet Friday Night to Protest NRA Code," *Harlem Liberator*, September 23, 1933, 2; Naison, *Communists in Harlem*, 46–47.

70. A. Thomas, "Negro Laundry Workers Are Organizing," *The Liberator*, October 20, 1932, 3; "Laundry Workers Meet on June 8," *Harlem Liberator*, June 10, 1933, 7; "Laundry Workers Meet Friday Night to Protest NRA Code," *Harlem Liberator*, September 23, 1933, 2; Smith, interview by the author, July 23, December 24, 2006, New York.

71. Harris, "Running with the Reds," 21–22; Gore, *Radicalism at the Crossroads*, 18, 25, 32, 81, 96, 102–3.

72. Maude White, "Negro Laundry Workers Are Organizing," *The Liberator*, October 20, 1932, 3 (quote); White, "Laundry Workers and the Fight," 5 (quote); Smith, interview by the author, July 23, December 24, 2006, New York.

73. "Six Men Must Face Court," *Bronx Home News*, March 2, 1933, 12; Smith, interview by Geiser, February 26, 2006, New York; "Laundry Workers Strike in N.Y.," *Daily Worker*, February 29, 1932, 2; "Laundry Strike on at Superfine Plant," *Daily Worker*, March 1, 1932, 2.

74. Smith, interview by the author, July 23, 27, 2006, New York; Sam Berland to the Central Committee Communist Party U.S.A., April 8, 1932, reel 232, Files of the Communist Party of the USA in the Comintern Archives, Tamiment Library and Robert F. Wagner Labor Archives at New York University, New York.

75. Quoted in Epstein, *The Jew and Communism*, 246–47, Marxist International Archive, https://www.marxists.org/subject/jewish/epstein-cpusa/index.htm.

76. "Laundry Workers in Bronx Decide to Join the TUUL," *Daily Worker*, May 9, 1932, 2; "Report of New York TUUC," July 13, 1932, 2–3, reel 230, Files of the Communist Party of the U.S.A. in the Comintern Archives, Tamiment Library, New York University, New York.

77. Zieger, *The CIO*, 16–19.

78. "Laundry Workers Strike," *New York Times*, June 27, 1933, 15; "14,000 Laundry Workers Strike for Higher Pay," *Bronx Home News*, June 27, 1933, 1; "Harlem Laundry Workers Strike against Wage Cuts," *Harlem Liberator*, July 1, 1933, 1; "Laundry Workers Fight Slave Code," *Harlem Liberator*, July 15, 1933, 2; A. Thomas, "The Laundry Workers March," *Harlem Liberator*, December 16, 1933, 2.

79. Biondi, *To Stand and Fight*, 1–7; Naison, *Communists in Harlem*, 47, 57–68, 74–89.

80. "Laundry Workers Strike," *New York Times*, June 27, 2933, 15; "Laundry Workers, Negro and White, Strike This Morning," *Daily Worker*, June 26, 1933, 3; "Rally Bronx Workers to Aid Laundry Strike," *Daily Worker*, June 29, 1933, 1, 3.

81. Smith, interview by the author, December 26, 2006, June 24, 2007, New York; "Laundry Workers, Negro and White, Strike This Morning," *Daily Worker*, June 26, 1933, 3.

82. Franklin, *The Negro Labor Unionist*, 209; Smith, interview by the author, December 24, 2006, New York.

83. Jessie Taft Smith, phone conversation with the author, July 23, 2006; Smith, interview by Geiser, February 26, 2006, New York.

84. "21 Seized in Bronx Laundry Strike," *Bronx Home News*, June 28, 1933, 3; "Laundry Driver Beaten in Strike," *Bronx Home News*, July 1, 1933, 2; Smith, interview by the author, June 24, 2007, New York.

85. "40 Negro and White Strike at 'Pretty' Laundry against Cut," *Daily Worker*, February 28, 1933, 1; "More Workers Join 'Pretty Laundry' Strike," *Daily Worker*, March 7, 1933, 2; "Strikers Foil Plan to Beat Laundry Union," *Daily Worker*, November 12, 1934, 4; "Workers of Adelphia L'ndry out on Strike," *Daily Worker*, March 26, 1934, 3.

86. Smith, interview by the author, December 24, 26, 2006, June 27, 2007, New York; "Rally Bronx Workers to Aid Laundry Strike," *Daily Worker*, June 29, 1933, 1, 3; Solomon, *The Cry Was Unity*, 148.

87. Smith, phone conversation with the author, July 23, 2006; Smith, interview by Geiser, February 26, 2006, New York; Orleck, *Common Sense*, 215–19, 241; Elizabeth Faue, "Paths of Unionization: Community, Bureaucracy, and Gender in the Minneapolis Labor Movement of the 1930s," in *Work Engendered: Toward a New History of American Labor*, ed. Ava Baron (Ithaca, NY: Cornell University Press, 1991), 298–99.

88. "Meet to Spread Laundry Strike," *Daily Worker*, May 25, 1932, 2; "Strike of N.Y. Laundry Workers in 2nd Week," *Daily Worker*, April 16, 1934, 3; "More Workers Join Pretty Laundry Strike," *Daily Worker*, March 7, 1933, 2.

89. "21 Seized in Bronx Laundry Strike," *Bronx Home News*, June 28, 1933, 3.

90. "Strikers in Laundry Turn Down Blacklist," *Daily Worker*, March 3, 1933, 2; "Parole Officer Gets $500 to Railroad Leon Blum," *Daily Worker*, June 22, 1933, 3; "Frame Worker in Laundry Strike," *Daily Worker*, April 12, 1933, 3; "ILD Calls for Mass Campaign to Free Leon Blum," *Daily Worker*, October 9, 1933, 4; "Leon Blum, Framed Laundry Union Head, Arrives in N.Y.," *Daily Worker*, May 14, 1934, 1.

91. Johanningsmeier, "The Trade Union Unity League," 159–60; Smith, interview by the author, June 28, 2007, New York.

92. "Not Making Necessary Headway Because of Our Sectarian Practices," *Daily Worker*, October 10, 1933, 4; Henry Shepard, "Trade Union Work among the Negro Masses," *Daily Worker*, March 29, 1934, 5; Naison, *Communists in Harlem*, 96–97; Solomon, *The Cry Was Unity*, 228–29.

93. Robinson, interview by Craig, 39 (quotes), TCTUW.

94. Pauli Murray, *Song in a Weary Throat: An American Pilgrimage* (New York: Harper and Row Publishers, 1987), 102–3.

95. Richards, *Conversations with Maida Springer*, 61, 86–91 (quotes); Eric Arnesen, "No 'Graver Danger': Black Anticommunism, the Communist Party, and the Race Question," *Labor: Studies in Working-Class History of the Americas* 3, no. 4 (2006): 24–29.

96. Smith, interview by the author, May 27, 2008, June 24, 2007, New York.

97. Naison, *Communists in Harlem*, 95–98.

98. Federal Writers' Project, *New York Panorama*, 150 (quote); Greenberg, *Or Does It Explode?*, 110.

99. Roi Ottley and William J. Weatherby, *The Negro in New York: An Informal Social History* (New York: Oceana Publications, 1967), 290–91.

100. Filley and Mitchell, *Consider the Laundry Workers*, 58; Greenberg, *Or Does It Explode?*, 108–13; Franklin, *Negro Labor Unionist*, 126–27.

101. Franklin, *Negro Labor Unionist*, 125–29 (quote), 158.

102. Wolman, *Ebb and Flow*, 144–45; "Union Wins Strike at Samac Laundry," *Daily Worker*, January 15, 1934, 2.

103. Naison, *Communists in Harlem*, 126–27, 158–59, 169–77; Robinson, interview by Craig, 48, TCTUW.

104. "Laundry Workers Get Unity in Strike Meet," *Daily Worker*, February 8, 1934, 3; "Laundry Workers to Hold Big Mass Meeting Sunday," *Harlem Liberator*, May 12, 1934, 2; "Unity Move in Laundry Union Gains," *Daily Worker*, June 4, 1934, 3; "Laundry Workers Plan Gen. Strike," *Daily Worker*, April 19, 1934, 4.

105. Wolman, *Ebb and Flow*, 144–45; "Laundry Workers Plan Gen. Strike," *Daily Worker*, April 19, 1934, 4; LSNR, untitled report, April 24, 1934, folder 5, box 1; Minutes of the Conference of Independent Trade Unions, 1935, 3, folder 5, box 2; and "The Open Letter," 1933, folder 8, box 1, all in Michelson Papers.

106. Letter to GEB of the LWIU, January 17, 1936, reel 39, AFL Records; Smith, interview by the author, December 24, 2006, June 28, 2007, New York; Franklin, *Negro Labor Unionist*, 208–10.

107. Franklin, *Negro Labor Unionist*, 208–10 (quote); Smith, interview by the author, December 24, 2006, June 24, 2007, New York.

108. Joseph Mackey, "Emergency Appeal," 1–2, Vertical File, Tamiment Library; Joseph Mackey to William Green, June 22, 1935, reel 39, AFL Records.

109. William Collins to Miss R. Lee Guard, January 20, 1936; and Mackey to Green, August 13, 1936, reel 39, both in AFL Records.

110. Franklin, *The Negro Labor Unionist*, 208–9; Smith, interview by the author, June 28, 2007, New York.

111. Joseph Mackey to William Green, November 23, 1935; Mackey to Green, April 5, 1936; and letter to GEB, January 17, 1936, reel 39, all in AFL Records; "Seek to Settle Laundry Dispute," *New York Amsterdam News*, January 25, 1936, 15.

112. William Collins to Miss R. Lee Guard, January 20, 1936; Mackey to Green, August 13, 1936, reel 39, both in AFL Records.

113. William Green to Matthew Woll, June 25, 1935; Mackey to Green, November 23, 1935; and letter to GEB, January 17, 1936, reel 39, all in AFL Records; Franklin, *The Negro Labor Unionist*, 208–210.

114. "Laundry Local Is Reorganized," *New York Amsterdam News*, January 11, 1936, 15; "Seek to Settle Laundry Dispute," *New York Amsterdam News*, January 25, 1936, 15.

115. "Union Gives Negroes Four Official Posts," *New York Amsterdam News*, October 12, 1935, 2.

116. Franklin, *The Negro Labor Unionist*, 210 (quote); Robinson, interview by Craig, 3, TCTUW.

Chapter Six. "Aristocrats of the Movement"

1. "Organization Report," 1934, 1, reel 3, NY WTUL Records; Robinson, interview by Craig, 1–2, TCTUW.

2. Mohun, *Steam Laundries*, 194; Orleck, *Common Sense*, 160–63.

3. Kathy Higgins, "Use Your Buying Power for Justice: The League of Women Shoppers and Innocuous Feminist Radicalism 1935–1948," *Chicago Journal of History* 6 (Spring

2016): 45; Ellen Cain, "'We Used to Be Patrons—Now We Are Pickets!': The League of Women Shoppers, the Picket Line, and Identity Formation, 1935–1949," *Journal of Women's History* 31, no. 3 (Fall 2019): 40–42.

4. Orleck, *Common Sense*, 144–63.

5. Nienburg and Blair, *Factors Affecting Wages*, 9–12; Mohun, *Steam Laundries*, 194–96.

6. Mohun, *Steam Laundries*, 196–97.

7. Elizabeth Lawson, "Negro Robbed Yet Again," 5, National Negro Congress Records, 1933–47, Schomburg Center for Research in Black Culture, New York; "Laundry Workers to Protest NRA Slavery Code," *Harlem Liberator*, September 16, 1933, 2.

8. Mary Anderson, "Statement on the Proposed Code for the Laundry Trade," November 20, 1933, 1–7, folder 2, box 9, NRA Transcripts of Hearings, 1735-2-10 (Vol. 3); "The Laundry Trade," November 20, 1933, 515–22, folder 7, box 7, United States National Archives and Records, Xerox Copies of Documentation Relating to Black Workers, Kheel Center, Cornell University, Ithaca, NY.

9. Mohun, *Steam Laundries*, 197; Orleck, *Common Sense*, 152–53.

10. Nienburg and Blair, *Factors Affecting Wages*, 9–10; Mohun, *Steam Laundries*, 197–217.

11. Nienburg and Blair, *Factors Affecting Wages*, 37, 42–43, 59–60.

12. Nestel, *Labor Relations*, 58; Mohun, *Steam Laundries*, 192–93; Orleck, *Common Sense*, 160–65.

13. New York Department of Labor, "New Release: Five out of Six Laundries Have Accepted State Minimum Wage Law," January 22, 1934, folder 60, box 2, National Consumers League Records, 5235, Kheel Center, Cornell University, Ithaca, NY; "Minimum Wage Commission Aims to Revive AFL in Laundry Industry," *Daily Worker*, June 7, 1933, 3.

14. New York Department of Labor, "Minimum Wage for Laundry Workers," folder 60, box 2; and Carrie Lou Allgood to the Industrial Club Girls, YWCA, December 10, 1936, folder 61, box 2, both in National Consumers League Records, 5235; Nestel, *Labor Relations*, 58.

15. New York Department of Labor, "Schedule of Hearing on Mandatory Laundry Wage Order," July 2, 1934, 3–4; New York State Department of Labor, "New Release: Five out of Six Laundries Have Accepted State Minimum Wage Law," January 22, 1934; and NY Minimum Wage, October 13, 1934, all in folder 60, box 2, National Consumers League Records, 5235.

16. "9 Laundries Cited as Wage Violators," *New York Times*, January 19, 1934, 15; "40 Laundries Put on Boycott List," *New York Times*, March 14, 1934, 12.

17. New York Department of Labor, "News," March 10, 1934; letter to Department of Labor, October 24, 1933; and NY Minimum Wage, October 13, 1934, all in folder 60, box 2, National Consumers League Records, 5235.

18. "Organization Report," January 8, 1934, 1, reel 3, NY WTUL Records.

19. "Laundry Union Wins War for Pay Boost," *New York Amsterdam News*, December 20, 1933, 11; "Brownsville Laundry Workers Build Union," *Harlem Liberator*, December 23, 1933, 3.

20. ACWA, "The Journal of the LWJB: 10th Anniversary Celebration," June 14, 1947, box 139, collection no. 5619, ACWA Records.

21. "Organization Report," January 8, 1934, 1, reel 3, NY WTUL Records.

22. Eleanor Mishnun, interview by Debra Bernhardt, March–May 1985, New York, 1–3, New Yorkers at Work Oral History Collection, 1979–2000, Tamiment Library, New York University, New York.

23. Edward P. Johanningsmeier, *Forging American Communism: The Life of William Z. Foster* (Princeton, NJ: Princeton University Press, 1994), 90; Mishnun, interview by Bernhardt, 1–18, 26, New Yorkers at Work Oral History Collection.

24. Mishnun, interview by Bernhardt, 1–18, 26, New Yorkers at Work Oral History Collection.

25. Kessler-Harris, "Rose Schneiderman," 80–88; Orleck, *Common Sense*, 123 (quote), 148–54.

26. Mishnun, interview by Bernhardt, 11 (quote), 12–18, 26, New Yorkers at Work Oral History Collection.

27. Orleck, *Common Sense*, 156–57.

28. "Educational Directors," undated, reel 2, Schneiderman Papers; Kessler-Harris, "Rose Schneiderman," 87–88; Orleck, *Common Sense*, 123–29, 155–56, 258–67.

29. Schneiderman with Goldthwaite, *All for One*, 216–17.

30. Smith, interview by the author, June 24, 27, 2007, New York.

31. "Report of the National Women's Department of the TUUL," January 1932, 2, reel 231; "Report of the Women's Department of the Central Committee," undated, reel 255, both in Files of the Communist Party of the U.S.A. in the Comintern Archives, Tamiment Library, New York University, New York.

32. Mishnun, interview by Bernhardt, 26–29, New Yorkers at Work Oral History Collection; "Organization Report," January 8, 1934, 1, reel 3, NY WTUL Records.

33. "Organization Report," January 8, 1934, reel 3, NY WTUL Records.

34. Robinson, interview by Craig, 12–16, 23, TCTUW; Richards, *Conversations with Maida Springer*, 120.

35. Ramona Lowe, "Tells of Laundry Union's War Work," *New York Amsterdam News*, April 10, 1943, 24; Robinson, interview by Craig, 1, 43, 55–56, 60, TCTUW.

36. "Organization Report," January 8, 1934, reel 3, NY WTUL Records; Mishnun, interview by Bernhardt, 27, New Yorkers at Work Oral History Collection.

37. Mishnun, interview by Bernhardt, 27, New Yorkers at Work Oral History Collection; "Mellon Admits Laundry Racket," *New York Times*, August 18, 1933, 32.

38. "Call Laundry Body Brooklyn 'Racket,'" *New York Times*, March 8, 1930, 22; "4 in Laundry 'Club' Indicted for Racket," *New York Times*, May 24, 1933, 12; "Jury Is Locked Up in Racket Trial," *New York Times*, August 8, 1933, 12; "Laundry Man Tells of Racket Reprisals," *New York Times*, August 11, 1933, 16.

39. "'Little Augie' Named in Laundry Racket," *New York Times*, August 9, 1933, 15; David Witwer, "The Scandal of George Scalise: A Case Study in the Rise of Labor Racketeering in the 1930s," *Journal of Social History* 36, no. 4 (Summer 2003): 917–40; Smith, interview by Geiser, February 26, 2006, New York.

40. Robinson, interview by Craig, 3, 10, 58–59, TCTUW; "Laundry Czar Loses in Suit over Racket," *New York Times*, July 8, 1936, 3; "Commissioner Puts Unionist on Wage Body," *New York Amsterdam News*, December 18, 1937, 23.

41. Mishnun, interview by Bernhardt, 26–29, 32, New Yorkers at Work Oral History Collection.

42. Robinson, interview by Craig, 1–2, TCTUW.

43. Mishnun, interview by Bernhardt, 29, New Yorkers at Work Oral History Collection.

44. Quoted in Cain, "'We Used to Be Patrons,'" 42 (quote); "The League's Work and the NRA," October 2, 1933, 1, reel 8, WTUL Publications.

45. Orleck, *Common Sense*, 154; McDuffie, *Sojourning Freedom*, 11.

46. Higginbotham, "African-American Women," 271-72; Harris, "Running with the Reds," 32.

47. Grace B. Klueg, "About the Strikers," March 1934 bulletin, reel 8, WTUL Publications.

48. "Minutes of the Executive Board," January 25, 1934, 1; and "Organization Report," February 1934, 1, both on reel 3, NY WTUL Records; Grace B. Klueg, "About the Strikers," March 1934 bulletin, reel 8, WTUL Publications.

49. "Johnson Labor Aide Off for Puerto Rico," *New York Times*, January 19, 1934, 3; "Organization Report," February 1934, 1, reel 3, NY WTUL Records.

50. "Rose Schneiderman Turns Sailing into Strikers' Rally," *World Telegram*, January 18, 1934, reel 2, National WTUL Papers, Arthur and Elizabeth Schlesinger Library on the History of Women in America, Radcliffe College, Cambridge, Massachusetts, microfilm version, *Papers of the Women's Trade Union League and Its Principal Leaders*, by Nancy Schrom Dye, Robin Miller Jacoby, and Edward T. James (Woodbridge, CT: Research Publications, [1985]).

51. "Organization Report," February 1934, 1, and March 1934, 2, reel 3, NY WTUL Records.

52. Mishnun, interview by Bernhardt, 32–33, New Yorkers at Work Oral History Collection.

53. Quoted in Cain, "'We Used to Be Patrons,'" 42 (quote).

54. "Mrs. R. S. Childs Aids Strike," *New York Times*, February 2, 1934, 6; "Mrs. Pinchot Joins Laundry Picket Line," *New York Times*, January 24, 1934, 2.

55. "Organization Report," February 1934, reel 3, NY WTUL Records; Schneiderman, untitled speech, undated, 6, reel 1, Schneiderman Papers; Landon R. Y. Storrs, *The Second Red Scare and the Unmaking of the New Deal Left* (Princeton, NJ: Princeton University Press, 2013), 54–55; Orleck, *Common Sense*, 62, 127–28, 151–52.

56. Mishnun, interview by Bernhardt, 29–30, 33–34, New Yorkers at Work Oral History Collection.

57. Ibid.

58. Ibid., 29–31; "Organization Report," March 1934, 1, reel 3, NY WTUL Records.

59. Schneiderman with Goldthwaite, *All for One*, 216 (quote); "Organization Report," March 1934, 1, reel 3, NY WTUL Records.

60. Thomas Kessner, *Fiorello LaGuardia and the Making of Modern New York* (New York: McGraw Hill, 1989), xii–xvi, 371–77.

61. ACWA, *Report of the GEB and Proceedings of the 12th Biennial Convention*, Atlantic City, May 1938, 327 (quote); Robinson, interview by Craig, 2 (quote), TCTUW.

62. "Organization Report," March 1934, 1–2, reel 3, NY WTUL Records; "Laundry Strike Ends as City Intervenes," *New York Times*, February 12, 1934, 3.

63. Mishnun, "Organization," *Annual Report*, 1934, 5–6, reel 8, NY WTUL Records.

64. Rose Schneiderman, "The WTUL Confronts the Situation of Women Workers Today," 1934, 2–3, reel 21, NY WTUL Records.

65. "Organization Report," April 1934, 2 (quote); and "Minutes of the Special Executive Board Meeting," May 18, 1934, 1, both on reel 3, NY WTUL Records.

66. "Organization Report," March 1934, 2; and "Organization Report," March 9, 1934, 1–2, both on reel 3, NY WTUL Records; "Laundries," undated, reel 2, Schneiderman Papers.

67. Robert H. Zieger and Gilbert J. Gall, *American Workers, American Unions*, 3rd ed. (Baltimore, MD: Johns Hopkins University Press, 2002), 75–79; Mohun, *Steam Laundries*, 211; "Organization Report," March 9, 1934; and "Organization Report," September 17, 1934, 1, both on reel 3, NY WTUL Records.

68. Mishnun, interview by Bernhardt, 31, New Yorkers at Work Oral History Collection.

69. Kessler-Harris, "Where Are the Organized Women Workers?," 30–37; Kessler-Harris, "Problems of Coalition-Building," 57–63; Orleck, *Common Sense*, 129–30, 150; Higgins, "Use Your Buying Power," 44–51.

70. Robinson, interview by Craig, 2, TCTUW.

71. "Meeting of the Membership Committee," January 13, 1936, reel 3, NY WTUL Records.

72. Dixon, Roscigno, and Hodson, "Unions, Solidarity, and Striking," 3–33; Dixon and Roscigno, "Status, Networks," 1292–1327.

Chapter Seven. "It Was Like the Salvation"

1. "Self-Made Prisoner," *Daily News*, October 26, 1936, 3, 24.

2. "The Journal of the Laundry Workers Joint Board: 10th Anniversary Celebration," box 139, collection no. 5619, ACWA Records; Adelmond to Members of the Board of Directors, LWJB, "Reasons for Resignation of Charlotte Adelmond," December 6, 1950, 1, folder 559, Pauli Murray Papers, Radcliffe Institute for Advanced Study, Schlesinger Library on the History of Women in America, Harvard University, Cambridge, MA.

3. Dixon, Roscigno, and Hodson, "Unions, Solidarity, and Striking," 3–33.

4. Zieger and Gall, *American Workers*, 80; Orleck, *Common Sense*, 165.

5. "Wage Slashing Laid to Laundry Owners," *New York Amsterdam News*, March 21, 1936, 3; Nestel, *Labor Relations*, 60–61; Filley and Mitchell, *Consider the Laundry Workers*, 40–43.

6. Worker letters compiled by Frieda Miller for Emily Marconnier, March 9, 1936, folder 61, box 2, collection no. 5235, National Consumers League Records; Georgette Johnson, "Plight of Laundry Workers," *New York Amsterdam News*, March 21, 1936, 12; Dorothy Maynard, "Minimum Wage Law," *New York Amsterdam News*, April 4, 1936, 12.

7. Higgins, "Use Your Buying Power," 44–51, 47 (quote); Cain, "'We Used to Be Patrons,'" 35–40; Storrs, *The Second Red Scare*, 54–55, 71, 75, 107.

8. Higgins, "Use Your Buying Power," 52–53.

9. Smith, interview by the author, December 26 and 27, 2006, New York.

10. Filley and Mitchell, *Consider the Laundry Workers*, 5–6; quoted in Higgins, "Use Your Buying Power," 44.

11. Zieger and Gall, *American Workers*, 79–82; Nelson Lichtenstein, *State of the Union: A Century of American Labor* (Princeton, NJ: Princeton University Press, 2003), 35–38; Zieger, *The CIO*, 63–64.

12. Robinson, interview by Craig, 2–3, 76, TCTUW; Stevenson, *Challenging the Roadblocks*, 40.

13. Julia Oestreich, "They Saw Themselves as Workers: Interracial Unionism in the ILGWU and the Development of Black Labor Organizations, 1933–1940" (PhD diss., Temple University, 2011), 262–80; Greenberg, *Or Does It Explode?*, 111–13, 129, 316.

14. Greenberg, *Or Does It Explode?*, 111–13, 129; Oestreich, "They Saw Themselves," 277–87, 313–17.

15. "Report of the Harlem Labor Committee," December 1, 1934–March 1935, reel 1, NLC Records; Oestreich, "They Saw Themselves," 263, 286.

16. Naison, *Communists in Harlem*, 39, 150, 198, 309; Bynum, *A. Philip Randolph*, 114, 150–52; Arnesen, "No 'Graver Danger,'" 19–20; Lumpkin, interview by the author, May 3, 2009, 9, Chicago.

17. "Minutes of the Harlem Labor Committee," August 12, 1935, reel 1, NLC Records.

18. "Minutes of the Special Executive Board Meeting," March 9, 1936, 1; "Organization 1935–1936"; and "Minutes of Special Meeting of the Executive Board," July 9, 1936, all on reel 3, NY WTUL Records.

19. "Laundry Union Gets Members in Harlem," *New York Amsterdam News*, September 5, 1936, 4; "Report of Organizer," February 1937, reel 4, NY WTUL Records; Smith, interview by the author, June 24, 2007, New York.

20. "Report of Organizer," December 1936, reel 3, NY WTUL Records; "Report of Organizer," January 1937; and "Annual Report of Organizer," April 1, 1936–March 30, 1937, 3, both on reel 4, NY WTUL Records; "Will Fight for Minimum Wages," *New York Amsterdam News*, March 7, 1936, 2.

21. Robinson, interview by Craig, 1, 43, 55–56, 60, TCTUW.

22. "Annual Report of Organizer," April 1, 1936–March 30, 1937, 3, reel 4, NY WTUL Records; Filley and Mitchell, *Consider the Laundry Workers*, 14; "Laundry Union Ready to Strike," *New York Amsterdam News*, February 20, 1937, 3; "Striking Workers Tie Up Laundries," *New York Amsterdam News*, April 3, 1937, 12.

23. "Loyal Friend of Laundry Workers Dies," *The Advance* 25, no. 7 (July 1939): 19.

24. "Report of Organizer," April 1937, 1–2; and "Annual Report of Organizer," April 1, 1936–March 30, 1937, 4–5, both on reel 4, NY WTUL Records.

25. New York Department of Labor, *Industrial Bulletin*, 15–16; Division of Women in Industry and Minimum Wage, *Women in Industry: Summary Report on Survey*, folder 5, box 52, collection no. 5619, ACWA Records.

26. NY WTUL, "Luncheon," undated; New York Department of Labor, "News Release," March 8, 1938, folder 61, box 2, collection no. 5235, National Consumers League Records.

27. "Report of Work," December 1, 1937, reel 4, NY WTUL Records; "Commissioner Puts Unionist on Wage Body," *New York Amsterdam News*, December 18, 1937, 23.

28. "Report of Work," December 1, 1937; "Executive Board Minutes," January 31, 1938, 2; and "Minutes of the Regular Membership Meeting of the WTUL," March 3 and 6, 1939, all on reel 4, NY WTUL Records.

29. "Executive Board Minutes," January 31, 1938, 2; "Report of Work," June 1–August 31, 1937; and "Special Committee on Organizers in Training," March 1, 1938, all on reel 4, NY WTUL Records.

30. "The Remarkable Twenty Year History of the Amalgamated Laundry Workers Joint Board," 1957, box 289, collection no. 5619, ACWA Records; "Report of Organization," June–September 1937, 1, reel 4, NY WTUL Records.

31. Zieger, *The CIO*, 19–27, 34–41.

32. Deslippe, *Rights Not Roses*, 25; Zieger, *The CIO*, 83–85; Greenberg, *Or Does It Explode?*, 112–13.

33. Zieger, *The CIO*, 85–88; Mary Margaret Fonow, *Union Women: Forging Feminism in the United Steelworkers of America* (Minneapolis: University of Minnesota Press, 2003), 42.

34. Charlotte Adelmond to Members of the Board of Directors, LWJB, "Reasons for Resignation of Charlotte Adelmond from the LWJB," December 6, 1950, 1, folder 559, Murray Papers.

35. George S. Schuyler, "Harlem Boasts 42,000 Negro Labor Unionists," *Pittsburgh Courier*, August 21, 1937, 14; Sabina Martinez, "A Black Union Organizer," in *Black Women in White America*, ed. Gerda Lerner (New York: Vintage, 1972), 263.

36. "Ten Thousand Laundry Workers Get ACWA Contract," *The Advance* 23, no. 9 (September 1937): 19; Zieger, *The CIO*, 68; "The Journal of the LWJB: Tenth Anniversary Celebration," box 139, collection no. 5619, ACWA Records.

37. Robinson, interview by Craig, 3, TCTUW; "Ten Thousand Laundry Workers Get ACWA Contract," *The Advance* 23, no. 9 (September 1937): 19.

38. Nestel, *Labor Relations*, 38–39; Faue, *Community of Suffering*, 73–99.

39. Nestel, *Labor Relations*, 12–15, 18, 39–41; "Ten Thousand Laundry Workers Get ACWA Contract," *The Advance* 23, no. 9 (September 1937): 19.

40. "How It Came About," *The Advance* 23, no. 9 (September 1937): 19; "Two Years of Laundry Labor Union," *The Advance* 25, no. 8 (August 1939): 20; "Laundry Workers Making Tremendous Strides," *The Advance* 23, no. 10 (October 1937): 10; "Ten Thousand Laundry Workers Get ACWA Contract," *The Advance* 23, no. 9 (September 1937): 19; Zieger, *The CIO*, 63–64.

41. "Laundry Workers Are Making Union History in New York," *The Advance* 23, no. 10 (October 1937): 2 (quote); "One Year of Laundry Labor Union," *The Advance* 24, no. 8 (August 1938): 3 (quote).

42. Pastorello, *A Power among Them*, 110–14.

43. Steven Fraser, *Labor Will Rule: Sidney Hillman and the Rise of American Labor* (Ithaca, NY: Cornell University Press, 1991), 240.

44. Schneiderman with Goldthwaite, *All for One*, 216–17.

45. Hedgeman, *The Trumpet Sounds*, 81; Maida Springer Kemp, interview by Elizabeth Balanoff, *The Black Woman Oral History Project (BWOHP)*, vol. 7, ed. Ruth Edmonds Hill (Westport, CT: Meckler, 1990), 71; Sabina Martinez, "Negro Women in Organization—Labor," *The Aframerican*, Summer and Fall 1941, in *Public Women, Public Words:*

A Documentary History of American Feminism, ed. Dawn Keetley and John Pettegrew (Oxford: Rowman and Littlefield, 2002), 408.

46. Robinson, interview by Craig, 1–2, TCTUW.

47. Belinda Robnett, "African-American Women in the Civil Rights Movement, 1954–1965: Gender, Leadership, and Micromobilization," *American Journal of Sociology* 101, no. 6 (May 1996): 1664–65.

48. Lumpkin, interview by the author, May 23, 2007, Chicago; Lumpkin, *Joy in the Struggle*, 80–95; Smith, phone conversation with author, Sept. 9, 2006.

49. Judith Stepan-Norris and Maurice Zeitlin, "'Who Gets the Bird?' or How the Communists Won Trust and Power in America's Unions: The Relative Autonomy of Intraclass Struggles," *American Sociological Review* 54, no. 4 (August 1989): 509.

50. Quoted in Yu, *To Save China*, 161.

51. "Laundry Workers Making Tremendous Strides," *The Advance* 23, no. 10 (October 1937): 10.

52. "Ten Thousand Laundry Workers Get ACWA Contract," *The Advance* 23, no. 9 (September 1937): 19.

53. Ibid., 16; "Report of the Laundry Minimum Wage Board to the Industrial Commissioner," January 14, 1938, folder 61, box 2, collection no. 5235, National Consumers League Records.

54. Gustave Strebel, "Independence Day for the Laundry Worker," *The Advance* 25, no. 7 (July 1939): 18 (quote); "Ten Thousand Laundry Workers Get ACWA Contract," *The Advance* 23, no. 9 (September 1937): 19.

55. John Lyons, "Stabilization Plan Set Up for Laundry Industry," *The Advance* 25, no. 1 (January 1939): 13.

56. "Ten Thousand Laundry Workers Get ACWA Contract," *The Advance*, 23, no. 9 (September 1937): 19; "Union and Management Get Together to Talk It Over," *The Advance* 28, no. 14 (July 1942): 9.

57. "Contracts Now Cover Over Twenty-Five Thousand," *The Advance* 23, no. 10 (October 1937): 11; Nestel, *Labor Relations*, 40–41; Lumpkin, *Joy in the Struggle,* 81.

58. Fraser, *Labor Will Rule*, 36–38, 343–48.

59. Lumpkin, *Joy in the Struggle*, 80; Lumpkin, interview by the author, May 23, 2007, Chicago.

60. "Laundry Workers Announce Growth," *New York Amsterdam News*, September 11, 1939, 7; "Laundry Workers Flocking into Union," *New York Amsterdam News*, October 9, 1937, 6.

61. Richards, *Conversations with Maida Springer,* 121; Robinson, interview by Craig, 3, 58–59, TCTUW.

62. Cecil Toppin speaking in *Dollie Lowther Robinson: The Woman and Her Times,* DVD, directed by Melvin McCray (New York: Media Genesis Productions / Melvin McCray, 2006).

63. Richards, *Conversations with Maida Springer,* 121–22; Robinson, interview by Craig, 3, 58–59, 59 (quote), TCTUW.

64. Lumpkin, interview by the author, May 23, 2007, Chicago; Smith, interview by the author, December 24, 2006, New York.

65. Lumpkin, interview by the author, May 23, 2007, Chicago; Lumpkin, *Joy in the Struggle*, 80; Beatrice Lumpkin, "I Helped Organize the CIO," *People's Weekly World Newspaper*, March 15, 2003.

66. George S. Schuyler, "Harlem Boasts 42,000 Negro Labor Unionists," *Pittsburgh Courier*, August 21, 1937, 14; Lester B. Granger, "Manhattan and Beyond," *New York Amsterdam News*, June 1, 1957, 8.

67. Lumpkin, interview by the author, May 23, 2007, Chicago; Jessie Smith, phone conversation with the author, July 23, 2006.

68. "Improved Conditions Won for Laundry Workers by Arbitration," *The Advance* 23, no. 12 (December 1937): 16: "Contracts Now Cover Over 25,000," *The Advance* 23, no. 10 (October 1937): 2.

69. "Westchester Agreement Signed," *The Advance* 23, no. 12 (December 1937): 17; "News from Laundry Workers Union, Local 300," *The Advance* 24, no. 2 (February 1938): 20; Michael Lantt, "A New Day for Laundry Workers in Westchester County," *The Advance* 24, no. 3 (March 1938): 14.

70. "Organizing Drive Progresses in Newark," *The Advance* 23, no. 12 (December 1937): 16; "News from the Laundry Workers Union, Local 300," *The Advance* 24, no. 2 (February 1938): 20; "Myer Bernstein, "New Gains Won by Campaign of ACWA Laundry Committee," *The Advance* 25, no. 4 (April 1939): 16.

71. "Laundry Workers Campaign Extends Drive into Other States," *The Advance* 24, no. 8 (August 1938): 17; Hyman Bookbinder, *They Promote the General Welfare: The Story of the Amalgamated* (ACWA, 1950), 62–63, folder 29, box 292, collection no. 5619, ACWA Records.

72. "Contracts Now Cover Over 25,000," *The Advance* 23, no. 10 (October 1937): 2; Nestel, *Labor Relations*, 44–45.

73. Nestel, *Labor Relations*, 46–47; LWJB, "Facts about Your Union," box 61, collection no. 5619, ACWA Records.

74. Nestel, *Labor Relations*, 47; Elizabeth Lindsey Dayton, "From the Heavy Iron Blues to I Pay My Union Dues" (master's thesis, Sarah Lawrence College, 2009), 151–52.

75. "Hand Laundries Next on the List," *The Advance* 23, no. 12 (December 1937): 17.

76. Nestel, *Labor Relations*, 41.

77. Louis Goldberg, "Hand Laundries Are Signed Up," *The Advance* 24, no. 12 (December 1938): 14.

78. "Agents Join Union," *The Advance* 23, no. 12 (December 1937): 16.

79. "Joint Board Events," *The Advance* 24, no. 3 (March 1938): 15; "Independent Drivers Local 324 Wins Many New Contracts," *The Advance* 24, no. 12 (December 1938): 15.

80. Meyer Bernstein, "Local 324, Laundry Drivers," *The Advance* 24, no. 8 (August 1938): 23; Nestel, *Labor Relations*, 45.

81. "Chinese Firms before Labor Board," *The Advance* 24, no. 4 (April 1938): 12; "Chinese Drive in Full Swing," *The Advance* 27, no. 4 (April 1941): 25.

82. "Sign First Agreement with Chinese Steam Laundry," *The Advance* 27, no. 1 (January 1941): 23; "Bronx Chinese Laundry Signs with Union," *The Advance* 27, no. 3 (March 1941): 24; "Fifth Chinese Laundry Signs Union Contract," *The Advance* 27, no. 9 (September 1941): 19; Nestel, *Labor Relations*, 73–74.

83. Quoted in Yu, *To Save China*, 156–62.

84. George S. Schuyler, "Harlem Boasts 42,000 Negro Labor Unionists," *Pittsburgh Courier*, August 21, 1937, 14; Nestel, *Labor Relations*, 42.

85. "The AFL Laundry Union's the Bunk," *The Advance* 15, no. 10 (October 1939): 24; Noah Walter, "A.F. of L. Laundry Union Is Disintegrating," *The Advance* 25, no. 8 (August 1939): 19; "Mayor Bans AFL Pickets in Ace Laundry Dispute," *The Advance* 26, no. 1 (January 1940): 22.

86. John D. McCarthy and Mayer N. Zald, "Resource Mobilization and Social Movements: A Partial Theory," in *Social Movements: Perspectives and Issues*, ed. Steven M. Buechler and F. Kurt Cylke (Mountain View: Mayfield Publishing Company, 1997), 149–72; Andrew Martin, "Resources for Success: Social Movements, Strategic Resource Allocation, and Union Organizing Outcomes," *Social Problems* 55 (2008): 501–24.

87. Kate Bronfenbrenner and Tom Juravich, "It Takes More Than House Calls: Organizing to Win with a Comprehensive Union-Building Strategy," in *Organizing to Win: New Research on Union Strategies*, ed. Kate Bronfenbrenner et al (Ithaca, NY: Cornell University Press, 1998), 19–36; Kate Bronfenbrenner and Robert Hickey, "Changing to Organize: A National Assessment of Union Strategies," in *Rebuilding Labor: Organizing and Organizers in the New Union Movement*, ed. Ruth Milkman and Kim Voss (Ithaca, NY: Cornell University Press, 2004), 17–61.

88. Dixon, Roscigno, and Hodson, "Unions, Solidarity, and Striking," 3–33; William A. Gamson, "The Social Psychology of Collective Action," in *Frontiers in Social Movement Theory*, ed. Aldon D. Morris and Carol M. Mueller (New Haven, CT: Yale University Press, 1992), 53–76; Teresa Sharpe, "Union Democracy and Successful Campaigns," in Milkman and Voss, *Rebuilding Labor*, 62–87.

89. Randy Hodson et al., "Is Worker Solidarity Undermined by Autonomy and Participation?," *American Sociological Review* 58 (1993): 398–416; Dixon and Roscigno, "Status, Networks," 1292–1327.

90. Ben Simon, "Local 300 Sets Up Housekeeping," *The Advance* 24, no. 2 (February 1938): 20.

91. Herman Brickman, Fourth Session, Proceedings of the Thirteenth Convention, in *Twenty-Fifth Anniversary Convention: Report of the GEB* (New York: ACWA, 1940), 291–92.

92. Hyman Blumberg, Fifth Session, Proceedings of the Thirteenth Convention, in *Twenty-Fifth Anniversary Convention*, 320.

93. Lumpkin, "I Helped Organize the CIO"; Lumpkin, interview by the author, May 23, 2007, Chicago; Robinson, interview by Craig, 45, TCTUW.

94. Greenberg, "The Politics of Disorder," 399–402.

95. Lumpkin, "I Helped Organize the CIO"; Lumpkin, interview by the author, June 2, 2008, Chicago; Lumpkin, *Joy in the Struggle*, 82–83.

96. Greenberg, "The Politics of Disorder," 402.

97. Mackey to Green, August 13, 1936; Mackey to Green, March 15, 1937, both in reel 39, AFL Records.

98. Florence Rice, "It Takes a While to Realize That It Is Discrimination," 272, 275–76; "Industrial Women March On," WEVD Radio script by the NY WTUL, November 24,

1938, 13, reel 2, Schneiderman Papers; "Dorothy Bailey on Radio Program," *The Advance* 25, no. 3 (March 1939): 17.

99. Division of Women in Industry and the Minimum Wage, *Women in Industry*; Nestel, *Labor Relations*, 56; Gabriel Winant, "'Hard Times Make for Hard Arteries and Hard Lives': Deindustrialization, Biopolitics, and the Making of a New Working Class," *Journal of Social History* 53, no. 1 (2019): 109.

100. Beatrice Lumpkin, "Sweating in a Union Shop," *People's Weekly World*, August 13, 2005; Lumpkin, "I Helped Organize the CIO"; Lumpkin, interview by the author, May 23, 2007, Chicago.

101. Quoted in Richards, *Conservations with Maida Springer*, 122.

102. "The Journal of the LWJB," box 139, collection no. 5619, ACWA Records; Roy Soden, "Employment Office Report," *The Advance* 24, no. 2 (February 1934): 21.

Chapter 8. The "Democratic Initiative"

1. Robinson, interview by Craig, 46–47, TCTUW.

2. "United Laundry Workers Union Chose Delegates and Officers Here," *New York Amsterdam News*, April 30, 1938, 4.

3. Louis Simon speaking in *Dollie Lowther Robinson*, DVD; Robinson, interview by Craig, 3–4, TCTUW.

4. "Commissioner Puts Unionists on Wage Body," *New York Amsterdam News*, December 18, 1937, 23; "Laundry Workers Charge Bias in Brooklyn Local," *New York Amsterdam News*, September 28, 1940, 4; "Back Wages Paid Workers," *The Advance* 24, no. 10 (October 1938): 24; "Local 327," *The Advance* 25, no. 3 (March 1939): 15.

5. "Officers of Locals Making Up the LWJB," *The Advance* 25, no. 5 (May 1938): 14; "The Journal of the Laundry Workers Joint Board: 10th Anniversary Celebration," box 139, collection no. 5619, ACWA Records.

6. "Laundry Workers Joint Board," *The Advance* 24, no. 10 (October 1938): 24; Nestel, *Labor Relations*, 46.

7. "Re-elected to Official Post in Laundry Workers' Union," *New York Amsterdam News*, June 4, 1938, 7; "In Union," *New York Amsterdam News*, November 20, 1937, 14.

8. Lumpkin, *Joy in the Struggle*, 85; Jessie Smith, interview by the author, December 24, 2006, New York; Stepan-Norris and Zeitlin, "Who Gets the Bird?," 512.

9. "One Year of Laundry Labor Union," *The Advance* 24, no. 8 (August 1938): 3; Walter M. Cook to Sidney Hillman, April 18, 1939, folder 1, box 59, collection no. 5619, ACWA Records; "To the General Board of the ACWA," April 21, 1939, folder 2, box 59, collection no. 5619, ACWA Records.

10. "To the General Board of the ACWA," April 21, 1939, 20–21, folder 2, box 59; and "The Journal of the LWJB: Tenth Anniversary Celebration," box 139, both in collection no. 5619, ACWA Records; "AFL-CIO Civil Rights Chairman Is Charged with Racial Bias," *New York Amsterdam News*, September 10, 1960, 1.

11. "One Year of Laundry Labor Union," *The Advance* 24, no. 8 (August 1938): 3.

12. "To the General Board of the ACWA," April 21, 1939, folder 2, box 59, collection no. 5619, ACWA Records.

13. Walter M. Cook to Sidney Hillman, April 18, 1939, folder 1, box 59, collection no. 5619, ACWA Records.

14. "To the General Board of the ACWA," April 21, 1939, folder 2, box 59, collection no. 5619, ACWA Records; Nestel, *Labor Relations*, 48–49.

15. "LWJB Managers' Report Reflects Fine Progress," *The Advance* 32, no. 24 (December 1946): 9.

16. Robinson, interview by Craig, 3, 50, TCTUW.

17. Nestel, *Labor Relations*, 46–50.

18. Division of Women in Industry and the Minimum Wage, *Women in Industry*; "Report of the Laundry Minimum Wage Board to the Industrial Commissioner," January 14, 1938, folder 61, box 2, collection no. 5235, National Consumers' League Records; "Ten Thousand Laundry Workers Get ACWA Contract," *The Advance* 23, no. 9 (September 1937): 16; Nestel, *Labor Relations*, 60. In 1944 the minimum wage was extended to cover men.

19. Freida Miller, "Public Hearing on the Report of the Laundry Minimum Wage Board," New York, February 5, 1938; State Department of Labor, "Public Hearings to Be Held Next Week," July 28, 1938; New York Department of Labor, "Laundry Wage Order Becomes Mandatory," August 19, 1938, folder 61, box 2, collection no. 5235, all from National Consumers' League Records.

20. "New Contract Ratified by Overwhelming Majority," *The Advance* 25, no. 12 (December 1939): 17.

21. "In the Matter of LWJB and Wholesale Laundry Board of Trade et al.," May 20, 1940, 66, folder 1, box 52, collection no. 5619, ACWA Records.

22. LWJB, "Study of Prevailing Wage Rates," July 21, 1939, folder 24, box 54, collection no. 5619, ACWA Records.

23. Nestel, *Labor Relations*, 72–73; "Award of Arbitrators," case no. 2612, July 1940, folder 21, box 54, collection no. 5619/016, ACWA Records.

24. "Award of Arbitrators," case no. 2612, July 1940, folder 21, box 54, collection no. 5619, ACWA Records.

25. "In the Matter of LWJB and Wholesale Laundry Board of Trade et al.," May 20, 1940, 48–52, folder 1, box 52, collection no. 5619, ACWA Papers; Lumpkin, "I Helped Organize."

26. Jack Barbash, "Economics and Organization of the Laundry Industry," *The Advance* 25, no. 3 (March 1939): 18; Barbash, "Economics and Organizing of the Laundry Industry," *The Advance* 25, no. 4 (April 1939): 18.

27. Charlotte Adelmond to Members of the Board of Directors, LWJB, "Reasons for Resignation of Charlotte Adelmond from the LWJB," December 6, 1950, 15–16, folder 559, Murray Papers.

28. Orleck, *Common Sense*, 76; Fraser, *Labor Will Rule*, 78–79; Katz, *All Together Different*, 59–63.

29. Fraser, *Labor Will Rule*, 205–37, 321–22; Pastorello, *A Power among Them*, 46–48; Zieger, *The CIO*, 15–18, 70–71.

30. "What Is Arbitration," *The Advance* 23, no. 11 (November 1937): 13.

31. "The Arbitration Court for the Laundry Industry," *The Advance* 24, no. 2 (February 1938): 21; Robinson, interview by Craig, 51–52 (quote), TCTUW.

32. "Chairlady Reinstated," *The Advance* 26, no. 9 (September 1940): 18; Amalgamated Joint Boards and Local Unions in New York, *The Book of the Amalgamated in New York, 1914–1940*, 73–76, box 289, collection no. 5619, ACWA Records.

33. "Local 327 Wins Back Jobs," *The Advance* 26, no. 3 (March 1940): 23; Louis Simon, "Check-Off System Being Adopted," *The Advance* 26, no. 4 (April 1940): 18, 20.

34. Nestel, *Labor Relations*, 71; Nell Geiser, "'The Democratic Initiative': Race, Gender and the Contradictions of Industrial Democracy in New York's Laundries, 1937–1950" (master's thesis, Columbia University, 2006), 45–46; Staughton Lynd, *"We Are All Leaders": The Alternative Unionism of the 1930s* (Urbana: University of Illinois Press, 1996), 5, 9.

35. Robinson, interview by Craig, 46–47, TCTUW.

36. Smith, interviews by the author, December 27, 2006, New York; Lumpkin, *Joy in the Struggle*, 85 (quote).

37. Noah Walter, "A Program to Meet the Drivers' Problems," *The Advance* 25, no. 5 (May 1939): 15; "Minutes of the Meeting of the GEB," April 19–22, 1939, 9, folder 23, box 165, collection no. 5619, ACWA Records.

38. Cohen, *Making a New Deal*, 324, 332–49.

39. Pastorello, *A Power among Them*, 24–56, 114–21.

40. Robinson, interview by Craig, 4, TCTUW.

41. "Laundry Workers: Get Happy! Get Busy! Get Wise—at Union Educational Classes," *The Advance* 23, no. 12 (December 1937): 16.

42. Orleck, *Common Sense*, 169–71; Pastorello, *A Power among Them*, 52–53, 111, 116.

43. "Extensive Educational Program Proposed for Laundry Workers," *The Advance* 23, no. 10 (October 1937): 11 (quote); "Laundry Workers: Get Happy! Get Busy! Get Wise—at Union Educational Classes," *The Advance* 23, no. 12 (December 1937): 16.

44. Bessie Hillman, "Educational Department," *The Advance* 24, no. 11 (November 1938): 15; Bessie Hillman, "Laundry Workers News," *The Advance* 24, no. 3 (March 1938): 15; Bessie Hillman, "Educational Department," *The Advance* 24, no. 12 (December 1938): 14 (quote); Bessie Hillman, "Educational Department," *The Advance* 25, no. 4 (April 1939): 17; Bessie Hillman, "Education Department," *The Advance* 25, no. 5 (May 1939): 16; Nestel, *Labor Relations*, 52.

45. "Laundry Workers All-Day Conference Lay Plans for Education," *The Advance* 24, no. 9 (September 1938): 18.

46. Hillman, "Education Department," *The Advance* 25, no. 6 (June 1939): 25.

47. Cohen, *Making a New Deal*, 339–42.

48. Northrup, *Organized Labor*, 135–36.

49. "The LWJB Chorus," *The Advance* 24, no. 8 (August 1938): 17; "Sing over National Station," *The Advance* 26, no. 3 (March 1940): 23; Lumpkin, interview by the author (quote), May 23, 2007, Chicago.

50. Pastorello, *A Power among Them*, 116–17.

51. Katz, *All Together Different*, 2–16, 84, 106–10; Orleck, *Common Sense*, 169–77, 181–84.

52. Nestel, *Labor Relations*, 54; Robinson, interview by Craig, 4, 36, TCTUW; Hillman, "News of Education Department," *The Advance* 25, no. 9 (September 1939): 26; Orleck, *Common Sense*, 177.

53. Orleck, *Common Sense*, 170–72, 181–84; Katz, *All Together Different*, 85–87, 108.

54. Hillman, "Educational Department," *The Advance* 25, no. 6 (June 1939): 25, 27; Hillman, "News of Education Department," *The Advance* 25, no. 9 (September 1939): 26.

55. Elizabeth Fones-Wolf, "Industrial Unionism and Labor Movement Culture in Depression-Era Philadelphia," *Pennsylvania Magazine of History and Biography* 109, no. 1 (January 1985): 24.

56. Nestel, *Labor Relations*, 52–53.

57. Oestreich, "They Saw Themselves," 186–89; Katz, *All Together Different*, 82.

58. Frank Crosswaith to the LWJB, August 20, 1943; and Crosswaith to Abe Miller, April 17, 1950, both on reel 8, NLC Records.

59. "3,000 Members Flock to Hear Crosswaith at Local 300 Meeting," *The Advance* 25, no. 11 (November 1939): 25.

60. Zieger, *The CIO*, 84 (quote), 85; Geiser, "The Democratic Initiative," 35–37.

61. Pastorello, *A Power among Them*, 122–24.

62. Gardner Taylor speaking in *Dollie Lowther Robinson*, DVD.

63. Donna Shalala speaking in *Dollie Lowther Robinson*, DVD.

64. Richards, *Conversations with Maida Springer*, 120.

65. Robinson, interview by Craig, 29–30, TCTUW.

66. Reta Oddi, "Dolly Robinson Gets Honor from Hudson Shore Labor School," *The Advance* 26, no. 9 (September 1940): 19.

67. "Laundry Worker Wins Scholarship," *New York Amsterdam News*, June 28, 1941, 11; Robinson, interview by Craig, 31, TCTUW.

68. Beatrice Lumpkin, e-mail message to the author, August 13, 2006; Robinson, interview by Craig, 63, TCTUW.

69. Robinson, interview by Craig, 28–32, TCTUW.

70. Ibid., 50, 58.

71. "Minutes of the Membership Meeting," April 1, 1940, 1–2; "Minutes of the Regular Meeting," March 3, 1941; "Minutes of the General Membership Meeting," December 14, 1942; "Committees, 1943-44," May 1943, all on reel 4, NY WTUL Records.

72. Robinson, interview by Craig, 7–8, 36, 57–58, TCTUW; Robinson speaking in *Dollie Lowther Robinson*, DVD; Melvin McCray, e-mail to the author, August 15, 2006.

73. Robinson, interview by Craig, 7–8, 25, 57, TCTUW; Christmas card, folder 10, box 115, collection no. 5619, ACWA Records.

74. Philoine Fried, interview by the author, July 7, 2007, New York.

75. Robinson, interview by Craig, 4, 25, TCTUW; Nestel, *Labor Relations*, 53; Ramona Lowe, "Tells of Laundry Union's War Work," *New York Amsterdam News*, April 10, 1943, 24.

76. Collins, *Black Feminist Thought*, 129–31, 151, 157–58; Battat, *Ain't Got No Home*, 107-8.

77. Ann Petry, *The Street* (Boston: Houghton Mifflin Company, 1946), 28–56, 55 (quotes).

78. Battat, *Ain't Got No Home*, 107–9; Katrina Myers Caldwell, "'It Will Be Social': Black Women Writers and the Postwar Era 1945–60" (master's thesis, University of Illinois at Chicago, 1995), 133–43.

79. Nestel, *Labor Relations*, 53–54; "N.Y. Laundry Workers Hold Varied Programs," *The Advance* 36, no. 3 (February 1950): 12.

80. Robnett, "African-American Women," 1680–83.

81. Collins, *Black Feminist Thought*, 157; Robnett, "African-American Women," 1680–83.

82. Richards, *Conversations with Maida Springer*, 121–22; Robinson, interview by Craig, 16, TCTUW. The quote in the subhead is from this same interview, page 58.

83. Robinson, interview by Craig, 3, TCTUW; Richards, *Conversations with Maida Springer*, 122.

84. Cecil Toppin speaking in *Dollie Lowther Robinson*, DVD; Judith Schuyf, "'Trousers with Flies!!': The Clothing and Subculture of Lesbians," *Textile History* 24, no. 1 (1993): 61–73; James F. Wilson, *Bulldaggers, Pansies, and Chocolate Babies: Performance, Race, and Sexuality in the Harlem Renaissance* (Ann Arbor: University of Michigan Press, 2010), 154–91.

85. Rosalind Rosenberg, *Jane Crow: The Life of Pauli Murray* (New York: Oxford University Press, 2017), 1–6, 49–51, 55–60, 80, 119–21, 184. There is likely a discrepancy in the file number of the Pauli Murray Papers from which this information is cited.

86. "Back Wages Paid Laundry Workers," *The Advance* 24, no. 10 (October 1938): 24; Robinson, interview by Craig, 58, TCTUW; "Local 327," *The Advance* 25, no. 5 (May 1939): 15; "Company Union Ordered Disbanded," *The Advance* 27, no. 8 (April 1941): 24.

87. "Local 327," *The Advance* 25, no. 2 (February 1939): 26.

88. Richards, *Maida Springer*, 68.

89. Bernice McNair Barnett, "Invisible Southern Black Women Leaders in the Civil Rights Movement: The Triple Constraints of Gender, Race, and Class," *Gender and Society* 7, no. 2 (June 1993): 176.

90. "Charlotte Is Ill," *The Advance* 25, no. 3 (March 1939): 15; "Thanks from Charlotte Adelmond," *The Advance* 25, no. 4 (April 1939): 15.

91. "Attend State CIO Unions Meet," *New York Amsterdam News*, September 24, 1938, 1, 17; "No Prejudices in CIO Unions," *New York Amsterdam News*, September 24, 1938, 1; "LWJB," *The Advance* 24, no. 10 (October 1938): 24.

92. "N. C. A. Walter Speaks at the Shoemaker Meeting," *The Advance* 24, no. 12 (December 1938): 13.

93. "Laundry Workers Charge Bias in Brooklyn Local," *New York Amsterdam News*, September 28, 1940, 4; "Officials Deny Jim Crowism in Laundry Workers Union," *New York Amsterdam News*, October 5, 1940, 11.

94. "Laundry Workers Charge Bias in Brooklyn Local," *New York Amsterdam News*, September 28, 1940, 4; Northrup, *Organized Labor*, 135; "Officials Deny Jim Crowism in Laundry Workers Union," *New York Amsterdam News*, October 5, 1940, 11.

95. "Laundry Workers Charge Bias in Brooklyn Local," *New York Amsterdam News*, September 28, 1940, 4; "Attend State CIO Unions Meet," *New York Amsterdam News*, September 24, 1938, 17; "No Prejudices in CIO Unions," *New York Amsterdam News*, September 24, 1938, 1.

96. Evelyn Brooks Higginbotham, *Righteous Discontent: The Women's Movement in the Black Baptist Church, 1880–1920* (Cambridge, MA: Harvard University Press, 1993),

187; Higginbotham, "African-American Women," 271–72; Harris, "Running with the Reds," 22–23, 37; Gore, *Radicalism at the Crossroads*, 100–106; McDuffie, *Sojourning for Freedom*, 8–11.

97. Harris, "Running with the Reds," 32–33.

98. "Officials Deny Jim Crowism in Laundry Workers Union," *New York Amsterdam News*, October 5, 1940, 11.

99. Robinson, interview by Craig, 53–54, TCTUW; Esther Peterson speaking in *Dollie Lowther Robinson*, DVD.

100. Charlotte Adelmond at http://www.fold3.com/document/7566013/.

101. Watkins-Owens, *Blood Relations*, 82–84.

102. "Union Honors Blumberg," *The Advance* 28, no. 7 (April 1942): 8.

103. Smith, interview by the author, June 24, 2007, New York.

104. Lumpkin, *Joy in the Struggle*, 37, 42–45, 84–89.

105. "News and Notes from Local 328," *The Advance* 25, no. 6 (June 1939): 24; Lumpkin, *Joy in the Struggle*, 43, 88–90.

106. "Local 328," *The Advance* 25, no. 3 (March 1939): 15; "Local 328 Pickets Fight New Imperial Lockout," *The Advance* 25, no. 9 (September 1939): 24; "New Imperial Laundry Signs with Local 328," *The Advance* 25, no. 11 (November 1939): 24.

107. Noah Walter, "Reports of the Local Unions," *The Advance* 24, no. 12 (December 1938): 12; "Local 327," *The Advance* 25, no. 4 (April 1939): 15.

108. "Local 327," *The Advance* 25, no. 4 (April 1939): 15; "Local 327," *The Advance* 25, no. 5 (May 1939): 16.

109. Lumpkin, *Joy in the Struggle*, 90–91; "Minutes of the Meeting of the GEB," April 19–22, 1939, 6, folder 23, box 165; and Cook to Hillman, April 18, 1939, 5, folder 1, box 59, both in collection no. 5619, ACWA Records.

110. "Minutes of the Meeting of the GEB," April 19–22, 1939, 6–9, folder 23, box 165; and "To the General Board of the ACWA," April 21, 1939, 17, folder 2, box 59, both in collection no. 5619, ACWA Records.

111. "Officers, Delegates Elected by Local 328," *The Advance* 25, no. 7 (July 1939): 8; Lumpkin, *Joy in the Struggle*, 90–91.

112. Lumpkin, *Joy in the Struggle*, 94; Fraser, *Labor Will Rule*, 445.

113. Fraser, *Labor Will Rule*, 434–35, 441–47; Biondi, *To Stand and Fight*, 144, 153–54; "Laundry Workers Get Out Full Registration," *The Advance* 26, no. 14 (October 1940): 6.

114. Lumpkin, *Joy in the Struggle*, 94; "Union Approves Decision Removing Business Agents," *The Advance* 27, no. 4 (April 1941): 25.

115. "Two Business Agents Suspended from Duties," *The Advance* 27, no. 3 (March 1941): 24–25; "Bans on Reds Voted by Laundry Union," *New York Times*, February 1, 1941, 19.

116. "Two Business Agents Suspended from Duties," *The Advance* 27, no. 3 (March 1941): 24; "Union Approves Decision Removing Business Agents," *The Advance* 27, no. 4 (April 1941): 25; Lumpkin, *Joy in the Struggle*, 95–96.

117. Lumpkin, interview by the author, May 23, 2007, Chicago; Lumpkin, *Joy in the Struggle*, 96–97; "Union Approves Decision Removing Business Agents," *The Advance* 27, no. 4 (April 1941): 25–26; Zieger, *The CIO*, 286–93.

118. Judith Stepan-Norris and Maurice Zeitlin, "Insurgency, Radicalism, and Democracy in America's Industrial Unions," *Social Forces* 75: 1 (September 1996), 11–12. Michael Goldfield, "Race and the CIO: The Possibilities for Racial Egalitarianism during the 1930s and 1940s," *International Labor and Working-Class History* 44 (Fall 1993): 10–13.

119. Lumpkin, interview by the author, May 23, 2007, Chicago.

120. Fraser, *Labor Will Rule*, 343–44, 434–52, 518–24; Zieger, *The CIO*, 256–61.

121. Zieger, *The CIO*, 24, 70–71, 247, 253–93; David Brody, *Workers in Industrial America* (Oxford: Oxford University Press, 1993), 148–51.

122. Stepan-Norris and Zeitlin, "Insurgency," 3–5, 15–16, 21–27.

123. Zieger, *The CIO*, 255; Lichtenstein, *State of the Union*, 117; Steve Rosswurm, *The CIO's Left-Led Unions* (New Brunswick, NJ: Rutgers University Press, 1992), 9, 12–14.

124. Biondi, *To Stand and Fight*, 27–32, 147, 164; Goldfield, "Race and the CIO," 13–22, 25–28; Zieger, *The CIO*, 255–56, 373–74; Cobble, *The Other Women's Movement*, 79–81; Kelley, *Hammer and Hoe*; Fonow, *Union Women*.

125. Arnesen, "No 'Graver Danger,'" 44–52.

Chapter Nine. "Putting Democracy into Action"

1. "Notes of the Month: Odell Waller," *New International* 7, no. 6 (July 1942): 164–66, quoted in Pauli Murray, *Song in a Weary Throat: An American Pilgrimage* (New York: Harper & Row, 1987), 174–76; Richards, *Conversations with Maida Springer*, 123–25. The quotation in the chapter title is from Noah Walter, "Putting Democracy into Action," *The Advance* 29, no. 5 (March 1943): 7.

2. Hall, "The Long Civil Rights Movement," 1246, 1254; Biondi, *To Stand and Fight*, 1–8; Korstad, "Civil Rights Unionism," 255.

3. Greenberg, "The Politics of Disorder," 419–22.

4. "Laundry Workers Get a Raise in New Pact," *The Advance* 28, no. 4 (February 1942): 11; "Linen Workers Cheer New Agreement," *The Advance* 28, no. 5 (March 1942): 11; Nestel, *Labor Relations*, 75–77.

5. Research Department, ACWA, "Changes in Minimum Wages of Time Workers in the Laundry Industry in New York City," October 30, 1945, folder 4, box 52, collection no. 5619, ACWA Records; Kessler-Harris, *A Woman's Wage*, 82–83.

6. "The Story of the Amalgamated Laundry Workers," *Amalgamated Laundry Workers Bulletin* 7, no. 1 (June 1964): 7, box 289, collection no. 5619, ACWA Records.

7. Florence Rice, "It Takes a While to Realize That It Is Discrimination," 272.

8. "Laundry Workers Ask Ten Cent an Hour Increase," *The Advance* 29, no. 13 (July 1943): 15; Research Department, ACWA, "Supplementary Statement Submitted by the LWJB of Greater NY," February 16, 1945, 3, folder 4, box 52, collection no. 5619, ACWA Records.

9. Nestel, *Labor Relations*, 29–30; Northrup, *Organized Labor*, 133–35.

10. Nestel, *Labor Relations*, 42.

11. "Make Wage Gains in Arbitration Award," *The Advance* 28, no. 22 (November 1942): 14; "Average 10 Percent Wage Increase Approved," *The Advance* 29, no. 2 (January 1943): 9; Zieger, *The CIO*, 145–151.

12. Research Department, ACWA, "Supplementary Statement," 6.

13. LWJB, "First Annual Report of the Laundry Workers Benefit Fund," reel 8, NLC Records; Nestel, *Labor Relations*, 50–51.

14. Greenberg, "The Politics of Disorder," 419–20, 428.

15. "Plans for March on Washington near Completion," *Norfolk New Journal and Guide*, June 21, 1941, 9; "Impressive Flag Meeting Held at Carolyn Laundry," *The Advance* 29, no. 5 (March 1943): 7.

16. "Soden and Gentile Made New Co-managers of LWJB," *The Advance* 32, no. 11 (June 1946): 5; "LWJB Managers' Report Reflects Fine Progress," *The Advance* 32, no. 24 (December 1946): 9; Biondi, *To Stand and Fight*, 50.

17. Thomas A. Guglielmo, "'Red Cross, Double Cross': Race and America's World War II-Era Blood Donor Service," *The Journal of American History*, 97: 1 (June 2010): 64. Robinson, interview by Craig, 5, TCTUW (quote); Guglielmo, "'Red Cross, Double Cross,'" 77–78.

18. Hedgeman, *The Trumpet Sounds*, 81.

19. Charlotte Adelmond to Members of the Board of Directors, LWJB, "Reasons for Resignation of Charlotte Adelmond from the LWJB," December 6, 1950, 23, folder 559, Murray Papers; James Q. Whitman, "Why the Nazis Studied American Race Laws for Inspiration," in *Beyond Bioethics: Towards a New Biopolitics*, ed. Osagie K. Obasogie and Marcy Darnovsky (Berkeley: University of California Press, 2018), 60–62.

20. Adelmond to Members of the Board of Directors, "Reasons for Resignation," 23.

21. Robinson, interview by Craig, 5–6, TCTUW; Richards, *Maida Springer*, 74.

22. Rosenberg, *Jane Crow*, 97–105, 177–79, 182–83.

23. Richards, *Maida Springer*, 75–76; Richards, *Conversations with Maida Springer*, 123–24; Collins, *Black Feminist Thought*, 96–97, 159; Biondi, *To Stand and Fight*, 37.

24. Adelmond to Members of the Board of Directors, "Reasons for Resignation," 18–20; Biondi, *To Stand and Fight*, 4, 8–10.

25. Biondi, *To Stand and Fight*, 38, 50.

26. Robinson, interview by Craig, 48, TCTUW.

27. "Laundry Workers Get Out Full Registration," *The Advance* 26, no. 14 (October 1940): 6; "Laundry Workers Rejoice over Election Results," *The Advance* 26, no. 17 (December 1940): 14; "Laundry Workers Increase Tempo of Political Action Campaign," *The Advance* 30, no. 21 (October 1944): 11.

28. "Laundry Workers Endorse Walter," *New York Amsterdam News*, September 7, 1940, 5.

29. "Soden and Gentile Made New Co-managers of LWJB," *The Advance* 32, no. 11 (June 1946): 5; "LWJB Managers' Report Reflects Fine Progress," *The Advance* 32, no. 24 (December 1946): 9; Biondi, *To Stand and Fight*, 38, 50–54.

30. "The Negro's Stake in American Victory," *The Advance* 29, no. 3 (February 1943): 11; Ervin, *Gateway to Equality*, 141.

31. Greenberg, "The Politics of Disorder," 425–28.

32. Nestel, *Labor Relations*, 54; "Joint Board Bomber Drive Goes into Full Swing," *The Advance* 29, no. 10 (May 1943): 12; "Bomber Drive Almost Doubles Quota," *The Advance* 29, no. 16 (August 1943): 4.

33. Ramona Lowe, "Tells of Laundry Union's War Work," *New York Amsterdam News*, April 10, 1943, 24.

34. Greenberg, "The Politics of Protest," 425–31.

35. "New Managers Settle Old Dispute," *The Advance* 29, no. 25 (January 1944): 8; "First Negro Named Union Co-manager," *Norfolk New Journal and Guide*, December 18, 1943, 1.

36. "Dewey Names Labor Leader to High Post," *New York Amsterdam News*, July 1, 1944, 1A; "Laundry Workers Given Raise; but May Abandon CIO," *New York Amsterdam News*, December 23, 1950, 3.

37. "The Journal of the Laundry Workers Joint Board: 10th Anniversary Celebration," box 139, collection no. 5619, ACWA Records.

38. James Guerin, "A Report to Bro. Sidney Hillman," folder 2, box 59, collection no. 5619, ACWA Records; "Laundry Maintenance Men's Local 446 Receives Charter," *The Advance* 30, no. 5 (April 1944): 8.

39. "Laundry Workers United as Negotiations Reach Climax," *The Advance* 31, no. 23 (December 1945): 3; "New York Laundry Workers Get Four and Five Cent Wage Raise," *The Advance* 31, no. 5 (March 1945): 1, 5; "Dues Increase Approved by All Locals," *The Advance* 29, no. 2 (January 1943): 9; "New York Laundry Workers Demand 40-Hour Week in New Contract," *The Advance* 31, no. 20 (October 1945): 8; "N.Y. Laundry Workers Deliver Strict Ultimatum to Employers," *The Advance* 31, no. 22 (November 1945): 6.

40. "N.Y. Laundry Workers Deliver Strict Ultimatum to Employers," *The Advance* 31, no. 22 (November 1945): 6; Zieger, *The CIO*, 150.

41. "N.Y. Laundry Workers Deliver Strict Ultimatum to Employers," *The Advance* 31, no. 22 (November 1945): 6.

42. "Laundry Workers Get 60.5 Cent Minimum," *The Advance* 31, no. 24 (December 1945): 4.

43. "Laundry Workers Ratify Settlement," *The Advance* 32, no. 1 (January 1946): 4.

44. ACWA, "The Increases Requested as Approvable under Present Wage Stabilization Policy," February 16, 1945, 8–10, folder 4, box 52, collection no. 5619, ACWA Records.

Chapter Ten. "Everybody's Libber"

1. Marilyn Bender, "Black Woman in Civil Rights: Is She a Second Class Citizen?," *New York Times*, September 2, 1969, 42; Robinson, interview by Craig, 37–38, 53, TCTUW.

2. Nestel, *Labor Relations*, 27–28; Mohun, *Steam Laundries*, 249–67.

3. "Soden and Gentile Made New Co-managers of LWJB," *The Advance* 32, no. 11 (June 1946): 5; Nestel, *Labor Relations*, 48–49.

4. "Settlement Announced at LWJB Meeting," *The Advance* 32, no. 29 (October 1946): 4; "N.Y. Laundry Workers Vote $5,000 for Hillman Fund," *The Advance* 33, no. 4 (February 1947): 8.

5. "N.Y. Laundry Workers Get More Wages, Less Hours," *The Advance* 32, no. 20 (October 1946): 4; Nestel, *Labor Relations*, 62–65.

6. Yu, *To Save China*, 138–39, 148–60.

7. "N.Y. Laundry Workers Hold Installation of New Officers," *The Advance* 33, no. 12

(June 1947): 6; "Drive Continues to Unionize Chinese Hand Laundries," *The Advance* 33, no. 6 (March 1947): 4.

8. "Laundry Workers Joint Board Wins Gains for 20,000 Members," *The Advance* 33, no. 15 (August 1947): 7; "New York Laundry Workers Contract Extended 2 Years," *The Advance* 33, no. 19 (October 1947): 3.

9. "New York Laundry Workers Contract Extended 2 Years," *The Advance* 33, no. 19 (October 1947): 3.

10. "The Journal of the LWJB: Tenth Anniversary Celebration," box 139, collection no. 5619, ACWA Records.

11. Nestel, *Labor Relations*, 83–84.

12. Charlotte Adelmond, "Local 327 vs. Impartial Chairman, Mr. Brickman, on the Conduct of His Court," July 10, 1947, 2–13, folder 559, Murray Papers; "LWJB Hears Review of Insurance Benefits," *The Advance* 34, no. 6 (March 1948): 3, 11; "Laundry Joint Board Reports Progress in Organizing Drive," *The Advance* 36, no. 22 (November 1950): 5.

13. "New York Laundry Workers Contract Extended Two Years," *The Advance* 33, no. 19 (October 1947): 3; Charlotte Adelmond to Members of the Board of Directors, LWJB, "Reasons for Resignation of Charlotte Adelmond from the LWJB," December 6, 1950, 23, folder 559, Murray Papers.

14. Adelmond, "Local 327 vs. Impartial Chairman," 1–12.

15. Dan Clawson, *The Next Upsurge: Labor and the New Social Movements* (Ithaca, NY: Cornell University Press, 2003), 32–35; Zieger and Gall, *American Workers*, 79–82.

16. "Laundry Meeting Decides to Spur Organizing Drive," *The Advance* 34, no. 1 (January 1948): 8.

17. Charlotte Adelmond, "Report on the History of the Proper Steam Laundry," April 20, 1949, folder 559, Murray Papers; and Adelmond, "Reasons for Resignation," 3, 35.

18. "Laundry Office Workers Local Gets Charter," *The Advance* 34, no. 3 (February 1948): 11; "N.Y. Laundry Workers Hear Manager's Report on Progress," *The Advance* 36, no. 20 (October 1950): 5.

19. "LWJB Reports Progress in Organizing Drive," *The Advance* 36, no. 22 (November 1950): 5.

20. Clawson, *The Next Upsurge*, 32–35; Lichtenstein, *State of the Union*, 98–99, 105, 136.

21. Nestel, *Labor Relations*, 62–65.

22. "Stipulation Regarding Minimum Rates," June 20, 1949, folder 21, box 54, collection no. 5619, ACWA Records; Marguerite J. Fisher, "Equal Pay for Equal Work Legislation," *ILR Review* 2, no. 1 (October 1948): 52–57.

23. "Discussion Points," April 20, 1949, folder 9, box 54; and Research Department, "Minimum Rates in the Linen Supply and Flatwork Divisions of the New York Laundry Industry," February 1, 1950, folder 7, box 52, both in collection no. 5619, ACWA Records; Adelmond, "Reasons for Resignation."

24. Adelmond, "Reasons for Resignation," 12–13.

25. Fonow, *Union Women*, 42–43.

26. Adelmond, "Reasons for Resignation," 12–13; Biondi, *To Stand and Fight*, 14, 60.

27. *Handbook of Information on Group Life Insurance and Group Accident and Sickness Insurance*, December 1950, 7–8, folder 559, Murray Papers; Adelmond, "Reasons for Resignation," 13–14.

28. Adelmond, "Reasons for Resignation," 18; Biondi, *To Stand and Fight*, 18–20.

29. Adelmond, "Reasons for Resignation," 18.

30. Pastorello, *A Power among Them*, 152–53; Dennis Deslippe, "Organized Labor, National Politics, and Second-Wave Feminism in the United States, 1963–1975," *ILWCH* 49 (Spring 1996): 146.

31. Smith, interviews by the author, December 26, 2006, New York; Beatrice Lumpkin, e-mail messages to the author, July 31, August 9, 2006.

32. Pastorello, *A Power among Them*, 150; Kessler-Harris, *A Woman's Wage*, 82–83; Dorothy Sue Cobble, "Lost Visions of Equality: The Labor Origins of the Next Women's Movement," *Labor's Heritage* 12, no. 1 (Winter/Spring 2003): 17; Cobble, *The Other Women's Movement*, 59, 98–99, 168–73.

33. The author thanks Alice Kessler-Harris for making these observations at the LAWCHA "Workers on the Move: Workers' Movements" conference, Duke University, May 31, 2019. See also Kessler-Harris, *A Woman's Wage*, 82–85.

34. Milkman, *Gender at Work*, 65–77.

35. Fonow, *Union Women*, 6, 16–19; Milkman, *Gender at Work*, 84, 89–94; Cobble, *The Other Women's Movement*, 98–99.

36. Lisa Kannenberg, "The Impact of the Cold War on Women's Trade Union Activism: The UE Experience," *Labor History* 34, no. 2–3 (2007): 311–13; Milkman, *Gender at Work*, 74–84, 89–94; Cobble, *The Other Women's Movement*, 88.

37. "Committee Representing the Maintenance Division of the LWJB to the GEB of the ACWA," October 22, 1943, 1–3, folder 2, box 59, collection no. 5619, ACWA Records.

38. Carl Lawrence, "Blame Union Bosses for Workers' Plight," *New York Amsterdam News*, March 25, 1950, 3; "Laundry Workers Given Raise; but May Abandon CIO," *New York Amsterdam News*, December 23, 1950, 3; Bernard Burton, "Laundry Workers Force ACW Poll," *Daily Worker*, June 6, 1950, 5.

39. Adelmond, "Reasons for Resignation," 11; "Laundry Workers Given Raise; but May Abandon CIO," *New York Amsterdam News*, December 23, 1950, 3.

40. "Laundry Workers Union Follows Real Democracy," *New York Amsterdam News*, October 20, 1951, 6; Earl Brown, "Odell Clark, Labor Pioneer," *New York Amsterdam News*, June 21, 1952, 18.

41. "Tribute Accorded Laundry Unit Aide," *The Advance* 36, no. 22 (November 1950): 10.

42. Earl Brown, "Odell Clark, Labor Pioneer," *New York Amsterdam News*, June 21, 1952, 18; "Tribute Accorded Laundry Unit Aide," *The Advance* 36, no. 22 (November 1950): 10; Carl Lawrence, "Blame Union Bosses for Workers' Plight," *New York Amsterdam News*, March 25, 1950, 3.

43. Bernard Burton, "Laundry Workers Force ACW Poll," *Daily Worker*, June 6, 1950, 5; Carl Lawrence, "Blame Union Bosses for Workers' Plight," *New York Amsterdam News*, March 25, 1950, 3; Adelmond, "Reasons for Resignation," 2.

44. Robinson, interview by Craig, 46, TCTUW.

45. Adelmond, "Reasons for Resignation," 2, 11–12, 17–18, 36.

46. Ibid., 24–26.

47. Pauli Murray, "The Liberation of Black Women," in *Words of Fire: An Anthology of African-American Feminist Thought*, ed. Beverly Guy-Sheftall (New York: New Press, 1995), 189–95; Collins, *Black Feminist Thought*, 74, 185–86.

48. Adelmond, "Reasons for Resignation," 2, 11–12, 17–18, 36.

49. "The Journal of the LWJB: Tenth Anniversary Celebration," box 139, collection no. 5619, ACWA Records.

50. Adelmond, "Reasons for Resignation," 25–26.

51. Biondi, *To Stand and Fight*, 14–15, 57–59.

52. Adelmond, "Reasons for Resignation," 20–22; McDuffie, *Sojourning for Freedom*, 95.

53. Adelmond, "Reasons for Resignation," 20–22; Keisha N. Blain, *Set the World on Fire: Black Nationalist Women and the Global Struggle for Freedom* (Philadelphia: University of Pennsylvania Press, 2018), 155–56 (quote).

54. "Laundry Workers Conduct Classes for New Members," *The Advance* 33, no. 7 (April 1947): 12.

55. Robinson, interview by Craig, 17–18, TCTUW; Ramona Lowe, "Tells of Laundry Union's War Work," *New York Amsterdam News*, April 10, 1943, 24; Nancy MacLean, *Freedom Is Not Enough: The Opening of the American Workplace* (Cambridge, MA: Harvard University Press, 2006), 119–23.

56. "Laundry Educational Department Ready for Summer Activities," *The Advance* 27, no. 5 (May 1941): 25; Robinson, interview by Craig, 40, TCTUW.

57. Robinson, interview by Craig, 9–10, 7, 23, TCTUW; "LWJB Aids Filing of Income Taxes," *The Advance* 33, no. 5 (March 1947): 12.

58. Robinson, interview by Craig, 13–14, 23–24, 32, 40–41, 60, TCTUW.

59. Ibid., 9–10.

60. "CIO Delegates at Columbus Meeting Stage 'Sit-In' against Jim-Crowism," *Cleveland Call and Post*, March 22, 1947, 1A; Biondi, *To Stand and Fight*, 81.

61. Biondi, *To Stand and Fight*, 71–72, 199–202.

62. "LWJB Hears Review of Insurance Benefits," *The Advance* 34, no. 6 (March 1948): 11; Cobble, *The Other Women's Movement*, 57.

63. Cecil Toppin speaking in *Dollie Lowther Robinson*, DVD; Robinson, interview by Craig, 37, 51, 63, TCTUW.

64. Marilyn Bender, "Black Woman in Civil Rights: Is She a Second Class Citizen?," *New York Times*, September 2, 1969, 42; Robinson, interview by Craig, 37, 50–53, TCTUW.

65. Elisabeth Petry, *At Home Inside: A Daughter's Tribute to Ann Petry* (Jackson: University of Mississippi Press, 2009), 163–65.

66. Robinson, interview by Craig, 50–51, TCTUW; Collins, *Black Feminist Thought*, 151, 158.

67. Naison, *Communists in Harlem*, 246, 312–13.

68. "Negro Women, Inc. to Buy Home in N.Y.," *Chicago Defender*, October 27, 1945, 15; Biondi, *To Stand and Fight*, 9–10, 41–42; Richards, *Conversations with Maida Springer*, 100, 129–30.

69. Quoted in Caldwell, "'It Will Be Social,'" 133–34; Richards, *Maida Springer*, 83; Gore, *Radicalism at the Crossroads*, 39.

70. Robinson, interview by Craig, 39, TCTUW; Biondi, *To Stand and Fight*, 147.

71. Robinson, interview by Craig, 48–49, TCTUW; Biondi, *To Stand and Fight*, 40, 55, 209.

72. Richards, *Conversations with Maida Springer*, 99, 119–22.

73. Richards, *Maida Springer*, 58; Richards, *Conversations with Maida Springer*, 121.

74. Marilyn Bender, "Black Woman in Civil Rights: Is She a Second Class Citizen?," *New York Times*, September 2, 1969, 42; Robinson, interview by Craig, 37, 53, TCTUW.

75. Marilyn Bender, "Black Woman in Civil Rights: Is She a Second Class Citizen?," *New York Times*, September 2, 1969, 42; Deborah K. King, "Multiple Jeopardy, Multiple Consciousness: The Context of a Black Feminist Ideology," *Signs* 14, no. 1 (Autumn 1988): 46.

76. Marilyn Bender, "Black Woman in Civil Rights: Is She a Second Class Citizen?," *New York Times*, September 2, 1969, 42; Robinson, interview by Craig, 53, TCTUW.

77. Murray quoted in Rosenberg, *Jane Crow*, 3.

78. Marilyn Bender, "Black Woman in Civil Rights: Is She a Second Class Citizen?," *New York Times*, September 2, 1969, 42.

79. Collins, *Black Feminist Thought*, 156; Premilla Nadasen, "Expanding the Boundaries of the Women's Movement: Black Feminism and the Struggle for Welfare Rights," *Feminist Studies* 28, no. 2 (Summer 2002): 273. Nadasen points out that civil rights leaders such as Fannie Lou Hamer similarly distanced themselves from the term "feminist" and from the feminist agenda.

80. King, "Multiple Jeopardy," 57–63; bell hooks, "Black Women: Shaping Feminist Theory," in Guy-Sheftall, *Words of Fire*, 270–72; Deslippe, "Organized Labor," 160.

81. Cobble, *The Other Women's Movement*, 71–78; hooks, "Black Women," 270, 278; Siobhan Brooks, "Black Feminism in Everyday Life: Race, Mental Illness, Poverty and Motherhood," in *Colonize This! Young Women of Color on Today's Feminism*, ed. Daisy Hernandez and Bushra Rehman (Berkeley, CA: Seal Press, 2002), 99–118.

82. Premilla Nadasen, "Expanding the Boundaries of the Women's Movement: Black Feminism and the Struggle for Welfare Rights," *Feminist Studies* 28, no. 2 (Summer 2002): 272 (quote), 284, 293.

83. Cobble, *The Other Women's Movement*, 3–9, 28, 50–60; Deslippe, "Organized Labor," 144.

84. Robinson, interview by Craig, 33–35, 53, TCTUW; Cobble, *The Other Women's Movement*, 61–66, 98–99, 114.

85. King, "Multiple Jeopardy," 72; Collins, *Black Feminist Thought*, 36.

86. Collins, *Black Feminist Thought*, 34–37, 160.

87. Springer, interview by Craig, 72, TCTUW; Adelmond, "Reasons for Resignation," 1.

88. Collins, *Black Feminist Thought*, 37, 39, 156.

89. Murray, "The Liberation of Black Women," 188 (quote), 197; Collins, *Black Feminist Thought*, 38–39.

90. Robinson quoted in Deslippe, *Rights Not Roses*, 143; Cobble, *The Other Women's Movement*, 185; Rosenberg, *Jane Crow*, 4–5, 298–300.

91. Eric Arnesen, *Brotherhoods of Color: Black Railroad Workers and Their Struggle for Equality* (Cambridge, MA: Harvard University Press, 2001); Beth Tompkins Bates, *Pullman Porters and the Rise of Protest Politics in Black America, 1925–1945* (Chapel Hill: University of North Carolina Press, 2001). Thank you to Nell Geiser for this observation.

Chapter Eleven. "We're Just Not Ready Yet"

1. Bernard Burton, "Laundry Workers Force ACW Poll," *Daily Worker*, June 6, 1950, 5; Carl Lawrence, "Laundry Outlook 'Damp' as CIO Confab Looms," *New York Amsterdam News*, May 13, 1950, 5.

2. Biondi, *To Stand and Fight*, 33–59, 141–47; Thomas J. Sugrue, *Sweet Land of Liberty: The Forgotten Struggle for Civil Rights in the North* (New York: Random House, 2008), 99–100.

3. Biondi, *To Stand and Fight*, 137, 143–47.

4. Harold Henderson, "Laundry Workers Given Raise; but May Abandon CIO," *New York Amsterdam News*, December 23, 1950, 3; Charlotte Adelmond to Members of the Board of Directors, LWJB, "Reasons for Resignation of Charlotte Adelmond from the LWJB," December 6, 1950, 15–16, folder 559, Murray Papers.

5. Bernard Burton, "Laundry Workers Force ACWA Poll," *Daily Worker*, June 6, 1950, 5.

6. Adelmond, "Statement by Charlotte Adelmond," April 18, 1950, 11–16, folder 592, Murray Papers; Adelmond, "Reasons for Resignation," 27–30.

7. Carl Lawrence, "Laundry Workers May Follow Lewis," *New York Amsterdam News*, April 22, 1950, 5; Adelmond, "Statement by Charlotte Adelmond," 15–16; Adelmond, "Reasons for Resignation," 27–30.

8. State of New York Department of Labor, "Employee Claim for Compensation," ca. 1933, folder 559, box 29, Murray Papers.

9. Charlotte Adelmond, "Description of Injury," undated, Workmen's Compensation Files; and Adelmond to Mary Doulan, August 7, 1947, both in folder 559, box 29, Murray Papers; Harris and Swartz, *The Cost of Clean Clothes*, 44–59.

10. Dr. Victor H. Raisman to Dr. Charles F. Nicol, State Insurance Fund, February 23, 1950, Workmen's Compensation Files; and Dr. Alvin Arkin, July 2, 1946, both in folder 559, box 29, Murray Papers.

11. M. Braverman and Sons Bill, June 20, 1950, Workmen's Compensation Files, folder 559, box 29, Murray Papers.

12. Adelmond, "Statement by Charlotte Adelmond," 16–19.

13. Carl Lawrence, "Woman Laundry Union Official Suspended," *New York Amsterdam News*, April 15, 1950, 3, 9; Adelmond, "Reasons for Resignation," 30.

14. Charlotte Adelmond retainer letter, February 21, 1950, folder 559, Murray Papers; Adelmond, "Reasons for Resignation," 30–33; Adelmond, "Statement by Charlotte Adelmond," 19–21; Carl Lawrence, "Laundry Workers May Follow Lewis," *New York Amsterdam News*, April 22, 1950, 5.

15. Carl Lawrence, "Drive to Organize New Laundry Union Going Strong," *New York Amsterdam News*, ca. 1950/1951, 3, reel 16, Negro Labor Committee Records, Schomburg

Center for Research in Black Culture, New York; Adelmond, "Reasons for Resignation,"
31–32.

16. Adelmond, "Statement by Charlotte Adelmond," 21–24; Lawrence, "Drive to Organize," 3; Carl Lawrence, "Laundry Outlook 'Damp' as CIO Confab Looms," *New York Amsterdam News*, May 13, 1950, 5.

17. Carl Lawrence, "Woman Laundry Union Official Suspended," *New York Amsterdam News*, April 15, 1950, 3, 9; Adelmond, "Statement by Charlotte Adelmond," 24; Adelmond, "Reasons for Resignation," 32.

18. Carl Lawrence, "Woman Laundry Union Official Suspended," *New York Amsterdam News*, April 15, 1950, 3, 9.

19. Bernard Burton, "Laundry Workers Force ACW Poll," *Daily Worker*, June 6, 1950, 5; Adelmond, "Reasons for Resignation," 34; ACWA, Seventeenth Biennial Convention, Cleveland, Ohio, May 15–19, 1950, box 286, collection no. 5619, ACWA Records.

20. Richards, *Maida Springer*, 70.

21. Bernard Burton, "Laundry Workers Force ACW Poll," *Daily Worker*, June 6, 1950, 5; Carl Lawrence, "Laundry Outlook 'Damp' as CIO Confab Looms," *New York Amsterdam News*, May 13, 1950, 5; Carl Lawrence, "Laundry Workers May Follow Lewis," *New York Amsterdam News*, April 22, 1950, 5.

22. Carl Lawrence, "Woman Laundry Union Official Suspended," *New York Amsterdam News*, April 15, 1950, 3, 9; Adelmond, "Reasons for Resignation," 32.

23. Carl Lawrence, "Laundry Workers May Follow Lewis," *New York Amsterdam News*, April 22, 1950, 5.

24. "NY Laundry Board Balks Raid Attempt," *The Advance* 36, no. 9 (May 1950): 12.

25. Lawrence, "Drive to Organize," 3; "Wait Final Count in Laundry Vote," *New York Amsterdam News*, June 17, 1950, 4; "Laundry Workers of New York," folder 5, box 54, collection no. 5619/016, ACWA Records.

26. Carl Lawrence, "Laundry Outlook 'Damp' as CIO Confab Looms," *New York Amsterdam News*, May 13, 1950, 5, 7.

27. Ibid.; "Laundry Workers—the Union Has Already Helped You," folder 5, box 54, collection no. 5619, ACWA Records.

28. "U.M.W. District 50 Hits O'Dwyer Rule," *New York Times*, June 14, 1950, 27; Robinson, interview by Craig, 49, TCTUW.

29. Carl Lawrence, "Laundry Workers Elections Looms," *New York Amsterdam News*, June 10, 1950, 3; "Laundrywork Union 'Rebels' Lose Fight," *New York Amsterdam News*, June 24, 1950, 4; Bernard Burton, "Laundry Workers Force ACW Poll," *Daily Worker*, June 6, 1950, 5.

30. Bernard Burton, "Laundry Workers Force ACW Poll," *Daily Worker*, June 6, 1950, 5.

31. Bernard Burton, "Bare Forged Leaflet in Laundry Poll," *Daily Worker*, June 13, 1950, 5; "Charge Vote Fraud in Union Election," *New York Amsterdam News*, July 22, 1950, 4.

32. Bernard Burton, "Bare Forged Leaflet in Laundry Poll," *Daily Worker*, June 13, 1950, 5; "NY Laundry Workers Elect Simon Manager," *The Advance* 36, no. 13 (July 1950): 4; Pastorello, *A Power among Them*, 143; Honest Ballot at https://www.honestballot.com/about-us/.

33. Adelmond, "Reasons for Resignation," 18.

34. Ibid., 2, 18.

35. "NY Laundry Workers Elect Simon Manager," *The Advance* 36, no. 13 (July 1950): 4; Adelmond, "Reasons for Resignation," 2–3.

36. "Equality Spokesman Defeated," *New York Amsterdam News*, September 16, 1950, 1.

37. Carl Lawrence, "Laundry Workers Elections Looms," *New York Amsterdam News*, June 10, 1950, 3; "Charge Vote Fraud in Union Election," *New York Amsterdam News*, July 22, 1950, 4; "Laundry Workers in Revolt over Harden," *New York Amsterdam News*, December 9, 1950, 4; Pastorello, *A Power among Them*, 114.

38. Carl Lawrence, "Laundry Workers Elections Looms," *New York Amsterdam News*, June 10, 1950, 3; "Charge Vote Fraud in Union Election," *New York Amsterdam News*, July 22, 1950, 4; "Referendum Results Show Largest Vote in ACW History," *The Advance* 36, no. 18 (September 1950): 3.

39. "Charge Vote Fraud in Union Election," *New York Amsterdam News*, July 22, 1950, 4; "Referendum Results Show Largest Vote in ACW History," *The Advance* 36, no. 18 (September 1950): 3; "Equality Spokesman Defeated," *New York Amsterdam News*, September 16, 1950, 1.

40. "Laundry Workers in Revolt over Harden," *New York Amsterdam News*, December 9, 1950, 4; "Laundry Workers Given Raise; but May Abandon CIO," *New York Amsterdam News*, December 23, 1950, 3.

41. Robinson, interview by Craig, 3, 59, TCTUW; "NY Laundry Workers Elect Simon Manager," *The Advance* 36, no. 13 (July 1950): 4; Adelmond, "Reasons for Resignation," 34.

42. Adelmond, "Reasons for Resignation," 1, 34; Adelmond to the Board of Directors, LWJB, and Mr. Louis Simon, December 8, 1950, folder 559, Murray Papers.

43. "Laundry Workers Defend Their Jobs and Union," *The Advance* 37, no. 7 (April 1951): 6; Carl Lawrence, "Woman Laundry Union Official Suspended," *New York Amsterdam News*, April 15, 1950, 3.

44. Adelmond, "Reasons for Resignation," 1, 19–20, 36.

45. Ibid., 2, 19.

46. Richards, *Conversations with Maida Springer*, 122 (quote); Biondi, *To Stand and Fight*, 57–58, 137–51.

47. Robinson, interview by Craig, 3, TCTUW.

48. Ibid., 29–33.

49. Pastorello, *A Power among Them*, 134–35, 157.

50. Robinson, interview by Craig, 35–37, TCTUW.

51. Bernice McNair Barnett, "Invisible Southern Black Women Leaders in the Civil Rights Movement: The Triple Constraints of Gender, Race, and Class," *Gender and Society* 7, no. 2 (June 1993): 176; Robnett, "African-American Women," 1670–71, 1678.

52. Robinson, interview by Craig, 35–37, TCTUW; Adelmond, "Reasons for Resignation," 1.

53. Richards, *Conversations with Maida Springer*, 122; Robinson, interview by Craig, 44, 50, TCTUW; Charlotte Adelmond, Genealogy Bank at http://www.genealogybank.com/gbnk/ssdi/?lname=Adelmond.

54. Robinson, interview by Craig, 50, TCTUW.

55. "N.Y. Laundry Worker Hold Varied Programs," *The Advance* 36, no. 3 (February 1950): 12.

56. Lawrence, "Drive to Organize," 3; Bernard Burton, "Laundry Workers Force ACW Poll," *Daily Worker*, June 6, 1950, 5.

57. "The Story of the Amalgamated Laundry Workers," *Amalgamated Laundry Workers Bulletin* 7, no. 1 (June 1964): 11, box 289, collection no. 5619, ACWA Records; "The Journal of the LWJB: 10th Anniversary Celebration," box 139, collection no. 5619, ACWA Records.

58. Jacob Schlitt Oral History interview by Christa Whitney, Yiddish Book Center's Wexler Oral History Project, Karmazin Recording Studio, Yiddish Book Center, December 12, 2010, http://archive.org/details/JacobSchlitt12dec2010YiddishBookCenter.

59. Dollie Robinson to Bessie Hillman, January 21, 1951; and Robinson to Hillman, April 25, 1951, both in folder 10, box 115, collection no. 5619, ACWA Records.

60. Robinson, interview by Craig, 36, TCTUW; Lawrence, "Drive to Organize," 9.

61. Robinson, interview by Craig, 12–14, 23–24, TCTUW; Richards, *Conversations with Maida Springer*, 120.

62. Robinson, interview by Craig, 12–16, TCTUW.

63. James, *Holding Aloft*, 50–51, 112.

64. Richards, *Conversations with Maida Springer*, 44; Jessie Taft Smith, phone conversation with the author, July 23, 2006.

65. James, *Holding Aloft*, 71, 78–85, 92–100, 113, 258.

66. Ibid., 187–88.

67. Robinson, interview by Craig, 42–43, TCTUW; Robinson to Hillman, February 28, 1951; and Robinson to Hillman, May 3, 1951, both in folder 10, box 115, collection no. 5619, ACWA Records.

68. Robinson to Hillman, April 25, 1951, folder 10, box 115, collection no. 5619, ACWA Records.

69. Robinson to Hillman, February 28, 1951, folder 10, box 115, collection no. 5619, ACWA Records; Robinson, interview by Craig, 11, 37, 44, TCTUW; Maida Springer and Jan Robinson speaking in *Dollie Lowther Robinson*, DVD.

70. Robinson, interview by Craig, 18–19, TCTUW.

71. Kimberly Springer, *Living for the Revolution: Black Feminist Organizations, 1968–1980* (Durham, NC: Duke University Press, 2005), 2; Robinson, interview by Craig, 18–19, 49, TCTUW.

72. Robinson, interview by Craig, 19, TCTUW; Milton Stewart to Bessie Hillman, January 17, 1955, folder 21, box 115, collection no. 5619, ACWA Records.

73. Richards, *Conversations with Maida Springer*, 100, 129–30; Robinson, interview by Craig, 20, TCTUW.

74. Esther Peterson, *Restless: The Memoirs of Labor and Consumer Activist Esther Peterson* (Washington, DC: Caring Publishing, 1995), 117.

75. Cobble, *The Other Women's Movement*, 34, 52, 159–61; Peterson, *Restless*, 117.

76. Robinson, interview by Craig, 20, TCTUW; "Brooklyn Woman Gets U.S. Labor Dept. Post," *New York Amsterdam News*, March 25, 1961, 21; Mamie L. Robinson, "Women in Politics," *Philadelphia Tribune*, May 27, 1961, 8.

77. Rosenberg, *Jane Crow*, 261–65.

78. Robinson, interview by Craig, 8, TCTUW.

79. "Mrs. Robinson Quits D.C. Post," *New York Amsterdam News*, June 8, 1963, 7.

80. "Woman Labor Assistant Takes Post with Union," *Chicago Defender*, June 8, 1963, 12; "Dollie Robinson Quits Labor Department Post," *Cleveland Call and Post*, June 15, 1963, 1.

81. Peterson, *Restless*, 117.

82. Ibid.

83. Ervin, *Gateway to Equality*, 10–11; Collins, *Black Feminist Thought*, 73–74.

84. Pauli Murray, "The Liberation of Black Women," in Guy-Sheftall, *Words of Fire*, 187, 192.

85. Ethel Payne speaking in *Dollie Lowther Robinson: The Woman and Her Times*, DVD; Melinda Chateauvert, "Organizing Gender: A. Philip Randolph and Women Activists," in *Reframing Randolph: Labor, Black Freedom, and the Legacies of A. Philip Randolph*, ed. Andrew E. Kersten and Clarence Lang (New York: New York University Press, 2015), 181, 186.

86. Cobble, *The Other Women's Movement*, 155.

87. Robinson, interview by Craig, 20, TCTUW.

88. Petry, *At Home Inside*, 163–65.

89. Robinson, interview by Craig, 20–22, TCTUW.

90. Ibid., 18–19, 49; Daphne Sheppard, "Who's Who in the Upcoming Primary Elections on June 18," *New York Amsterdam News*, June 8, 1968, 25.

91. Robinson, interview by Craig, 27–28, TCTUW; Richards, *Conversations with Maida Springer*, 121; obituary, *New York Times*, March 19, 1984.

92. Robinson, interview by Craig, 54–55, TCTUW.

93. George Morris, "A Lot of Dirty Laundry in ACW's Laundry Union," *Daily Worker*, April 28, 1950, 6; "Laundry Workers Given Raise; but May Abandon CIO," *New York Amsterdam News*, December 23, 1950, 3.

94. "Simon Outlines Program for N.Y. Laundry Union," *The Advance* 36, no. 14 (July 1950): 4; "N.Y. Laundry Workers Hear Manager's Report on Progress," *The Advance* 36, no. 20 (October 1950): 4; "Rosenblum Hails Solidarity of Laundry Workers in N.Y.," *The Advance* 38, no. 13 (July 1952): 4.

95. "Laundry Joint Board Reports Progress in Organizing Drive," *The Advance* 36, no. 22 (November 1950): 5.

96. "New Laundry Workers Health Center Is a Tribute to Management, Labor," reel 8, NLC Records.

97. "N.Y. Laundry Locals Install Officers," *The Advance* 36, no. 15 (August 1950): 5; "Laundry Joint Board Reports Progress in Organizing Drive," *The Advance* 36, no. 22 (November 1950): 5.

98. "Laundry Deserters Beaten—Simon," *The Advance* 37, no. 6 (March 1951): 8, 10; "Laundry Joint Board Overwhelmingly Defeats AFL Union in NY Bargaining Election," *The Advance* 37, no. 4 (February 1952): 16.

99. "Laundry Deserters Beaten—Simon," *The Advance* 37, no. 6 (March 1951): 8, 10; "Potofsky Addresses N.Y. Laundry Union," *The Advance* 37, no. 21 (November 1951): 4.

100. "N.Y. Laundry Board Revises Procedure for Business Agents," *The Advance,* October 1, 1952, 7.

101. "Laundry Deserters Beaten—Simon," *The Advance* 37, no. 6 (March 1951): 8, 10; "Simon Outlines Program for N.Y. Laundry Union," *The Advance* 36, no. 14 (July 1950): 4; Odell Clark, "$250 Laundry Workers' Check Given to NAACP," *New York Amsterdam News,* January 26, 1952, 16; Biondi, *To Stand and Fight,* 168–69.

102. "Labor Leader Addresses Eli Student Body," *New York Amsterdam News,* April 4, 1953, 3.

103. "Odell Clark Dropped by Labor Union," *New York Amsterdam News,* May 30, 1959, 1, 11.

104. "AFL-CIO Civil Rights Chairman Is Charged with Racial Bias," *New York Amsterdam News,* September 10, 1960, 1.

105. "Paging Laundry Workers! Odell Clark Is Now Labor Investigator," *New York Amsterdam News,* March 11, 1961, 11.

106. Sylvia Cullman, "You're Welcome," *New York Amsterdam News,* October 22, 1960, 10.

107. "Louis Simon Labor Leader, 97," *New York Times,* October 2, 1992, http://www.nytimes.com/1992/10/02/obituaries/louis-simon-labor-leader-97.html; Sylvia Cullman, "You're Welcome," *New York Amsterdam News,* October 22, 1960, 10.

108. "Who Watches Simon? Name Simon as Rights Watchdog," *New York Amsterdam News,* May 28, 1960, 38; "The Story of the Amalgamated Laundry Workers," *Amalgamated Laundry Workers Bulletin* 7, no. 1 (June 1964): 10, box 289, collection no. 5619, ACWA Records; Gore, *Radicalism at the Crossroads,* 100–101, 117.

109. Biondi, *To Stand and Fight,* 256–58; "Nationalists Picket Laundry Workers Head," *New York Amsterdam News,* May 13, 1961, 1; "The Story of the Amalgamated Laundry Workers," *Amalgamated Laundry Workers Bulletin* 7, no. 1 (June 1964): 10–11, box 289, collection no. 5619, ACWA Records; Sam Reiss, "Louis Simon, Frank Rosenblum, Bayard Rustin," undated photograph, folder 1, box 33, collection no. 5743P, ACWA Photographs, Kheel Center, Cornell University, Ithaca, NY.

110. "Nationalists Picket Laundry Workers Head," *New York Amsterdam News,* May 13, 1961, 1.

111. Nathan Glazer and Daniel Patrick Moynihan, *Beyond the Melting Pot: The Negroes, Puerto Ricans, Jews, Italians, and Irish of New York City,* 2nd ed. (Cambridge, MA: MIT Press, 1970), 72.

112. Carmen Western, interview by the author, May 30, 2008, New York.

113. Joan Boyce, interview by the author, May 30, 2008, New York.

114. Fraser, *Labor Will Rule,* 343–44; Kim Moody, *An Injury to All: The Decline of American Unionism* (London: Verso, 1988), 41, 45–47; Faue, *Community of Suffering,* 13–15.

115. Faue, "Paths of Unionization," 296–301, 310–19; Lichtenstein, *State of the Union,* 90.

116. "Laundry, Dry Cleaning Workers May Strike," *New York Amsterdam News,* November 26, 1966, 32.

Epilogue

1. Robinson, interview by Craig, 6, TCTUW; "The Story of the Amalgamated Laundry Workers," *Amalgamated Laundry Workers Bulletin* 7, no. 1 (June 1964): 23, box 289, collection no. 5619, ACWA Records.

2. Lichtenstein, *State of the Union*, 30, 142; Joan Boyce, interview by the author, May 30, 2008, New York.

3. Boyce, interview by the author, May 30, 2008, New York.

4. Mohun, *Steam Laundries*, 249–67; US Department of Labor, Bureau of Labor Statistics, *Occupational Employment and Wages*, May 2018, 51-6011 Laundry and Dry-Cleaning Workers, https://www.bls.gov/oes/current/oes516011.htm.

5. US Department of Labor, Wage and Hour and Public Contracts Division, *Laundry and Cleaning Services* (Washington, DC: Government Printing Office, 1962), 1–13.

6. David Molphus, "Dirty Work: Washing Hospital Laundry," *National Public Radio*, September 2, 2002; Katie Unger, interview by the author, May 29, 2008, New York; Annette Bernhardt, Siobhan McGrath, and James DeFilippis, *Unregulated Work in the Global City: Employment and Labor Law Violations in New York City* (New York: Brennan Center for Justice / New York University School of Law, 2007), 81; Cintas, corporate profile, https://www.cintas.com/company/.

7. Fabrice Robinet, "$7 an Hour, 72 Hours a Week: Why Laundry Workers Have Had Enough," *New York Times*, August 23, 2019.

8. US Department of Labor, *Laundry and Cleaning Services*, 12–13; Jorge Deschamps, interview by the author, May 30, 2008, New York.

9. Manville Personal Injury Settlement Trust, Verified Shareholder Derivative Complaint, Case No. A0806822, Common Pleas Court, Hamilton County, Ohio, 2008, 6, 25; National Interfaith Community for Worker Justice, *Airing Dirty Laundry: A Report on Cintas Worker Concerns*, June 23, 2004; Unger, interview by the author, May 29, 2008, New York.

10. Kevin Osborne, "Cintas Fine Highest Ever," *Porkopolis*, August 17, 2007; Sandy Smith, "Another Cintas Worker Dies in Incident Related to Industrial Dryer," *EHS Today*, November 3, 2011.

11. Bernhardt, McGrath, and DeFilippis, *Unregulated Work*, 81; Molphus, "Dirty Work."

12. Clean, "Report: Alarming Lack of Cleanliness Standards," May 14, 2015, http://cleannyc.org/2015/05/report-alarming-lack-of-cleanliness-standards-at-industrial-laundry-plants-handling-linens-that-new-york-city-restaurants-hotels-and-hospitals-use/.

13. US Department of Labor, *Women in the Labor Force: A Databook*, Report 1002, http://www.bls.gov/cps/wlf-databook-2007.pdf; Bernhardt, McGrath, and DeFilippis, *Unregulated Work*, 81–82; UNITE HERE and Teamsters, "The 'Spirit' Is the Problem: Systemic Racial and Gender Discrimination at Cintas Corporation," December 2004, 9.

14. Winant, "'Hard Times,'" 108–10.

15. Quoted in Bernhardt, McGrath, and DeFilippis, *Unregulated Work*, 82; US Department of Labor, *Occupational Employment and Wages*, https://www.bls.gov/oes/current/oes516011.htm.

16. UNITE HERE, "The 'Spirit' Is the Problem," 1.

17. Unger, interview by the author, May 29, 2008, New York; Milkman, *Gender at Work*, 3–8.

18. Doria Barrera, interview by the author, May 4, 2009; UNITE HERE, "The 'Spirit' Is the Problem," 1–5; Jenny Carson, "'Taking on Corporate Bullies': Laundry Worker Organizing in the 1930s and 21st Century," *Labor Studies Journal* 35, no. 4 (2010): 462–64. The location of the Barrera interview is not noted to protect the anonymity of the workers interviewed in the same city (at the workers' request).

19. Barrera, interview by the author, May 4, 2009; UNITE HERE, "The 'Spirit' Is the Problem," 1, 5–6.

20. Boyce, interview by the author, May 30, 2008, Chicago; Unger, interview by the author, May 29, 2008, New York.

21. Robinet, "$7 an Hour"; Laundry Workers Center, http://laundryworkerscenter. org/.

22. Laundry Workers Center, "Report on Working Conditions in the Retail Laundromat Industry," New York City, http://laundryworkerscenter.org/wp-content/uploads/2018/06/Eng-Laundry-Workers-Center-Report-2.pdf; Robinet, "$7 an Hour."

23. Clean, "Report"; Matt Poe, "Laundry Licensing Bill Adopted by Unanimous Vote," *American Laundry News*, July 25, 2016, https://americanlaundrynews.com/articles/nyc-council-passes-clean-act.

24. J. Stewart Dalzell, memorandum in Pichler et al. v. UNITE et al., United States District Court for the Eastern District of Pennsylvania, No. 04-2841, August 30, 2006; Cintas Corp. v. UNITE HERE et al., Civil Action, United States District Court Southern District of New York, March 5, 2008.

25. Carson, "Taking on Corporate Bullies," 463–67. I would like to thank Annelise Orleck for making this observation to me.

26. Carmen, interview by the author, 2009; Carson, "Taking on Corporate Bullies," 466–67. Cintas workers I interviewed requested anonymity because of fears of employer retaliation.

27. Carson, "Taking on Corporate Bullies," 467–69; Roberto, interview by the author, 2009.

28. Manville Personal Injury Settlement Trust, Verified Shareholder Derivative Complaint, Case No. A0806822; Carson, "Taking on Corporate Bullies," 467–69; Clawson, *The Next Upsurge*, 34–42; Bernabe, interview by the author, 2009.

29. Lumpkin, *Joy in the Struggle*, 57.

30. Carson, "Taking on Corporate Bullies," 463–67; Steven H. Lopez, "Overcoming Legacies of Business Unionism: Why Grassroots Organizing Tactics Succeed," in Milkman and Voss, *Rebuilding Labor*, 124.

31. Carson, "Taking on Corporate Bullies," 468–70.

32. Robinson, interview by Craig, 55–56, TCTUW.

33. Smith, interview by the author, December 26, 2006, July 14, 2007, New York.

34. Robinson, interview by Craig, 55–56, TCTUW.

35. Robinson, interview by Craig, 6–7, 63, TCTUW.

36. Lumpkin, e-mail message to the author, August 13, 2006; Robinson, interview by Craig, 63, TCTUW.

37. Clawson, *The Next Upsurge*, 13–25; Julie Martinez Ortega, "Why We Should Support the Employee Free Choice Act," *Labor Studies Journal* 31, no. 4 (2007): 23–30.

38. Beatrice Lumpkin, *"Always Bring a Crowd!": The Story of Frank Lumpkin, Steelworker* (New York: International Publishers Co., 1999).

39. Lumpkin, *Joy in the Struggle*, 167; Paulina Firozi, "She's Voted in Every Election Since 1940. A Pandemic Wasn't Going to Stop Her This Year," *Washington Post*, October 6, 2020, https://www.washingtonpost.com/lifestyle/2020/10/06/102-year-old-hazmat-voter/.

40. Alliance for Retired Americans, "Chicago Metro Chapter Joins Youth Activists in Intergenerational Alliance," July 14, 2017, https://retiredamericans.org/chicago-metro-chapter-joins-youth-activists-intergenerational-alliance/.

41. Jessie Taft Smith, phone conversation with the author, July 23, 2006.

42. Robinson, interview by Craig, 7, TCTUW.

Index

abusive treatment, 1, 28–29, 124–26, 214; employer, 4, 55, 119; strike against, 51, 107

Addams, Jane, 78

Adelmond, Charlotte, 1–9, *144*, 216, 218; accidents, 189–90; and ACWA union, 97, 107, 115, 127, 172–73; against AFL, 1–2, 107; banishment of, 195–98; Black female business agent, 128; Black nationalist movement, 53; blood policy, 159–60; Bomber drive, 162–63; Brickman's proemployer bias, 169–70; Chinanki physically assaulted, 190; CIO convention, 146; death, 198; democratic initiative, 149, 159; discrimination, eradication of, 185; homeland, 54; initiative and LWJB, 190–92; intersectional and fluid approach, 167; Laundry Minimum Wage Board, 132; lesbian, 146; Local, 327 137, *144*, 177, 190–91; negotiating committee, 164; New York City, moved to, 200; ousted Negro leader, 198; pan-Africanism and international solidarity, 177; Pan-Africanist Garvey movement, 53, 65; rank-and-file empowerment, 146; reassignment of, 188–90; seamstress, 54–55; union movement, 4; working life, beginning, 3; WTUL's executive board, 112, 142. *See also* Robinson, Dollie Lowther; Springer, Maida

African American laundresses, 14, 18; employmen,t 19; laundry union in Brooklyn, 97; old women, 19; unionist, 85

African American women, 3, 39; laundry work, 14, 20; proletarianization, 4, 21–23; sexual harassment, 28–29. *See also* Black women laundry workers' activism

Always Bring a Crowd!: The Story of Frank Lumpkin, Steelworker (Lumpkin), 223

Amalgamated Clothing Workers of America (ACWA), 2, 97, 107, 127, 159; and Adelmond, Charlotte, 97, 107, 115, 127, 172–73; Baron, William, 163; biennial convention in 1938, 104; Biennial Convention in Atlantic City, 177; Biennial Convention in Cleveland, Ohio, 190–91; Blumberg, Hyman, 132; and communist laundry workers, 149–53; Cook, Walter, 130; Declaration of Independence, 117; Dickason, Gladys, 132; Hillman, Sidney, 113, 115; laundry industry, dominance in, 123–25; laundry union, 116, 192; laundry workers joining, 114–16; leadership, 8; and leftists, 129; Local 300, 120–23; LWJB, 120–23; LWJB's Education Department, 135–40; LWOC, 118–20; Messina, Vincent, 119; New York City's laundry workers, 114–16, 118–20; racial justice, commitment to, 194–96; racism and, 149; Research Department, 131; resources for campaign, 107; Rosenblum, Frank, *211*; sexual division of labor, 174; union election under, 128–31; unionization of New York City's laundry workers, 6

American Federation of Labor (AFL), 1–2, 41, 110. *See also* Committee for Industrial Organization (CIO)

American Fund for Public Service, 63

American Labor Education Service, 141

American Labor Party (ALP), 113, 159, 161

Anderson, Alberta, 86

Anderson, Mathilene, 23

Anthony, Susan B., 78, 100, 179

JENNY CARSON is an associate professor of history at Ryerson University.

The University of Illinois Press
is a founding member of the
Association of University Presses.

———————————————

University of Illinois Press
1325 South Oak Street
Champaign, IL 61820-6903
www.press.uillinois.edu